TAMALPAIS TRAILS

∧ ∧ ∧

Barry Spitz

Potrero Meadow Publishing Company

First Edition, Second Printing

Maps: Dewey Livingston
Cover Design: Jil Weil
Front Cover Photo: Mt. Tamalpais from Yolanda Trail, Jim Vitek
Back Cover Photo: Girl in Muir Woods, Randy Hogue

Library of Congress Cataloging-in-Publication Data

Spitz, Barry, 1948-
Tamalpais Trails / by Barry Spitz.
p. 320
Includes index.
ISBN 0-9620715-0-1 : $16.95
1. Hiking--California--Tamalpais, Mount--Guide-books.
2. Trails--California--Tamalpais, Mount--Guide-books.
3. Tamalpais, Mount (Calif.)--Description and travel-Guide-books.
I. Title.
GV199.42.C22T367 1989
917.94'62--dc20   89-8739
                                               CIP

Published by   Potrero Meadow Publishing Co.
               P.O. Box 3007
               San Anselmo, CA 94960

Printed in the United States of America

THIS BOOK IS DEDICATED TO THE MEMORY
OF MY SISTER, SYDELLE,
WHO WAS GRANTED BUT ONE VISIT
TO THE TOP OF MT. TAMALPAIS

*"Climb the mountains and get their good
tidings. Nature's peace will flow into
you as sunshine flows into trees. The
winds will blow their freshness into you,
and the storms their energy, while cares
will drop off like autumn leaves."*
- John Muir

ACKNOWLEDGMENTS

I wish to thank the following people, who, along with many others, helped make this book possible:

JIM VITEK, the grand old man of the Mountain's north side, painstakingly read the manuscript and made countless corrections;

NANCY SKINNER, the Mountain's unofficial archivist, shared her files and also pored through the full manuscript;

DEWEY LIVINGSTON, the Mountain's best mapmaker, who, when he agreed to do the maps, gave impetus to the project;

FRED SANDROCK, dean of Tam's historians, supported the effort from the start;

BEN SCHMIDT, who perhaps knows Mt. Tamalpais better than anyone, shared some of his reminiscences and personal maps;

KEN WILSON measured dozens of north side trails;

PATTI BREITMAN hiked many of the trails with me;

RANDY HOGUE offered his outstanding photographs;

DICK and BRUN LIEBES closely read the full text;

PAMELA NEILL SPITZ bore with me throughout;

LINCOLN FAIRLEY, who walked these paths before me;

FRAN BRIGMAN, FAITH DUNCAN, WILMA FOLLETTE, GLENN FULLER, JAY GALLOWAY, BOB LETHBRIDGE, CASEY MAY, MIA MONROE, STEVE PETTERLE, SALEM RICE, BRIAN SANDFORD, and DAVID WIMPFHEIMER all read sections of the manuscript and offered valuable suggestions.

Errors that remain are entirely my own.

A special thank you goes to the thousands of volunteers who built, maintained, and still work on Tamalpais' trails.

This is a record of Tamalpais' trails at press-time, in early 1990. The reader is forewarned that there will be changes, and should always be prepared when on the Mountain.

TAMALPAIS TRAILS

My sturdy lad, with the shining eyes,
Comes back from an overnight hike,
And tries to tell me, in stumbling words
What Tamalpais trails are like.

He speaks of the glories of sunset skies,
And mists of the early morn –
Things that I knew and loved full well
In days before he was born.

Ah, well I remember those Tamalpais trails,
Mounting toward the far sky,
Wandering through valley and woodland dim,
Then over the ridges dry.

'Neath trees where the flickering sunlight weaves
A lacework of shadow and gold,
Then over long stretches of rockland bare,
Gray rocks all lichened and old.

Sometimes by the borders of valleys so deep,
Looking out o'er the sea, darkly blue,
With white specks of sails in the distance far,
And cloud shadows always on view.

Ever new, ever changing, all upward they climb,
The trails, their grit sharp 'neath one's feet;
The winds that blow ever, o'er uplands and trails
All laden with wood odors sweet.

I remember, remember and love them –
Those trails, now forbidden to me,
For I'm old, and now chained to the valley –
Those trails ne'er again shall I see.

But memories, rainbowed and fragrant
Shall linger with me to the end –
Each memory, happy and vivid,
Still keeping the mountain my friend.

- A.H. Hutchinson
As published in "California Out of Doors," 1933.

CONTENTS

OVERVIEW MAP
SHOWING
ACCESS and TRAILHEADS
To accompany the maps in
"Tamalpais Trails"

KEY TO TRAILHEAD MAPS

ALL MAPS: NORTH IS TOP OF PAGE

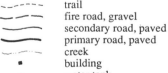

- - - - - - trail
————— fire road, gravel
————— secondary road, paved
————— primary road, paved
- - - - - creek
• building
• water tank
⅌ picnic tables

INDEX TO MAPS

All maps ©1990 by Dewey Livingston

MOUNT TAMALPAIS

It would be difficult to overstate the importance of Mount Tamalpais to the quality of life in the San Francisco Bay Area. For the Mountain veterans who have come to know it intimately over the years, it has assumed a mythic quality. Many couples marry on the Mountain; others will their ashes to be scattered on its slopes. Thousands of others come regularly to hike, run, ride bikes or horses, to look at plants and birds, to fly kites or hang glide, to escape the pressures of urban life and modern times. Hundreds of thousands more come occasionally; some only to see the Mountain Play, others never leave their cars. Tamalpais' presence — immutable, ever green, pristine, visible from so wide an area — provides an assurance of nature's timelessness in a world rapidly changing. Few mountains anywhere are more beloved or more zealously guarded. Few have inspired more legends, poems or paintings. Just why is Mount Tamalpais, but 2,571 feet high and not even the tallest peak in the Bay Area, so special?

One reason is Tamalpais' stunning setting. Straddling the Marin Peninsula, Tam overlooks the Pacific Ocean to the west, the Marin Headlands and the Golden Gate to the south, San Francisco Bay to the east, and seemingly limitless open rolling hills to the north. A second is the famous "Sleeping Maiden" profile of its summit ridge, visible from so much of of the Bay Area. It is, with the Golden Gate, perhaps the quintessential natural feature of the region.

Another factor is Tamalpais' accessibility. Generations of San Franciscans have used the Mountain as their playground; Tam lies barely ten miles from the City's downtown. A road crosses the Mountain, another winds to near the summit. Also, most of the Mountain is publicly owned. It is open every day, without charge, to all.

The Mountain retains a natural environment. True, nearly all Tam's old growth redwoods have been logged; the bears, elk, coyotes, and mountain lions extirpated; its largest creek dammed several times; and countless structures, including a railroad, built on it. Still, much of the Mountain's setting remains wild, with forests, streams, grassy slopes, marshes, meadows, chaparral, and rock outcroppings. A uniquely diverse flora and fauna remains.

Unmeasurable but no less real is a special quality long associated with the Mountain. The native Americans who lived beside it revered Tam, perhaps unwilling to tred on its summit. Many who regularly visit Tamalpais develop a similar veneration. For example, in 1989, the Dalai Lama, spiritual leader of Tibetan Buddhists, chose to hold a service on Tam's West Peak.

Another factor is that Mt. Tamalpais does hold several impressive physical honors. It is the tallest mountain bordering San Francisco Bay. It is the highest point directly on the California coast from Big Sur north into Mendocino County, a distance of over 250 miles. There is no other peak over 2,000 feet in a 30 mile radius of Tamalpais, making it the most prominent feature in a circle of nearly 3,000 square miles.

And then, of course, there are the trails. Perhaps no wilderness area of comparable size in the world has a greater number of, or more richly diversified, or consistently lovelier, trails than Mt. Tamalpais. You can spend your whole life on the Mountain and still discover new trails and new treasures on familiar routes.

This book is about Mt. Tamalpais and those trails that help open its pleasures, its secrets. All of the Mountain's some 160 reasonably maintained trails and fire roads, totaling over 200 miles in length, are described in detail. (Though I don't doubt that, despite my years of research, a few other hidden trails exist on Tamalpais.) Presented are the distances, elevations, intersecting trails, flowers and trees and creeks and other natural features passed along the way, the man-made changes, the story of each trail's name. Each description is intended to be interesting in its own right and, more, an invitation and a guide for exploration. Hopefully all Mountain users; hikers, runners, cyclists, horse riders, historians, and naturalists, plus armchair mountaineers, will find the book of value.

The thought that I could play some role in helping open, even to one person, the rich experiences that Mt. Tamalpais has to offer is what motivated me to write this book. I describe some of the things I've seen and that you might see. If you give it the chance, the Mountain will work a special magic upon you, and your experiences and discoveries will be like no one else's.

Come, let us explore.

How To Use This Book

Each of the 160 trails and fire roads in this book are presented in a standardized format. First, they are grouped into eleven major trailheads, then listed alphabetically. Below each trail's heading are, in italics, five (sometimes six) subheadings. First is the trail's start and end points, with the total mileage. The second line briefly describes the type of terrain the trail traverses, and gives the managing jurisdiction. Line three gives the elevation of the start and end points, and the steepness. On line four are, in order, all the intersecting trails. The last line gives directions to the trail's start. Those trails that have spurs, or branches, carry an additional line. Each of these elements is explained later in this section. Beneath the capsule summary is the full trail description.

In the back of the book are chapters on Tamalpais' creeks, lakes, rocks, weather, flora, fauna, history, key trail junctions, jurisdictions, and recreational opportunities.

THE BOUNDARIES OF MT. TAMALPAIS

Mt. Tamalpais can be described as an L-shaped ridge which runs east-west from East Peak to Bolinas Ridge, then northwest. The east-west ridge has three distinct peaks; East at 2,571', Middle at 2,490', and West at 2,567', separated by saddles. West of West Peak, Tamalpa Ridge extends to Bolinas Ridge. Bolinas Ridge, which runs northwest, is a separate rock formation from the rest of Tamalpais. Among Mt. Tamalpais' several prominent spurs are Throckmorton Ridge on the south side, Blithedale Ridge to the southeast, and Rocky Ridge on the north side.

Except on the southwest, where the Mountain drops to the Pacific Ocean, Tamalpais' physical boundaries are not clear-cut. The Mountain does not neatly descend steadily to low-lying ground. The boundaries used in this book are based on a combination of factors. They include the drops to sea level, creek drainages (particularly Redwood Creek to the south and Lagunitas Creek to the north), public open space boundaries, roads (which usually follow natural contours), traditional maps, and popular conceptions. These boundaries are given below.

North - Fairfax-Bolinas Road, north of which is a separate watershed from Mt. Tamalpais.

Northeast - The borders of Marin Municipal Water District lands.

East - The Magnolia Avenue-Corte Madera Avenue-Camino Alto corridor (the route of Marin's original Highway 101).

Southeast - The Dipsea Trail.

South - Muir Woods (Frank Valley) Road, which follows Redwood Creek.

Southwest - Pacific Ocean.

West - Highway 1 (which borders Bolinas Lagoon).

Northwest - The property of Audubon Canyon Ranch, which is not regularly open to the public.

This is a roughly 60 square mile area, around 8.5 miles east-west and 7.5 miles north-south. It covers some 12% of Marin County. Since around 200 miles of trails are described in this book, Mt. Tamalpais can be said to average just over three miles of trails and fire roads per square mile.

TRAIL STANDARDS

The trails and fire roads on Mt. Tamalpais included in this book all meet a minimum set of standards. Each trail and fire road is:

* Unpaved all, or most, its length.
* Closed to motor vehicles.
* At least 2-3 feet wide.
* Reasonably clear to follow.
* Entirely on public land, or has a public easement through any privately owned sections.
* At least occasionally maintained.
* At least a quarter-mile long (a few important shorter trails are included as well).
* Reasonably safe regarding such hazards as steepness, poison-oak, sharp-pointed shrubs, and the like.
* Not specifically posted as closed by the managing jurisdiction.

TRAILHEADS

All trails are grouped into eleven major trailheads. Some trails depart directly from the trailhead, others are reached by following one or more trails from the trailhead. Trailheads may be a single place (Deer Park, Mountain Home, Muir Woods, Phoenix Lake, Pantoll, Rock Spring) or an area (East Ridgecrest Boulevard, Old Highway 101, Mill Valley, Sky Oaks, West Slope). Each is accessible by automobile. Besides parking areas, there are usually restrooms, water fountains, and telephones at trailheads. The Sky Oaks, Pantoll, and Muir Woods trailheads are staffed.

Each trailhead introduction has directions from Highway 101, Marin's main artery. Each introduction also presents a number of suggested loop walks, arranged by distance, from the trailhead. One of the principal purposes of this book is to enable all users to plan, by themselves, an almost limitless number of loop or other trip options. Still, these suggestions are offered to get beginners started, to highlight some of the classical routes, and to possibly give new ideas to experienced Mountain users. Loop descriptions are quite concise; refer to the individual trail sections for full detail.

Opposite each introduction is a trailhead area map. These maps overlap in coverage to accommodate long distance hikers, runners, bike riders, and equestrians.

TRAIL NAMES

Trail names are among the most colorful features of Mt. Tamalpais. While most trails have one generally agreed upon name, many carry multiple names and some have no name at all. There is no central naming authority for the trails. Given the several jurisdictions into which the Mountain is divided, and the cherished place of the alternate names, standardization is not likely soon.

When a trail carries more than one name, I use what I believe to be the most accepted in the trail's heading, then cite the alternates. The names used by those managing Mountain lands — Marin Municipal Water District (MMWD), Mount Tamalpais State Park (MTSP), Marin County Open Space District (MCOSD), Muir Woods National Monument (MWNM), Golden Gate National Recreation Area (GGNRA), and Marin communities — on their own maps and signs generally take precedence. Maps published by The Olmsted Bros. Map Co. (referred to as "Olmsted"), by T. O. Erickson Maps ("Erickson"), and by the Tamalpais Conservation Club ("TCC") are also key sources. Unnamed trails were a difficulty. For these, I searched for names used by local users or Mountain old-timers. In a handful of cases, I coined a name based on the trail's most characteristic feature.

For some trails, the origin of the name is obscure. This too is part of the Mountain's lore and appeal. I talked with many Mountain veterans, and read both published and unpublished references, but I've no doubt others can expand upon my stories.

There is even less agreement about the "surnames" of trails. The terms "trail," "road," "fire road," "fire trail," and "grade" have been attached to names without standardization, and often vary on different maps. Following is a summary of the surname conventions used in this book.

Trail - This is the standard surname. If no surname is given for a route, "trail" is assumed.

Fire Road - Trails wide enough to accommodate vehicles are called fire roads, whether or not they were built to help in fire control. Many are labeled "protection roads" on signs at their gates.

Grade - Four fire roads have traditionally been, and continue to be, called "grades." They are Old Railroad, Eldridge, Fish, and Shaver.

Road - Three fire roads that are partly paved are called roads. They are Old Stage Road, Camp Eastwood Road, and Steep Ravine Road.

Fire Trail - These were originally broad cuts on ridge lines, carved to help block the spread of fires and to provide access when fighting fires. They are now classified either as a trail if advancing vegetation has narrowed them, or as a fire road if they are still wide.

Spur - A few trails have shorter, unnamed branches, which are called "spurs." They are cited in the second line of the trail summary.

Connector - A trail or fire road that meets minimum standards but is not described separately — usually because it is too short (under a quarter-mile) — is called a connector. Connectors are described with a "from" or "to," or with both.

Path - Any route beneath this book's standards of safety, steepness, or ease of following is considered a path. These include the myriad of deer paths, abandoned older trails, paths improperly worn in as shortcuts, and the like. Paths are only mentioned when they are prominent enough to cause confusion. Their use is discouraged because of the environmental damage that can be caused, and for the dangers of getting lost, brushing poison oak, and the like.

For clarity, the words "trail," "fire road," "grade," "road," and "fire trail" are capitalized when referring to the specific route of the chapter heading.

FROM. . .TO

A trail can, obviously, be followed in either direction. Still, the given "start" and "end" points were not selected arbitrarily. Generally, the end at or nearer an auto-access trailhead is considered the "from" of the heading. When both ends of a trail are auto-accessible, or both are remote, the trail is generally described going uphill. A few exceptions to these rules were made when one end of a trail was much easier to spot than the other, when one direction was deemed unsafe, or when the trail formed a likely loop partner with another trail.

DISTANCE

Over two-thirds of the trails in this book were measured with a surveyor's wheel, either personally or by my friend Ken Wilson. These are so noted in the Appendix. For the others, the distances cited are a blend of my own estimates, the estimates of other users, and what is shown on signposts. Thus, the precise lengths of at least a few trails will remain lively sources of debate.

Distances are expressed in tenths of miles (e.g., .4 miles or .4m). Distances of less than .1 mile are sometimes given in feet or yards, rounded off. Admittedly vague terms, such as "immediately," "directly," and "shortly," are used for some variety. They imply distances of less than 25 yards or so, and indicate the reader should be alert for the noted intersection or point of interest.

TERRAIN

The "terrain" line contains very brief descriptions of the trail's nature. The vegetation summary is based on the plant communities as presented in the "Flora" chapter in the back of the book. "Woodland" and "forest" imply shade, "chaparral" and "grassland" connote openness. "Riparian" means the trail passes beside a creek or lake. "Unimproved" means that the trail is not maintained by the governing jurisdiction, so is likely to be unmarked and have some rough spots. If the trail has exceptional views, that is cited, though there is hardly a trail on Tam without good views and my opinion may differ from yours. If horses are permitted on the trail (they are presumed allowed on fire roads), it is noted here. Also, for those who want (or don't want!) to encounter others, the most visited trails and fire roads are described as "heavily used." At the end of the terrain line is an abbreviation for the jurisdiction(s) through which the trail passes. See the "Jurisdictions" chapter in the back for greater detail.

ELEVATION

For each trail, the elevation in feet is given for the start and end point, and for any significantly higher or lower places passed in between. These elevations come largely from the United States Geological Survey topographic map of the Mt. Tamalpais 15' quadrangle (1954, photorevised 1980). Most elevations are given to the nearest 40 feet, the Survey map's contour line interval.

Along with the elevation is a word or two on the trail's steepness. Since what, for example, is "very steep" to some may be no problem to others, the following rather conservative guidelines are used. They apply to the general nature of the trail; significant sections that differ are noted.

Extremely steep - Elevation changes greater than 850 feet per mile. Stretches may require use of the hands for safety. There is significant risk of falling if attempted downhill. Trails with "extremely steep" sections should be avoided by all but very fit and nimble users.

Very steep - Elevation changes of 600-850 feet per mile. These trails might be a problem for those with concerns about their cardiovascular fitness or sureness of foot.

Steep - Elevation changes of 350-600 feet per mile. When taken slowly, these trails can be comfortably handled by almost all Mountain users.

Gradual - Elevation changes of 100-350 feet per mile. These trails would be considered easy by almost all users.

Almost level - Elevation changes of under 100 feet per mile. While no trail on Mt. Tamalpais is perfectly flat, these come the closest.

Rolling - The route has significantly more uphill and downhill than the net change in elevation indicates.

INTERSECTING TRAILS

Each intersecting trail, with its mileage (expressed as x.xm) from the starting point, is given. With this feature, readers can design for themselves an all but infinite number of fully described trip possibilities. Intersecting fire roads are designated as "F.R." Intersecting connectors are described with "to" or "from."

DIRECTIONS

This is the shortest or easiest-to-follow route to the trail's starting point from the sectional trailhead. If parking is usually a problem, it is noted. "Limited or no parking" means that there are no, or very few, legal spaces by the trail's start. Try to carpool.

ABBREVIATIONS

Below are the abbreviations used in this book. Mount Tamalpais itself is interchangeably referred to as "Mt. Tamalpais," "Tamalpais," "Tam," and "the Mountain." To avoid ambiguity, the words "trail," "grade," "fire road," "road," and "fire trail" are capitalized when they refer to the specific route of the chapter heading.

CHARETTE - "Mt. Tamalpais Map," published by B.Q. Charette Map Co.

ERICKSON - "Trail Map of the Mt. Tamalpais Region," published by Erickson Maps

FAA - Federal Aviation Administration, specifically referring to their tracking facility atop West Peak

F.R. - Fire Road

FAIRLEY - Lincoln Fairley in his book "Mount Tamalpais, A History," published by Scottwall Associates

FREESE - "Trail Map of the Mt. Tamalpais Region," formerly published by Harry Freese

GGNRA - Golden Gate National Recreation Area

HOWELL - John Thomas Howell in his book "Marin Flora," published by the University of California Press

m - mile

MCOSD - Marin County Open Space District

MMWD - Marin Municipal Water District (also called "the Water District")

MTIA - Mt. Tamalpais Interpretive Association

MTSP - Mount Tamalpais State Park (also called "the State Park")

MWNM - Muir Woods National Monument

OLMSTED - "A Rambler's Guide to the Trails of Mt. Tamalpais," a map published by Olmsted Bros. Map Co.

SANBORN - "Tourists' Map of Mt. Tamalpais," published by A.H. Sanborn and P.C. Knapp in 1898

TCC - Tamalpais Conservation Club

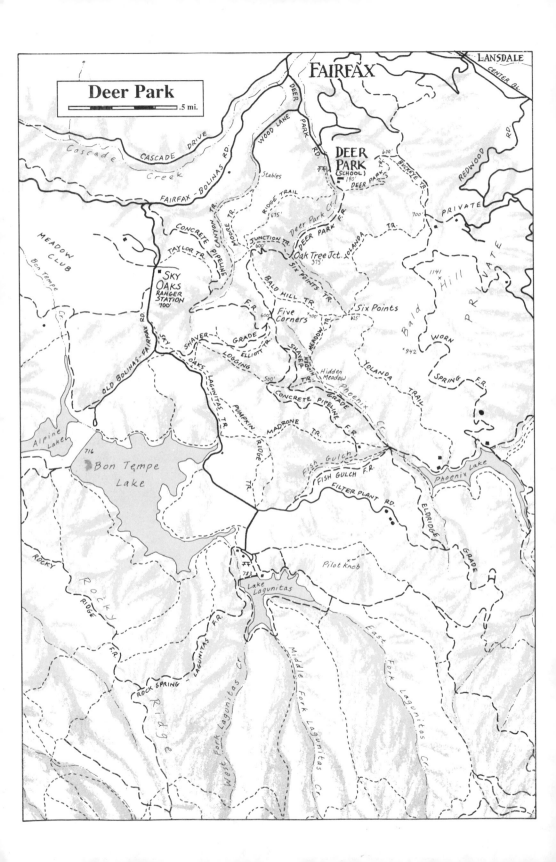

DEER PARK TRAILHEAD

Directions to Deer Park:

Highway 101 - Sir Francis Drake Blvd. (exit) west, Greenbrae, to San Anselmo - left on Center Blvd. to Broadway, Fairfax - left on Bolinas Road - left on Porteous Ave. to end, or to Wood Lane

Deer Park, a delightful picnic area, serves as access to the northernmost trails in this book. The park is maintained by Marin County but is surrounded by Water District land. The adjacent Deer Park School, owned by the Ross Valley School District, is leased to the Fairfax-San Anselmo Children's Center. Pass through the school grounds, to the left or right, to enter the trail network. There are outhouses and fountains near the parking area, and picnic tables, shaded by oaks, on both sides of Deer Park Creek.

Deer Park Fire Road and Deer Park and Ridge trails leave from near the parking area. The Deer Park F.R. is the most used route. It leads, in 1/3 mile, to four-way Oak Tree Junction and, in 2/3 miles, to seven-way Boy Scout Junction.

A second, nearby public access to the Mountain is through the Marin Stables at the end of Wood Lane, a street passed on the way to Deer Park. Please be quiet when going through the stables so as not to startle the horses.

There is a completely separate Deer Park area, and fire road, on the south side of Tamalpais.

Suggested loops from Deer Park - elevation 190'

*Deer Park Trail, .8m, to Worn Spring F.R. - right, .4m to Yolanda Trail - right, .9m, to Six Points Junction - right, .4m, on Bald Hill Trail and fire road connector to Five Corners - right, 1.1m, on Deer Park F.R. to start / **3.6 miles.***

*Deer Park F.R., .4m, to Junction Trail - right, .3m, to Moore Trail - right, .5m, to Canyon Trail - left, .7m, to Concrete Pipeline F.R. - left, .6m, to Five Corners - left on Deer Park F.R., 1.1m, to start / **3.6 miles.***

*Deer Park F.R., 1.1m, to Five Corners - left (east) on Concrete Pipeline F.R., 1.4m, to Fish Gulch Trail - left, .4m, to Phoenix Junction - left on Shaver Grade, .4m, to Hidden Meadow Trail - right, .8m, to Six Points Junction - left on Bald Hill Trail, .7m, to Boy Scout Junction - right on Deer Park F.R., .7m, to to start / **5.5 miles.***

BALD HILL TRAIL

From Boy Scout Junction to Six Points Junction / .7 miles
Terrain: Mostly madrone woodland, parts through redwoods, grassland; horses permitted / MMWD
Elevation: From 380' to 550' / gradual, short part very steep
Intersecting Trails: Connector fire road to Five Corners (.4m), spur of Hidden Meadow (.6m)
Directions: Deer Park trailhead - Deer Park F.R., .7 miles

Bald Hill Trail begins at a seven-way intersection, passes a connector to Five Corners (which has six options), and ends at a five-way junction called Six Points! We'll try to untangle things.

When arriving at Boy Scout Junction on Deer Park F.R. from Deer Park, Bald Hill Trail is the left-most fork. The others, in order clockwise, are: Deer Park F.R. continuing to Five Corners, a connector fire road dropping to Canyon Trail, Moore Trail, Ridge Trail, and Junction Trail.

Bald Hill Trail starts steeply uphill on the western flank of Bald Hill or Baldy. The Trail is covered with wildflowers in spring. At the first leveling, under madrones, note, in spring, the deep blues and purples of the irises. Further along on the Trail the shadings are more pink and white. Yet they are all the same species of the wonderfully variable Marin iris.

In just under .4 miles, the Trail hits a ridge line at a T-intersection. To the right, a connector fire road drops .1 mile to Five Corners. There are splendid views of Mt. Tam. Bald Hill Trail continues left, along the spine of what is sometimes called Kentucky Ridge. It skirts an area closed for erosion control, then veers left into a redwood forest at another rerouting. Bald Hill Trail re-emerges onto the ridge by the top of a spur, marked by a sign, of Hidden Meadow Trail.

In another .1 mile, Bald Hill Trail ends at Six Points. The four other trails are, clockwise: Six Points dropping to Deer Park F.R., Yolanda going to Worn Spring F.R., Yolanda towards Phoenix Lake, and Hidden Meadow Trail dropping to Hidden Meadow. The pristine upper reaches of Bald Hill rise to the northeast. The now overgrown sixth trail out of Six Points ascended Baldy.

BUCKEYE TRAIL

Between Worn Spring Fire Road | .2 miles
Terrain: Grassy hillside; narrow | MMWD
Elevation: Around 540' | almost level
Intersecting Trails: None
Directions: Deer Park Trail to end

This short Trail, named on the Erickson map but not found on Olmsted, cuts off a stiff up and down section on the Worn Spring Fire Road.

Buckeye's northern end is 100 feet above the top of Deer Park Trail. Buckeye is quite narrow, difficult to run on but fine for walking. Pause to enjoy the views of the top of Bald Hill and of the miles of open space. In fall, the Trail still is colored by late-blooming wildflowers; pink from willow-herbs and yellow from madias. Except for an oak or two, all the trees passed along the way are buckeyes, in several small stands. The buckeye's palmate leaves, fragrant candle-like blossoms, the seed capsules clinging to the tree in fall, and the bare limbs in winter are all highly distinctive.

The aptly named Buckeye Trail ends at Worn Spring Fire Road in a saddle. To the right, the fire road passes the north end of Yolanda Trail and continues up Baldy.

CANYON TRAIL

From Marin Stables to Concrete Pipeline Fire Road | .7 miles
Terrain: Riparian; woodland; muddy in winter; horses permitted | MMWD
Elevation: 190' to 480' | gradual, last part very steep
Intersecting Trails: Moore (.1m), connector F.R. to Boy Scout Junction (.5m)
Directions: Wood Lane to end

Canyon Trail begins directly behind Fairfax' Marin Stables, to the left of the last stable when entering from Wood Lane. Be quiet as you walk past the horses. The stables are privately run, though on MMWD land. The Trail, through a peaceful, tree lined canyon, is used principally by horseback riders to and from the stables.

Canyon Trail is basically level for its first .5 miles. One hundred yards past the stables, the (Ethel and Harry) Moore Trail forks left while Canyon continues right, beside the stream. The main stream is crossed once, to the left bank, at around .2 miles. Just after, a feeder stream is also crossed. The trees are mostly laurels, with some madrones. Farther in, redwoods dominate.

In .5 miles, a connector fire road to Boy Scout Junction rises to the left across the stream. Canyon Trail continues straight. It now climbs very steeply over a series of switchbacks. The Trail ends when it meets Concrete Pipeline F.R. To the right is Taylor Trail and Fairfax-Bolinas Road. To the left, it is .8 miles to Five Corners.

The canyon and stream that this Trail follows are unnamed. The Trail itself dates at least to the 1930's.

DEER PARK FIRE ROAD

From Deer Park to Five Corners / 1.1 miles
Terrain: Wooded; riparian; heavily used / Marin County Park & MMWD
Elevation: From 190' to 520' / first half level, second half very steep
Intersecting Trails: Six Points (.4m), Junction (.4m), Bald Hill (.7m), connector fire road to Canyon (.7m), Moore (.7m), Junction (.7m), Ridge (.7m)
Directions: Deer Park

Deer Park Fire Road is the principal route from the Deer Park trailhead. It is popular both for just strolling out and back and as an entry to many other trails on the west side of Bald Hill.

The Fire Road begins from a gate across the playing field behind the old Deer Park School (now the Fairfax-San Anselmo Children's Center). The separate Deer Park Trail goes left from the near side of the field. The Fire Road is level at first, through oak woodland. Deer Park Creek is to the right. Don't venture off, as poison-oak is rampant.

In .3 miles, at a sign, the Fire Road leaves the land leased to the County and enters Water District jurisdiction. Just beyond is the four-way Oak Tree Junction, dominated by a large oak. To the left is Six Points Trail, rising to Six Points. To the right, beside the oak, is the short Junction Trail, an alternate route up to Boy Scout Junction.

Deer Park F.R. then begins climbing steeply under a lovely madrone-laurel canopy. After the stiff rise, the Fire Road levels and opens up as it meets seven-way Boy Scout Junction. The intersecting trails, clockwise, are: Bald Hill rising to Six Points, Deer Park F.R. continuing, a connector fire road down to Canyon Trail, Ridge Trail, Moore Trail to Marin Stables, and the top end of Junction Trail.

Deer Park F.R. continues to climb, but less steeply. This is a lovely area, with views of pristine wooded hills. The Fire Road ends at six-way Five Corners. The trails meeting here are, clockwise: a connector fire road uphill to Bald Hill Trail, the combined Shaver Grade and Concrete Pipeline F.R. going downhill, Elliott going uphill, Shaver Grade going uphill, and Concrete Pipeline towards Fairfax-Bolinas Road.

The Fire Road was built by the Marin County Fire Department in 1948. There is a completely separate Deer Park Fire Road on Tamalpais' southwest slope.

DEER PARK TRAIL

From Deer Park School to Worn Spring Fire Road / .8 miles
Terrain: Lower part riparian and wooded, upper part grassland; horses permitted /
MMWD
Elevation: From 190' to 520' / steep
Intersecting Trails: None
Directions: Deer Park

Deer Park Trail offers serenity within minutes of the popular Deer Park trailhead. Its warm southern exposure helps make it outstanding for wildflowers. The Trail is part of one of the basic routes to the summit of Bald Hill.

To reach the trailhead from the Deer Park parking area, go left past the school, which is now a day care center. You enter an open playing field. Deer Park Trail rises from it, signed, to the left by a black oak. Straight across the field, behind the gate, is the start of the separate Deer Park F.R.

The Trail steadily winds its way up the northwest flank of Bald Hill. The area is quite pretty and peaceful. A stream runs alongside in the lower part. Wildflowers are particularly abundant in the open area just above. You can count on milk-maids and hound's-tongue to lead the annual parade, beginning in January. Several deer paths cut through the area. Views open.

Deer Park Trail ends at Worn Spring Fire Road. To the left, an extremely steep path leads back to the Deer Park parking lot. Uphill, Worn Spring rises past the north end of Buckeye Trail, then bends right on its way to the top of Bald Hill. There is a separate Deer Park on the southwest side of Tamalpais.

ELLIOTT TRAIL

From Five Corners to Sky Oaks-Lagunitas Trail / .6 miles
Terrain: Madrone woodland; horses permitted / MMWD
Elevation: 520' to 700' / parts very steep
Intersecting Trails: Shaver Grade (.3m, .5m)
Directions: Deer Park F.R. to Five Corners

Elliott is the only trail option at the Five Corners junction; the other spokes are fire road width. It winds its way uphill as a secluded bypass of Shaver Grade.

Elliott starts up a few wooden steps, between the two arms of Shaver Grade. It ascends through a madrone-dominated woodland, becoming very steep for a stretch. Shaver Grade, running roughly parallel to the right, is visible.

In .3 miles, Elliott crosses Shaver Grade. The Trail passes through a quintessential California oak woodland, then forks. The path right leads to a lovely, isolated grassy knoll. Elliott continues to the left. It crosses Shaver Grade again, then, immediately, veers right and uphill. The left option at the Shaver junction is the top of Logging Trail. Elliott ends at Sky Oaks-Lagunitas Trail just below Sky Oaks Road.

R. Walter and Harriet Elliott built the nearby Marin Stables, and were guiding forces among the Tamalpais Trail Riders. The Trail is used largely by horse riders. Walter Elliott died while riding in 1962; the Trail was built soon after. The trail signs and many maps misspell the name.

JUNCTION TRAIL

Between Deer Park F.R., Oak Tree Junction to Boy Scout Junction / .3 miles
Terrain: Lightly wooded grass hillside; narrow / MMWD
Elevation: From 200' to 380' / steep
Intersecting Trails: None
Directions: Deer Park F.R., .3 miles

This quarter-mile trail provides an alternate to Deer Park Fire Road between Oak Tree and Boy Scout junctions. Junction Trail begins at Oak Tree Junction, the four-way intersection on Deer Park F.R. just west of the MMWD boundary sign. Junction Trail sets off north (to the right when coming from Deer Park); across the fire road is Six Points Trail.

Junction Trail immediately passes the huge oak that gives the junction its name. It crosses a short bridge. The Trail then rises steeply, with some rocky sections. Its southern exposure helps spring wildflowers, including a mass of baby-blue-eyes near the top, to bloom early. The Trail is at its best on warm summer evenings, when it catches the last sunlight in the canyon.

The Trail ends at Boy Scout Junction. The other six spokes here are, clockwise: Deer Park F.R. from Deer Park, Bald Hill Trail, Deer Park F.R. continuing on to Five Corners, a connector fire road down to Canyon Trail, Moore Trail, and Ridge Trail.

Erickson uses the name Junction Trail, as it connects two key junctions.

MOORE TRAIL

From Canyon Trail to Boy Scout Junction | .4 miles
Terrain: Laurel dominated woodland; muddy in winter; horses permitted | MMWD
Elevation: 220' to 380' | gradual
Intersecting Trails: None
Directions: End of Wood Lane to Marin Stables - Canyon Trail, .1m

One hundred yards behind the Marin Stables, Canyon Trail meets a fork. Canyon continues to the right, along the stream. Left and uphill is the start of Moore Trail. A sign names it for both Ethel and Harry Moore. Naturally, the Trail is quite popular with equestrians.

Moore Trail climbs steadily through a forest of mostly laurels, with occasional madrones. In winter it can be muddy from horse traffic. In summer dust may be a problem, though the Trail's welcome shade more than compensates.

The Trail climbs gradually for just under .5 miles. A few yards before its end, a sign reads only "Ethel Moore Trail." Behind a MMWD sign, the nearly invisible last part of Ridge Trail enters. Moore Trail ends at Boy Scout Junction. The other intersecting trails are, clockwise: Junction to Deer Park F.R., Deer Park F.R. down to Deer Park, Bald Hill, Deer Park F.R. up to Five Corners, and a short connector fire road down to Canyon Trail.

The Moores were horse lovers closely associated with Marin Stables, and were charter members of the Tamalpais Trail Riders. Harry Moore died in 1944. The Trail was built a few years later and named for him. Ethel Moore, then 86, was present during the dedication ceremony.

RIDGE TRAIL

From Deer Park to Boy Scout Junction / 1.1 miles
Terrain: Oak-madrone woodland; narrow; lined with poison oak; unimproved;
horses permitted / MMWD
Elevation: From 200' to 560' to 380' / very steep
Intersecting Trails: None
Directions: Deer Park

Ridge Trail is at this book's both northern geographic limits and quality standard limits, and is rapidly passing beyond the latter. It has not been maintained since the mid-1970's and is now overgrown with broom in sections, unsigned, and has several tricky intersections. The Trail is included because it leaves from a popular trailhead, is found on the Erickson map, passes through an otherwise trackless area, and hits a pair of knolls offering outstanding Mt. Tamalpais views.

The Trail sets off from the Deer Park sign, to the right as you enter the parking area. In under .1 mile it passes the shaded picnic area by the bridge across Deer Park Creek. Ridge Trail continues along the creek's left bank. Beware of poison oak along the margins here and all the rest of the way. Bypass four paths up to the right; they all connect to Ridge Trail but are even steeper and more overgrown than the main Trail. In .3 miles, there is another fork. Left drops down to the creek; take the uphill fork to the right.

Ridge Trail rises very steeply. Irises dot the hillside in spring. Scotch broom lines the Trail. Madrones and oaks are the common trees. Many paths branch off both left and right but the true route, ever uphill, can still be discerned. The climbing leads to a clearing with an excellent Tam vista. The Trail is then heavily overgrown with French broom, but passable.

Press on to reach the spine of Deer Park Ridge. At a knoll, there is a stunning view of Tamalpais. The vista is pristine, nary a sign of a residence. Go another .1 mile to a slightly higher knoll, and another great Mountain shot. Bald Hill is to the left. The Trail then fades a bit as it veers left and drops very sharply. The lowest yards are a bare trace. One fork meets the Moore Trail sign just uphill from Boy Scout Junction, another drops to the junction itself.

The ridge the Trail follows separates the canyon of Deer Park Creek from the one housing Canyon Trail. Ridge Trail was built during World War II by the Tamalpais Trail Riders. They wanted to provide additional equestrian routes to replace the many that were closed off by the military. The Trail was originally called Harry Scott Trail, for the man who built nearby Crest Farm and who was a founder, and the first president, of the Trail Riders.

SIX POINTS TRAIL

From Deer Park Fire Road at Oak Tree Junction to Six Points Junction / .6 miles
Terrain: Deeply wooded; riparian / MMWD
Elevation: From 220' to 550' / steep
Intersecting Trails: None
Directions: Deer Park Fire Road, .3 miles

Six Points Trail offers easy access to the peaceful west face of Bald Hill. It plays a role in several loop possibilities out of Deer Park. And it is a lovely trail, alongside a stream through deep woods, in its own right.

The Trail rises to the left (south) of the Deer Park F.R., .3 miles from the fire road's start. On the other side of the four-way intersection, called Oak Tree Junction for a large oak to the right, Junction Trail departs uphill.

Six Points Trail heads off into a quiet creekside woodland, with redwoods amidst madrones and laurels. It quickly begins ascending steeply alongside Deer Park Creek. The vegetation in this cool, wet forest is lush. Ferns are abundant among the redwoods. In mid-summer, you may be lucky enough to spot the small greenish-white flowers of rein-orchis, a member of the always special orchid family. Switchbacks ease the uphill climb.

The Trail veers right, away from and above the headwaters of the creek. It ends at five-way Six Points Junction, on a ridge with striking Mt. Tam views. The other four trails are, clockwise: Yolanda heading to Worn Spring Fire Road, Yolanda towards Phoenix Lake, Hidden Meadow downhill, and Bald Hill Trail on to Boy Scout Junction. The missing sixth point is a now overgrown path up Bald Hill.

The Trail has also been known as Redwood Trail, particularly among equestrians.

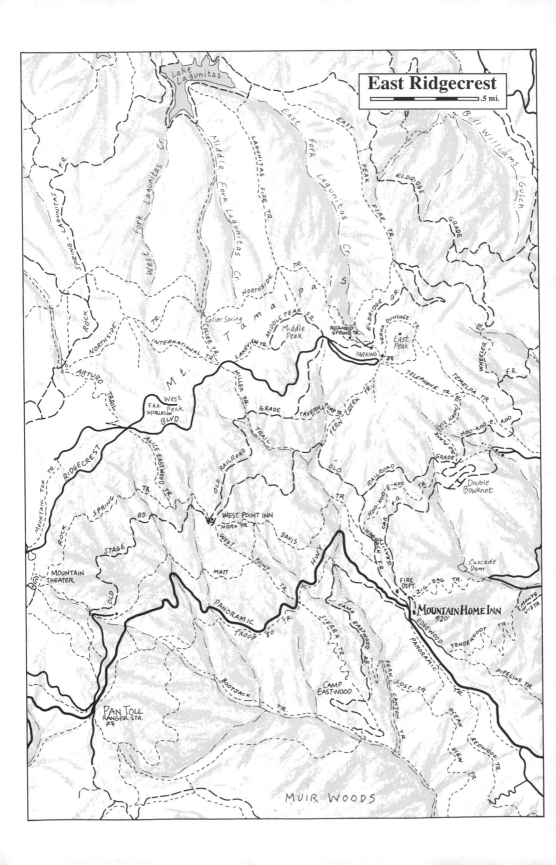

EAST RIDGECREST BLVD. TRAILHEAD

Directions to East Ridgecrest Boulevard:
Highway 101 - Highway 1 - Panoramic Highway - Southside (Pantoll) Road to Rock Spring, or
Fairfax-Bolinas Road, from either downtown Fairfax (where it is called Bolinas Road) or from Highway 1 at north end of Bolinas Lagoon - West Ridgecrest Blvd. to Rock Spring

Ridgecrest Boulevard runs 6.6 miles from Fairfax-Bolinas Road to the East Peak parking area. Some 20 trails intersect it. The road's scenic appeal is known world-wide as many automobile, and other, commercials have been filmed on it. The boulevard was built as a toll road in the 1920's. Tolls were collected at the Fairfax-Bolinas Road junction at a site called Ridgecrest. A sign there proclaimed that the road was among the most beautiful in the world. At the start of World War II, the military closed the boulevard. Ridgecrest reopened after the war as a public road, free of charge.

Ridgecrest Boulevard is often divided into two sections. The 3.7 mile stretch along Bolinas Ridge from Fairfax-Bolinas Road to Rock Spring is known as West Ridgecrest. Trails off West Ridgecrest are described in the West Slope Trailhead. The 2.9 mile section of Ridgecrest from Rock Spring to the East Peak parking lot is referred to as East Ridgecrest. It is the highest road in the County, and the access for trails in this section. Rock Spring itself is treated as a separate trailhead.

Gates at Fairfax-Bolinas Road and at Pantoll bar vehicular access to Ridgecrest Boulevard at night; call Pantoll Ranger Station at 415/388-2070 to check gate closing and opening times. At press-time, there were plans to institute a $3 parking fee at East Peak.

Suggested loops from East Peak parking area - elevation 2,360'

Verna Dunshee Trail loop / .7 miles.

Fern Creek Trail, .7m, to Old Railroad Grade - right, .1m, to Miller Trail - right, .5m, to across Ridgecrest Boulevard - right on Lakeview Trail, .2m, to Middle Peak F.R. - left, .7m, to Ridgecrest Boulevard and start / 2.2 miles.

Eldridge Grade, 1.2m, to Northside Trail - left, 1.6m, to Colier Trail - left (uphill), .4m, to International Trail - left, .1m, to across Ridgecrest Blvd. - Miller Trail, .3m, to Old Railroad Grade - left, .8m, to start / 4.4 miles.

ARTURO TRAIL

From FAA base on Tamalpa Ridge to Rifle Camp / .5 miles
Terrain: Deep woodland / GGNRA & MMWD
Elevation: From 2,360' to 2,000' / very steep
Intersecting Trails: None
Directions: Rock Spring - East Ridgecrest Boulevard to FAA gate; limited parking

The reopening of Arturo Trail in 1985 was a source of joy to Mountain veterans. The Trail was long part of a popular route between Tam's north and south sides. From 1951, after the construction of the Mill Valley Air Force Station on Tamalpa (West Peak) Ridge, it was closed for 34 years. It is now again a key north-south link.

To reach the upper end of Arturo, enter the main FAA gate off Ridgecrest Boulevard. Veer left, through a gap in the gate. Follow the hiker symbol sign down the left fork of the paved road. Another hiker sign, to the right, marks the trailhead.

In World War II, the military secured long-term leases to Water District lands here. In 1983, the remaining leases, save for the parcel on the very top of West Peak, were turned over to the Golden Gate National Recreation Area. After a spirited debate, a decision was made to remove the structures and return the area to open space. (At press-time, the volunteer effort to dismantle the buildings was halted because high levels of asbestos were found. Professional removal of the asbestos was awaiting funding.) The West Peak summit, uphill to the right, remains, however, fenced and off-limits. The two prominent, five-story white "golf ball" radar domes atop it are used by the Federal Aviation Administration and the Air Force. Their plans to replace the two domes with a larger but less conspicuous single dome were meeting with opposition from environmental groups and the MMWD at press-time. The MMWD, scheduled to resume stewardship of the land when the leases expire in the year 2005, is concerned that a new facility will unlikely be abandoned then.

Arturo drops sharply at its start. It returns to the edge of the Air Force base's old fence, then enters a Douglas fir-dominated forest. Over a hundred years ago, the area was rather open, perhaps the result of a fire. Manzanitas came in, enjoying the full sunlight. Then the Douglas firs invaded, crowding out the manzanita, whose skeletons remain. Some of the huge, older firs, which grew here without competition for sunlight, have sizable lower limbs. These monarchs are called "wolf trees," because they choke out competing plant growth. An impressive pair beside the Trail have been named Romulus and Remus. Above them, a path, the old Potrero Cutoff, sets off for Potrero Meadow. Quiet is assured here in this delightful woodland. Lower down, bays, tanbark oaks, and madrones resist the Douglas firs' ascendancy.

The Trail ends when it hits Rock Spring-Lagunitas Fire Road at Rifle Camp. Also at this junction, Northside Trail departs toward Eldridge Grade and, across the fire road, Azalea Meadow Trail begins its descent to Kent Trail. Potrero Meadow, definitely worth visiting, is a few yards to the left.

Arthur, or Arturo, Oettl, a member of the Cross-Country Boys Club, built the Trail in the 1920's. It was a partial reroute of the old Coyote Trail, the first ever constructed by the Tamalpais Conservation Club. The Marin Conservation Corps, the GGNRA, the MMWD, and the Mt. Tamalpais History Project all played key roles in the Arturo's reopening.

EASTWOOD TRAIL

From Ridgecrest Boulevard to Rock Spring Trail | .5 miles
Terrain: Chaparral; rocky; views | MMWD
Elevation: From 2,400' to 1,920' | extremely steep
Intersecting Trails: None
Directions: Rock Spring - East Ridgecrest Boulevard to 25 yards past FAA gate

Only Plankwalk Trail and Middle Peak Fire Road run higher on the Mountain than Eastwood Trail. Correspondingly, Eastwood offers some of the best views in the Bay Area. However, you may find yourself watching your footing, as the Trail is extremely steep and rocky.

The upper end of Eastwood (or Alice Eastwood) Trail is across Ridgecrest Boulevard from the gate into the Federal Aviation Administration tracking facility. The start is marked only by a sign with the hiking figure symbol used by the GGNRA; a narrow strip beside the boulevard is GGNRA property. The Trail immediately enters Water District land.

Eastwood Trail skirts a small grove of isolated Sargent cypress trees. It meets an open area of reddish rock amid blue-green serpentine. The views here, of ocean, Marin Headlands, San Francisco skyline and Bay, and East Bay are spectacular. The distant Farallon Islands are not on the horizon; ocean is visible beyond them.

The Trail bends right (a shortcut path rises left) and begins its precipitous descent through chaparral shrub. You'll probably be gripping the chamise and manzanita for safety if you're descending. The Trail ends when it meets Rock Spring Trail at a well marked junction. It is .4 miles left to West Point Inn and 1.1 miles right to the Mountain Theater.

Alice Eastwood was one of the most beloved of all people associated with Mt. Tamalpais. She was an outstanding botanist, Curator of Botany at the California Academy of Sciences in San Francisco for 47 years. She did much of her field research on Tamalpais, from 1891 to her death, at 94, in 1953. Her particular passion was manzanita, and she described and named five of the Mountain's six species. She walked with the swiftest and ruggedest of the Mountain's male hikers, often over 30 miles a day carrying plant presses, and was accepted as an equal. Alice Eastwood is honored on Tamalpais by this manzanita-lined Trail, by Camp Eastwood, and by Camp Eastwood Road. Mountain veteran John Colier is said to have built the trail.

FERN CREEK TRAIL

From Ridgecrest Boulevard to Old Railroad Grade / .7 miles
Terrain: Upper half through chaparral over loose rock; lower part riparian and heavily wooded; slippery sections / MMWD
Elevation: From 2,340' to 1,580' / extremely steep
Intersecting Trails: Tavern Pump (.5m)
Directions: Rock Spring - East Ridgecrest Boulevard to end

Fern Creek flows nearly the entire height of Mt. Tamalpais, from around 2,200' down to Redwood Creek in Muir Woods at below 200'. Fern Creek Trail follows the creek's upper reaches. A separate trail, Fern Canyon (also sometimes called Fern Creek Trail), follows the creek much lower, in Muir Woods. Fern Creek Trail is important as a shortcut to and from the top of the Mountain, bypassing three miles of the gentler graded but more circuitous Old Railroad Grade. Since its upper end is accessible by car, the Trail will be described downhill. Be careful; the route is quite steep and slippery.

Fern Creek Trail starts southbound from just below the East Peak parking lot. The winding, 125 yard topmost section, between the one-way upper and lower arms of Ridgecrest Boulevard, is little used. The crossing of lower Ridgecrest is marked by white lines and a State Park sign. Fern Creek then descends very steeply through chaparral. There are fine southern views over the canyon. A water pipeline follows the trail.

In .4 miles, the Trail meets a water tank and a blue building, which houses a working pump, the Tavern Pump. The pump sends water through the pipeline, on a narrow sliver of State Park property in the midst of MMWD lands, to the East Peak area. Steps lead down left to the pump. Tavern Pump Trail, rising to Old Railroad Grade, sets off to the right. Fern Creek Trail continues straight.

In less than .1 mile, after a big bend left, the Trail crosses Fern Creek. Here only an easy rock hop is required; below, in Muir Woods, bridges are needed to cross. There is a distinctive stand of chain (or Woodwardia) ferns at the crossing, one of several fern species encountered along the creek. Chain ferns are Marin's largest ferns, reaching nine feet in height elsewhere on the Mountain. Look on the undersides of the fronds (leaves) and you might see the fern's next generation of spore clusters (called sori) lined in the chain-like formation that gives the plant its name.

The Trail follows the creek down. This forested canyon is quite lovely. Several short drops over rocks must be negotiated. Loose dirt, slippery tanbark oak acorns, and exposed roots also slow the descent. Fern Creek Trail ends at a bend in Old Railroad Grade. Hogback F.R. is .4 miles to the left, West Point around a mile right. Fern Creek itself goes under the Grade through a culvert.

INTERNATIONAL TRAIL

From Ridgecrest Boulevard to Northside Trail / .5 miles
Terrain: Forest; lowest yards open serpentine / MMWD
Elevation: From 2,300' to 2,060' / gradual, parts steep
Intersecting Trails: Colier (.1m)
Directions: Rock Spring - East Ridgecrest Boulevard 1.9 miles to saddle between West and Middle peaks

International Trail starts at one of Tamalpais' best view spots, and ends at another. The signed trailhead is on the north side of Ridgecrest Boulevard at a turnout. Here, in the dip between West and Middle peaks, is a rare vista to both the north and south. A few yards up Ridgecrest toward Middle Peak is a presently unsigned entrance to Lakeview Trail. Across the pavement, south, is the upper end of Miller Trail.

International Trail quickly sets off into the trees. In 100 yards the upper end of the extremely steep Colier Trail, which drops all the way to Lake Lagunitas, enters on the right, unsigned. The downhill steepens, and is very steep over a root-covered stretch. Just before a huge Douglas-fir on the left edge of the Trail, a path goes left. Called Birthday Trail (not separately described) by some, it rises 1/6 mile to Rocky Ridge Fire Trail.

International continues down, less steeply. It leaves the forest when it hits serpentine rock. There are again excellent views, to the north. In another 50 yards, International ends as it meets Northside Trail. Some 100 yards to the left, Northside crosses broad Rocky Ridge Fire Trail. To the right, Northside heads to Colier Spring and Trail, offering a nice loop option.

International was built in the 1940's as a replacement north-south route over the Mountain's summit ridge for Arturo Trail, which was closed during World War II. One story relates that it was named in a spirit of harmony to reflect the many backgrounds of those who worked on it. Another story has it that MMWD patrolman Joe Zapella remarked, when planning to talk to those responsible for the Trail's unauthorized construction, there would be an "international situation" because of the many nationalities of the builders.

LAKEVIEW TRAIL

From Ridgecrest Boulevard to Middle Peak Fire Road | .2 miles
Terrain: Light woodland and chaparral | MMWD
Elevation: From 2,300' to 2,400' | gradual
Intersecting Trails: None
Directions: Rock Spring - East Ridgecrest Boulevard 1.9 miles to saddle between West and Middle peaks

Lakeview Trail (completely separate from Lakeview Fire Road, which connects Lake Lagunitas to Eldridge Grade) is one of Tamalpais' oldest. It once ran between the two saddles of Tamalpais' summit ridge. Now its eastern half has been covered by Middle Peak Fire Road. What is left of Lakeview Trail is short, but appealing.

Lakeview sets off on the north side of Ridgecrest Boulevard at the special vista point of the West-Middle Peak saddle. Its trailhead is presently unsigned. International Trail sets off a few yards below Lakeview, and Miller Trail descends from the opposite, south side of the road.

Lakeview gently rises along the northern face of Middle Peak. Between the shrubs and trees are splendid views, but not as sweeping as years ago, when fires regularly kept the foliage lower. Lake Lagunitas, the closest of the three visible lakes and the "view lake" that gave the Trail its name, can now just barely be glimpsed. Bon Tempe Lake is most prominent, with a bit of Alpine Lake visible beyond Bon Tempe Dam.

Lakeview Trail ends at its unsigned junction with Middle Peak Fire Road. Straight ahead, the fire road, over the original Lakeview Trail route, descends to Ridgecrest Boulevard at the saddle between East and Middle peaks. To the right, the fire road rises .2 miles to Middle Peak's summit.

LOWER NORTHSIDE TRAIL

From Rocky Ridge Fire Trail to Colier Spring / .9 miles
Terrain: Heavily wooded; parts open and rocky / MMWD
Elevation: From 1,840' to 1,800' / almost level
Intersecting Trails: None
Directions: Rock Spring - East Ridgecrest Blvd. - International Trail - Colier Trail to Colier Spring

Lower Northside Trail runs, all but level, through a remote area high on the Mountain's north face. To reach the trailhead, follow Colier Trail down to the delightful, traditional hiker's resting spot of Colier Spring. The other intersecting trails there are, clockwise: Northside (or Upper Northside) heading west to Rifle Camp, Lower Northside, Colier Trail descending to Lake Lagunitas, and Northside going east to Eldridge Grade. We take the well-marked Lower Northside.

Lower Northside begins amidst towering redwoods. There is a brief opening, another redwood grove, then a somewhat rocky stretch. The Trail gently rises to another view site, with Pilot Knob and Bald Hill framed between the trees. A short rise brings Lower Northside to another stand of redwoods, and the crossing of the upper reaches of the West Fork of Lagunitas Creek.

Just about all the most common trees of Tam are to be found in the woodland ahead: huge Douglas-firs and redwoods along with bay, madrone, live oak, tanbark oak, and nutmeg. The Trail leaves the forest to enter an open area of serpentine rock. Here only shrubs and stunted Sargent cypress trees grow. The views north and west are outstanding.

Lower Northside ends at its junction with Rocky Ridge Fire Trail. One-third mile uphill (left), Northside Trail crosses Rocky Ridge, offering an easy loop opportunity. Seventy-five yards downhill is Rock Spring-Lagunitas Fire Road. The Trail, often spelled Lower North Side, was built in the 1930's.

MIDDLE PEAK FIRE ROAD

From Ridgecrest Boulevard to Middle Peak | .6 miles
Terrain: Mostly chaparral; views | MMWD
Elevation: From 2,240' to 2,480' | gradual
Intersecting Trails: Lagunitas Fire (.2m), Lakeview (.4m)
Directions: Rock Spring - East Ridgecrest Boulevard 2.5 miles to saddle between Middle and East peaks

A Fire Road, not named on any of the maps, climbs to the top of Middle Peak. It starts on the north side of Ridgecrest Boulevard, opposite the top of Old Railroad Grade and a few yards below the top of Eldridge Grade. This saddle between East Peak and Middle Peak is quite visible from, for example, the Ross Valley. The area was once known as Pieville. A funicular from here to Middle Peak was built in 1905; its route up the peak's face is now overgrown.

Middle Peak F.R. begins rising gradually beyond the gate. There are fine views to the north between gaps in the foliage; be patient, the vistas will soon open completely. In .2 miles, the unsigned, easy to miss Lagunitas Fire Trail comes in on the right. There are a rectangular metal cover, a power line pole, and a boulder at the junction. The fire trail drops extremely steeply all the way to Lake Lagunitas.

The Fire Road bends sharply to the left. Lakeview Trail sets off straight ahead, to Ridgecrest Boulevard at the saddle between Middle and West peaks. Middle Peak Fire Road continues uphill. It passes a couple of paths to the left before reaching the summit area. Middle Peak's crest is at 2,490 feet in elevation. The nearly 360 degree panorama, only slightly blocked by East and West peaks, taller by 91 and 87 feet, respectively, is stunning.

To the left is a futuristic-looking green building, built in 1981. It is the hub of a privately run microwave communications network used by several government agencies and private firms, and is off-limits to the public. To the right, also not to be disturbed, is an array of Federal Aviation Administration equipment. Use of Middle Peak for communication purposes has a long history. Two 300 foot tall wooden radio transmission towers were erected, using the funicular, on the peak in 1905. They blew over the next year.

Middle Peak Fire Road was built over the eastern half of old Lakeview Trail to access the new facilities on the summit.

MILLER TRAIL

From Ridgecrest Boulevard to Old Railroad Grade / .8 miles
Terrain: Upper half chaparral, lower half riparian and heavily wooded; parts rocky /
MMWD
Elevation: From 2,300' to 1,580' / very steep
Intersecting Trails: Old Railroad Grade (.3m)
Directions: Rock Spring - East Ridgecrest Boulevard 1.9 miles to saddle between West
and Middle peaks

Miller Trail has two completely different characters. Its upper half is through chaparral, with excellent views from high on the Mountain. Its lower half is heavily wooded, alongside a stream in a deep canyon. Each part contributes to make Miller one of Tamalpais' lovelier trails. East Ridgecrest Boulevard drops to a saddle, or dip, between West and Middle peaks. There are paved parking turnouts, and splendid views, on both sides of the road. To the north are accesses to both the International and Lakeview trails. On the south side is the top of Miller Trail.

Miller starts with a few downhill steps, and continues dropping very steeply. The canyon of the headwaters of the west fork of Fern Creek is to the right. Chaparral shrubs line the Trail as it passes over serpentine rock. A couple of pioneeering Douglas firs stand out; they may dominate the canyon one day.

In 1/3 mile, Miller hits Old Railroad Grade; the last few yards before the junction are quite steep. A new wooden signpost, and the remains of an old metal one, mark the intersection. West Point is to the right, East Peak to the left. Miller continues across the Grade. It offers an almost one mile shortcut downhill compared to the less steep Grade.

Miller again is steep and rocky. In .1 mile, the Trail meets a creek bed and enters forest. Soon, a more heavily flowing feeder of the west fork of Fern Creek enters on the far right. The Trail plunges deeper into the forest, where it remains. Keep a sharp eye right to spot where the Trail crosses to the other bank. A clump of large chain ferns and several blue elderberry bushes mark the site, and rocks help to ford the water. The Trail continues down. A large, fallen tanbark oak forces you to bend. Soon the Trail recrosses back to the creek's left bank (the creek is now to the right). Redwoods tower above.

The Trail encounters a slide, already being covered by monkeyflower, from the great storm of January 1982. Redwoods lie fallen across the creek. The

Trail was repaired here in 1989 with wooden steps added to ease the descent. There is a huge rock on the left. A pipe, which once carried water from the creek, lays broken off at both ends. The Trail drops its final yards through more towering redwoods.

Miller ends at its second junction with Old Railroad Grade. The junction is easy to spot as Old Railroad Grade rises on both sides of the redwood-lined bend. This rarity on the Grade also dates from January 1982. The raging creek tore off 40 feet of the fire road, which was then refilled. Fern Creek Trail is .1 mile to the left and West Point is about a mile to the right.

John Miller was a native of Canada who came to San Francisco in 1895, at age 29. He joined the Tamalpais Conservation Club in 1921, and worked tirelessly on the Mountain's trails until his death in 1951. When he was 80, he badly injured his back while prying a boulder on this Trail. The accident left him bedridden for most of the final three years of his life, and the Trail was named in his honor. He left a sizable bequest to the TCC, which helped toward purchase of additions to the State Park, notably the area around O'Rourke's Bench. To Miller is attributed the wonderful quote, "Why should I deserve praise? Hasn't the Mountain always repaid whatever work I did on it, giving me health, happiness and friendships?"

MOUNTAIN TOP TRAIL

From Ridgecrest Boulevard to former Air Force base on Tamalpa Ridge / .5 miles
Terrain: Rocky; overgrown; lightly wooded; unimproved; views / MMWD & GGNRA
Elevation: From 2,100' to 2,400' / steep
Intersecting Trails: None
Directions: Rock Spring - East Ridgecrest Blvd. .4 miles

Mountain Top Trail originally did go to the highest point on Tam, the 2,604 foot summit of West Peak. In 1951, West Peak was bulldozed and leveled down to 2,567 feet, four feet below East Peak, during construction of the Air Force base. A California Alpine Club memorial cairn, for those who died in the Great War, that stood at the summit was plowed under. Mountain Top Trail was cut off. Only a half-mile of its westernmost section remains.

The Trail begins at a gate on the north side of Ridgecrest Boulevard across from a parking area for the Mountain Theater. Rock Spring-Lagunitas Fire Road also begins here; it immediately veers left while Mountain Top Trail continues straight. The broad Trail climbs parallel to, and above, Ridgecrest Boulevard.

Some ducking may be required beneath overgrown trees and shrubs but the Trail is otherwise fine. The air base's old fence line is still evident. In openings between trees, many of them Sargent cypress, are superb southern and eastern panoramas. The Trail is blocked by overgrowth in around a half-mile. Scramble uphill left to the top of the ridge, known as West Peak Ridge, Tamalpa Ridge, or, earlier, Bill Williams Ridge.

Many buildings remain from the Air Force station; the one directly above left housed a bowling alley and a movie theater. After considerable public debate, the GGNRA, which inherited the Air Force's lease of the Water District land, agreed to have the buildings torn down and the area returned to open space. They were being cleared by volunteers when high levels of asbestos were discovered. Work remains halted until funds to remove the asbestos are allocated. Because of the disrepair, the area is posted as closed. Arturo descends to Rifle Camp from the other side of the base.

A trail, called Bill Williams (though separate from the Bill Williams Trail that connects Phoenix Lake to Tucker Trail), ran along Tamalpa Ridge to West Peak since the late 1800's. A parallel fire trail just south of Bill Williams appears on the 1914 map published by the Tamalpais Fire Association. It is apparently this fire trail, later used as a road into the military installation, that survives today as Mountain Top Trail. The Trail, like most of the top of Tam, was closed by the military during World War II.

NORTHSIDE TRAIL

From Rifle Camp to Eldridge Grade / 2.7 miles
Terrain: Light woods, parts deep forest, rocky chaparral; horses permitted / MMWD
Elevation: Around 2,000' / almost level
Intersecting Trails: Rocky Ridge (.5m), International (.6m), Lower Northside (1.1m), Colier (1.1m), Lagunitas Fire (1.6m), Redwood Spring (2.1m), East Peak Fire (2.7m)
Directions: Rock Spring - East Ridgecrest Boulevard to FAA gate - Arturo Trail

No trail in Marin runs longer above 1,800 feet than Northside. It ranks with Coastal as the longest of the almost level trails on Tam. Northside, in total or in part, usually plays a role in most circuit routes of Tam. Traversing the full length of Northside is one of Mt. Tamalpais' treats.

Northside Trail departs from the base of Arturo Trail, on the south side of Rock Spring-Lagunitas Fire Road at Rifle Camp. This section of Northside, to Colier Spring, is commonly called Upper Northside. Douglas-fir dominates in the deep woodland. Soon laurel become the principal forest tree. In 1/3 mile, the Trail enters an open serpentine rock area. The views from this short section, just above 2,000 feet, are spectacular. They sweep from Point Reyes across Marin into Sonoma and Napa Counties. The only trees are Sargent cypress, growing shrub-like beside the manzanita.

Northside crosses Rocky Ridge Trail beneath a telephone line. Rocky Ridge goes uphill to the fence around the old Air Force base and downhill to Lower Northside Trail and Rock Spring-Lagunitas F.R. Northside continues across at a wood signpost. In 120 yards, still on the open serpentine, International Trail comes in from the right. It rises to Ridgecrest Boulevard. Just beyond, at the edge of the forest, look carefully in spring for fragrant wild onion, with its six pink-purple petals in clusters on a thick, leafless stalk. Northside returns to woodland. It passes through a grove of short redwoods. In the next grove, near Colier Spring, the redwoods are towering.

Colier Spring was once a reliable source of water. Since a storm shifted its underground source away from the pipe, it is usually dry. Still, it is one of the best loved resting spots on the Mountain. Five routes converge. Clockwise from Northside, they are: Lower Northside dropping to Rock Spring-Lagunitas F.R., Colier descending extremely steeply down the canyon to Lake Lagunitas, Northside continuing, and Colier going uphill to International Trail.

Northside Trail rises slightly as it leaves the redwood forest. At 1/4 mile past Colier is a pipe tapping a now more reliable spring. Chain ferns mark the damp site. Shortly past are azalea bushes, on both sides of the Trail. Their striking, and fragrant, pinkish-white flowers bloom in late spring. Earlier, irises abound here. Back in the chaparral, the unsigned, extremely steep Lagunitas Fire Trail crosses Northside. Left leads down to Lake Lagunitas, right up to Middle Peak Fire Road.

The last mile of Northside offers many outstanding views. Attention to footing as well becomes important as the Trail passes through a 1/4 mile band of loose, broken rocks. Two hundred yards past the end of the rock scree is the unsigned lower end of Redwood Spring Trail. It rises on the right to Redwood Spring and Eldridge Grade.

Northside crosses the East Fork of Lagunitas Creek. The Trail has now passed all three forks of the Mountain's most important creek, the one that is dammed to form, in order, Lakes Lagunitas, Bon Tempe, Alpine, and Kent. Madrone and nutmeg become the most common trees. A clearing offers a fine view down the canyon to Pilot Knob and beyond.

Northside then hits Inspiration Point, a rock ledge with a splendid northern panorama. Here the precipitous East Peak Fire Trail crosses, left down to Lakeview F.R., right to high on Eldridge Grade. Northside goes on, wider, for about another 100 yards. It ends at a bend in Eldridge Grade roughly halfway between the Wheeler Trail intersection below and the top of East Peak Fire Trail above. A classic old sign marks the spot.

Mountain veteran Ted Abeel began working on Northside in 1926, to improve the hiking possibilites on the Mountain's less visited north face. Other sources credit the Sierra Club and the Civilian Conservation Corps as playing key roles. The Trail's name is often spelled North Side.

PLANKWALK TRAIL

From East Peak parking area to East Peak / .2 miles
Terrain: Chaparral; loose rock; views; heavily used / MMWD & MTSP
Elevation: From 2,390' to 2,571' / very steep to extremely steep
Intersecting Trails: None
Directions: Rock Spring - East Ridgecrest Blvd. to end

Plankwalk Trail reaches the highest point in Marin County, the 2,571' summit of Mt. Tamalpais. The lure of reaching the top of Tam makes Plankwalk one of the most used trails on the Mountain. It also provides an example of how changes occur on the Mountain's trails.

Plankwalk begins as a wide, rock-strewn route up from the Verna Dunshee Trail loop behind the East Peak refreshment stand. In around 50 yards, there is a bend to the right which the traditional way to the top followed. In 1989, the State Park closed that broad route by erecting wooden barriers. They were reacting to lawsuits filed by visitors, some in inappropriate footwear, who had fallen on the very slippery terrain. The alternate, safer route, now the only access to the summit, departs left from the bend as a narrow trail. It too is called Plankwalk on the MTSP signpost.

Plankwalk continues upward on the north, then the east side, of the Mountain. The views are splendid, unsurpassed. The Trail bends right. At the next bend left, an overgrown and precipitous "path" continues straight. It leads, in a few yards beside a pipe, to one of the Mountain's hidden treasures. Just yards below the northwest corner of the lookout tower is an old bench and plaque. The well preserved plaque reads:

BENEATH THIS PLATE ARE THE NAMES OF THOSE HEROES OF THE AIR WHO HAVE FALLEN IN THE PURSUIT OF THE SCIENCE OF AVIATION, ERECTED BY THE CITIZENS OF MILL VALLEY, MAY 30, 1915.

Return to the stone steps for the final yards up Plankwalk, to the door of Gardner Lookout atop the Mountain. The panorama is now complete. On clear days, the snowcapped wall of the Sierra, 160 miles away, tops the eastern horizon. There are older reports that the golden dome of the State Capitol in Sacramento used to be visible. Mt. Diablo, 34 miles to the east, and Mt. St. Helena, 48 miles northeast, appear as neighbors. Strong winds are common, but there are perfectly calm days as well.

The Gardner Lookout atop the East Peak summit was built by the Civilian Conservation Corps in 1935-36. The residents of the lookout play an important role in spotting fires on the Mountain and in other parts of the County. An earlier structure here, built in 1901 through financing by the San Francisco Examiner, was used for marine communications until 1919 and as a fire lookout from 1921. It was blown down by high winds in the early 1930's. Edwin B. Gardner was the first chief warden of the Tamalpais Fire District.

A photograph in the Mt. Tam Visitor Center clearly shows the line of wood planks that once lined the original summit route to provide surer footing.

REDWOOD SPRING TRAIL

From Mt. Tam Visitor Center to Northside Trail / .4 miles
Terrain: Woodland; parts rocky / MMWD
Elevation: From 2,380' to 2,000' / very steep
Intersecting Trails: None
Directions: Rock Spring - East Ridgecrest Blvd. to end

In recent years, Redwood Spring Trail was used only as a shortcut between East Peak and Eldridge Grade. In 1989, the Trail's lower half was cleared, reopening the route to Redwood Spring itself, and to Northside Trail for loop possibilities.

The Trail sets off below the two water fountains by the East Peak parking lot. It immediately passes the Mt. Tam Visitor Center, a one-time bathroom that was most recently renovated in 1988. The center is presently open on weekends all year, and on Fridays in summer. Inside are displays on the Mountain's flowers, on the railroad, and other aspects of Tam. The center is cheerfully staffed by knowledgeable volunteers from the Mt. Tamalpais Interpretive Association. Proceeds from the sale of the books, shirts, and maps help support the State Park.

The Trail continues below the small, shaded picnic area. It then drops steeply. The few feet just above Eldridge Grade have been covered by a slide, making them dangerous to descend. The crossing of Eldridge Grade is unsigned.

The lower section of Redwood Spring Trail is little-known, and delightful. It drops through a woodland of nutmegs, madrones, and oaks. Then, almost magically, is a stand of redwoods, the highest on Mt. Tamalpais. Watering the redwoods is Redwood Spring, flowing out from an old broken pipe to the left. This is a special place.

The Trail's remaining .1 mile descent is extremely steep; be cautious. Redwood Spring Trail ends at Northside Trail. The unsigned junction is hard to spot. A young nutmeg and a mature madrone frame the entrance. The rock-strewn band on Northside Trail is 200 yards to the left. Lagunitas Fire Trail and East Peak Fire Trail are each about a half-mile away on Northside, to the left and right, respectively.

TAVERN PUMP TRAIL

From Old Railroad Grade to Fern Creek Trail | .3 miles
Terrain: Woodland | MMWD
Elevation: From 2,080' to 1,920' | steep
Intersecting Trails: None
Directions: Rock Spring - East Ridgecrest Boulevard - Old Railroad Grade, .6 miles

Tavern Pump Trail is little used; most visitors opt for the nearby, easier to reach Fern Creek Trail. Still, Tavern Pump is attractive and does open a couple of loop options.

A new MMWD signpost has been placed on Tavern Pump Trail's upper end, on Old Railroad Grade 1/4 mile above Miller Trail. The Trail starts down very steeply for a few yards, then eases. Steps were placed at the top in 1989. Around half-way down, Tavern Pump Trail crosses a seep; veer left across it through a stand of chain ferns. The Trail ends at Fern Creek Trail, which rises left to the East Peak parking lot and drops right to Old Railroad Grade. Azaleas add fragrance here in late spring.

Steps lead down to a water tank and a blue building, which houses the "tavern pump." Water from Fern Creek was once pumped up to the Tavern of Tamalpais that stood at the terminus of the Mt. Tamalpais Railway, near the present East Peak parking lot. The renown tavern was built in 1896 as part of the railway project, and rebuilt in 1923 after a fire. In 1950, twenty years after the railway ceased operations, officials deliberately burned the tavern down because it had fallen into such extreme disrepair. The foundations are still visible. The pump, meanwhile, still delivers water via a pipeline, on a sliver of State Park property amidst Water District land, up to the East Peak area.

VERNA DUNSHEE TRAIL

Loop around East Peak | .7 miles
Terrain: Asphalt covered; views; heavily used; wheelchair accessible | MMWD & MTSP
Elevation: Around 2,400' | almost level
Intersecting Trails: Temelpa (.3m), Plankwalk (.7m)
Directions: Rock Spring - East Ridgecrest Blvd. to end

Tens of thousands of visitors take this loop Trail around the summit of East Peak each year, and are treated to unsurpassed views. We'll follow the Verna Dunshee loop counterclockwise from the bathrooms. A plaque names Verna Dunshee as "The First Lady of the State Park System, She Did So Much For So Many." A display identifies the landmarks visible in this initial south-southeast vista. The start was where the Tavern of Tamalpais once stood. It was the terminus of the railway up Tam from 1896 until the line ceased operations in 1930. After falling into extreme disrepair, the Tavern was razed by the Water District in 1950. Its stone foundations are quite evident.

At .2 miles, a railing surrounds Sunrise Point. At this famous site was the Tamalpais Locator, a spotting scope through which visitors gazed to identify distant landmarks. A stone bench, carved with the letters "Sunrise Point," offers a place to sit and enjoy the classic eastern views. The double peak of Mt. Diablo, 50% taller than Tam, in Contra Costa County is often prominent. On the clearest of winter days, the snow covered Sierra is visible, some 160 miles away.

A few feet beyond Sunrise Point, the Trail edges beneath the famous "Profile Rock." At .3 miles, Dunshee meets the signed top of Temelpa Trail, which drops very precipitously to Hoo-Koo-E-Koo Fire Road. Only the nimblest of hikers should attempt it. Fifty yards beyond, Devil's Slide is shored up by railroad ties that are dubbed, on a small signpost, "the great wall of Mt. Tamalpais." The slide is visible from much of central Marin. Next is the upper end of Indian Fire Trail. This extremely steep trail is closed from entry points below (so is not described in this book) for erosion and safety reasons, and to give vegetation a chance to cover it. The overgrown section here leads to the rock outcropping known as North Knee.

Views open north, to Mendocino County on clear days. At .6 miles, a plaque on a rock to the right carries the inscription:

BACK TO THE MOUNTAIN IN THE FULLNESS OF LIFE.

It is dedicated to George Grant, who died at 72 in 1914, and his wife, Grace Adelaide, who passed away the following year. George Grant was a former "Cariboo" gold miner who came to be called the "old man of the Mountain." There was once a Grant Trail up from West Point; it is now overgrown.

Beyond the plaque are steps, a problem for wheelchair users. The original, more level trail ran up to 16 feet higher, but it was rerouted after a slide. There is talk of improving this section for those in wheelchairs. At the end of the loop, the broad, rocky Plankwalk Trail rises a quarter-mile to the lookout tower atop East Peak.

Verna Dunshee first hiked on Tam in 1913 while a student at the University of California, Berkeley. She and her husband Bertram moved to Ross in 1920. Both became leading activists in preserving Marin's open space for State and County parks. Mrs. Dunshee was president of the Tamalpais Conservation Club in 1950-51. The Trail was dedicated to her by the California State Parks Rangers Association in 1973, the year she died at age 80. The Trail is sometimes called the "Twenty Minute," because of a sign indicating that's how long it takes to walk. It was also once known as Race Track Trail.

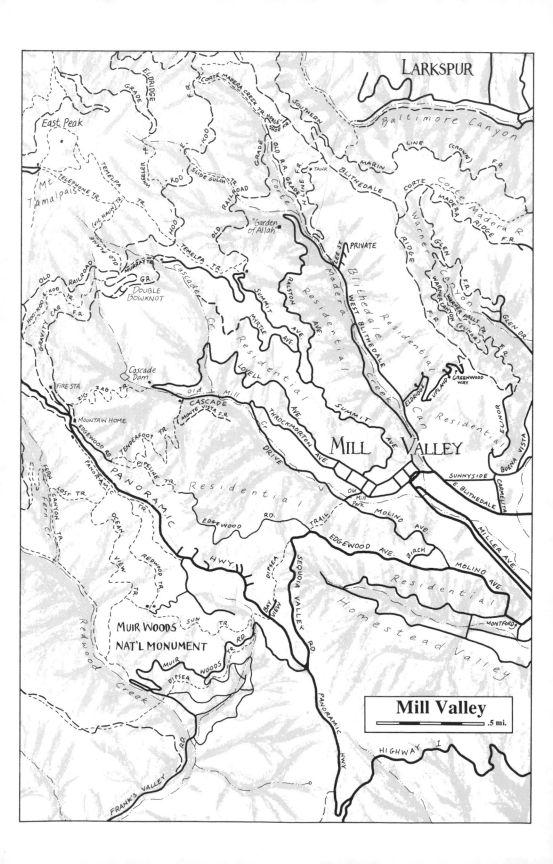

Mill Valley

.5 mi.

MILL VALLEY TRAILHEAD

Directions to downtown Mill Valley:
Highway 101 - East Blithedale Ave. (exit), Mill Valley - left on Throckmorton Ave. to Lytton Square (or continue to Old Mill Park or Cascade Drive)

Directions to start of Old Railroad Grade:
Downtown Mill Valley - West Blithedale Ave. to just past Lee Street

Directions to Fern Canyon Road:
Downtown Mill Valley - Throckmorton Ave. - right on Old Mill St. - left on Lovell Ave. - right on Summit Ave. to top

Mill Valley is nestled on the southeast slope of Mt. Tamalpais and offers several access points. The town has long been the principal entry route for visitors from San Francisco. For decades, they took a ferry to Sausalito, then the Northwestern Pacific Railroad to the depot in downtown Mill Valley. The railroad service was suspended in 1940; driving over the newly built Golden Gate Bridge proved more popular. From 1896 to 1930, the separate Mt. Tamalpais Railway ran from the same depot to near East Peak. The depot site (called "downtown Mill Valley" in the text) is known as Lytton Square, for the first Mill Valley resident killed in World War I, or as the Depot, for the bookstore/cafe there of that name. A two-hour time limit is enforced at downtown parking meters on weekends.

A second popular trailhead in Mill Valley is at the start of the present Old Railroad Grade, off West Blithedale above Lee Street. A third is past lovely Cascade Falls at the far end of Cascade Drive, from which both the Tenderfoot and Zig-Zag trails rise. A higher access is at the upper end of Fern Canyon Road, which is a paved section of Old Railroad Grade. Parking is limited at these trailheads, and is not permitted on Fern Canyon Road after dark.

Mill Valley also contains several potential new trailheads onto adjacent Marin County Open Space District properties. Paths set off from Fairway Drive, Val Vista Avenue, Tartan Road, Manor Drive, Del Casa Avenue, and other locations on the east side of Mill Valley. At least some of these paths, all currently beneath this book's minimum standards, may be cleared and signed.

Suggested loops from Mill Valley:

Old Railroad Grade trailhead (elevation 280') - Grade, .6m, to Horseshoe F.R. - right, .1m, to Corte Madera Trail - left, .6m, to Hoo-Koo-E-Koo Trail - right, .5m, to

*Blithedale Ridge F.R. - right, .5m, to H-Line F.R. - right, .6m, to Railroad Grade - left, .1m, to start | **3.0 miles.***

*Old Mill Park (elevation 100') - Dipsea Trail, .5m, to Edgewood Ave. - right on Edgewood Ave. and Pipeline Trail, 2.0m, to Mountain Home - right on Zig-Zag Trail, .6m, to Cascade Drive - right, 1.2m, to start | **4.3 miles.***

*Fern Canyon Road at Summit Ave. (elevation 820') - Temelpa Trail, .4m, to Hoo-Koo-E-Koo F.R. - right, 1.8m, to Blithedale Ridge F.R. - right, .8m, to Horseshoe F.R. - right, .3m, to Old Railroad Grade - right, 1.6m, to start | **4.9 miles.***

BLITHEDALE RIDGE FIRE ROAD

From Via Van Dyke off Elinor Avenue, Mill Valley, to Indian Fire Road | 2.3 miles
Terrain: Chaparral; views | MCOSD & MMWD
Elevation: From 540' to 880' | rolling, parts steep
Intersecting Trails: Connector fire road to Greenwood Way, Mill Valley (.1m), Corte Madera Ridge F.R. (.9m), H-Line F.R. (1.4m), Horseshoe F.R. (1.6m), Hoo-Koo-E-Koo Trail (1.9m), Hoo-Koo-E-Koo F.R. (2.3m)
Directions: Highway 101 - East Blithedale Ave. (exit), Mill Valley - right on Oakdale Ave. - left on Elinor Ave. to Via Van Dyke; very limited parking

Blithedale Ridge runs down the eastern flank of Mt. Tamalpais to just east of downtown Mill Valley. It forms an imposing wall dividing Blithedale and Warner canyons. Homes off narrow, winding Mill Valley streets cover the lowest reaches of Blithedale Ridge but a fire road tops its pristine upper two and a half miles. Some of the most dramatic views of Mt. Tamalpais' summit are found while traversing it, making the Fire Road a favorite among photographers.

At press-time, significant changes were occurring at the traditional access route to the southeast end of Blithedale Ridge Fire Road. For years, visitors entered by climbing 50 yards up a private driveway on Via Van Dyke, off Elinor Avenue, then cutting right by the water tank. A path led up to the gate marking the start of Blithedale Ridge F.R. and the boundary of Marin County Open Space land. In the summer of 1989, the property owner placed a gate across the base of Via Van Dyke, closing the access. Representatives from MCOSD, who bought the ridge line some ten years ago as the heart of the four million dollar Northridge acquisition, are trying to secure a public easement. The Via Van Dyke entry is therefore still shown here in the hope of a resolution to the impasse, but the reader is cautioned that this access may not be available.

(The only alternate Mill Valley access to Blithedale Ridge F.R. is Greenwood Way. It is reached by taking West Blithedale Avenue from downtown Mill Valley, going right on Eldridge Avenue to Woodbine Drive, then right to Upland, then uphill on Greenwood past house numbers 24-60, 70, 74, and 78. There is some parking, actually more than on Elinor. Continue up Greenwood past the water tank. Both a connector fire road, beyond the gate with an MCOSD sign, and a steep path rise to the ridge line. The actual start of Blithedale Ridge Fire Road is 150 yards to the right.)

At the Via Van Dyke start, there is an MCOSD trail sign immediately to the right. The shaded path it marks parallels the Fire Road, rejoining it in under .3 miles at another MCOSD sign. The path was cleared by a local boy scout troop.

Views of the Mountain on this opening up and down part of Blithedale Ridge, one of several stretches on Tam designated as "the roller coaster," are striking. Atop the first rise, in .1 mile, is the path left down to the water tank atop Greenwood Way. Just beyond, before the next rise, is the fire road connector to Greenwood. Blithedale Ridge F.R. briefly touches the edge of private property; MCOSD signs mark the return to public open space. The second fire road left, barred by an orange gate covered with warning messages, does lead to a private residence; keep out.

Climb some more to get another particularly stunning Tam shot. In few other places is the full scale of the Mountain's East Peak framed so dramatically. Northern vistas open. The canyon to the left is Blithedale, cut by Corte Madera Creek. The canyon right is Warner, carved by Warner Creek. At .9 miles, Corte Madera Ridge Fire Road, which tops the opposite wall of Warner Canyon, comes in from the right. It runs 1.7 miles to Corte Madera Avenue, and offers an alternate access to Blithedale Ridge.

Though there are more uphills, the Fire Road now generally descends, in parts steeply. It enters redwood forest. At 1.4 miles, in a saddle, the Fire Road meets a gate. Thirty yards beyond, Blithedale Ridge F.R. crosses H-Line F.R. The H-Line drops left to Old Railroad Grade and Mill Valley; right to Southern Marin Line (Crown) F.R. Blithedale Ridge F.R. continues uphill between the arms of H-Line.

Climb and return to summit views. After another roller coaster, Horseshoe Fire Road departs left. It too drops to Old Railroad Grade. In another quarter-mile, Hoo-Koo-E-Koo Trail crosses Blithedale Ridge. Right leads to Crown Road, left to Hoo-Koo-E-Koo F.R. There's a stiff uphill, rewarded by great views to the south from the head of Blithedale Canyon.

The Fire Road leaves MCOSD lands and enters Marin Municipal Water District jurisdiction. Just above is the 1,091' summit of Knob Hill. To the left, at a gate, is the top of Hoo-Koo-E-Koo Fire Road. Climb the remaining yards to the end of Blithedale Ridge Fire Road at its junction with Indian Fire Road. Left leads up to Eldridge Grade, right down to Kent Woodlands.

In the 1870's, Dr. John Cushing, a pioneering Mill Valley homeopathic physician, built a sanitarium. He called it "Blithedale" after a novel he had just read, Nathaniel Hawthorne's "Blithedale Romance." After Dr. Cushing's death in 1879, his son Sidney converted Blithedale, near the present 205 West Blithedale Avenue, into a hotel. Sidney then became the chief mover behind the construction of the railway up Mt. Tamalpais, partly to boost patronage in the track-side hotel. The Mountain Theater is named for him. Blithedale Ridge Fire Road was built in 1914 over an older trail.

CORTE MADERA TRAIL

From Horseshoe Fire Road to Hoo-Koo-E-Koo Fire Road | .4 miles
Terrain: Deep redwood forest; riparian; several unbridged stream crossings | MCOSD & MMWD
Elevation: From 500' to 950' | extremely steep
Intersecting Trails: None
Directions: Old Railroad Grade trailhead - Grade, .6 miles

Corte Madera Trail follows the upper reaches of the creek called Corte Madera del Presidio, or Corte Madera Creek. It is not to be confused with the larger Corte Madera Creek that flows through the College of Marin and enters the bay near Larkspur Landing. The Trail is quite lovely, entirely through dense redwoods. It is, however, very steep, in some disrepair, and does require some potentially tricky stream crossings after winter rains.

To reach the lower end of Corte Madera Trail, follow the Railroad Grade uphill from its start off West Blithedale Avenue. The first fire road on the right is H-Line. A half-mile later, at a horseshoe curve over Corte Madera Creek, Horseshoe Fire Road also sets off on the right up to Blithedale Ridge. Follow it .1 mile to an MCOSD sign, on the left, that simply says

"Trail," the start of Corte Madera Trail. There is also a very steep path to the trailhead from Old Railroad Grade up the creek's right bank.

The Trail, rising beside the creek, immediately enters MMWD land. The first of four creek crossings, all without benefit of a bridge, is from the left to the right bank. The next crossing is at the confluence of two forks. A slide after the storm of January 1982 forces walking on a log; use particular caution. So, while the stream isn't deep, some may wish to avoid this Trail altogether in winter and early spring. Others will enjoy the challenge and the beauty associated with such a lively, woodland creek. The rock wall to the left of the crossing was painstakingly built by a young artist in 1988.

Continue climbing the left-hand creek through the quiet woods. The redwoods and the water muffle outside noise. There are two more crossings. The Trail ends when it merges with Hoo-Koo-E-Koo Trail, coming in from Echo Rock on the right. A short scramble uphill leads to Hoo-Koo-E-Koo F.R. To the right is Blithedale Ridge F.R., to the left, Wheeler Trail. A new MMWD signpost was placed here in June 1988.

"Corte Madera del Presidio" means "cut wood for the Presidio." Logging of the area's redwoods began soon after the arrival, in the late 1700's, of the first Spanish settlers. The lumber was used in the building of San Francisco's Presidio and other structures. The creek is also sometimes called "Widow Reed Creek," for Hilaria Sanchez de Garcia. Her husband, Irishman John Reed, was granted the 8,000 acre Rancho Corte Madera del Presidio, which included today's Mill Valley, in 1834.

DIPSEA TRAIL

From Old Mill Park, Mill Valley, to intersection of Highway 1 and Panoramic Highway, Stinson Beach / 6.8 miles
Terrain: Varied; deep and light woodland, grassland, riparian, and coastal scrub; views / City of Mill Valley, private (easement), MTSP, MWNM, GGNRA
Elevation: From 90' to 760' to 160' to 1,350' to 80' / parts very steep, almost no parts level
Intersecting Trails: Sun (1.3m), Deer Park F.R. (several times between miles 2.9m and 4.1m), Ben Johnson (3.9m), TCC (4.1m), Coastal F.R. (4.2m), Lone Tree F.R. (4.4m, 4.6m, 4.8m), Steep Ravine (5.6m-5.7m), fire road connector to Panoramic Highway (5.7m), Hill 640 F.R. (5.9m)
Directions: Downtown Mill Valley - Throckmorton Ave. to Old Mill Park

There is no more famous, or infamous, trail in Marin or the Bay Area than the Dipsea. Its beauty, ruggedness, variety, and history would themselves make it special; the race held over it has made it unique. Mark Reese, in his wonderful (but unfortunately out-of-print) book, "The Dipsea Race," says the Trail was probably first blazed by the Coast Miwok Indians. It was popular, under the name Lone Tree Trail, with the County's first pleasure hikers in the 1880's. In 1905 it became the route of the Dipsea Race, which continues as one of the nation's best known runs.

Reese, after much research, still cannot pinpoint with certainty the origin of the word "Dipsea." A Dipsea Inn was built at Stinson Beach (called Willow Camp until 1920) in 1904 on property owned by William Kent. A group from San Francisco's Olympic Club, conceiving the idea of a race from Mill Valley to the inn, called themselves the Dipsea Indians. But whether "Dipsea" itself refers to the practice of taking a plunge in the Pacific after trekking the Trail, or to the Trail's apparent drop to the ocean as viewed from Lone Tree, or to a name Kent picked up on his travels to British seaside resorts, remains a mystery.

It must be pointed out that the course of the Dipsea Race (technically the runners can take any itinerary to Stinson that is not specifically excluded, but most use a standard route) differs somewhat from the true Dipsea Trail. For one, it is shorter. Since the race is so closely tied to the Trail, I'll describe both ways. I will, however, omit a few environmentally dubious shortcuts used on race day. Two other cautions are in order. The Dipsea is arduous and may not be for everyone. And it's a one way affair. Return options include Golden Gate Transit bus service back to Mill Valley (weekends only), a car shuttle, and a doubly tiring round trip. Another option is to hike or run the Trail out and back in shorter sections, say from the start to Muir Woods or to the top of Cardiac Hill.

The Dipsea Race, now held the second Sunday each June, begins at Lytton Square besides the Depot Bookstore & Cafe in downtown Mill Valley. The contestants run up Throckmorton to Old Mill Park, which still houses the remains of John Reed's sawmill that gave the town its name. Cut through the park and cross Old Mill Creek on the bridge. Continue straight to encounter the Dipsea steps (the first steps visible, to the left, lead to a private home; go up a few more yards right). These steps (technically Cascade Way), .3 miles into the race, mark the start of the Dipsea Trail.

No part of the Dipsea Trail is better known than these both dreaded and beloved 671 steps. Originally of logs, they were all replaced in 1936 and subsequently as needed. They are in three flights. Private homes line the whole way. The first flight is the longest, 307 steps. At its top, go right on the road, then immediately left (white Dipsea arrows, sometimes faint, are painted on the pavement here and elsewhere) on Marion Avenue, to climb the second flight, also the middle in length (221 steps). At the top, go left on Hazel Avenue a few yards to the third and shortest flight (143 steps). Think of the runners, who jam the steps to over-capacity, fatigued yet still short of the one mile mark. A famous quote by Jack Kirk, the legendary "Dipsea Demon" who has run every race since 1930, goes, "Old Dipsea runners never die. They just reach the 672nd step."

At the top of the steps, at a junction once known as Inspiration Point for the views, go right on Sequoia Valley Road (not Edgewood Avenue). This is a short but dangerous (due to cars) 100 yards. The Dipsea then rises through the gates of the new Flying Y development on what is now called Walsh Drive. This area is fondly remembered by generations of Dipsea runners and hikers as the site of the Flying Y Ranch, where horses peacefully grazed.

The pavement ends at around the race's one mile (the Trail's .7 mile) mark. The Trail then rejoins pavement as the upper half of Bayview Drive. Go right at the top, and cross Panoramic Highway. This first of the route's two main summits is called Windy Gap. In under 50 yards, go left off the pavement at a Dipsea Trail signpost. The Trail is now in Mount Tamalpais State Park, and remains on public land the rest of the way.

After the first big bend left on the downhill, a few yards past a small wooden bridge, is a signed junction. Sun Trail veers right, towards the Tourist Club. The Dipsea takes the left fork and drops steeply to paved Muir Woods Road. All the runners go right here, flying down the road. The true Dipsea Trail is marked by a post directly across the road. This section, not used by any of the racers because it is slower to run on than the pavement, is a little known part of the Dipsea. It follows a stream in the woods, and is quite attractive. The Trail and race route meet at a dirt road, Camino del Canyon, marked by a row of mailboxes. The Dipsea continues straight across the dirt road (or to the right when coming off Muir Woods Road), at trail width. Camino del Canyon is a private, unpaved access to several residences.

This next section of the Dipsea Trail was built in the late 1970's to replace the precipitous, 45 degree descent known as Suicide. The downhill is moderately steep. Beware of poison oak, particularly in late winter and spring. Good samaritans usually cut it back just before race day. The Trail meets a service road, then crosses Muir Woods Road again. This was the site of a snack bar and dance pavilion called Joe's Place, which was quite popular in the 1920's and '30's. The main entrance to Muir Woods National Monument is to the right.

The Dipsea Trail passes through the Monument's overflow parking lot. It then drops a few steps to cross Redwood Creek on a footbridge. This crucial bridge is, however, only moved into place in spring, after the rainy season. The significantly longer alternative is to go left a half-mile on Muir Woods (Frank Valley) Road, then right, uphill, on Deer Park Fire Road to rejoin the Dipsea Trail.

Across Redwood Creek, the Dipsea Trail begins an almost continuous climb to its highest point. This first part, called Dynamite, is the steepest long section, around a half-mile. It is through a lush, fern-lined forest in the southwest corner of Muir Woods National Monument. It replaced an even steeper, more direct route, long known as Butler's Pride, that is now off-limits. The climb eases a bit as the Trail leaves the deep forest and Muir Woods to again enter Mount Tamalpais State Park. A few feet to the left is Deer Park F.R. This is around mile 3 of the race.

The Trail stays to the right of the fire road at first. The two then merge before the Trail departs left at a marked Dipsea sign post. Don't worry whether you should be on the fire road or the Trail; the two run near each other for almost 1 1/2 miles to their last junction just below Cardiac Hill.

The uphill eases at this stretch through open grassland called the Hogsback, for its appearance in profile. Splendid panoramas open. The Trail then again merges with and crosses Deer Park F.R. After passing through a small grove, the Trail leaves the grassland left of the fire road. This next heavily wooded mile, back in Muir Woods National Monument, is called the Rainforest. In summer, water drips off the fog-laden

Douglas-firs and redwoods. It is another special stretch of the Dipsea. Here is one of the likeliest places on Tam to see orchids.

There is a bit more gradual uphill. Ben Johnson Trail, which also rose from Muir Woods, meets the Dipsea on the right and ends. The Dipsea Trail joins Deer Park Fire Road for the last time. Go left around 100 yards on the merged pair, then right as the Trail branches off. This final stiff, 300 yard uphill is called Cardiac, not because it is that much steeper or longer than what has come before, but because the runners are already fatigued from the continuous climb out of Muir Woods. TCC Trail, from Pantoll, comes in on the right. The Dipsea re-enters Mt. Tamalpais State Park. There is a last push to the summit, one of the most spectacular places on the Mountain.

The top of Cardiac Hill (formerly known as the Sugar Lump) is just below 1,400'. The vistas of San Francisco and of the Pacific are quite dramatic. The knowledge that the Trail is now almost all downhill, plus the usual cooling ocean breezes, the views, and the water station here on race day, make this a place welcome to all Dipsea veterans. Here the Dipsea crosses Coastal Fire Road. Just downhill to the left is the end of the now familiar Deer Park Fire Road and, well beyond, Muir Beach. To the right is Pantoll Ranger Station.

The narrow Dipsea Trail continues west, skirting the hillside. It then briefly merges with Lone Tree F.R. at what is actually the highest point on the Dipsea course. This is "Farren's Rest," named for James Farren, Jr., a young althlete whose ashes were scattered here. Early photos of this area show a single redwood, the "Lone Tree" that once gave its name to the Dipsea Trail. The redwood still stands, but the hillside above is covered with Douglas firs. Beneath the redwood, on a short path to the right, is a stone cairn. A pipe tapping into Lone Tree Spring here provides the only drinking water (untreated) on the Dipsea. The Tamalpais Conservation Club built the fountain in 1917.

The Dipsea Trail departs left from the fire road in a few yards. The two merge again for a down and up stretch. The Dipsea Trail leaves Lone Tree F.R. for the last time, to the right, at a post. Gone too, for a while, are the ocean views.

At a wooden fence, less than .1 mile below Lone Tree F.R., the runners leave the regular Dipsea Trail to plunge down the nearly vertical Swoop Hollow, so named by Kirk. Today's "official" Dipsea Trail is to the right (north). This gentler graded section, built in 1977 by the Youth Conservation Corps, is all but unknown to the racers. Yet it is one of the loveliest parts of the route, deeply wooded and quiet. The bent laurels and the erect redwoods form separate, seemingly magical forests. A few Douglas firs rise to enormous heights. The shortcut and Trail meet again 1/4 mile below.

The Trail goes to the right of the wood fence and enters the cool, wet forest of Steep Ravine. The Trail certainly is steep here, with protruding rocks and roots. Stone and wooden steps, which Dipsea champions have been known to descend four at a time, help but caution is very much in order. This area, in deep woods, is enchanting.

The Dipsea crosses Webb Creek over a substantial wood bridge. On the other bank, going right, is Steep Ravine Trail rising to Pantoll. The combined Dipsea and Steep Ravine trails go left. They pass a pond, part of the Stinson Beach water supply.

The short stiff uphill now encountered is called Insult. It is the last uphill of note in the Dipsea Race (but not on the regular Dipsea Trail); the course's final "insult" to those who thought it was all downhill to the finish line. Steep Ravine Trail branches left, to Highway 1. Old timers refer to the area at the top of the hill as White Barn, part of the old White Gate Ranch.

Knowledgeable Dipsea competitors depart the Trail here for the first of two stretches on Panoramic Highway. These well known shortcuts avoid the Trail's remaining uphills, but also cut off one of the Trail's most attractive sections. This rolling grassland is known as the Moors for its appearance during the frequent summer fogs. When the weather is clear there are striking views of Stinson Beach, tantalizingly close below. Stay on the narrow Trail. The intersecting Hill 640 Fire Road goes right to Panoramic Highway and left to a deadend above a series of old military bunkers. Then an old ranch road criss-crosses.

The Trail descends to woodland, meeting the second of the two shortcuts through an old wood fence. A bridge crosses the last creek. A short, open downhill leads to the end of the Dipsea Trail at its junction with Panoramic Highway, just above Highway 1. There is a large trail sign. (The Dipsea Race route veers left from the Trail a few yards before this end, hitting Highway 1. The runners leap over a fence, go right on Highway 1, left on Marine Way, then left again through the Stinson Beach parking lot to the finish line.)

The Dipsea Trail offers a special experience, among the best the Mountain has to offer, any time of year. It gets a trifle crowded with runners practicing on the several weekends before the race. Do come on race day to cheer the runners on. The race uses a handicap format, with women and older and younger entrants starting ahead, in one minute intervals, of the "scratch" runners. Women, men in their fifties and sixties, even a ten year old girl, have been champions, first across the finish line. The race record is an amazingly quick 44 minutes, 49 seconds, run by Ron Elijah in 1974. Later in June, the Double Dipsea Race is held, from Stinson Beach to Mill Valley and back. In November, a Quadruple Dipsea, four crossings, is contested. There's even been a "Dipsea 'Til You Drop." In 1987 the winner did eight Dipseas!

GLEN FIRE ROAD

From Glen Drive, Mill Valley, to Corte Madera Ridge Fire Road at Huckleberry Trail / .9 miles
Terrain: Broom-lined hillside / MCOSD
Elevation: From 280' to 800' / steep
Intersecting Trails: Warner Canyon (Elinor) F.R. (.4m)
Directions: Highway 101 - East Blithedale Ave. (exit), Mill Valley - right on Carmelita Ave. - right on Buena Vista Ave. - Glen Drive to end

Fire roads rise on both the west (from Elinor Avenue) and east (from Glen Drive) sides of Mill Valley's Warner Canyon. The two fire roads merge and continue up the canyon to Corte Madera Ridge.

Glen Fire Road starts from an MCOSD-signed gate at the upper end of Glen Drive. Broom is dominant at the Fire Road's edge in the early going. The Fire Road rises fairly steeply. Warner Canyon (Elinor) F.R., across Warner Canyon, is visible most of the time. The two merge in .4 miles. Left leads, in 1.2 miles, to the top of Elinor Avenue in Mill Valley. The continuation straight, uphill, is considered as Glen Fire Road here.

Sage and monkeyflower hold out against the invasive broom. Look behind to get views of the San Francisco skyline. Glen Fire Road ends at the top of Warner Canyon at a four-way intersection. Corte Madera Ridge F.R. goes left to Blithedale Ridge and right to Summit Avenue, Corte Madera. Huckleberry Trail, straight ahead, drops to the east end of Southern Marin Line Fire Road. Make sure to go a few yards left for an outstanding view of Tam's East Peak.

H-LINE FIRE ROAD

From Old Railroad Grade to Southern Marin Line Fire Road / .9 miles
Terrain: Chaparral / MCOSD
Elevation: From 320' to 660' to 510' / very steep
Intersecting Trails: Blithedale Ridge F.R. (.6m)
Directions: Start of Old Railroad Grade - Grade, .1 mile

H-Line is the first fire road that rises off Old Railroad Grade, some 200 yards up the Grade from West Blithedale Avenue. H-Line departs to the right. The lower yards were being paved at press-time. The Fire Road leaves the canyon's forest canopy into chaparral. In .1 mile, H-Line passes the first of two water tanks, called "Lower Tank." Just beyond, splendid views of the summit of Mt. Tamalpais open.

The Fire Road climbs relentlessly. In .5 miles, the "Upper Tank" is passed. There is a last bend, and a leveling. H-Line then crosses Blithedale Ridge F.R. at a key intersection. Blithedale rises on both sides, to the left toward Indian Fire Road and to the right, past a gate, toward Corte Madera Ridge. Between these two branches, H-Line F.R. continues, downhill.

The remaining steep quarter-mile descent is lined with madrones and manzanita. H-Line Fire Road ends at its junction with Southern Marin Line F.R., by a pump station. It is 1.2 miles left to Crown Road in Kentfield, 1.6 miles right to Sunrise Lane in Larkspur.

H-Line was built just after World War II as part of the Southern Marin Line project, which brings water from the lakes on the north side of Tamalpais, through the Bon Tempe treatment plant, to users in southern Marin. The pipeline from the treatment plant that follows Southern Marin Line Fire Road branches at the H-Line F.R. intersection. One of the branches adjoins H-Line. Water is pumped across Blithedale Ridge to the two storage tanks and on to central Mill Valley. The name H-Line, which is used only by Water District personnel, arose when sections of the Southern Marin Line pipeline were marked by a grid; A-Line, B-Line, etc. This Fire Road lay, obviously, along the H-Line. The part of H-Line F.R. between Old Railroad Grade and Blithedale Ridge is called Water Tank Fire Road by many users.

HORSESHOE FIRE ROAD

From Old Railroad Grade to Blithedale Ridge Fire Road / .3 miles
Terrain: Chaparral / MCOSD
Elevation: From 440' to 700' / very steep
Intersecting Trails: Corte Madera (.1m)
Directions: Start of Old Railroad Grade - Grade, .6 miles

H orseshoe is the second of the two fire roads that rise from the lower part of Old Railroad Grade to Blithedale Ridge. It sets off a half-mile past the first, H-Line. The start is at Old Railroad Grade's crossing over Corte Madera Creek, at a big bend known from railroad days as Horseshoe Curve. It was the sharpest turn on the over eight miles of track.

The uphill is a tough one. In .1 mile, at a green MCOSD trail sign post, Corte Madera Trail departs left to begin its very steep climb to Hoo-Koo-E-Koo Fire Road. Horseshoe F.R. leaves the redwood forest into open chaparral. Views of both Mt. Tamalpais and of the San Francisco skyline open. Horseshoe ends when it hits Blithedale Ridge F.R., which goes left to Hoo-Koo-E-Koo Trail and right to Mill Valley.

MONTE VISTA FIRE ROAD

From Cascade Drive to Rose Avenue, Mill Valley / .5 miles
Terrain: Redwood forest / City of Mill Valley
Elevation: From 240' to 360' / gradual
Intersecting Trails: Tenderfoot (<.1m)
Directions: Cascade Drive to #477

T his delightful, redwood-lined Fire Road has not appeared on trail maps because it is bordered throughout by private property. Yet the route itself is public, part of Mill Valley, and passage is open. Whether this section of Monte Vista Avenue will remain unpaved and undeveloped is not certain but, for now, it serves as a reminder of how the canyons of Mill Valley once looked.

The trailhead is the same as for Tenderfoot Trail, beside #477 Cascade around 1.2 miles in from Old Mill Park. Enter quietly, respecting the adjacent homeowner's privacy. There is a chain across the Fire Road in some 200 feet. Less than twenty yards beyond, historic Tenderfoot Trail, heading toward Mountain Home, branches off to the right. Continue up the creek canyon.

Monte Vista bends left over the creek at .2 miles. A huge, double-trunked redwood stands sentinel at the crossing. The uphill is now quite gentle. Redwoods dominate. A common shrub is California hazel, with its drooping catkins, velvety soft leaves, and tasty nuts. Where the forest thins, look left for the views of Mt. Tamalpais that gave the Fire Road its name.

The Fire Road ends at another chain just before #420 Monte Vista Avenue. The intersection with Rose Avenue is about 100 yards ahead. Both Monte Vista and Rose connect to Hazel Avenue. There are no all-trail loop possibilities.

MURRAY TRAIL

From Old Railroad Grade to Hoo-Koo-E-Koo F.R. / .2 miles
Terrain: Lower part redwoods, upper part lightly wooded / MMWD
Elevation: From 1,000' to 1,220' / very steep, bottom yards extremely steep
Intersecting Trails: None
Directions: Upper end of Fern Canyon Road - Old Railroad Grade, .1 mile

This steep, unsigned Trail cuts almost a half-mile off the ascent or descent of Old Railroad Grade. To reach the Murray trailhead, follow Old Railroad Grade from the upper end of Fern Canyon Road. Around 100 yards past the end of the pavement, just beyond milepost #4, the Grade crosses over Cascade Creek. Trails ascend both banks of the creek. On the near (left) bank is a path that is presently below minimum standards. Across the creek (up the right bank) is the start of Murray Trail.

The steepest part of Murray Trail is at the beginning. Ascend through the dense redwood forest. The Trail continues to rise, but less sharply, as it veers away from the creek. Huckleberries abound. The principal trees are introduced Bishop and Monterey pines. Ten yards before the Trail's top, a shortcut path forks left to lower on the Double Bow Knot.

The end of Murray is at its junction with Hoo-Koo-E-Koo Fire Road. Right leads to the east side of the Mountain. Fifteen yards to the left is Old Railroad Grade in the middle of the uppermost bend of the Bow Knot, and the base of Old Plane (Vic Haun) Trail.

Frank J. Murray was a one-time chairman of the TCC Trails Committee, an important position to this day. He signed the visitor register atop East Peak in November 1881, at age 14, noting that it was his second visit. Murray helped build this Trail, and it was named for him after his death in 1922.

MYRTLE AVENUE FIRE ROAD

From Myrtle Avenue, Mill Valley, to Cascade Creek / .6 miles
Terrain: Mostly chaparral, part redwood forest / City of Mill Valley
Elevation: Around 600' / almost level
Intersecting Trails: None
Directions: Downtown Mill Valley - Summit Ave. - left on Myrtle Ave. to end; limited or no parking

This Fire Road is used almost exclusively by local residents as it is unsigned, offers virtually no parking, intersects no other trails, and meets a deadend. It sets off from the west end of Mill Valley's residential Myrtle Avenue at a gate. The Fire Road rolls through a mixture of chaparral and exotic vegetation. There are fine head-on views of the south face of Tamalpais. To the right above are homes on Fern Canyon Road, the paved section of Old Railroad Grade. Below is heavily wooded Cascade Canyon.

In a half-mile, Myrtle Avenue Fire Road narrows to trail width. It then enters a forest of redwood and bay. A couple of old intake water pipes still rest in the crossing of Cascade Creek. A path takes off uphill right 15 yards past the next crossing of a seep. It climbs very steeply through a redwood forest to Old Railroad Grade by the Double Bow Knot. The continuing path straight ahead, winding toward Mill Valley's Lovell Avenue, is heavily overgrown.

The head of Cascade Canyon is specifically cited in Howell's classic 1948 book, "Marin Flora," as one of the Tamalpais locales for the small tree California wax-myrtle *(Myrica californica)*. The tree was introduced to science by the botanist Chamisso when he spent a month collecting specimens in San Francisco's Presidio during 1816. The trees' elongated, saw-toothed, aromatic leaves are broadest near the pointed tips. The wax-coated fruits are borne in clusters. Wax-myrtles are in the bayberry family. The only true members of the myrtle family found on Mt. Tamalpais are the non-native eucalyptus, introduced from Australia.

OLD PLANE TRAIL

From junction of Old Railroad Grade and Hoo-Koo-E-Koo Fire Road to junction of Temelpa and Telephone trails / .5 miles
Terrain: Mostly chaparral, parts wooded; views / MMWD
Elevation: From 1,220' to 1,580' / steep
Intersecting Trails: None
Directions: Upper end of Fern Canyon Rd. - Old Railroad Grade uphill - Murray Trail

This Trail is little used because it has been unmarked, is very steep, and ends at even steeper trails. Yet it offers great views, passes through some haunting woodlands near an old plane crash site, and leads to one of the Mountain's jewels, the Sitting Bull plaque. The Erickson map calls the Trail the Old Plane since its lower half was cut in 1944 specifically to reach a plane wreck site. The Olmsted map uses Vic Haun Trail; Victor Emmanuel Haun was one of the founders of the California Alpine Club.

The unmarked start of Old Plane is easy to miss. To reach the trailhead, climb Murray Trail to its top, then go left fifteen yards on Hoo-Koo-E-Koo F.R. to Old Railroad Grade. Old Plane sets off uphill, between manzanita bushes, from the Grade some ten feet above the junction's signpost. Because the steep Old Plane Trail is relatively free of loose rocks, going up or down is fairly easy. If you are planning to make a loop with Temelpa Trail and Hoo-Koo-E-Koo F.R., it is safer to take the rocky Temelpa uphill and Old Plane downhill.

Splendid vistas of San Francisco, Mt. Diablo, and the Golden Gate Bridge open up immediately on Old Plane. The Trail enters a wonderful forest. Short, rigidly upright laurels line the left border, redwoods the right edge. In 1/3 mile, at the bottom of a brief drop in the Trail, a path forks sharply right. It is readily noticeable only when descending Old Plane, when it can be mistakenly followed. This path leads down a creek bed to the largest remaining debris from the 1944 crash.

Old Plane Trail then crosses Cascade Creek. Keep a sharp eye out for any signs left from the Navy plane that went down near here in 1944, killing its eight crew members. The plane was flying from Alameda to Kaneohe on Oahu, Hawaii when it slammed into the fog shrouded Mountain. Remember, it is unlawful to remove any historic artifacts from the Mountain.

The continuation of the Trail beyond the crash site was built a few years later. A level rock offers a resting site with a choice southern panorama.

Take a closer look at the evergreens ahead. Most are introduced Bishop pines, a tree rarely found growing naturally on this eastern side of San Andreas Fault. Distinctive is the thickly furrowed bark, the needles in bunches of two (nearby Monterey pines, also introduced, have needles in threes), and the closed cones clinging directly to the branches and trunks. These stout cones, around 3" long and tipped with prickles, generally open only from the heat of a fire. They then release their seeds, starting a new generation.

Old Plane ends when it hits Temelpa Trail. Uphill to the left is the start of the extremely steep Telephone Trail, heading to the East Peak parking lot. Uphill right is the continuation of the equally steep Temelpa Trail, climbing to Verna Dunshee Trail. Straight ahead is an overgrown path. Go downhill 25 yards on Temelpa to see the wonderful Sitting Bull plaque (see Temelpa Trail) embedded in a boulder.

OLD RAILROAD GRADE

From West Blithedale Avenue, Mill Valley, to Ridgecrest Boulevard / 6.7 miles
Terrain: Lower part deeply wooded, upper part mostly chaparral; heavily used / MCOSD & MMWD
Elevation: From 240' to 2,220' / gradual the whole length
Intersecting Trails: H-Line F.R. (.1m), Horseshoe F.R. (.6m), Slide Gulch (1.1m), Temelpa (1.8m), Murray (2.6m), Gravity Car Grade (2.9m), Hoo-Koo-E-Koo (3.1m), Hoo-Koo-E-Koo F.R. (3.2m), Old Plane (3.2m), Hogback F.R. (3.8m), Fern Creek (4.2m), Miller (4.3m, 6.0m), Nora (5.3m), West Point (5.3m), Old Stage Road (5.3m), Rock Spring (5.3m), Tavern Pump (6.2m)
Directions: Downtown Mill Valley - West Blithedale Ave., just above Lee Street

A strong case can be made that Old Railroad Grade is the most important route on Mt. Tamalpais. From 1896 to 1930 it was covered with the tracks of the Mt. Tamalpais and Muir Woods Railway, "the world's crookedest railroad." The railway carried millions of people to the summit, and brought itself and the Mountain world-wide fame. The Grade remains the most heavily used base-to-summit route on the Mountain, particularly for mountain bikers. Because it intersects so many trails, the Grade usually plays a part in most all visits to the Mountain's southern side.

The train to near East Peak departed from a depot (now The Depot Bookstore & Cafe) at Lytton Square in downtown Mill Valley. This depot also was the terminus of a spur of the Northwestern Pacific Railroad from Sausalito. The 8+ miles of track up the Mountain rounded a total of 281 curves, the equivalent of 42 full circles. The longest straight section, ironically in the middle of the celebrated series of turns known as Double Bow Knot, was only 413 feet. The uphill never exceeded a modest 7 degree grade. There were originally 22 trestles.

The line's first 1.2 miles, besides Corte Madera Creek, are no longer a trail. Some glimpses of the bygone era can be captured by walking past the stately mansions on Corte Madera Avenue. A local train, nicknamed the "Dinky", ran on the tracks from the depot to Lee Street. Around fifty yards beyond Lee, going right off West Blithedale Avenue at a gate, is the beginning of today's Old Railroad Grade.

This lower section passes beside privately held property, but passage is open. The Grade rises above Corte Madera Creek, and is well wooded and attractive. The many big-leaf maple trees lend New England colors to the area in fall. In some 200 yards, the steep H-Line Fire Road (also called Water Tank F.R.) rises on the right. It passes two water tanks on its way up Blithedale Ridge. Farther along, a fence adjoins the Grade on the left.

The Grade reaches a bend called Horseshoe Curve, the sharpest on the entire route, at Corte Madera Creek. On the near side of the creek, Horseshoe Fire Road, also going to Blithedale Ridge, sets off uphill to the right. Corte Madera Trail splits from Horseshoe F.R. some 100 yards up. The path on the far (right) bank of the creek also connects to Corte Madera Trail. There is a rare dip in the Grade, the result of storm damage, as it crosses the creek. Here too the Grade leaves the Marin County Open Space District to enter the jurisdiction of the Marin Municipal Water District, where it remains the rest of the way.

The first of several old wood post mileage markers, Mile 2 (as calibrated from the Mill Valley depot; deduct 1.2 miles to match our start), is passed. The Grade skirts a fence line on the left. Less than 50 yards beyond the fence line, an unnamed trail, not described in this book because it is entirely through private property, drops to the left. It descends to Chaparral Trail (also not described because it is on private land) and on to the Ralston L. White Memorial Retreat Center. This huge estate, originally named the Garden of Allah after a book popular when it was constructed around 1910, borders the Grade for a considerable distance. Indeed, supplies to build it came via the railroad. The property was deeded to the United Church of Christ in 1957 by the Barnard family.

Around 150 yards beyond, at a bend that takes the Grade over a creek, the unsigned, unmaintained Slide Gulch Trail departs uphill on the right. It follows an old water pipeline, then continues extremely steeply up to Hoo-Koo-E-Koo Fire Road.

Around 60 yards before Milepost 3 the Grade enters its largest road cut, the McKinley Cut. Look to the left on a large rock to see the words, periodically repainted by railroad buffs, "McKinley Cut." President McKinley was scheduled to ride on the railroad in 1900 and the Mill Valley depot was properly festooned, but his wife became ill and the trip was cancelled. Milepost 3 is at 700 foot elevation.

Around .3 miles above, the Grade meets a gate and, immediately after, a private residence. Just higher, ten yards before the Grade meets the junction of Summit Avenue and Fern Canyon Road, the unmarked Temelpa Trail sets off uphill toward the Mountain's summit.

The original Grade is paved and open to auto traffic for .6 miles along Fern Canyon Road, but is included to avoid a discontinuity. Sweeping views, including of the San Francisco skyline, help compensate. This stretch can be reached by car via Summit Avenue from downtown Mill Valley. Temelpa Trail again touches Fern Canyon Road, on the right. A classic old sign marks the junction by a yellow fire hydrant.

The Grade reenters woodland, and its surface is again dirt, beyond a gate at the upper end of Fern Canyon Road. A fence on the left marks the boundary of a private estate. Cascade Creek is just past the wood Milepost 4 (which supports a "dogs on leash" sign). On the near bank (the creek's left bank), a path, just below this book's minimum standards, climbs past a water tank. Across the creek, the unmarked Murray Trail sets off uphill, heading to the Bow Knot. It offers a shortcut to the Grade. The Grade leaves the tree cover for the chaparral that characterizes virtually the whole rest of the route. Views to the east, south, and west become ever more expansive.

The Grade then enters the famous Double Bow Knot (also spelled as Bow-Knot and Bowknot, and without the "Double"). Here the tracks ran parallel to themselves five times, over a straight line distance of just 600 feet, to gain 168 feet of elevation. It used to be easy to go wrong in the maze here, losing the Grade by not bending right and ending up on Gravity Car Fire Road toward Mountain Home. New signposts should end the problem.

The Grade passes the stone platform remnant of Mesa Station, at Milepost 4.5, elevation 1,120'. Here, beginning in 1907, passengers could switch to gravity cars to descend to the Muir Woods Inn, above the newly opened Muir Woods National Monument. A couple of small paths left and right offer Bow Knot shortcuts for impatient hikers.

Just before the Bow Knot's final bend, Hoo-Koo-E-Koo Trail branches sharply left to Hogback (Throckmorton) F.R. A shortcut path to higher on the Grade rises from the same junction. One hundred yards beyond on the Grade, Hoo-Koo-E-Koo departs right, as a fire road. The top of Murray Trail is fifteen yards away on it, unmarked and on the right. The Grade itself bends left, west. At this bend the unmarked Old Plane (Vic Haun) Trail sets off uphill to Temelpa Trail.

The Grade is now on a steady course west. A shortcut path back to the Bow Knot leaves left. Past Milepost 5 is the intersection with Hogback (Throckmorton) Fire Road, which drops directly to Mountain Home. To the right is a now closed precipitous, rocky route to the East Peak parking lot.

The Grade re-enters woodland. Fern Creek Trail rises to the right from a marked signpost at the bend over Fern Creek itself. A usually reliable spring, which flows down a rock to the right, is just ahead. At the next big bend, rebuilding after a washout in the major storm of January 1982 has introduced a second brief downhill to the Grade. Here, near where the now gone Milepost 6 was, Miller Trail begins its very steep climb. It crosses the Grade again higher up, offersing a steep, shaded, shortcut.

The Grade approaches the cluster of buildings of West Point Inn, barely visible until the last yards. The inn sits at the western-most edge of Old Railroad Grade. It was built by the railroad company in 1904 to provide lodging for visitors, and still does provide rustic accommodations (call 415/388-9955 well in advance for reservations). West Point was also the transfer point for passengers taking the stagecoach on to Bolinas; a proposed rail line to Bolinas was never built. The inn is run by the West Point Inn Association, which also hosts a series of popular Sunday pancake breakfasts that are open to all. At the inn are public bathrooms, picnic tables with great views, a fountain, and interesting exhibits on the Mountain's geology, flora and fauna, and history.

Four trails meet the Grade at West Point. Clockwise, they are: Nora dropping steeply to Matt Davis, West Point very steeply down to Matt Davis, Old Stage Road descending to Pantoll, and Rock Spring heading to the Mountain Theater. There was a siding here for the extra railway cars used on Mountain Play weekends. Playgoers then walked to the theater.

The Grade rounds the inn and soon passes Milepost 7. The final stretch is nearly treeless, as virtually all the upper two-thirds of the original route was, and often hot in summer. Miller Trail again meets the Grade. It continues left uphill to Ridgecrest Boulevard. One-quarter mile after, Tavern Pump Trail joins from the right, having risen from Fern Creek Trail. You pass Milepost 8 (6.8 miles from our start). The Grade ends at paved

Ridgecrest Boulevard. Across the pavement is Middle Peak Fire Road and, to the right, the top of Eldridge Grade.

The tracks used to continue east to what is now the East Peak parking lot. Here was the famous Tavern of Tamalpais, or Summit Tavern. The tavern, which offered overnight accomodations, was built as part of the railway project. Fires, often started by cinders from the train, were a constant problem. The tavern burned to the ground in 1923, was rebuilt, and then survived the Mountain's 1929 conflagration. The tavern continued as a commercial enterprise until 1942, 12 years after the railroad's demise. It was then leased to the Army as a barracks. The structure fell into such disrepair after World War II that it was deliberately burned down in 1950. Its foundation now blends into the overlook picnic area.

The story of the Mt. Tamalpais and Muir Woods Railway is one of the Mountain's most colorful. It is well told in the book, "The Crookedest Railroad in the World," by Ted Wurm and Al Graves. The Railway's flavor is also splendidly recaptured in the 1988 film "Steaming up Tamalpais," by Cris Chater.

Among the private railroad's principal financial backers were: Sidney Cushing, who owned the Blithedale Hotel near the start; William Kent, who went on to donate Muir Woods to the public; and the Tamalpais Land and Water Co., which was then developing its Mill Valley holdings. The route was graded and the tracks laid in less than eight months. The groundbreaking was on February 5, 1896, the formal opening that August 27. Improvements continued to be made, including filling in of all the trestles. Visitors from San Francisco came by ferry, then rail to Mill Valley, where they boarded the train. During the Pan-American Exposition year of 1915, over 100,000 people took the ride to the top. Descent was by the even more thrilling gravity cars. The railroad fell victim to the increased popularity of the automobile, and construction of Ridgecrest Boulevard (partly financed by the railway) and Panoramic Highway in the 1920's made it possible to drive to the top. The fire of 1929 was a final blow. The tracks were pulled up in 1930 but it is still possible, if you're sharp eyed and lucky, to find old spikes along the Grade.

SLIDE GULCH TRAIL

From Old Railroad Grade to Hoo-Koo-E-Koo Fire Road / .4 miles
Terrain: Deep redwood forest; riparian; unimproved / MMWD
Elevation: From 560' to 1,040' / extremely steep
Intersecting Trails: None
Directions: Start of Old Railroad Grade - Grade, 1.1 miles

This unmaintained Trail is not on the maps. It is quite steep and would be too dangerous to include in this book were it not for the relatively good footing that a redwood forest provides.

To find the unsigned lower end of the Trail, ascend Old Railroad Grade from West Blithedale Avenue. A half-mile past Horseshoe Curve and Fire Road, and 200 yards past a fence, the grade crosses a creek. There is a prominent slide on the left. Slide Gulch Trail heads right, beside the creek, into the redwoods. It follows an old pipeline and, in 50 yards, meets a small water tank. Above is a remnant of a small diversion dam, used as a water source from 1890 until it was completely abandoned in 1967. The Trail crosses the stream and continues up its left bank, where it remains the rest of the trip.

The Trail rises extremely steeply through deep forest. Almost halfway up, there is a path right; veer left. The Trail follows the stream up to Hoo-Koo-E-Koo Fire Road. The junction is in a redwood grove. Since there are several similar looking groves along this section of Hoo-Koo-E-Koo, and the junction is unsigned, identify it by a riveted water pipe that bears the logos of both Kaiser Steel and United States Steel (USS). Wheeler Trail is 1/3 mile to the left on Hoo-Koo-E-Koo F.R., and Corte Madera Trail is 1/2 mile to the right.

Slide Gulch has been a named feature on Tam since the 1800's. Two forks of a creek flow southeast in the Slide Gulch area. They merge just below Old Railroad Grade, then empty into Corte Madera Creek. Slide Gulch Trail follows one of these forks; the main Slide Gulch channel is to the southwest.

SUPPORT THE M.T.I.A.

With a name whose meaning is shrouded by the mists of time, Mt. Tamalpais has been revered and loved by countless people over the years, and the establishment of the Mount Tamalpais Interpretive Association in 1983 has served to promote the conservation of this "Magic Mountain" through education.

This dedicated group of volunteers has become a servant to the Mountain by sharing its knowledge and enthusiasm with park visitors. At the Visitors Center at East Peak, M.T.I.A. volunteers answer questions and share facts relating to the natural and cultural history of the Mountain. Meeting thousands of people from all over the world, the M.T.I.A. takes the opportunity to share with people the magic of nature.

In addition, the Association makes "interpretive walks" available to the public, free of charge, on a regular basis. The purpose of these walks is to give people, particularly those not comfortable venturing alone, an opportunity to explore Mt. Tamalpais. During these moderately paced walks, M.T.I.A. volunteers stop frequently to point out and discuss interesting features such as the flowers, birds, animal tracks, geologic formations and the fascinating cultural history.

The not-for-profit M.T.I.A. is funded solely through donations and the sale of shirts and educational items at the Visitors Center and at community events. All proceeds go to support the Association and to purchase interpretive equipment for use by the State Park rangers at Mt. Tamalpais.

Most of all, the Mt. Tamalpais Interpretive Association is a group of volunteers whose interests, backgrounds and ages vary greatly but who are strongly linked by a love of the Mountain. And it is their hope, by sharing this love and enthusiasm, they can impart a deeper sense of responsibility for preserving Mt. Tamalpais and other wondrous resources.

For information about the M.T.I.A.'s hike programs, or about volunteering, please call the Pantoll Ranger Station at Mt. Tamalpais, (415) 388-2070.

TELEPHONE TRAIL

From Temelpa Trail to East Peak parking area / .6 miles
Terrain: Chaparral; loose rocks; overgrown; views / MMWD
Elevation: 1,600' to 2,320' / extremely steep
Intersecting Trails: None
Directions: Fern Canyon Rd. at Summit Ave. - Temelpa Trail, .8 miles

Telephone Trail is one of the steepest on Mt. Tamalpais. Loose rock on its upper half makes it extremely dangerous to descend; don't try it unless you're a mountaineer. It is also overgrown (Olmsted omits it entirely), so wear protective clothing or you may be scratched by chaparral shrubs. On the positive side, the Trail does provide unique, spectacular vistas from high on the Mountain.

Two trails, both unsigned, branch left off Temelpa Trail about 25 yards above the Sitting Bull plaque and boulder. First is Old Plane (Vic Haun), heading to Old Railroad Grade. A few feet beyond is the bottom of Telephone Trail. Telephone Trail climbs the Mountain on the other side of a ridge from Temelpa. From the start, the views are extraordinary. Shortly, a path branches left, downhill. In less than .2 miles, the Trail meets the row of telephone poles that give it its name. This active line to the summit is a companion the rest of the way. The wires are sometimes little more than five feet above the Trail. The poles are visible from many places south of the Mountain.

Halfway up, the Trail meets a stand of laurels, and they line the remainder of the ascent. A couple of paths set off right, back to Temelpa. The route becomes quite rocky, requiring agility to mount the boulders on the path and delicate balance should you be descending. It is also closely lined with sharp-pointed manzanita. Sounds from the summit parking area carry down. The Trail passes a Monterey pine, then makes a final bend to the right. Remnants of the long-gone Tavern on Tamalpais, the terminus of the railroad line, are visible. Telephone Trail ends at the stop sign by the edge of the East Peak parking lot. Plankwalk Trail, to the East Peak summit, is straight ahead.

Telephone Trail apparently dates from the early 1930's, perhaps tied to the rebuilding of the lookout tower atop East Peak then. There used to be another Telephone Trail, labelled #2 on some maps, running from the Mountain Theater area to Old Stage Road. It is now overgrown.

TEMELPA TRAIL

From Old Railroad Grade at Summit Avenue, Mill Valley, to Verna Dunshee Trail / 1.5 miles
Terrain: Overgrown chaparral; loose rocks; views / MMWD
Elevation: From 820' to 2,380' / extremely steep
Intersecting Trails: Connector to Hoo-Koo-E-Koo F.R. (.3m), Hoo-Koo-E-Koo F.R. (.4m), Old Plane (.8m), Telephone (.8m)
Directions: Fern Canyon Rd. at Summit Ave.; limited parking

Temelpa Trail is probably the steepest on Mt. Tamalpais, rising almost 1,600' in 1.5 miles. As a corollary, it is part of the fastest route from the Mountain's base to its summit. In 1987, Tom Borschel ran from Lytton Square in downtown Mill Valley, elevation 64', to the East Peak fire lookout, elevation 2,571', via Summit Avenue and Temelpa Trail in 30 minutes, 32 seconds during a Tamalpa Runners Club time trial. Needless to say, Temelpa Trail is only for the very fittest hikers and should not be taken downhill at all because of the loose rock, which makes the footing treacherous. It is also somewhat difficult to follow, with many unsigned intersections. Those who do venture onto Temelpa not only receive a fast, scenic trip up the Mountain, but also get to see a little known treasure, the Sitting Bull plaque.

Temelpa Trail presently starts uphill, unmarked, off Old Railroad Grade a few feet below the junction of Summit Avenue and Fern Canyon Road. Earlier, Temelpa started in Blithedale Canyon. The spur the Trail climbs is known as Middle Ridge. In .2 miles, Temelpa Trail meets an access path coming from Fern Canyon Road on the left. Continue right, ever steeply uphill.

As compensation for the effort, the views are outstanding even low, and get ever better. An old 2" pipeline cuts through the Trail in the early going, creating a gully. At .3 miles, a short connector to Hoo-Koo-E-Koo F.R. branches right. It is mistakenly called McKinley Cut Trail on the Olmsted map; some call it Easter Lily Trail. Stay left. In just under a half-mile, Temelpa crosses Hoo-Koo-E-Koo Fire Road. A sign points the way left to Bootjack, right to Kentfield. Cross the fire road and keep climbing. The most common shrub lining the way is manzanita.

In another 1/3 mile, a gray plaque is affixed to a large boulder on the left. The boulder itself, a block of erosion-resistant quartz tourmaline that fell from East Peak during a slide in the distant past, is wonderful enough; the plaque is one of the Mountain's jewels. It contains one of the most eloquent environmental statements ever made, expressed by the Sioux chief Sitting Bull in 1877. The quote is found in "The Portable North American Indian Reader" edited by Frederick W. Turner III (Viking Press, 1974). The plaque (which was maliciously defaced during the winter of 1989-90) reads in full:

> BEHOLD MY BROTHERS, THE SPRING HAS COME; THE EARTH HAS RECEIVED THE EMBRACES OF THE SUN AND WE SHALL SOON SEE THE RESULT OF ALL THAT LOVE! EVERY SEED IS AWAKENED AND SO HAS ALL ANIMAL LIFE. IT IS THROUGH THIS MYSTERIOUS POWER THAT WE TOO HAVE OUR BEING AND WE THEREFORE YIELD TO OUR NEIGHBORS, EVEN OUR ANIMAL NEIGHBORS, THE SAME RIGHT AS OURSELVES, TO INHABIT THIS LAND. YET HEAR ME, PEOPLE, WE HAVE NOW TO DEAL WITH ANOTHER RACE; SMALL AND FEEBLE WHEN OUR FATHERS FIRST MET THEM BUT NOW GREAT AND OVERBEARING. STRANGELY ENOUGH THEY HAVE A MIND TO TILL THE SOIL AND THE LOVE OF POSSESSION IS A DISEASE TO THEM. THESE PEOPLE HAVE MADE MANY RULES THAT THE RICH MAY BREAK BUT THE POOR MAY NOT. THEY TAKE TITHES FROM THE POOR AND WEAK TO SUPPORT THE RICH WHO RULE. THEY CLAIM THIS MOTHER OF OURS, THE EARTH, FOR THEIR OWN AND FENCE THEIR NEIGHBORS AWAY; THEY DEFACE HER WITH THEIR BUILDINGS AND THEIR REFUSE. THAT NATION IS LIKE A SPRING FRESHET THAT OVERRUNS ITS BANKS AND DESTROYS ALL WHO ARE IN ITS PATH.

> SITTING BULL 1877

Twenty-five yards uphill, two trails depart to the left. First is Old Plane (Vic Haun) going sharply left, downhill, to Double Bow Knot. A few feet above, Telephone Trail begins an extremely steep, rocky climb to the East Peak parking lot. Veer right, uphill (there is another overgrown path farther to the right). Continue the steep rock scrambling. Many years of slides and use have made for several reroutings and a host of intersections with unnamed paths. Keep veering right and uphill.

At 1.1 miles Temelpa crosses the jumbled rocks of Devil's Slide. Bend left without crossing. The remaining .4 miles are only gently uphill; there are even a few feet of downhill. If you somehow stuck to the true Temelpa you'll reach the Verna Dunshee, an asphalt covered loop around East Peak, at a sign. If not, you may end up a bit to the left or right; no matter.

It's a bit quicker to reach the East Peak parking lot, with its bathrooms, fountains, food stand, visitor center, and trail to the summit, by going left.

The origin of the word "Tamalpais" has been long debated; the subject of literally hundreds of articles. Many hold that the name is of Coast Miwok Indian origin. "Tamal" meant either "coast," "bay," or "west," and "pa" (later corrupted by the Spanish to "pais") meant "mountain" or "near." Others believe the name is entirely of Spanish origin, stemming either from: "country ("pais") of the Tamals," their name for a local Indian tribe; "mal pais," a common Spanish term for barren, rocky terrain; the Aztec place name "Tamaulipas," transferred from Mexico; or even the dish "tamales." The name Tamalpais was officially applied to the Mountain around 1860. Most earlier survey maps referred to it as Table Hill or Mountain, but other names were used as well.

Temelpa (variously spelled) is one name for the legendary lovelorn Indian "Sleeping Maiden" who reposes on the Mountain to give the summit ridge its famous profile. This legend, inspiration for countless poems and stories, may or may not be of Indian origin (there is a lively debate). The most famous recounting of the myth is Dan Totheroh's play, "Tamalpa," which has been presented a record eight seasons at the Mountain Theater. Its closing line, recited as the maiden Tamalpa is borne to her final resting place, is, "Throw over her the purple cloak that she will always wear — a shroud of amethyst from tip of toe to crown of hair."

Temelpa Trail was formerly part of the Summit Trail, one of Tamalpais' oldest, dating from around 1875. The name was changed in 1914. It has also been called Cushing's Trail, because it led up from the Cushing family's hotel in Blithedale Canyon. The ridge west of West Peak has also been known as Tamalpa, or Temelpa, Ridge.

TENDERFOOT TRAIL

From Cascade Drive, Mill Valley, to Pipeline Trail / 1.1 miles
Terrain: Deep woodland / City of Mill Valley, MCOSD, & private (easement)
Elevation: From 270' to 840'; steep
Intersecting Trails: Monte Vista F.R. (<.1m)
Directions: Downtown Mill Valley - Throckmorton Ave. - Cascade Drive to #477

A pair of trails, Zig-Zag and Tenderfoot, rise toward Mountain Home from the west end of Mill Valley's Cascade Drive. Taking one up and the other down makes for a pleasant loop walk, with rest and refreshments available halfway through at Mountain Home Inn.

Cascade Drive is a quintessential Mill Valley street; alongside a creek and lined with redwoods and attractive older homes. To reach Tenderfoot, follow Cascade Drive just over a mile from Old Mill Park and .2 miles past Cascade Falls. A sign beside the driveway of #477 Cascade, at unmarked Monte Vista Avenue, reads "Tenderfoot Trails." The plural is no mistake; the hillside south of Cascade is laced with paths and tricky, unmarked intersections. Start the climb by quietly passing to the left of the private residence. A chain marks the broad start of Tenderfoot.

The first junction on Tenderfoot is in just 30 yards. Left (straight) is half-mile long Monte Vista Fire Road. Veer right. In another 50 yards is a recently installed gate; there is room to pass. The second fork is at .2 miles. The spine-covered fruits from a chinquapin tree at the intersection cover the ground here in early fall. The right path immediately enters private property; veer left. Fork #3, by an old corrugated iron switchback siding, is at .4 miles. The left path, narrow and laced with poison oak, winds along for over a mile parallel to and below Edgewood Avenue. Veer right.

At a brief clearing in Tenderfoot's woodland canopy, a spectacular vista of East Peak opens. Around 75 yards beyond is fork #4. The upper, right option ends in 25 yards; veer left. The fifth and last fork, at .7 miles, is in the deep woodland. The left branch narrows to an overgrown path. Go right. Therefore, Tenderfoot's sequence of turns is, fortuitously: right, left, right, left, right.

Tenderfoot's remaining climb is through a quiet redwood forest. A slide is bypassed. A few yards later, the Trail crosses a stream over a bridge of roughly lashed redwood logs. The top of Tenderfoot is at the northwest end of Pipeline Trail. The junction is unmarked and easy to miss. Look for it where narrow Pipeline Trail meets broader Edgewood Road in a small, rather open grove of redwoods. To the left is Pipeline heading toward the Dipsea. To the right, a half-mile along Edgewood, is Mountain Home. Loops can be made with both options.

There have been various proposals over the years to develop homesites along Tenderfoot Trail. In 1980, a major effort to keep the Trail open was mounted by concerned citizens. Evidence was cited that Tenderfoot had been used by local Coast Miwok Indians, then by the earliest loggers. Now much of Tenderfoot Trail has been acquired by the City of Mill Valley and the Marin County Open Space District, and easements secured through private holdings. In 1989, approvals were granted to build a couple of homes on a private parcel at the top of Tenderfoot; the Trail will be slightly rerouted. The name Tenderfoot may refer to the Trail being gentler graded than the Dipsea steps, Zig-Zag Trail (which is twice as steep), the overgrown adjacent Mill Creek Fire Trail (not separately described), or other old routes up out of Mill Valley. At press-time, Tenderfoot Trail is open to bicylists; rules changes, however, are being considered.

WARNER CANYON FIRE ROAD

From Elinor Avenue, Mill Valley, to Glen Fire Road / 1.2 miles
Terrain: Lower part redwood forest; upper part chaparral / MCOSD & private (easement)
Elevation: From 360' to 580' / lower part steep, upper part almost level
Intersecting Trails: Warner (Elinor) Falls (.3m)
Directions: Highway 101 - East Blithedale Avenue (exit), Mill Valley - right on Carmelita Ave. - left on Oakdale Ave.- right on Elinor Ave. to past #245; limited or no parking

W arner Canyon, cut by Warner Creek, lies between Corte Madera Ridge and Blithedale Ridge. Its lower end is the site of the Mill Valley Municipal Golf Course. A fire road runs down from the head of the canyon and splits into two forks, descending on the east and west sides of Warner Creek. The east branch, called Glen Fire Road, meets Glen Drive in Mill Valley. The other fork is here called Warner Canyon Fire Road; it is just as commonly called Elinor Fire Road.

To reach Warner Canyon F.R., follow Mill Valley's Elinor Avenue to the end of the pavement and continue on the dirt. At the first junction, veer right; left goes up to a private residence. In 30 yards there is a gate marking the start of Warner Canyon Fire Road. The opening yards of the Fire Road are through private property, then the route enters MCOSD land.

The Fire Road is level at first. A path drops right to Bay Tree Lane in Mill Valley. The Fire Road alternates between being lined with broom and, at creek crossings, with redwoods. In .2 miles, a path branches right through the broom and drops to the end of Tartan Road in Mill Valley. In another 100 yards, in the middle of a horseshoe bend amidst the redwoods, unsigned Warner Falls Trail departs to the right. It runs a half-mile to a lovely, little known waterfall.

The uphill steepens. Warner Canyon F.R. passes in and out of redwood groves. The grade lessens, and there is even a short downhill. After the last quarter-mile long stretch of redwoods, the Fire Road opens. There are views of the San Francisco skyline. To the left, a delightful little "shrine" has been cut into the hillside; anyone disturbing it should expect years of bad luck!

The Fire Road ends at its junction with Glen Fire Road. Downhill leads, in less than .4 miles, to Mill Valley's Glen Drive. The remaining half-mile of uphill, to Corte Madera Ridge F.R., is treated as part of Glen Fire Road in this book, but can just as logically still be considered as Warner Canyon F.R.

Alexander Warner was a San Francisco physician who brought his large family to a summer home in the canyon beginning in 1885. Elinor Burt was a granddaughter of one of Mill Valley's first settlers, Jack Gardner. Her father, John Gardner, was a member of the Tamalpais Land & Water Co., which owned much of Mill Valley in the 1890's. The company had a policy of letting members name a street after a female relative. Burt was a widely respected teacher, a dietitian for the U.S. Air Corps during World War II, and the author of two cookbooks, "Olla Podrida" and "Far Eastern Cooking." She died in 1973 at age 74. Her oral history is found in the Mill Valley Public Library. The Marin County Open Space District began making acquisitions in Warner Canyon in the 1970's.

WARNER FALLS TRAIL

From Warner Canyon (Elinor) Fire Road to Warner Falls / .5 miles
Terrain: Riparian; largely redwood forest, parts lined with broom / MCOSD
Elevation: Around 380' / almost level
Intersecting Trails: None
Directions: Highway 101 - East Blithedale Ave. (exit), Mill Valley - right on Carmelita Ave. - left on Oakdale Ave. - right on Elinor Ave. to end (limited or no parking) - Warner Canyon F.R., .3 miles

There is a lovely waterfall on Warner Creek and a Trail to it, both little visited except by local residents. The falls are known both as Warner, for the canyon, and as Elinor, because access is by Elinor Avenue. The Trail, unsigned and unnamed, is usually simply referred to as "the trail to the falls."

To reach the trailhead, follow Warner Canyon (Elinor) Fire Road around .3 miles from its start off Elinor Avenue. A few paths are passed along the way but a noticeably more prominent trail branches right in the first big horseshoe bend. This is the start of Warner Falls Trail. It was once a fire road but, like some other old road cuts in this area, has became heavily overgrown with French broom. Continued use by visitors to the falls has kept it open, though the broom appears winning at press-time.

Redwood and hazel line the Trail in the wetter stretches, broom elsewhere. Poison oak also intrudes, so be careful. Beginning halfway in, the broom must be brushed aside to pass. The Trail rises slightly as it follows Warner Creek upstream. Paths branch off. The Trail returns to redwoods, then ends beside the falls. The flow is lively after a winter rain; nonexistent in summer. The deep woods help make this a special picnic spot.

Background on Alexander Warner and on Elinor Burt is found in the Warner Canyon Fire Road description.

WHEELER TRAIL

From Hoo-Koo-E-Koo Fire Road to Eldridge Grade / .7 miles
Terrain: Light woods, chaparral / MMWD
Elevation: From 1,120' to 1,580' / very steep
Intersecting Trails: None
Directions: Fern Canyon Rd. at Summit Ave. - Temelpa Trail - right on Hoo-Koo-E-Koo F.R., .2 miles

Wheeler Trail often plays a role in circuit routes around Tamalpais as it provides a key link on the Mountain's east face. Otherwise it is little used, being far from any trailhead.

Wheeler sets off uphill from Hoo-Koo-E-Koo Fire Road at Slide Gulch. The gulch, a named feature on the Mountain for some 100 years, is a long, prominent slide that runs southeast from below East Peak. At Wheeler's base are a dam and pipeline, remnants of the old Slide Gulch water intake. Bear sharply right a few feet up the Trail, not crossing the creek. Wheeler rises very steeply. There are old paths left and right but Wheeler is easy enough to follow. The Trail passes through a forest of young redwoods. Tree cover alternates with longer stretches through chaparral. There are sweeping eastern views.

Keep climbing over the rocky terrain. There is, at last, a welcome downhill. Fifty yards later Wheeler ends at a horseshoe curve in Eldridge Grade. Right leads down to the lakes, left up to East Peak.

The Trail was largely built by Alfred Wheeler. He was an attorney who sailed to San Francisco from New York in 1849. In the 1850's, he accumulated large parcels of San Francisco real estate. He loved to hike on Tam, and, seeing the need for a connection between the north and south sides of the Mountain, decided to do the work himself. The San Francisco Chronicle covered the dedication ceremony in September 1902 when bronze tablets honoring Wheeler were placed at both ends of the Trail. The account reads, in part, "For over two years, through summer's heat and winter's cold, this philanthropist, 80 years of age, toiled away with pick and shovel on the stubborn slopes of Tamalpais. He pursued his end with infinite patience, clearing a path over flinty rocks, hewing away the resisting chaparral, prying boulders out of the way, and all for a labor of love. . .He is now only able to move about with the help of crutches, and will probably never see his trail again. . .His thoughts dwell constantly on the heights of Tamalpais, and in his dreams he is still working away. . .on the winding path." Wheeler died 11 months later. His Chronicle obituary said, "the (trail) work cost him his life."

ZIG-ZAG TRAIL

From Cascade Drive, Mill Valley, to Mountain Home | .5 miles
Terrain: Mostly redwood forest, some chaparral | MCOSD & private (easement)
Elevation: From 290' to 900' | extremely steep
Intersecting Trails: None
Directions: Cascade Drive to end at Lovell Avenue

Zig-Zag Trail is part of the quickest route from Mill Valley to Mountain Home, and to Tam's network of trails. Indeed, in the mid-1980's, some runners in the Dipsea Race used it as part of a faster route to Stinson Beach than the Dipsea Trail itself. The trailhead is to the left of the driveway for the private residence of 550 Cascade Drive. Please be courteous. A separate road leads to Cascade Dam, a pond above it, and the now overgrown Cascade Fire Trail. The dam area is presently signed as closed.

Zig-Zag starts by crossing a bridge over Old Mill Creek. The Trail goes uphill, beside a fence surrounding the hundred year old, covered, Cascade Reservoir. The nine-foot-deep reservoir can hold 68,000 gallons. Uphill is the key word, for the climb up Throckmorton Ridge is quite steep throughout. Descending Zig-Zag is difficult as well. Several switchbacks bring the Trail its name. At the bottom and at the top are forests of young redwoods. In between, in a rocky gully amidst chaparral shrubs, there are some nice views. Huckleberry is abundant much of the way.

Zig Zag ends at an old signpost on a private drive; go right. In 50 yards is Gravity Car Grade, heading right to Double Bow Knot. Mountain Home Inn and Panoramic Highway are just uphill to the left.

Zig-Zag Trail is shown unnamed on the 1898 Sanborn map and named on the 1914 Tamalpais Fire Association map. The Trail was long part of a popular route over Throckmorton (Old Mine) Ridge and down to Muir Woods.

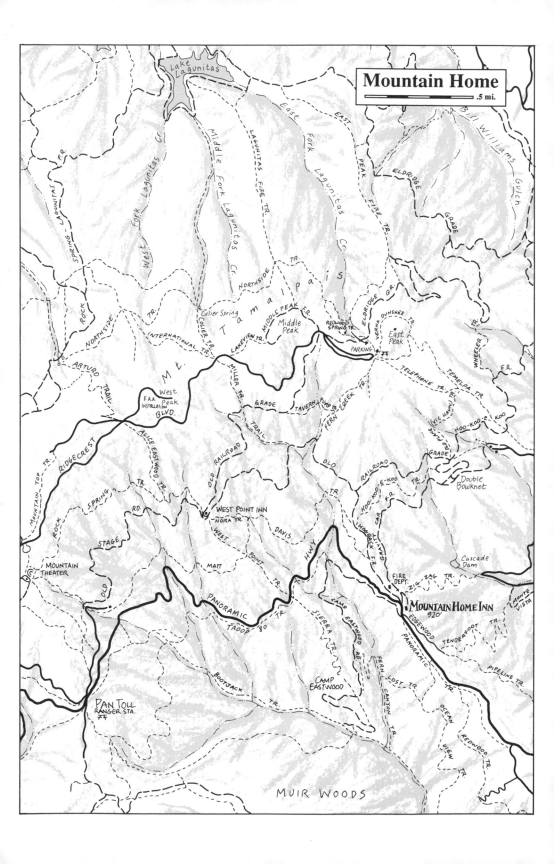

MOUNTAIN HOME TRAILHEAD

Directions to Mountain Home:
Highway 101 - Highway 1 - Panoramic Highway

M ountain Home has been a popular Tamalpais trailhead for over 75 years. Six trails set off from here, with several more nearby, fanning out to cover the Mountain's south side. Many organized hikes start here and each Saturday morning for over 20 years now a hardy group of runners gathers for a long jaunt. The parking lot often fills early on weekends. There is some off-road parking to the south and a small overflow lot (which the MMWD is considering closing) just north across Panoramic Highway down the dirt road. The trailhead has a fountain, built by the Tamalpa Runners in 1982, and outhouses. Golden Gate Transit bus #63 stops here on weekends.

The Mountain Home Inn, which gives the area its name, was built in 1912 by a Swiss couple, Claus and Martha Meyer. The inn had an Alpine flavor and fare, and was a popular dining spot for decades. Later, guest rooms and a beer garden were added. After several ownership changes, and a few years of being closed altogether, the inn was completely and attractively remodeled in the early 1980's. Today it offers both light refreshments and elegant, full course dining, served indoors and outside on the splendid patio. Ten guest rooms, each with a spectacular view, are available for overnight stays.

There are other trail access points closer to Mill Valley along Panoramic Highway. One is at the Dipsea Trail crossing opposite Bayview Drive, another is at Ridge Avenue.

Suggested loops from Mountain Home - elevation 920'

*Hogback F.R., .3m, to Matt Davis Trail - left, .9m, to Nora Trail - right .5m, to West Point - right (downhill), 1.6m, on Old Railroad Grade to Hogback F.R. - right, .7m, to start / **4.0 miles.***

*Hogback F.R., .3m, to Matt Davis Trail - left, 2.3m, to Bootjack Picnic Area - left on Bootjack Trail, .4m, to Troop 80 Trail - left, 1.5m, to Camp Eastwood Road - left, .5m, to start / **5.0 miles.***

*Panoramic Trail, .5m, to Redwood Trail - right, .7m, to Tourist Club - Sun Trail, .7m, to Dipsea Trail - right, 1.1m, to Frank Valley Road - right, .9m, into Muir Woods to Camp Eastwood Road - right, 2.2 miles, to start / **6.1 miles.***

Circuit of Mt. Tamalpais

*Gravity Car Grade, .9m, to Old Railroad Grade - left (uphill), .2m, to Hoo-Koo-E-Koo F.R. - right, .7m, to Wheeler Trail - left, .7m, to Eldridge Grade - left (uphill), .5m, to Northside Trail - right, 2.7m, to Rifle Camp - left on Rock Spring-Lagunitas F.R., 1.2m, across Ridgecrest Boulevard to Mountain Theater - left on Rock Spring Trail, 1.7m, to West Point - Old Railroad Grade downhill, 1.5m, to Hogback F.R. - right, .7m, to start / **10.8 miles.***

CAMP EASTWOOD ROAD

From Panoramic Highway to Muir Woods Road / 2.3 miles
Terrain: Mostly redwood forest; upper half paved; bicycles not permitted / MTSP & MWNM
Elevation: From 900' to 220' / gradual
Intersecting Trails: Connector to Mountain Home (.1m), Troop 80 (.6m), Sierra (1.3m), Fern Canyon (1.4m), Plevin Cut (1.4, 1.9m), Bootjack Spur (2.1m)
Directions: Mountain Home

This broad and gradual connection between Mountain Home and Muir Woods carries a bevy of names. Mt. Tamalpais State Park signs refer to it both as Old Railroad Grade and Alice Eastwood Road. Olmsted calls it the Gravity Car Grade; Erickson, the Camp Eastwood Road; Charette, the Old Railroad Grade; the TCC map uses Alice Eastwood Road. The current edition of the State Park map has Camp Eastwood Road. The now paved upper part of Camp Eastwood Road was the route of a gravity car rail line, built in 1907, from Double Bow Knot. However, the line never descended all the way to the floor of Muir Woods, as Camp Eastwood Road does. Also, the gravity car's route below Mountain Home was cut off by the construction of Panoramic Highway and later paved. Therefore, I use the name Gravity Car Grade only for the fire road between Mountain Home and Double Bow Knot.

Camp Eastwood Road begins at a gate to the left of Panoramic Highway (coming from Mill Valley) just before Mountain Home Inn. The sign on the gate indicates it is 1.4 miles to the Alice Eastwood Group Camp, and gives the Pantoll phone number (415/388-2070) to call for information.

The Road is paved. The highway shoulder signs found along the way are recycled safety markers from other Marin roads.

In around 1/6 mile, the Road passes below the Mountain Home trailhead parking lot; the outhouses are visible above. The very short connection, up steps, to the parking lot bears a name on the signpost, Trestle Trail; it's all of .03 miles long. A trestle carried a water pipeline over the rail tracks before Panoramic Highway was built.

The Road continues its gradual descent. Douglas fir, laurel, ceanothus, and madrone mix with the occasional redwood. The Road crosses over Fern Creek, which can be quite a torrent in winter. Just on the other side of the creek, to the right, is one end of the Troop 80 Trail, heading to Bootjack Trail. The woodland is denser, with towering redwoods now dominant. On the right side of the road, by a highway sign reading "C107, 1.96," is a section of the old railroad track. One hundred yards below, the Road crosses Laguna Creek by a water tank that serves Camp Eastwood. The deep canyon left of the now combined Fern and Laguna creeks is variously called Redwood or, on old maps, Sequoia Canyon. Beside a blank road marker on the right, look for tree poppies, a shrub with lovely large yellow flowers in spring.

After 1.4 miles, the Road meets a broad paved clearing, Camp Alice Eastwood. This was the site of the first Muir Woods Inn, built in 1907 and the original terminus of the gravity car line. The inn was destroyed by fire in 1913. In the 1930's, the Civilian Conservation Corps built their Camp Mt. Tamalpais here. It contained some 14 buildings and the foundations of some are still visible. On May 1 1949, Alice Eastwood's 90th birthday, the area was renamed in her honor as a group campground. Eastwood was present for the dedication.

Several trails meet here. Just past the bathrooms, to the left, are the Plevin Cut and Fern Canyon (Creek) trails. The former cuts around .4 miles off the descent of the Camp Eastwood Road while the latter is an alternate route to Muir Woods. To the right of Camp Eastwood Road is Sierra Trail, which rises to Troop 80 Trail and Panoramic Highway.

Camp Eastwood Road, continuing to the right beyond a gate, is now unpaved. Runners might enjoy flying down its perfect grade. The rail line extended a short way down it until 1913. The balance of the trip to Muir Woods could then be taken by stagecoach, and some old maps call this the Stage Road. The Road passes through the actual Plevin Cut of the rail line, then, a few yards later, meets the bottom of Plevin Cut Trail. Plevin Cut Trail goes uphill sharply left; look to its right for an overgrown old road. This is the lower section of the rail line that was extended down to the second Muir Woods Inn in 1914. Its continuation, overgrown but traceable, is across Camp Eastwood Road some ten yards below.

Around a half mile below the camp, the Road makes a bend right at a slight clearing. A Douglas fir stands somewhat alone to the left. This was the site of the second Muir Woods Inn, from 1914 until it was torn down in 1932. The inn had a view down to Muir Woods. That view is now blocked by trees that have since grown taller. A bit farther along, at another bend and beside a redwood of enormous girth, is the signed top of Bootjack Spur. It drops .1 mile to Bootjack Trail.

Soon the asphalt-covered, often crowded Muir Woods Trail becomes visible. Camp Eastwood Road meets it and ends. Just to the left is the bottom of Fern Canyon (Creek) Trail and, beyond, the Muir Woods visitor center. Bridge #4 and the Ben Johnson and Bootjack trails are to the right.

GRAVITY CAR GRADE

From Mountain Home to Old Railroad Grade at Double Bow Knot / 1.0 mile
Terrain: Hillside road cut; mostly chaparral, lightly wooded; heavily used / MMWD
Elevation: From 900' to 1,100' / gradual
Intersecting Trails: Connector to Hogback F.R. (.1m)
Directions: Mountain Home

The Mount Tamalpais Railway, from downtown Mill Valley to near East Peak, was built and opened in 1896. Its route is today's Old Railroad Grade. In 1907, a branch line, from Mesa Station in the Double Bow Knot down to the Muir Woods Inn, was added, and the Railway was renamed the Mt. Tamalpais and Muir Woods. The descent to Muir Woods was by an engineless gravity car. The ride was both scenic and thrilling, with the posted top speed of 12 miles per hour often surpassed. The return to Mesa Station was by steam power. Later, gravity cars were used for the full descent of the main line to Mill Valley. The railway, its financial condition weakened by the new auto road to the summit, the Depression, and the huge fire of 1929, ceased operations in 1930. Gravity Car Grade, now a dirt fire road with the tracks long gone, remains as a remnant of those special days. (Note that the section of the gravity car line below Mountain Home is called Camp Eastwood Road in this book; see Camp Eastwood Road for the explanation.)

A few yards above Mountain Home Inn on Panoramic Highway, a paved road rises to the right. Within a couple of yards, Gravity Car Grade branches off, down a short hill. No, the downhill gravity cars did not have to go over the hill. Instead, the tracks crossed the ridge through the Mine Ridge Cut, which was subsequently filled during construction of Panoramic Highway. Within a few yards, a private driveway branches right to the top of Zig-Zag Trail. The Grade passes an overflow parking area and then a gate. (The MMWD is considering placing a gate closer to Panoramic, which would cut off this parking area.)

The ascent is very gentle. In .1 mile, a connector fire road rises to the left; it goes the few yards to the rear of the fire station on Old Mine, or Throckmorton, Ridge. The Grade leaves the forest, and views of San Francisco open. Shrubs then line most of the way, though the Grade passes through some half-dozen redwood groves at stream crossings.

Gravity Car Grade splits just before its end. Both forks hit, in 100 yards, Old Railroad Grade as it makes a horseshoe turn through Double Bow Knot. The left fork leads to Mesa Station and higher on the Mountain; right leads down to Mill Valley.

HOGBACK FIRE ROAD

From Mountain Home to Old Railroad Grade / .6 miles
Terrain: Chaparral; ridgetop; views; bicycles not permitted / MMWD
Elevation: 940' to 1,460' / very steep
Intersecting Trails: Matt Davis (.3m), Hoo-Koo-E-Koo (.5m)
Directions: Mountain Home

This broad, dirt, very steep Fire Road is well used, as it is part of direct routes from the Mountain Home trailhead to popular destinations such as West Point, Bootjack, and Pantoll. It is one of the Mountain's oldest routes, and was once even more renown when it was the principal hikers' access to East Peak from Mill Valley. However, its upper end, above Old Railroad Grade, is now closed for erosion control.

A paved road up to a fire station departs from Panoramic Highway 50 yards above Mountain Home Inn. In twenty yards, Gravity Car Grade forks to the right while Hogback F.R. climbs the ridge line. Many users, however, simply stay on the paved road until the fire station. The Fire Road meets Throckmorton Ridge Fire Station #2, built in 1959, at the end of the pavement. There is a water fountain beside the building. Continue up beyond the gate. The views are outstanding. Just above the fire station on Hogback is said to be the lowest point in elevation on Tamalpais from which the Sierra Nevada, 160 miles east, can be seen. The snowcapped peaks are visible only on the clearest of winter days.

In spring, you'll see lovely yellow flowers of the shrub bush poppy near the first water tank. The Fire Road meets two more water tanks, called the Mine Ridge tanks. There is a water spigot beside the fenced tank on the left. Just beyond the tanks is the start of Matt Davis Trail, heading left (west) to Bootjack. One of the signs still indicates the Throckmorton continues up to East Peak. An uphill path at the start of Matt Davis rejoins Hogback.

The tough uphill continues and the views get even more sweeping. Hoo-Koo-E-Koo Trail crosses left and right, marked by new signposts. Left connects to Matt Davis in around .2 miles, right goes to Double Bow Knot. It is another stiff .2 miles to the top of Hogback at Old Railroad Grade. Left leads to West Point, right to Bow Knot. The Hogback's rocky uphill continuation across the Grade, quite visible when looking at the Mountain from Mill Valley, is now closed.

Many people call this Fire Road the Throckmorton, an alternate name for the prominent ridge it climbs. The new MMWD signpost at the Railroad Grade junction labels the Fire Road as Hogback, another long-used name due to the ridge's shape in profile. The ridge has also been called Mine Ridge; there was a quicksilver (mercury) claim near the present California Alpine Club headquarters just south of Mountain Home.

San Francisco financier Samuel Throckmorton took over the huge Rancho Sausalito land grant, which covered much of southern Marin, from debt-ridden William Richardson in 1856. He then built and lived in the second house in Mill Valley (John Reed's was the first) near the present junction of Montford Avenue and Linden Lane. Much of the estate was divided into some 24 dairy ranches, mostly rented by Portuguese settlers. Throckmorton died at in 1883 at age 75. His daughter, Susanna, ceded 3,790 acres, including much of Mill Valley, to the San Francisco Savings Union to settle debts against the Throckmorton estate. In 1890, much of the downtown Mill Valley land was auctioned off in lots.

Though a fire road, the steep Hogback is closed to bicycles. Gravity Car Grade and Old Railroad Grade serve as alternates.

MATT DAVIS TRAIL

From Hogback Fire Road to Belvedere Avenue, Stinson Beach / 6.7 miles
Spur: Between Matt Davis Trail and Buena Vista Avenue, Stinson Beach / .1 mile
Terrain: Mostly heavily wooded; parts open with broad panoramas / MMWD, MTSP,
& GGNRA; part of Bay Area Ridge Trail
Elevation: 1,100' to 1,500' to 60' / gradual with western section very steep
Intersecting Trails: Hoo-Koo-E-Koo (.3m), Nora (1.0m), West Point (1.2m),
Bootjack (2.3m), Easy Grade (2.6m), Old Stage Road (2.7m), Coastal (2.7m-4.3m)
Directions: Mountain Home - Hogback F.R., .3m

Matt Davis Trail offers a wonderful east-west passage across the Mountain. The Trail passes through redwoods, chaparral, magnificent open grassland, forests of towering Douglas fir, and coastal flora on its passage to Stinson Beach. Because of the Trail's 6.7 mile length, and because all return routes back to Mountain Home involve at least 1,500' of uphill, taking Matt Davis its full length requires some planning. One option is to place a car at Mountain Home, another at Stinson, and take the Trail one way downhill. Another option, available weekends only, is to ride a Golden Gate Transit bus back from Stinson Beach. Many loop possibilities cover sections of the Trail.

Though the west end of Matt Davis is accessible by car, most users join the Trail at its east end, so we will too. From Mountain Home, climb .3 miles via Hogback (Throckmorton) F.R. past the fire station, a water tank, then two more water tanks. The Matt Davis trailhead is on the left; a sign indicates it is 2.3 miles to Bootjack. A path, connecting to higher on Hogback, immediately branches right.

Matt Davis is initially quite wide for a trail; two can easily walk abreast. This opening section was a later addition, built to provide access for MMWD vehicles to the water intake at Fern Creek. Tall chaparral shrubs alternate with redwood groves. The going is level to gently uphill. In .3 miles, beside a splendid redwood with spiraled bark, Hoo-Koo-E-Koo Trail joins on the right. This is the start of the original Matt Davis Trail. Look above to see a pair of very old outhouses.

A bridge ahead fords Fern Creek, which is halfway down on its nearly 2,000 foot drop into Muir Woods. Remnants of the old intake, a one-time water source, are visible. The Trail narrows to the usual single file width. Stands of densely packed young redwoods are passed. There are fine southern vistas in the clearings. A small meadow known as Azalea Flat lies a few yards to the left of Matt Davis just before the prominent uphill. A few azaleas mark the overgrown entry. The meadow itself is being encroached by trees and shrubs.

In nearly a mile, at a bend just before a bridge over Laguna Creek, is the bottom end of Nora Trail. It goes uphill to West Point. Matt Davis levels and opens. Ten yards past a line of pine trees, planted here around 1930, is the easy-to-miss, unmarked crossing of West Point Trail. It goes left downhill to Panoramic Highway and right uphill to West Point.

At around 1.5 miles are the charred remains of chamise and manzanita shrubs, victims of an experimental controlled burn in 1984. Controlled burning, to clear the Mountain of volatile brush, is an issue that arouses passions pro and con. Fires on Tam, sometimes raging for days, were once more common. Modern fire control techniques have prevented serious conflagrations; the last was in 1945. Some people want a return of the old cycle through controlled burnings while others oppose any tampering.

The Trail crosses Spike Buck Creek on a bridge. Traffic noise from nearby Panoramic Highway becomes more evident. Next are crossings of two forks of Rattlesnake Creek. Matt Davis then enters delightful Bootjack Camp, a favorite picnic area for decades, and crosses Bootjack Trail. Matt Davis' continuation, to Pantoll, is momentarily hard to follow; stay just above the bathroom. The Trail follows a grassy hillside between Panoramic Highway below and Old Stage Road above.

In .3 miles from Bootjack, Easy Grade Trail, going uphill to the Mountain Theater, departs right. Climb a few steps to join and cross paved Old Stage Road. It goes right to West Point, left to Pantoll. To continue west on Matt Davis, cross the higher Pantoll (Southside) auto road, not Panoramic Highway. Coastal Trail joins Matt Davis here. The 1.6 miles that Matt Davis and Coastal run together is a pedestrian section of the newly formed Bay Area Ridge Trail. Matt Davis' entire remaining 4.0 mile length to Stinson Beach is commonly called, as on the Erickson map, Matt Davis Extension, since it was built later.

In the opening yards, on serpentine rock, the striking yellow mariposa lily can be spotted in late spring. Matt Davis quickly enters a cool, deep Douglas-fir dominated forest, where it remains for 1.0 miles. This nearly level stretch is one of the best places to see orchids; calypso (invariably associated with Douglas-firs on Tam), spotted-coralroot, and others, but you'll have to look carefully.

Matt Davis then emerges onto the open grasslands of the Mountain's west shoulder. This is one of the most spectacular sites in the Bay Area. The summit ridge towers behind, the Pacific stretches below, the views are sweeping. A photo from here graced the cover of Dorothy Whitnah's well-researched "An Outdoor Guide to the San Francisco Bay Area." If the weather is mild, these gentle knolls are an impossible-to-resist picnic site. At a trail sign, a path branches left to a grove of trees atop "the Knolls," or "Big Knoll." The Tamalpa Runners run to it each New Year's Day. Another path here heads right, steeply up.

Twenty yards after passing through a grove of laurels, Matt Davis splits from Coastal Trail. Coastal continues high and open for miles. Matt Davis veers left, down and into woodland. The distance to Stinson Beach is 2.4 miles, not the 1.7 miles of the signpost; the Trail was rerouted in 1968, using more switchbacks to make the descent gentler. Between laurel groves are great views, to Bodega Head beyond Point Reyes on clear days.

Next is a magical downhill through a Douglas fir forest. One of the more striking firs, though battered by lightning, has sent several massive candelabra-like limbs skyward. The ocean surf becomes audible. Numerous paths, traces of the former, steeper trail, branch left and right.

The Trail veers left at a fence post beside a rock outcropping. Leave the Trail to go a few feet right, to the top of Table Rock. It offers a great resting spot, with commanding views over the town of Stinson Beach. California buckeye is the common tree around the rock. The Trail continues steeply down as it passes the base of Table Rock. The vegetation increasingly shows the ocean's influence.

The Trail briefly exits the woods for a hillside covered with morning-glory. Back in the woods, Matt Davis crosses Table Rock Creek over a bridge. After a few more passages in and out of the forest, and a second creek crossing, the Trail hits a junction at a red fire plug. Right is a .1 mile spur to the junction of Belvedere, Buena Vista, and Laurel avenues, at one of Matt Davis' two signed trailheads in Stinson Beach. Continue left. At the next fork, veer right. Left is a short path through grassland onto private property.

Matt Davis ends on Belvedere Avenue above the community center and fire station. There is a large trailhead signpost with the distances to Coastal and Pantoll greatly understated. From the base of the street, downtown Stinson Beach is just to the right. Panoramic Highway and the western end of the Dipsea Trail are 1/4 mile to the left.

Perhaps no one has influenced Mt. Tamalpais' trails more than Matt Davis. Lincoln Fairley's book, "Mount Tamalpais, A History," has a picture of Matt Davis and calls him "champion trailbuilder." The TCC labeled him "the dean of trail workers," no small accolade from that club. Davis, a one time upholsterer, was for years the TCC's paid trails man. Davis built and lived in a couple of cabins in the Bootjack-Mountain Theater area from the

1920's to his death. Davis suffered a heart attack on the Mountain in 1938; he died on the Golden Gate Bridge while being transported to a hospital. He worked on the Trail that bears his name in 1929. The Extension was constructed in 1931.

NORA TRAIL

From Matt Davis Trail to West Point / .5 miles
Terrain: Mostly heavily wooded; lower part riparian / MMWD
Elevation: From 1,360' to 1,780' / very steep
Intersecting Trails: None
Directions: Mountain Home - Hogback Fire Road - Matt Davis Trail, .9 miles

N ora Trail is part of a well-traveled route between Mountain Home and West Point, and, with Matt Davis Trail and Old Railroad Grade, offers a very popular loop option.

Nora sets off uphill to the right of Matt Davis Trail, when coming from Mountain Home, just before the bridge over lively Laguna Creek. Elk clover, a common Tam shrub with huge leaves that die back each year, and chain ferns line the creek bed. Nora goes over the creek on a bridge some 50 yards above and continues up the right bank.

The Trail veers west, away from the creek and out of the redwood forest. San Francisco can be seen in clearings. The Trail goes over a second bridge. It winds into and out of tree cover. The going is very steep. Nora crosses a small bridge, then another more sizable one. The opening around West Point becomes visible above. Near its top, the Trail passes some wood posts, once part of a stile to keep horses from passing through.

Nora ends at a signpost beside the picnic tables at West Point. A few feet to the left is the bench with the loving dedication to hiker Robert Schneider, "who touched our lives as he passed this way." To the left is the top of the steep, unmarked West Point Trail. Old Stage Road, Rock Spring Trail, and Old Railroad Grade also meet at West Point.

Nora and Bob Stanton helped build the Trail while they were caretakers of the West Point Inn during World War I. They later operated a restaurant in San Francisco at the corner of Pine and Montgomery Streets. The Mount Tamalpais History Project file conjectures that Nora was a sister of Mickey O'Brien, who also has a trail named for him.

PANORAMIC TRAIL

From junction of Panoramic Highway and Ridge Avenue, Mill Valley, to Camp Eastwood Road / .9 miles
Terrain: Hillside; disturbed vegetation / MTSP
Elevation: Around 900' / almost level
Intersecting Trails: Redwood (.5m), Ocean View (.8m)
Directions: Panoramic Highway to Ridge Avenue

P anoramic Trail, though within yards of busy Panoramic Highway, is well used because of the easy access and the excellent views. It also plays a role in several loop possibilities. Both ends of the Trail are accessible by car, and by Golden Gate Transit bus on weekends. Starting from Ridge Avenue offers outstanding Mt. Tamalpais vistas; starting from Camp Eastwood Road gives ocean views. The Trail will be described from Ridge Avenue, closer to downtown Mill Valley.

The Panoramic trailhead is at the northwest corner of Ridge Avenue and Panoramic Highway, at a State Park signpost. Ridge Avenue leads to both the M.W.P.I.A. (Muir Woods Park Improvement Association) hall and a road down to the Tourist Club.

The Trail sets off parallel to the highway through a dense growth of blackberry bushes. The tasty berries ripen around July, and are invariably picked quickly. After passing the last private residence on the west side of the highway, the Trail drops lower on the hillside, somewhat escaping the traffic sounds. The Tourist Club can be glimpsed to the left. There are paths right, to the road, and left. An old rusted automobile sits on the left. In a half-mile, beside introduced Monterey pines, is the upper end of Redwood Trail. It goes sharply left, to the Tourist Club. Broom, having crowded out the native vegetation, then dominates Panoramic Trail. There are periodic organized broom pulls. Acacias are another common exotic. The Trail passes a prominent rock. Just beyond, Panoramic meets the top of Ocean View Trail, which descends 1.5 miles to Muir Woods.

Directly across Panoramic Highway here is Alpine Lodge, headquarters of the California Alpine Club, which was founded in 1914. The Lodge's Henry Hertenstein Hall, added in 1953, can be rented for parties. Dormitory-style accommodations upstairs can also be booked; call (415) 388-9940. The Trail ends when it hits paved Camp Eastwood Road, which drops to Muir Woods, at a gate. Mountain Home Inn is a few yards farther ahead across Panoramic Highway.

Panoramic Highway was built in the 1920's. This Trail, a way to avoid walking on the highway, was completed in 1969, largely by Ben Schmidt. It originally extended south to the Dipsea at Windy Gap, but private residences now block that section. Muir Woods maps and trail signs label Ocean View Trail as the Panoramic Trail, and the Panoramic Trail as the Panoramic Highway Trail.

PIPELINE TRAIL

Between the two sections of Edgewood Avenue, Mill Valley / .3 miles
Terrain: Redwood forest / City of Mill Valley
Elevation: Around 820' / almost level
Intersecting Trails: None
Directions: Mountain Home Inn - Edgewood Avenue, .5 miles

Pipeline Trail was once "the most traveled and fondly remembered of all approaches to the Mountain" (Fred Sandrock, "Mill Valley Historical Review," Spring 1985). It went from the top of the Dipsea steps to Mountain Home, crossed over the railroad tracks on a bridge, then split into an Upper Pipeline to Bootjack Camp and a lower branch to Rattlesnake Camp. Hikers would come from San Francisco via ferry to Sausalito, take the Northwestern Pacific Railroad to Mill Valley, climb the Dipsea steps, then head deep into the Mountain on the Pipeline. It was so popular that refreshment stands were set up along the way on weekends.

Today Pipeline Trail, covered and carved up by Panoramic Highway and Edgewood Avenue and replaced by the Matt Davis and Troop 80 trails, remains a public access, closed to cars, dirt trail for barely one-third mile. It connects two segments of Edgewood Avenue. To pick it up, follow unpaved Edgewood Road south of the Mountain Home Inn guest parking lot. The road is used by local residents so this segment is no longer considered a trail here.

In about a half-mile, the road narrows. Here, where Tenderfoot Trail drops left down to Cascade Drive in Mill Valley, begins the surviving section of Pipeline. The lovely Trail winds along the hillside. Redwoods dominate in the quiet canyon below. The old pipeline itself, badly battered, is still very evident. The Trail ends when it widens and is again open to cars as Edgewood Avenue. Edgewood continues to Sequoia Valley Road at the top of the Dipsea steps, passing several homes, the Swiss Club Tell, a native plant garden, and a huge water tank (the former Belvedere Reservoir).

Pipeline Trail, and the adjacent eight inch riveted steel pipeline, were built in 1904. The pipeline brought water from intakes at Rattlesnake, Spike Buck, Laguna, and Fern creeks to the Belvedere Reservoir, to serve the then developing community of Belvedere. The three acre, open reservoir, plagued with leakage and a diminishing supply from the intakes, was replaced by a five million gallon steel tank in 1967. The pipeline was completely abandoned soon after. Many other segments of the old pipeline remain, such as alongside Troop 80 Trail.

Helen Wild wrote a charming poem entitled "The Pipe Line Trail" that was published in California Out of Doors at the time the Trail was being carved up, in 1927. The poem concludes: "Dear little brown trail among the green, Your allurement your own destruction has been."

PLEVIN CUT TRAIL

From Camp Eastwood to Camp Eastwood Fire Road / .2 miles
Terrain: Deep woodland / MTSP
Elevation: From 580' to 400' / very steep
Intersecting Trails: None
Directions: Mountain Home - Camp Eastwood Fire Road, 1.3 miles

Plevin Cut Trail cuts off .3 miles on the Camp Eastwood Fire Road route between Muir Woods and Camp Eastwood. Two parallel branches of Plevin Cut, only one signed, descend from Camp Eastwood. They set off behind the outhouses at the top of Fern Canyon Trail and merge in around 75 yards.

Halfway down, Plevin Cut Trail crosses an overgrown remnant of a railroad grade. It is part of the extension of the Mt. Tamalpais & Muir Woods Railway gravity car line down to the second Muir Woods Inn. Both the extension and the inn were built after the higher, first Muir Woods Inn burned in 1913. Plevin Cut ends at the crossing of this now abandoned grade with Camp Eastwood F.R. The actual Plevin Cut, a gap dynamited through the hill for the rail line, is a few yards to the right.

W. T. "Dad" Plevin, a plumbing contractor in San Francisco, was a Mountain regular who served as the first custodian of Muir Woods and as a president of the Tamalpais Conservation Club. When he could no longer hike, he spent his Sundays at Bootjack Camp chatting with Mountain visitors. He died in 1947 at age 81.

REDWOOD TRAIL

From Panoramic Highway to the Tourist Club / .7 miles
Terrain: Largely open hillside, some woodland / MTSP
Elevation: From 900' to 700' / gradual
Intersecting Trails: None
Directions: Panoramic Highway across from Marin View Ave., Mill Valley - Ocean
View Trail, .2 miles

Redwood Trail has lovely views, but few redwoods. To reach it, pick up Panoramic Trail at Panoramic Highway, across from Marin View Avenue and the Alpine Lodge. The first fork off Panoramic, to the right, is the top of Ocean View Trail, which drops to Muir Woods. The second fork, also to the right and signed, is the start of Redwood Trail. An introduced Monterey pine marks the junction.

At the start there are fine views of the Pacific, and of the green hills rolling down to the ocean. The downhill briefly steepens. The Trail enters a grove of bay trees. Poison oak is abundant. Below are some redwoods. In .3 miles, back in the open, the Trail passes old fence posts and, to the left, a bench commanding a splendid vista. It invites a rest. The Tourist Club is visible, and you may hear German music on weekends.

The Trail re-enters woodland. After crossing over a bridge beneath a huge rock, Redwood Trail finally enters a redwood forest. The next creek bed shows remains of an old water intake. Redwood Trail passes above the main Tourist Club building; steps on the right lead down to it. Refreshments are sold here on weekends, and there are restrooms on the other side of the veranda.

Redwood Trail continues a bit farther through Tourist Club property before ending at the broad road, which is not open to regular traffic, that rises to Ridge Avenue. There are several Tourist Club signs at the intersection. To the right is the top of a path that drops to Ocean View Trail. Fifty yards uphill on the road is one end of Sun Trail, going towards the Dipsea Trail. Redwood Trail, in a different routing, dates to 1900 or earlier. It has also been called Tourist Club Trail. The Club, whose full name is "Touristen Verein - Die Naturfreunde" (Tourist Club - Nature Friends), established its Tamalpais chapter in 1912 (see Sun Trail). The world-wide organization itself was founded in Vienna in 1882. Two of its most popular weekends here are the beer fests in May and October. There once were plans to widen Redwood Trail to a road and to build homes along it.

SIERRA TRAIL

From Panoramic Highway to Camp Eastwood / 1.1 miles
Terrain: Woodland, with redwoods / MTSP
Elevation: From 1,000' to 600' / steep
Intersecting Trails: Troop 80 (.1m)
Directions: Panoramic Highway to milepost 3.66 sign (between Mountain Home and Bootjack); limited or no off-road parking

Sierra Trail was once part of of a broad fire break called West Point Fire Trail. That old route was severed by Panoramic Highway. The top of today's Sierra Trail is on the south side of Panoramic Highway near milepost marker 3.66. Across the highway is a turnout and the unmarked entry to the old route's upper section, the present West Point Trail. Sierra's trailhead sign says it is .7 miles to Camp Eastwood; subsequent reroutings of the Trail make the distance now slightly over one mile.

Just 40 yards down, Sierra crosses Troop 80 Trail; left leads to Mountain Home, right to Bootjack. Sierra goes straight ahead. There is a short, lone uphill on the otherwise steady descent. Huckleberry is abundant. The Trail occasionally leaves the woodland and fine southern views open. A sign recognizes that the Youth Conservation Corps worked on and rerouted Sierra Trail in 1980. There was an earlier rerouting in 1972. Five yards beyond the sign is the first of many chinquapin trees. Squaw-grass (*Xerophyllum tenax*), which sends up tall flower-laden stalks from a grass-like base, was in bloom here in 1988. It usually blossoms only after fires.

Switchbacks wind the route downhill. The Trail encounters a few stands of short, thin redwoods. Just above its terminus, Sierra passes a stone octagon-shaped water tank and widens to fire road-width. The Trail meets the upper, Camp B, section of Camp Alice Eastwood. Seventy yards below, Sierra ends at the main clearing of Camp Eastwood. There are outhouses to the left, a small amphitheater, and several picnic tables. The first Muir Woods Inn, original terminus of the gravity car rail line from Double Bow Knot, stood here. Also meeting at the camp are the Fern Canyon and Plevin Cut trails and Camp Eastwood Fire Road.

The Sierra Club, which has been active in Tamalpais trail work and conservation since it was co-founded by John Muir in 1892, rebuilt this Trail in 1946. The Sierra Club offers over one hundred hikes, all without charge, annually on Tamalpais, introducing thousands to the Mountain.

SUN TRAIL

From Dipsea Trail to the Tourist Club | .7 miles
Terrain: Open, grassy hillside; views | MTSP
Elevation: 680' to 700' | almost level
Intersecting Trails: None
Directions: Panoramic Highway to Bayview Drive, Mill Valley - Dipsea Trail toward Muir Woods, .1 mile

For wildflower color in spring, and gorgeous views any time, the Sun Trail is outstanding. Though the Trail has limited loop possibilities (basically only with the Dipsea), it is still well used because it begins near Mill Valley, is fairly level, goes to the Tourist Club, and is so attractive.

Just under .1 mile down the Dipsea Trail from Panoramic Highway, past a wood plank bridge, a path goes right. Then, in another 20 yards, the marked Sun Trail itself veers right off the Dipsea. Broom crowds the opening yards but then sweeping views open, of the pristine hills to the west and of the Pacific. The Trail remains a visual treat as it skirts the grassy hillside. Spring brings a riot of color. Against the green grass are the orange poppies; yellows of buttercup, broom, and wyethia; blues and purples of blue-eyed-grass, lupine, and blue-dicks; pinks and reds from mallow, vetch, and paintbrush; and whites from the abundant morning-glory and wild cucumber.

The Trail passes through a few small laurel groves but is otherwise open. Though largely level, there is some rolling terrain. Sun Trail, now lined with introduced flora, then descends. The Trail ends at the road that connects the Tourist Club with Ridge Avenue. The main club building and Redwood Trail are just to the left.

The local branch of the Tourist Club, or, properly reflecting its German roots, "Touristen Verein - Die Naturfreunde," was established here in 1912. There are over 800 club branches in Germany, Austria, and Switzerland, plus several scattered elsewhere, devoted to the outdoors ("nature friends") and fellowship. The club and its buildings are private. The main lodge, however, is open to all passing through on weekends, when drinks and light refreshments can be ordered from a well-stocked bar.

Sun Trail was long known as Cow Trail for the dairies in the area.

Coastal Trail winds toward Willow Camp Fire Road. Stinson Beach and Bolinas are in the background (Steve Ottaway)

North side of Tam and an almost 100 mile vista, as seen from near West Peak (Randall Hogue)

The trail, built in 1879, around Lake Lagunitas remains one of Tam's loveliest and most popular (Dewey Livingston)

A mountain biker ascends Bald Hill via Worn Spring F.R. (Kennard Wilson)

A group of runners follow the Dipsea Trail beyond its crossing of Coastal Fire Road atop Cardiac Hill. Mt. Diablo, 38 miles away, is on the horizon. (Eric Mohr)

The Mountain Theater before the stone seats were installed (Courtesy Nancy Skinner)

Dedication ceremony of Wheeler Trail, 1902 (Courtesy Nancy Skinner)

ravity car begins descent on tracks that covered Railroad Grade (Calif. Historical Society)

ohn Muir, William Kent, and J.H. Cutter (l. to r.) at Muir Woods Inn (Courtesy N. Skinner)

John Muir touches Kent Tree, beside Fern Creek Trail, 1910 (Courtesy N. Skinner)

Ruedy Niemela, Ethel Moore, J.W. Crawford at Sky Oaks, 1941 (Courtesy Connie Berto)

MTHP members on Rock Spring Trail after reopening Arturo Trail, 12/28/85 (D. Livingston)

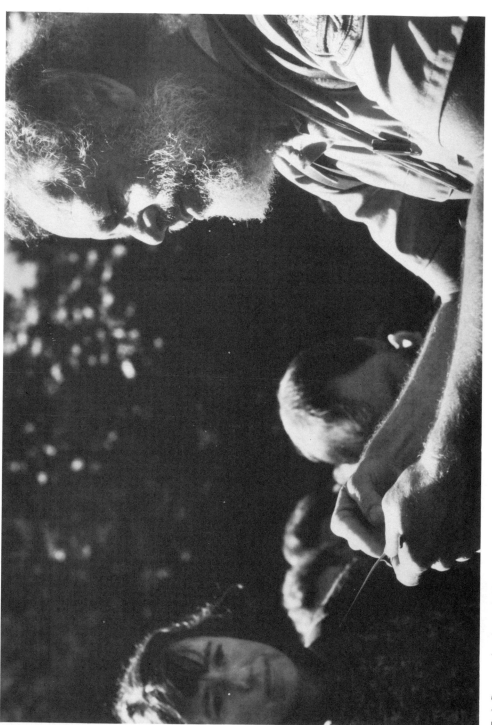

Bob Stewart leads a wildflower walk at Rock Spring for the Mt. Tamalpais Interpretive Association (Randall Hogue)

Three truly "stellar jays" at the misspelled sign in Van Wyck Meadow, junction of Bootjack and TCC Trails (Randall Hogue)

Dipsea Trail

Steep Ravine Trail	1.9 km
Coastal Trail	4.1
Muir Beach	10.6
Tenn. Valley	15.0
Rodeo Cove	21.0
Frank Valley	8.0
Miwok Trail	8.0
Mill Valley	11.0

Stinson Beach end of the Dipsea, the most fabled Trail on Mt. Tamalpais. (Eric Mohr)

Snowfall on Verna Dunshee Trail at the top of Temelpa Trail, March '89 (R. Hogue)

Kent Falls, top of Kent Canyon Trail (Randall Hogue)

A hiker crosses Webb Creek at the junction of the Dipsea and Steep Ravine Trails (Barry Spitz)

San Francisco skyline as seen above the fog from high on the Mountain (R. Hogue)

TROOP 80 TRAIL

From Camp Eastwood Road to Bootjack Trail | 1.5 miles
Spur: Between Troop 80 Trail and Van Wyck Meadow | .1 mile
Terrain: Light woodland | MMWD & MTSP
Elevation: From 780' to 1,120' | gradual
Intersecting Trails: Sierra (.5m), Troop 80 Spur (1.3m)
Direction: Mountain Home - Camp Eastwood Road, .4 miles

Troop 80 Trail, because it is near the Mountain Home trailhead and is fairly level, is well trod. It plays a part in many loop trips. It also offers some fine view sites. The drawback is its proximity to Panoramic Highway, with the concomitant road noise.

To reach Troop 80, take the short path down from the north edge (by the telephone) of the Mountain Home trailhead parking lot to Camp Eastwood Road. This short path is called Trestle Trail, for the trestle that once spanned the railroad cut through the ridge here. Follow Camp Eastwood Road (called Old Railroad Grade on the MTSP signs) downhill to Fern Creek, which flows below in a culvert. On the far bank, Troop 80 departs to the right. This short initial stretch, rerouted in 1971, beside Fern Creek is Troop 80's steepest. Switchbacks quickly bring the Trail to more level terrain.

Troop 80 is heavily forested in this eastern part. The Trail crosses Laguna Creek, flowing down to join Fern Creek, over a bridge. An old steel water pipeline is embedded in the Trail. It once brought water from several south side creeks (Rattlesnake, Spike Buck, Laguna, and Fern) to the Belvedere Reservoir in Mill Valley, then on to Belvedere (see Pipeline Trail).

In .5 miles, Troop 80 crosses Sierra Trail. Downhill left leads to Camp Eastwood, while Panoramic Highway is a few yards uphill. Shortly after is another stream crossing and redwood grove, a common Mountain combination. Just ahead is an old wooden bench and a water trough in which hikers used to dip their cups. Continuing west, next up is a 60-foot-long curved, boardwalk-like footbridge, built by Matt Davis. East Bay views open. Troop 80 crosses Spike Buck Creek at around 1.2 miles. In another .2 miles is Rattlesnake Creek, the westernmost creek tapped and the start for the pipeline. Again the Trail is in dense redwoods. A steep, heavily wooded canyon drops to the left.

At 1.5 miles, there is a clearing and an old wood bench sign with yellow lettering. Troop 80 Spur (also called Van Wyck Trail) sets off from here .1

mile to delightful Van Wyck Meadow. The meadow was the site of Lower Rattlesnake Camp.

Look behind you at the junction to spot the steps down to the Memorial Tree. A plaque beside the huge Douglas-fir reads:

DEDICATED MAY 2, 1920 BY THE TAMALPAIS CONSERVATION CLUB IN HONOR OF THE SERVICES RENDERED BY ITS MEMBERS DURING WORLD WAR I.

Some 300 people attended the dedication service. The plaque is clearly not the original because the term "World War I" did not come into use until after the second World War.

Troop 80 continues to the right of the fork, passing above Van Wyck Meadow. It ends at a poorly-marked intersection with Bootjack Trail. The area is the old Upper Rattlesnake Camp. Rattlesnake was "certainly the most popular hikers' camp on Mount Tam" (Mt. Tamalpais History Project's newsletter "Facts and Fancies," #15) during the 1920's and '30's. The Bootjack Trail goes left downhill to Muir Woods, and right, uphill to Alpine Trail and Bootjack Camp.

The Trail was built in 1931 largely by the Troop 80 Boy Scouts from the Ingleside district of San Francisco. It basically replaced the very popular Lower Pipeline Trail, which was disrupted when Panoramic Highway was constructed in the late 1920's.

SUPPORT OPEN SPACE

Marin County's splendid green and gold hills offer peace, beauty and recreation. However, not all of these areas are protected as public open space. Fortunately there is an organization, Health & Habitat, which helps to acquire land for permanent preservation.

Founded by Sandra Ross, Ph.D., this not-for-profit, public benefit corporation works tirelessly to save areas of scenic beauty and ecological importance, to conserve natural resources, and to preserve and restore native species and habitats.

Mt. Tamalpais is a center of endemism, a meeting place of the flora and fauna from the north and the south. It comprises a great diversity of habitats due to its varied altitudes and slope exposures. To quote from Dr. Peter Raven, leading American botanist, "It contains threatened and endangered species of plants and animals."

Aided by a panel of distinguished scientists, Health & Habitat encourages and sponsors research on the biosphere with special emphasis on maintaining natural balance. It educates people about the unique ecosystem of Mt. Tamalpais and how to appreciate and care for it.

Presently, Health & Habitat is collecting funds to help buy several sites for public open space such as: Horse Hill and Warner Ridge on Mt. Tamalpais' southeast slope; Bald Hill to the Mountain's north; and part of the railroad right of way in Corte Madera/Larkspur. In addition, Health & Habitat encourages paths which connect neighborhoods with town centers and with open space.

Readers are encouraged to support Health & Habitat in its environmental endeavors by making tax-deductible donations to: Health & Habitat, 76 Lee Street, Mill Valley, CA 94941, (415) 383-6130.

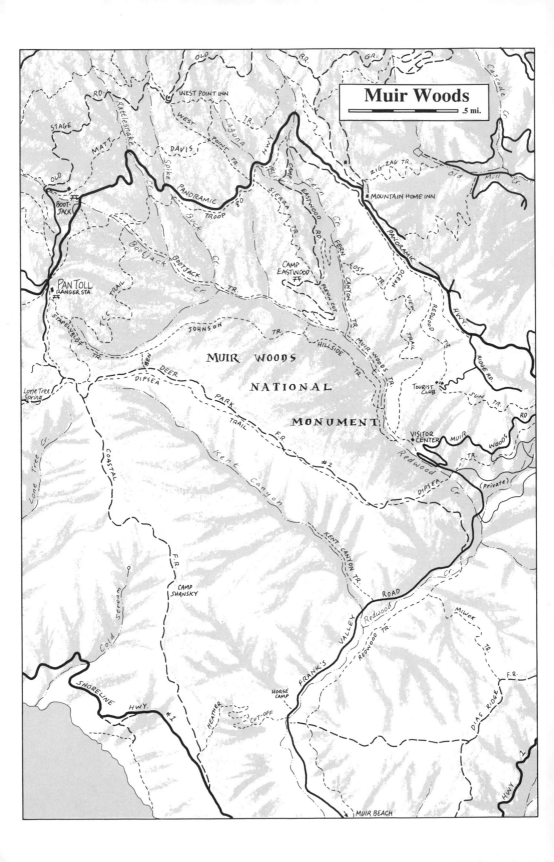

Muir Woods

.5 mi.

MUIR WOODS TRAILHEAD

Directions to Muir Woods National Monument main entrance:
Highway 101 - Highway 1 - Panoramic Highway to the Four Corners intersection -
left on Muir Woods Road to parking area

Most of Mt. Tamalpais' redwood trees were logged in the years after the California Gold Rush. To save an important surviving stand, William and Elizabeth Kent purchased 295 acres in 1905 of what had been known as Sequoia, or Redwood, Canyon. In 1908, they donated the land to the United States Government as a National Monument and insisted it be named for naturalist and conservationist John Muir. Muir said, "This is the best tree lover's monument that could be found in all the forests of the world."

The Monument is today the most popular part of Mt. Tamalpais, with almost two million visitors yearly. The grandeur of the redwoods, many over 200 feet tall, along pristine Redwood Creek makes this a unique place on this special Mountain, and a national treasure.

A new visitor center , opened in December 1989, stands at the main Muir Woods entrance. The Monument opens at 8 a.m. and closes at sunset. Admission is free but donations are welcomed. Just inside the new entrance arch are a gift shop, cafeteria, and the Park's administrative headquarters. There are restrooms in the parking lot and by the cafeteria, and several water fountains along the Muir Woods Trail.

On Muir Woods (Frank Valley) Road between the monument and Muir Beach are access points to Deer Park Fire Road (at milepost 2.09) and to Kent Canyon Trail (past milepost 2.56).

Suggested loops from Muir Woods main entrance - elevation 160'

*Muir Woods Trail, .9m, to bridge #4 and Hillside Trail - left, .7m, to bridge #2 - right .3m, on Muir Woods Trail to start / **1.9 miles.***

*Muir Woods Trail, .2m, to Ocean View (Panoramic) Trail - right, 1.2m, to Lost Trail - left, .6m, to Fern Canyon (Creek) Trail - left, .4m, to Muir Woods Trail - left, .7m, to start / **3.1 miles***

*Dipsea Trail west from overflow parking lot (or Deer Park F. R. when Redwood Creek is impassable), 1.6m, to Ben Johnson Trail - right, 1.3m, to Muir Woods Trail - right, 1.0m to start (1.5m to Deer Park F.R.) / **3.9 miles.***

Muir Woods Trail, .9m, to Bootjack Trail - right (straight), 1.5m, to Van Wyck Meadow - right, .9m, on Troop 80 Spur and Trail to Sierra Trail - right, 1.0m, to Camp Eastwood - right(downhill), .9m, on Camp Eastwood Road to Muir Woods Trail - left, .7m, to start / 5.9 miles.

Muir Woods Trail, .9m, to bridge #4 and Ben Johnson Trail - left, 1.3m, to Dipsea Trail - right, .3m, to TCC Trail - right, 1.8m, to Van Wyck Meadow - right on Bootjack Trail, 1.5m, to Muir Woods Trail - left (straight), .8m, to start / 6.6 miles.

BEN JOHNSON TRAIL

From Muir Woods Trail to Dipsea Trail / 1.3 miles
Terrain: *Redwood forest / MWNM*
Elevation: *From 230' to 860' / very steep*
Intersecting Trails: *Hillside (<.1m), Deer Park F.R. (1.2m)*
Directions: *Muir Woods Trail, .9 miles to bridge #4*

Ben Johnson Trail passes through one of the quietest, deepest, wettest forests on Mt. Tamalpais. It plays a role in several lovely loop walks out of Muir Woods.

To reach the Ben Johnson trailhead, take the main, asphalt-covered trail into Muir Woods to its end at bridge #4, the fourth bridge over Redwood Creek from the main entrance. Bootjack Trail continues straight ahead while the Ben Johnson rises to the left across a bridge. A signpost points the way toward the Dipsea Trail, Pantoll, and Stinson Beach. Just on the other side of the bridge, to the left, is the north end of Hillside Trail, which connects to bridge #2. Ben Johnson veers right, steeply uphill.

The climb is a stiff one, but the certain coolness of the woods brings relief. The Trail begins steep; the incline eases in about 1/2 mile. Rivulets are crossed on old bridges cut from redwood trunks. The redwoods and Douglas firs are enormous; several of the former, opened by fire, can be entered. Huckleberry is abundant.

At .9 miles, where there was once a welcome bench, several huge redwoods lie fallen. The small clearing in the tree canopy permits glimpses of Mine Ridge, above to the right. In another .1 mile, Ben Johnson meets a signed, three-way junction. A pause at the bench here in the deep woods is obligatory. Straight ahead is the start of Stapelveldt Trail, rising to Pantoll. Ben Johnson continues left, following the sign to the Dipsea Trail and Stinson Beach. Switchbacks carry it uphill another .2 miles.

Ben Johnson crests a ridge. It crosses Deer Park Fire Road in the magical area known as Deer Park. To the left is a magnificent stand of virgin redwoods. Just to the right is the fire road's junction with the Dipsea Trail. Ben Johnson Trail goes another 100 feet straight ahead to end at the Dipsea.

Ben Johnson was born in what is now Mill Valley in 1852, possibly the first white child born there. Later he was the superintendent of Samuel Throckmorton's dairy ranches in Southern Marin. He then moved to a cabin just downstream from the present bridge #4. Indeed, the creek was once known as Johnson's Creek. Ben Johnson built the Trail that carries his name around 1900, when he became the gamekeeper for the Tamalpais Sportsman's Club. The Trail was built to provide hunters access to the club's extensive lands to the west. All the Mountain's grizzly bears had been killed off by around 1850, and black bears, elk, and almost all bobcats and mountain lions were hunted out by the 1880's. Deer and quail remained as quarry. Johnson was retained as caretaker when William Kent bought Muir Woods in 1905 but died the year after. The Ben Johnson is one of the few trails named on the current U.S. Geological Survey Mt. Tamalpais map (15' Quadrangle, 1954, photorevised 1980). The Trail has been known as Dead Horse Trail and as Sequoia Trail.

BOOTJACK TRAIL

From Muir Woods Trail to the Mountain Theater | 2.7 miles
Spur: From Bootjack Trail to Camp Eastwood F.R. | .1 mile
Terrain: Mostly riparian, redwood forest; upper parts tanbark oak woodland with some open grassland | MTSP & MMWD
Elevation: From 230' to 1,980' | steep
Intersecting Trails: Troop 80 Spur (1.5m), TCC (1.5m), Troop 80 (1.6m), Alpine (1.9m), Matt Davis (2.0m), Old Stage Road (2.2m)
Directions: Muir Woods Trail to end

No trail, and only three fire roads (Willow Camp, and the Eldridge and Old Railroad grades), has a greater differential between its start and end elevations than Bootjack does. Along the way, Bootjack climbs through some of the Mountain's loveliest and most diverse areas, touching such important landmarks as Muir Woods, Van Wyck Meadow, Bootjack picnic area, and the Mountain Theater. It is one of the most appealing of Tam's trails.

Bootjack Trail can be said to begin at the Muir Woods entrance, but the initial asphalt-covered .9 miles are considered as the Muir Woods Trail in this book. Bootjack proper starts at the end of the asphalt, at bridge #4. Here, too, left across the bridge, Ben Johnson Trail begins its climb. Bootjack immediately leaves Muir Woods National Monument into Mount Tamalpais State Park.

The early going, along the left bank of Redwood Creek, is fairly level. Giant redwoods, rivals to those passed on the approach walk, tower above. Beside one is a plaque dedicating the tree to "the memory of Andrew Jay Cross, Pioneer in Optometry, 1855-1925."

In .1 mile, Bootjack Spur departs to the right. It climbs .1 mile to meet Camp Eastwood Fire Road beside a particularly huge redwood. That upper junction was the site of the second Muir Woods Inn, which was built in 1914 and torn down in 1932. The Spur was used by visitors walking between the inn and Muir Woods.

There is not another trail intersection for 1.4 miles, one of the longest such stretches on the Mountain. Bootjack passes through wondrous terrain; deep in forest, beside a vigorous, waterfall-laden stream. The crowds of Muir Woods seem miles away. Here Bootjack rivals the Cataract and Steep Ravine trails as Tam's best waterfall walk after a heavy rain. Azalea bushes are abundant. The Trail crosses several feeder streams over bridges. Around 1/3 mile in, the Trail has been rerouted; keep off the blocked path. In this area, millions of ladybugs (*Hippodomia convergens,* also called ladybird beetles) congregate each summer, covering rocks, bridges, live and dead branches and trunks, and ferns.

Now the uphill is more noticeable, and it relents only infrequently. The common shrub with the enormous leaves is elk clover. There is a welcome bench. The Trail crosses Spike Buck Creek, then Rattlesnake Creek. A "Surf Unsafe" is embedded in the railing of the bridge over the latter. The going gets steeper. Panoramic Highway can be glimpsed as the forest cover thins a bit. There are more steps, some of them made from old trail signs (like a rather incongruous "No Dogs, 8 p.m.-7 a.m" message on one step). A few yards below Van Wyck Meadow, you may, in mid-summer, be lucky enough to see Indian pink, one of the Mountain's showiest plants. It has deeply cleft, bright red petals and sepals.

Van Wyck Meadow is a delightful, grassy clearing. On one side is the charming (and misspelled) sign "Population, 3 Stellar Jays." In the middle of the meadow is a large sandstone boulder, Council Rock. A plaque dedicated to the Tamalpais Conservation Club, "Guardian of the Mountain," was placed on the old stone fireplace. The meadow was the site of Lower Rattlesnake Camp, later called Van Wyck Camp, one of the most popular of the Mountain's old gathering spots.

Sidney M. Van Wyck, Jr. (1869-1931) was a lawyer who helped the TCC during one of the most important crises for conservation on the Mountain. Donating his services, he headed the condemnation proceedings in 1927-28 against James Newlands and William Magee of the North Coast Water Company. They had refused to sell their over-500 acre parcel, between Mountain Home and Bootjack, to the State, hoping instead to develop it. The land, when finally purchased for $52,000, became the initial acreage of Mount Tamalpais State Park. Van Wyck, a graduate of the University of California, Berkeley, was also a TCC president, in 1921-22. He ran unsuccessfully for governor of California.

A signed trail through the grass to the right is Troop 80 Spur (also called Van Wyck Trail) leading to Troop 80 Trail at the Memorial Tree. At the meadow's left, TCC Trail begins a 1.4 mile trip to Stapelveldt Trail.

Bootjack continues uphill past a huge rock. The Trail is back in woods, largely tanbark oak and redwood. The next intersection is with the west end of Troop 80 Trail; it goes right, to Mountain Home. Just beyond is a bench made from an old trail sign, and the remains of an old fountain. This was the site of Upper Rattlesnake Camp. Alpine Trail comes in from the left; it rises to Pantoll. A bench at this junction is made from a classic old Rattlesnake Camp sign.

The sound of cars on Panoramic Highway becomes evident. After crossing a couple of bridges, Bootjack Trail meets the highway at a Golden Gate Transit bus stop. Cross the road into the parking lot and go right, up steps past a fountain, into the Bootjack picnic area. There are picnic tables and restrooms at this historic resting site, long known as Bootjack Camp. There were 29 State Park campsites here until the early 1970's. Wind your way through, passing a huge stone grill, to pick up the Trail at its intersection with Matt Davis Trail. Matt Davis goes left to Pantoll and right toward Mountain Home while Bootjack continues straight up.

The Trail passes below a MTSP residence, originally built by the TCC for their trails man Matt Davis and enlarged in 1955. Bootjack then crosses an asphalt road. To the far right is the entry to the residence. Above is Old Stage Road, to the right heading to West Point and left to Pantoll. A few yards to the left is the bottom of Riding and Hiking Trail. There is a drinking fountain beside the chlorinator building.

Bootjack continues steeply uphill. Above a rocky stretch, the Trail hits a grassy hillside. This clearing is prominent from many vantage points south of the Mountain. It once struck someone as having the shape of a bootjack, a device used to help remove boots, particularly riding boots, and the name has stuck since at least the 1880's. In late spring, the clearing is ablaze with yellow from poppies and mariposa lilies. There are splendid southeast vistas. The view from a bench, carved "RANGER," is slowly being blocked by a spreading Douglas fir.

This is a good area to see, in late spring, the Tamalpais jewelflower, a plant unique to Marin. It has odd, four-petaled purple flowers. The upper leaves are perfoliate; that is, they surround the stalk. Switchbacks, one with a small sign dubbing it "the Gucci," carry the Trail into chaparral. The next bench was made out of the "STATION" part of the same sign as the lower bench. Just below the Mountain Theater is a three-way intersection. Right leads to the theater. Fifty yards to the left is Bootjack Trail's upper terminus, at a junction with Easy Grade Trail. The Mountain Theater is just to the right.

Bootjack Trail appeared on the 1898 Sanborn map.

DEER PARK FIRE ROAD

From Coastal F.R. to Muir Woods Road | 2.4 miles
Terrain: Upper part redwood forest, middle part grassland, lower part lightly wooded | MTSP & MWNM ; part of Bay Area Ridge Trail
Elevation: From 1,300' to 140' | steep
Intersecting Trails: Dipsea (.2m, .3m, 1.0m, 1.1m, 1.2m, 1.3m, 1.4, 1.5m), Ben Johnson (.4m)
Directions: Pantoll - Coastal Fire Road, .6 miles

The lovely Deer Park Fire Road is a neighbor of the Dipsea Trail; they run together for four stretches and intersect several other times. Since the Dipsea Trail is described, and is usually taken, uphill from Muir Woods, I'll describe Deer Park F.R. downhill for the splendid loop opportunity, even though its lower end is the one accessible by car. Note that there is a completely separate Deer Park Fire Road and Deer Park Trail out of Deer Park in Fairfax.

To reach the trailhead, follow Coastal (Old Mine) Fire Road downhill from Pantoll. The fire road leaves the forest at one of the Mountain's more dramatic view sites. Just beyond are three intersections. The first is with

Lone Tree Fire Road (called Dipsea F.R. on the signpost), which departs to the right. Next, the Dipsea Trail crosses left and right. In seventy-five more yards, Deer Park F.R. begins its long downhill to the left (east).

The Fire Road quickly leaves the open grassland to enter deep forest and the westernmost tip of Muir Woods National Monument. Huge redwoods and Douglas firs tower above. One of the latter, on the right, is particularly enormous, with a huge girth supporting three tall trunks.

Deer Park Fire Road crosses the Dipsea Trail, which rises left to the top of Cardiac Hill. Deer Park F.R. and the Dipsea run together for around one hundred yards, then the Dipsea departs to the right. Shortly after, at a wordy signpost, Ben Johnson Trail crosses. It ends a few yards to the right, and drops to the main, lower part of Muir Woods to the left.

Deer Park Fire Road then enters one of the special parts of Tam; an unexpected stand of giant, virgin redwoods high on the Mountain. Presumably their relative inaccessibility spared these giants from the loggers who felled virtually all the Mountain's other redwood groves. Among many treasures is a redwood cluster with four fused trunks. This magic section, once called Kent's Deer Park, is little known even to Mountain veterans, as most visitors follow the Dipsea Trail. George Lucas filmed part of his movie "Willow" here.

The Fire Road leaves the forest, and Muir Woods National Monument, to re-enter grassland and Mount Tamalpais State Park. There are splendid views east and south. The Dipsea Trail is visible to the right and is soon met. The Fire Road and trail run together briefly, then the Dipsea goes right. There are more outstanding views on this stretch, called the Hogsback for its appearance in profile. The common shrub that lines the Fire Road here and below is baccharis, or coyote bush. The Dipsea again enters from the right, then shortly departs to the right. The two routes intersect one more time, with the Dipsea coming in on the right and leaving to the left, where it stays.

The ever descending Deer Park Fire Road swings wide right, then comes back within a couple of feet of the Dipsea Trail. The two finally completely part ways when the grassland gives way to forest at the top of Dynamite Hill. The Fire Road's remaining half-mile has woodland to the left and shrub-covered hillside right. Blackberries are common.

Well down, there is a poison oak-laden shortcut path left through Rocky Canyon. In another .1 mile, Deer Park F.R. ends at Muir Woods (Frank Valley) Road. The junction is at a gate between highway mile signs 2.09 and 2.10. To the left, .4 miles beside the paved road, is the Dipsea Trail to complete a loop. The main Muir Woods entrance is just beyond. Muir

Beach is to the right. Across the road, and therefore just outside this book's boundary (though still part of Mt. Tamalpais State Park), is one end of Redwood Creek Trail, which also winds its way to Muir Beach.

On September 23, 1989, the full length of Deer Park Fire Road was formally dedicated as part of the Bay Area Ridge Trail, a 400 mile multi-use route that will, when complete, circle San Francisco Bay. New blue Ridge Trail signs have been installed. The Ridge Trail continues south on Miwok Trail (across Frank Valley Road) and north on Coastal Fire Road.

Deer Park Fire Road appears on the 1898 Sanborn map. It has been known as Old Mine Truck Road, because it went on to the old mine below Pantoll.

FERN CANYON TRAIL

From Muir Woods to Camp Alice Eastwood | 1.0 mile
Terrain: Redwood forest; riparian | MWNM & MTSP
Elevation: 210' to 580' | lower part gradual, upper part steep
Intersecting Trails: Lost (.4m), Plevin Cut (1.0m)
Directions: Muir Woods Trail, .7 miles

The lovely trail that rises beside Fern Creek in Muir Woods is called Fern Canyon Trail on the MTSP, Erickson, and Olmsted maps and Fern Creek Trail on the Muir Woods, Charette, and TCC maps. Since another, unconnected trail near the creek's headwaters, some 2,000' higher in elevation, is called Fern Creek Trail by all authorities, I'll use Fern Canyon Trail here. By any name, it is one of the more delightful trails on the Mountain, wild in winter and refreshingly cool in summer.

The trailhead sign (saying Fern Creek Trail) is a quarter-mile past Cathedral Grove and bridge #3 when coming from the main Muir Woods entrance. It is here that Fern Creek itself, one of the longest and liveliest streams on Tamalpais, ends at its junction with Redwood Creek. The sign says that the Trail goes to Camp Eastwood, and that it is 92 meters to the Kent Memorial. The Memorial is a plaque on a boulder beside a huge Douglas fir. It reads:

WILLIAM KENT, WHO GAVE THESE WOODS AND OTHER NATURAL BEAUTY SITES TO PERPETUATE THEM FOR PEOPLE WHO LOVE THE OUT-OF-DOORS, 1864-1928. . .TCC.

The three-ton boulder was brought to Muir Woods Inn by railroad car, then farther down the canyon by wagon. On the journey, the boulder fell into the creek and had to be rolled to its present site by hikers. The dedication ceremony was in May, 1929.

William Kent (see Kent Trail) donated Muir Woods to the United States in 1908, having purchased it three years earlier. The massive Douglas fir to the left of the plaque was said to be Kent's favorite tree, and it is called the Kent Tree. It was once measured at 273 feet, making it the tallest tree in Marin County. Subsequent remeasurements show it somewhat shorter — its top apparently fell in a storm — and it is no longer the champ. (Marin's tallest tree is in Roy's Redwoods, off Nicasio Road.) With a circumference of 26 feet, 8 inches, it remains Tam's biggest fir.

The Trail heads into the canyon of Fern Creek, seemingly a world apart from the sometimes bustle of Muir Woods. The Trail actually does leave MWNM in .1 mile, to enter Mt. Tamalpais State Park. Bridges cross first to the creek's right bank, then back to the left. There is a distinctive clump of horsetails beside a sandy stretch of bank. The uphill begins.

The Trail crosses a feeder stream. It then meets Lost Trail, which heads right .6 miles to Ocean View Trail. Fern Canyon Trail crosses a wonderful bridge, at 100 feet the longest on Tam, to Fern Creek's right bank. The bridge is buttressed by a fallen tree. On the other side, some steps cut a few yards out of a switchback. The Trail leaves the canyon of Fern Creek here.

The uphill steepens. Several huge redwoods, many showing scars from the fire of 1929 and some joined at the base to form double or triple trees, are passed. Old Mine Ridge is occasionally visible. There are remnants of the asphalt which once covered the Trail. Near its top, the Trail meets a concrete foundation from the Civilian Conservation Corps camp that was here in the 1930's. A few yards farther is the signed Plevin Cut Trail, a steep downhill shortcut to Camp Eastwood Road.

Fern Canyon Trail ends 30 yards above at the paved, open clearing of Camp Alice Eastwood, near the outhouses. Here stood, from 1907 to 1913, the first Muir Woods Inn at the terminus of the gravity car line from Double Bow Knot. The other trails meeting here are, clockwise: a spur of Plevin Cut, Camp Eastwood Road downhill (a nice loop option), Sierra, and Camp Eastwood Road uphill.

The Trail appears on the 1898 Sanborn map. It was considered as the western half of Zig-Zag Trail until construction of Panoramic Highway severed the two.

HEATHER CUTOFF TRAIL

From Muir Woods Road to Coastal Fire Road / 1.2 miles
Terrain: Coastal grassland; terraced switchbacks; horses permitted / MTSP
Elevation: From 60' to 440' / gradual
Intersecting Trails: None
Directions: Muir Woods Road at milepost 3.21

This unusual Trail consists of 21 gentle switchbacks cut into a hillside. It was built in 1982 primarily for the many horseback riders in the Muir Beach area. Heather Cutoff plays a role for those on foot as well as part of the only all-trail loop in a large area of southwest Mt. Tamalpais.

The Trail begins from a gate north of the Muir Woods (Frank Valley) Road at milepost 3.21. Straight ahead, by the trees, is a picnic area and a new three site camp, geared to equestrians, that opened in 1989. Heather Cutoff Trail veers left at the edge of the parking lot, toward the corral. At the fence, the Trail sets off to the right, uphill, past a "No Dogs" sign.

The next section is sometimes overgrown with cat-tails (*Typha latifolia*), easy to brush aside. Then the switchbacks, which bring the Trail ever gradually upward for about a mile, begin. Prevalent among the thimbleberry, monkeyflower, baccharis, sage, thistles, and other trail-side plants is poison oak. Midway up the Trail are a few bay trees.

The Trail keeps rising. You can see how far you've climbed, and what remains. Near the top of the switchbacks, views of San Francisco and beyond open. Heather Cutoff ends at its junction with Coastal Fire Road, which goes left to Highway 1 and right up to Pantoll. Also just to the left is the MTSP-GGNRA boundary. There are lovely ocean vistas at this often windy site.

Heather Farm is to the left (south). The farm, on GGNRA land leased to the Banducci family, is an important supplier of ornamental heather and other flowers. In late winter, the hills below the east side of Highway 1 here are covered with the pink-purple of heather, which is not a native Marin plant. Some maps note a "Perkins Bypass" in the area; it has been closed due to erosion problems and replaced by Heather Cutoff.

HILLSIDE TRAIL

Between Muir Woods Trail from bridge #2 to bridge #4 / .7 miles
Terrain: Redwood forest; heavily used / MWNM
Elevation: From 180' to 360' to 240' / gradual
Intersecting Trails: None
Directions: Muir Woods Trail, .3 miles

Since Hillside offers the easiest dirt trail loop from the main Muir Woods entrance, it is heavily used. Indeed, probably more people cover its full length each year than any other dirt trail in this book. The signed entrance to Hillside Trail is at bridge #2 over Redwood Creek, about a quarter-mile from the main Muir Woods National Monument entrance. The Trail immediately climbs some steps, perhaps frightening off some Monument visitors, but the going later is easy, almost level.

The Trail skirts a hillside, earning its name. Redwoods dominate. The main Muir Woods Trail is visible below. In .2 miles, on the right, is a redwood with a huge root burl. At .4 miles, a new set of steps, up and then immediately down, bypasses a fallen redwood. There is a bench at a bend in the Trail. One of the redwoods there has trillium growing right out of its trunk, several feet above the soil.

Hillside Trail descends to, and ends at, its junction with Ben Johnson Trail, which is beginning its climb left to the Dipsea Trail. A few steps lead down to bridge #4 over Redwood Creek. Cross and go right to return to the Muir Woods headquarters. Left is the start of the long Bootjack Trail, which rises to the Mountain Theater.

Hillside Trail, which appears on maps from the 1920's, was restored in the mid-'30's and renamed Hillside Nature Trail. There were signs for a self-guided nature tour along it until 1964.

KENT CANYON TRAIL

From Muir Woods Road to Kent Canyon Falls / *.5 miles*
Terrain: Riparian; deep woods / MTSP
Elevation: Around 140' / almost level
Intersecting Trails: None
Directions: Muir Woods Road to "Kerri Lane," between mileposts 2.56 and 2.67

In 1914, a trail was opened from Frank Valley up Kent Canyon to the Dipsea (then called Lone Tree) Trail. It was designed to provide a new shaded route for walking to the Mountain Theater. The trail was named for its builders, F.S. Robbins and W. Higgins. Fred Robbins was a newspaperman who wrote books and articles about the outdoors. Logging in the 1950's contributed to the trail's disrepair and abandonment. Today only a remnant remains as Kent Canyon Trail.

The Trail begins at a driveway, marked by a sign "Kerri Lane," between a pair of State Park residences off Muir Woods (Frank Valley) Road. Kerri is State Park ranger Randy Hogue's daughter; the lane's name is unofficial. This was the site of the old Brazil Ranch before it was added to the State Park. Veer right around the aluminum-sided barn. The Trail is initially fire road-width as it follows the creek. In .2 miles is a clearing used as a ranger target practice range. Kent Canyon Trail narrows and crosses the creek. Visible here is the first of three "Kent Canyon Blow Off" water valves.

The Trail enters a laurel forest, and one huge fallen but still alive laurel must be ducked under. An overgrown ranch road branches left. It can be followed for about 1/6 mile before it deteriorates to a deer path. Kent Canyon Trail hits the creek again, and ends, just before a rocky gorge and waterfall. This is one of the loveliest, most peaceful, and little visited parts of Mt. Tamalpais. It gives a hint of how delightful the rest of the trail up Kent Canyon (also called Kent Ravine) must have been. The upper part of the canyon is now one of the major trail-less areas on the Mountain.

This is one of three trails, among other features, on Mt. Tamalpais named for the Kent family (see Kent Trail).

LOST TRAIL

From Fern Canyon Trail to Ocean View Trail / .6 miles
Terrain: Deeply wooded, lower half redwood, upper half Douglas fir / MTSP
Elevation: From 310' to 750' / very steep
Intersecting Trails: None
Directions: Muir Woods Trail - Fern Canyon Trail, .4 miles

Lost Trail, when combined with Ocean View and Fern Canyon trails, offers a lovely loop walk out of Muir Woods. Lost Trail leaves Fern Canyon Trail (called Fern Creek Trail on the signpost) to the right at a marked intersection, .4 miles above the main Muir Woods Trail. The junction is immediately before the long bridge over Fern Creek.

Lost Trail opens with steps and remains very steep, with few respites, throughout. The Trail, in deep woods, is quiet and peaceful. At the fifth set of steps, a giant Douglas fir sits above the top step. Fir replaces redwood as the dominant tree.

The forest canopy opens slightly. The stiff climb continues to Lost Trail's end at its junction with Ocean View Trail, which goes left uphill to Panoramic Trail and Panoramic Highway and right downhill back to Muir Woods.

The Trail dates to around 1914. It was partly buried by a landslide in the 1930's and "lost" for some 30 years until it was cleared again and given the name "Lost." What has been lost, ironically, is the Lost Trail sign at the upper trailhead; at press-time the name is handwritten on the wooden post.

MUIR WOODS TRAIL

From Muir Woods entrance to junction of Ben Johnson and Bootjack Trails / .9 miles
Spur: Between bridges #1 and #3 / .4 miles
Terrain: Redwood forest; riparian; asphalt surface; heavily used; wheelchair accessible / MWNM
Elevation: Around 160' / almost level
Intersecting Trails: Ocean View-Panoramic (.2m), Hillside (.3m), Fern Canyon-Fern Creek (.7m), Camp Eastwood Road (.7m)
Directions: Muir Woods trailhead; parking lots overflow summer weekends

No Mt. Tamalpais trail is used more than this one. Close to two million visitors a year, from scores of countries and speaking dozens of languages, follow it along Redwood Creek north from the main Muir Woods National Monument entrance. Along the Trail tower some of the County's tallest and oldest trees. Salmon and steelhead trout still swim up the pristine stream to their spawning grounds. Come to the Monument early (it opens at 8 a.m.) or in winter to enjoy the area in relative solitude, or take pleasure in sharing this very special place with others. Adjoining trails, which head high on the Mountain, are uncrowded any time of the year.

Oddly, this busiest of trails, which was once open to auto traffic, does not have a single, widely accepted name. Some maps (e.g., Erickson) consider it part of Bootjack Trail. The Muir Woods staff refers to it as the Main Trail. The Spur of the Trail on Redwood Creek's right bank between bridges #1 and #3 has also been called the Nature Trail.

The asphalt-covered Muir Woods Trail begins from the new main entry building, constructed in the style used by the Works Progress Administration in the 1930's, to the Monument. There is no admission fee but donations are welcomed. An informative brochure is available here. There are maps and attractive natural history signs along the way as well. The Trail is presently the only one on Mt. Tamalpais completely accessible to those in wheelchairs.

Immediately on the right are the gift shop and cafeteria (both run by a concessionaire), restrooms, and the Monument's staff offices. In a few more yards is a bridge, signed #1, across Redwood Creek. The Muir Woods Trail runs on both sides of the creek between bridges #1 and #3 (the right bank route is considered as a Spur here), but don't cross yet. Traces of no fewer than 16 bridges across Redwood Creek in Muir Woods have been uncovered.

Redwoods are, of course, the stars of this Trail. These long-lived monarchs have exceptionally thick bark, up to 12 inches, which keeps out enemies such as insects and fungi. The bark also helps make redwoods exceptionally fire-resistant; many healthy redwoods still show evidence of the last great fire to sweep through the area, in 1845. In winter, the tree's male cones release their clouds of pollen, imparting a golden cast to the area.

By a water fountain, Ocean View Trail (called Panoramic on the Monument's maps and signs), departs uphill to the right. Opposite is a plaque dedicating a redwood to Gifford Pinchot, first head of the National Forest Service. The plaque, placed by some members of the Sierra Club in 1910, reads:

FRIEND   OF   THE   FOREST,   PRESERVER   OF   THE COMMON-WEALTH

Ironically, Pinchot soon after became the club's, and John Muir's, foe when he supported the damming of Hetch Hetchy in Yosemite. Just behind the Pinchot Tree is a double-trunked giant, the Emerson Tree. A plaque, still affixed to its far side, was placed in 1903 to mark the 100th anniversary of the birth of Ralph Waldo Emerson. Jack London was among those attending the ceremony. The plaque simply reads:

1803 EMERSON 1903

This plaque may be the oldest on Mount Tam.

Across bridge #2, the gently rolling Hillside Trail begins. It goes to bridge #4, and offers a popular loop option. The bridges are good spots to look, in December and January, for the salmon and steelhead trout heading upstream to spawn. The adult salmon then die. Only the young return downstream, after the first heavy fall rains open the way back to the ocean. After a few years in the Pacific, they, too, return to this same Redwood Creek, and complete their own life cycle. Steelhead, however, can spawn more than once and both the adults and the young return to the ocean. Note the large rocks along the creek bank. They were placed there by the Civilian Conservation Corps in the 1930's to control erosion.

Bridge #3 (.4 miles in) offers an easy loop back on the creek's opposite bank but we'll continue further without crossing. The Trail forks around Cathedral Grove, which contains some of the Monument's largest trees. On the right fork is the site, marked by a plaque, where delegates from around the world, meeting in San Francisco to frame the United Nations charter, came on May 19, 1945. They were honoring President Franklin D. Roosevelt, who had died a month earlier. Azaleas grow beside the creek.

At .7 miles, the Fern Canyon (also called Fern Creek) Trail goes uphill to the right. It offers excellent loop options with the Ocean View (Panoramic) Trail or with Camp Eastwood Fire Road. In 100 yards, on the left, a turnout marks the site of the old Muir Woods Cabin. Just beyond, Camp Eastwood F. R. begins its climb to Mountain Home.

Muir Woods Trail ends at bridge #4 by the Monument's boundary, exactly .88 miles from the entrance. The unpaved trail straight ahead is the Bootjack, which climbs all the way to the Mountain Theater. Ben Johnson Trail sets off left on its way to the Dipsea Trail. A few yards up on the Ben Johnson, just over the bridge, is the northwest end of Hillside Trail.

On the return, cross Redwood Creek at bridge #3 to make a loop back. There was a self guided nature walk here and along the Hillside Trail from 1956-64; a new one is being planned. Look on the right for a redwood with a particularly large burl, about 20 feet up, some 15 yards before bridge #2. Burls, which can weigh up to 50 tons each, are swollen masses of undeveloped buds. Why some trees grow burls and others don't is still not well understood.

At bridge #2 is Hillside Trail and the Bohemian Grove. The Bohemian Club had its annual summer camp here in 1902. The members decided that Muir Woods was too cold, so they purchased a permanent camp in Sonoma County. In the Bohemian Grove is Muir Woods' tallest tree, a redwood measured at 252 feet. A bit farther on is a plaque marking the Bicentennial Tree, estimated to have sprouted in 1776, the year the Declaration of Independence was signed. The redwood is now a full-fledged giant. The loop ends at bridge #1.

President Theodore Roosevelt wanted to name the park Kent Monument in honor of William Kent, who donated its initial acreage to the nation in 1908. Kent declined, saying, "I have five good husky boys. . .if (they) cannot keep the name of Kent alive, I am willing it should be forgotten." He also said of his donation, "I deserve no more credit than if I had protected my children from a kidnaper." Kent suggested honoring John Muir, then 70 and the dean of American conservationists.

OCEAN VIEW TRAIL

From Muir Woods to Panoramic Trail / 1.5 miles
Terrain: Deeply wooded except at top / MWNM & MTSP
Elevation: 180' to 900' / steep
Intersecting Trails: Lost (1.2m)
Directions: Muir Woods Trail, .1 mile

There is some confusion about the name of this important, well used, lovely Trail. It has been known as Ocean View since it first appeared on a hiking map in 1914. But maps in Muir Woods, where most users pick up the Trail, call it Panoramic Trail because it leads to Panoramic Highway. The State Park sign at the upper trailhead still reads Ocean View at press-time, and still labels the separate trail beside Panoramic Highway as Panoramic Trail. In any case, the growth of forest trees to the west has obscured any ocean views, or panoramas, except at the Trail's very top.

The Trail begins .1 mile in from the Muir Woods Visitor Center. The trailhead, on the right, is opposite the tree dedicated to National Forest Service founder Gifford Pinchot. Ocean View begins its long uphill on steps. Towering redwoods line the Trail along with associated forest plants such as trillium, fairy-bells, and sword ferns. Unfortunately, poison oak is also abundant, so be cautious. In .1 mile a large Douglas fir straddles the Trail's left margin; firs become more common above.

At .4 miles, the Trail levels somewhat as it leaves Muir Woods National Monument and enters Mt. Tamalpais State Park. Thirty yards past the sign, on the right, is a steep path up to the Tourist Club. Its use is discouraged because of erosion problems. Soon after crossing a creek, Ocean View steepens. In .8 miles, at a clearing called "Fir Tree Point" on the Erickson map, the Trail opens. Look here for highly aromatic pitcher sages (*Lepechinia calycina*). They are woody shrubs, one to four feet tall, with two-lipped white flowers in spring. Rub the opposite leaves to capture the mint fragrance.

There is another stand of redwoods, then the first major incursion of broom. Just beyond, at a signpost, Lost Trail departs to the left. It offers, with Fern Canyon (Creek) Trail, a loop possibility back to Muir Woods. The Trail encounters open, broom-laden grassland. First there is a view of Tam's summit ridge. A few yards later look back to see the Pacific, and how the Trail got its name. The Trail passes beneath a huge rock; a few feet to the left is a lovely picnic site.

Ocean View ends when it meets Panoramic Trail. To the left is Mountain Home and to the right, Ridge Avenue. A few yards up is Panoramic Highway and, directly across, Alpine Lodge, headquarters of the California Alpine Club.

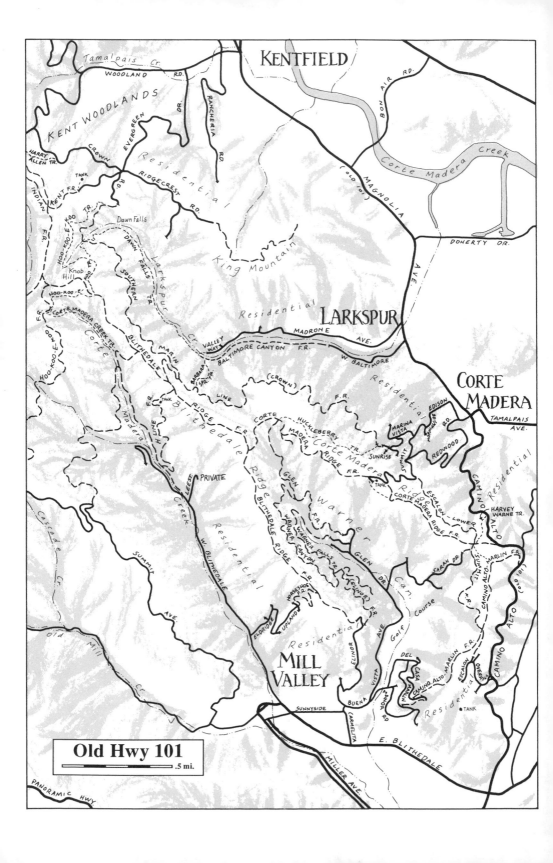

Old Hwy 101

⊢━━━━━━━━━━┥ .5 mi.

OLD HIGHWAY 101 TRAILHEAD

Directions to Southern Marin Line (Crown) F.R., Kent Woodlands:
Highway 101 - west on Sir Francis Drake Blvd. (exit), Greenbrae - left on College
Ave., Kentfield - right on Woodland Road - left on Evergreen Drive - left on Crown
Road (or straight to end)

Directions to northern Crown Road, Kent Woodlands:
Same as above to Woodland Road - right on Goodhill Road - left on Crown Road to
Phoenix Road

Directions to Baltimore Canyon, Larkspur:
Highway 101 - west on Tamalpais Drive (exit), Corte Madera to Redwood Ave. -
right on Corte Madera Ave. (which becomes Magnolia Ave.) - left on Madrone Ave.
to Valley Way

Directions to Summit Drive, Corte Madera:
Same as above but Redwood Ave. to Summit Drive

Directions to Escalon Drive, Mill Valley:
Highway 101 - East Blithedale Ave. (exit), Mill Valley - right on Camino Alto - left on
Overhill Road - right on Escalon Drive

Marin's original Highway 101 now has four different names through
the four communities it passes; College in Kentfield, Magnolia in
Larkspur, Corte Madera in Corte Madera, and Camino Alto in Mill Valley.
The road paralleled the tracks of the Northwestern Pacific Railroad line
that ran from Sausalito to San Anselmo. The old highway route has
traditionally been the eastern boundary of Mt. Tamalpais maps, such as
Erickson's and Olmsted's. Several trails depart to the west from the
corridor, either directly or off nearby roads, generally into lands of the
Marin County Open Space District.

A few trailheads are in Kent Woodlands, an elegant residential area of
Kentfield that the Kent family began subdividing in 1936. The most
popular, to Southern Marin Line Fire Road, is at the southern end of
Crown Road. There are other public access points near the north end of
Crown Road and at the top of Evergreen Drive.

In Larkspur, shaded, creek-side Baltimore Canyon, southwest of
downtown, is another favorite starting point. In Corte Madera, there are
three fire road access points off steep Summit Drive, the most used one
being at the road's top. Continuing south, there are three public open
space entries beside the road near the Corte Madera-Mill Valley border.
Two are just before the road's crest (where Corte Madera Avenue changes

its name to Camino Alto), and one just after. Still further south along Old Highway 101, there is a popular access at the end of Escalon Drive, off Overhill Road. None of these access points offers any facilities.

Suggested loops from Old Highway 101:

---

*Baltimore Canyon trailhead (elevation 160') - Dawn Falls Trail, .1m to Barbara Spring Trail - left, .3m, to Southern Marin Line F.R. - right, 1.3m, to Dawn Falls Trail - right, 1.2m, to start / **2.9 miles**.*

---

*Southern Marin Line F.R. trailhead (elevation 510') - Southern Marin Line F.R., 2.8m, to Huckleberry Trail - right, .6m, to Corte Madera Ridge F.R. - right, .5m, to Blithedale Ridge F.R. - right, .8m, to Hoo-Koo-E-Koo Trail - right, .9m, to Southern Marin Line F.R. - left, .1m, to start / **5.7 miles**.*

BALTIMORE CANYON FIRE ROAD

From Dawn Falls Trail to West Baltimore Avenue / .5 miles
Terrain: Riparian; heavily wooded / MCOSD
Elevation: From 160' to 120' / almost level
Intersecting Trails: None
Directions: Baltimore Canyon trailhead - cross bridge; limited parking

---

Within a mile from one of Marin's busiest streets is lovely, redwood-lined Baltimore Canyon. At the head of the canyon is Dawn Falls. Baltimore Canyon Fire Road and Dawn Falls Trail follow the right bank of Larkspur Creek the length of the canyon. Access to the Fire Road is from the end of charming Madrone Avenue, at Valley Way. Drop the 50 yards to Larkspur Creek, and cross a wood bridge, built by Boy Scouts. Baltimore Canyon F.R. goes left to a deadend. To the right is Dawn Falls Trail. (This convenient demarcation is somewhat arbitrary as the route remains fire road width for .2 miles to the right.)

Walk downstream, left. Larkspur Creek, once also known as Arroyo Holon, flows quite strongly after winter rains. In summer, while the creek may be nearly dry, the redwood forest still makes for a pleasant escape. The Fire Road winds its way east. Homes line the opposite, left bank.

Baltimore Canyon F.R. ends at a MCOSD sign by a private residence known to local residents as the house where rock star Janis Joplin once lived. There is no public through passage here but some visitors follow, water flow permitting, a crude path along the creek bank around the house to West Baltimore Avenue.

The name Baltimore Canyon comes from a Maryland firm, the Baltimore & Frederick Mining and Trading Co. The firm brought a sawmill around Cape Horn to the head of the heavily wooded canyon in 1849. Company employees took the shorter route across the Isthmus of Panama, which proved miserable, and several died. They began logging the canyon's giant redwoods, some said to be nearly 300 feet high with one reputed to be the tallest tree ever found. The lumber was carted by oxen to an estuary of Corte Madera Creek, then shipped to San Francisco. The firm, its workers afflicted by gold fever, sold its equipment after just five months. Baltimore Canyon's virgin forest was logged out by around 1860. Today's Baltimore Canyon Fire Road follows the original logging road.

BARBARA SPRING TRAIL

From Dawn Falls Trail to Southern Marin Line F.R. / .3 miles
Terrain: Riparian; deep woodland; dangerous to descend / MCOSD
Elevation: From 170' to 490' / extremely steep
Intersecting Trails: None
Directions: Baltimore Canyon trailhead - Dawn Falls Trail (right), 50 yards

Few trails are so accessible yet pass through such deep forest as Barbara Spring. Combined with Dawn Falls Trail and Southern Marin Line Fire Road, it offers a wilderness loop walk within minutes of a main population corridor. The Trail has extremely steep sections which can be quite slippery when taken downhill.

Barbara Spring Trail rises, unnamed, from a MCOSD signpost around 50 yards upstream from the bridge over Larkspur Creek. The Trail's steep, slide-prone early yards are typical. The Trail climbs beside a deep creek canyon. In .1 mile, two feeder rivulets merge at a small waterfall. The Trail follows the left-hand feeder. The forest, muffling any urban noise, shifts from tanbark oak-madrone to redwood as the elevation increases. Barbara Spring Trail squeezes past downed trees; new routings get worn around them.

The Trail ends when it meets level Southern Marin Line Fire Road. An MCOSD signpost, again without a name shown, marks the intersection. It is around 1.2 miles left to the fire road's Larkspur end and .3 miles right to H-Line Fire Road.

The "Barbara" of the Trail's name is unknown. It is also called "S" Trail, for its shape.

CAMINO ALTO-MARLIN FIRE ROAD

From Camino Alto to Marlin Avenue, Mill Valley / 1.2 miles
Terrain: Broom-dominated chaparral; views / MCOSD
Elevation: From 350' to 490' to 200' / rolling, parts very steep
Intersecting Trails: Escalon-Lower Summit F.R. (.6m)
Directions: Highway 101 - East Blithedale Avenue (exit), Mill Valley - right on Camino Alto to just below Mill Valley town limits sign

This rolling, unnamed Fire Road is designated here by its start and end points. It begins at a gate just below the summit of Camino Alto, to the left when coming from Mill Valley. There is limited parking at the adjacent turnout and across Camino Alto.

Camino Alto-Marlin Fire Road opens with a very steep climb to a water tank. Immediately there are fine views of the San Francisco skyline. Several paths branch to the right. The Fire Road drops. In .6 miles the Fire Road crosses a four-way junction dubbed "the Escalon Octopus" by MCOSD rangers. The Escalon-Lower Summit F.R. goes left to Escalon Drive in Mill Valley and right, past another junction known simply as "the Octopus," to Summit Drive in Corte Madera.

Camino Alto-Marlin F.R. rises again. A few yards up, a path goes right, into deeply wooded MCOSD lands above the Mill Valley golf course. The Fire Road crests again beside a row of private homes. There are excellent views of Mt. Tamalpais, towering over the nearer ridge called Little Tamalpais.

The Fire Road bends right, then drops very steeply. Lupine, clover, and yarrow hold out against the generally all-pervasive broom. The Fire Road meets a gate, marked with a MCOSD sign, at the crest of Mill Valley's Del Casa Drive. A new home, completed in 1990, sits here. Del Casa is an alternate access to the Fire Road. The unpaved route continues downhill to the left, again very steep. This last section was only added to the Open Space District in 1989. Camino Alto-Marlin Fire Road ends at a gate beside the private residence of #150 Marlin Drive.

CORTE MADERA RIDGE FIRE ROAD

From Corte Madera Avenue, Corte Madera, to Blithedale Ridge Fire Road / 1.7 miles
Terrain: Chaparral and light woodland; views / MCOSD
Elevation: From 300' to 850' / rolling, parts very steep
Intersecting Trails: Harvey Warne (.1m), Escalon-Lower Summit F.R. (.1m),
Huckleberry (1.6m), Glen F.R. (1.6m)
Directions: Highway 101 - west on Tamalpais Drive (exit), Corte Madera - left on
Corte Madera Avenue to opposite Chapman Avenue

Corte Madera Ridge Fire Road provides access to the main Mountain trail network. It also offers, most of its length, excellent Mt. Tam views. On the negative side, the Fire Road is very steep, is bordered largely by the weed French broom, and has a one-fifth-mile-long discontinuity that is paved and open to automobiles.

The Fire Road begins from an MCOSD-signed gate to the right, when going up Corte Madera Avenue from Corte Madera, a few yards before the Mill Valley town limits sign. There is very limited off-road parking at the turnout.

The initial uphill is through dense woods. In .1 mile, on the right, is the top of Harvey Warne Trail. It too connects with Corte Madera Avenue. Ten yards beyond, by a pump house, is a major, currently completely unsigned trail junction, dubbed the "Octopus" by MCOSD rangers. Corte Madera Ridge F.R. continues uphill, the level Escalon-Lower Summit F.R. goes left and right, and a short connector fire road drops to Mill Valley's Sarah Drive. Three paths complete the eight-option Octopus.

Continue the very steep climb. French broom, a native of southern France (its specific name, *"monspessulanus,"* means "of Montpelier") that was introduced to Tam, lines both sides of the Fire Road. Despite its colorful yellow flowers, it has become, with its somewhat less ubiquitous cousin, Scotch broom (which has smaller, needle-like leaves), anathema to many Mountain visitors. There are organized broom pulls. The shrub earned this disdain by being so successful an intruder, crowding out other wildflowers. Howell said of it, as early as 1948, "(French broom is). . .a pernicious shrub weed exhibiting an aggressive vigor that the native vegetation cannot withstand."

At the bottom of a dip in the Fire Road, a path branches left back to Sarah Drive at the Octopus. In .7 miles, the Fire Road meets, and joins, the uppermost part of Corte Madera's Summit Drive. There are two options up: an overgrown path left a few yards below the junction or the asphalt.

The steep paved road (shown as a fire road on the Olmsted map) rises .2 miles past several homes. The path and road meet near the gate and MCOSD sign that mark the continuation of Corte Madera Ridge F.R., straight ahead. The road to the left of the gate leads to a private residence.

The Fire Road circles high above Warner Canyon. The actual ridge top of what is called Little Tamalpais is a few yards up on the right; a path traverses it. The fire road that Olmsted, Erickson, and Charette all show as branching left from Corte Madera Ridge F.R. is completely overgrown by broom in its early yards, and at several places later. As the maps show, the path simply ends and disappears; you've been warned!

There are several outstanding Mt. Tam vista points. In .6 miles from the last gate, the Fire Road meets a four-way intersection. Huckleberry Trail drops right to Southern Marin Line (Crown) Fire Road. To the left, Glen Fire Road descends Warner Canyon.

Corte Madera Ridge F.R. rises to command a glorious view to the north and south. It drops, then rises again. The Fire Road ends at the junction, called Judy's Corner by some equestrians, with Blithedale Ridge F.R. The top of 937' Blithedale Knoll is just above. This is a stunning view site. Blithedale Ridge F.R. goes left to Mill Valley and right to Indian Fire Road.

Corte Madera del Presidio ("cut wood for the Presidio" in Spanish) was the name of the nearly 8,000 acre rancho, covering much of the southeast of the Mountain, that was granted to John Reed by the Mexican government in 1834. There is a separate Corte Madera Trail running between Hoo-Koo-E-Koo F.R. and Old Railroad Grade.

DAWN FALLS TRAIL

From Baltimore Canyon F.R. to Hoo-Koo-E-Koo Trail / 1.4 miles
Terrain: Deep woodland; riparian / MCOSD & private (easement)
Elevation: 160' to 640' / half almost level, half very steep
Intersecting Trails: Southern Marin Line F.R. (1.2m)
Directions: Baltimore Canyon trailhead - cross bridge

Dawn Falls is one of the more accessible of the Mountain's larger waterfalls. It is just 1.5 miles west of busy Magnolia Avenue, and .7 miles from a trailhead. This popular Trail to the falls is quite lovely.

There is no clear demarcation between Baltimore Canyon Fire Road and Dawn Falls Trail. The two form a continuous route, partly over an old logging road that dates to around 1850, along the right bank of Larkspur Creek. In this book, the public-access footbridge across Larkspur Creek below Valley Way is considered the divide. To the left (east and downstream) is Baltimore Canyon F.R; to the right is Dawn Falls Trail.

Head upstream, to the right and west. In around fifty yards is the lower end of Barbara Spring Trail, marked by a generic MCOSD "Trail" sign. Barbara Spring rises very steeply to Southern Marin Line (Crown) F.R. In another .1 mile is a fence, with a sign saying the area ahead is closed after sunset. Public outcry over blocking of the route here led to an easement through this stretch of private property. Just beyond, the Trail goes over a short hill. In the creek below are remnants of a dam originally built to provide drinking water for Larkspur. After a drowning here in the 1920's, the dam, no longer in use, was dynamited.

Dawn Falls Trail narrows. The Trail skirts the edge of lively Larkspur Creek. After a good rain, the creek overruns sections of the Trail, requiring some scrambling along the bank. The old Blue Rock Quarry, which provided the blue basalt for the dam, the refacing of Larkspur's historic Blue Rock Inn, and other Marin projects, is still visible on the left. Redwoods line the way. Many of the fallen trees are madrones, losers in the arboreal competition for light. Urban sights and sounds fade far behind.

In a small meadow on the right is a wintering ground for ladybugs; they can cover the vegetation. An old trail on the other side of the creek here went up to King Mountain. If plans to acquire King Mountain for open space are completed (an agreement was reached in March 1990) that old trail and this junction may become more prominent.

The Trail now begins to steeply climb. Switchbacks, cut in the mid-1980's, help. Then Dawn Falls themselves are reached. Two streams converge and promptly plummet 25'. Come after a sizable mid-winter rain and you'll be rewarded with a torrent; in the summer the falls are barely a trickle. There are rocks on which to sit and enjoy this special place.

More switchbacks and steps then lead up to Southern Marin Line F.R. The junction is signed. It is .3 miles right to Kentfield's Crown Road, an alternate trailhead to reach Dawn Falls. Cross the fire road to another MCOSD post. This upper part of Dawn Falls Trail, though old, was improved and signed only in 1988; it isn't yet on the Erickson or Olmsted maps. The Trail rises very steeply up a redwood-lined canyon, passing a path to the right. Dawn Falls Trail ends at its junction with Hoo-Koo-E-Koo Trail. To the right is a downhill to Southern Marin Line F.R., to the left a climb to Blithedale Ridge.

Since Dawn Falls and Baltimore Canyon face southeast, the "Dawn" perhaps refers to the wooded area's early morning light.

ESCALON-LOWER SUMMIT FIRE ROAD

From Escalon Drive, Mill Valley, to Summit Drive, Corte Madera / 1.3 miles
Terrain: Southern half grassland, northern half woodland / MCOSD
Elevation: Around 400' / almost level
Intersecting Trails: Camino Alto-Marlin F.R. (.1m), Corte Madera Ridge F.R. (.7m),
Harvey Warne (.7m)
Directions: Escalon Drive trailhead

A nearly level fire road runs from one end of Escalon Drive in the Northridge subdivision off Mill Valley's Camino Alto to between #151 and #155 Summit Drive in Corte Madera. It bears no official name but the MCOSD rangers who patrol the area call it Escalon-Lower Summit Fire Road. There is adequate street parking only on the Escalon end, our starting point.

Pass the gate and almost immediately, behind, are lovely views of the San Francisco skyline. Broom, which thrives along road cuts in this part of Tam, lines the way. In .1 mile, the Fire Road crosses Camino Alto-Marlin F.R. This four-way junction is called the "Escalon Octopus" by the rangers. Left and uphill leads to Marlin Avenue and Del Casa Drive in Mill Valley while right and uphill connects to Camino Alto.

The next virtually flat stretch is lightly wooded. Madrone is the most common tree, with some redwoods. There are striking Mt. Tamalpais vistas. The Fire Road then meets, at a water pump station, the "Octopus" junction. There are indeed eight options; five fire roads and three paths. The Fire Road continues directly across the Octopus.

The last half-mile, slightly uphill, is well-wooded. Madrone, laurel, redwood and the shrub hazel are most common. Paths veer off left up to Corte Madera Ridge Fire Road and right down to Corte Madera Avenue.

The Fire Road ends at a gate with an MCOSD "Northridge, Blithedale Summit" sign between the private residences of #151 and #155 Summit Drive in Corte Madera. Parking is extremely limited, or non-existent, on this end. The access here is called Lower Summit by the rangers because there are two MCOSD entry gates higher, designated as Middle Summit and Upper Summit.

The Fire Road was built around 1950 as part of the Southern Marin Line project, bringing a water pipeline from the Bon Tempe treatment plant to the Alto Tank and on to southern Marin users. Escalon Drive was constructed in the 1960's. Escalon is the name of a city in Mexico where a key battle in that country's war for independence was fought. The name has come to signify "stepping stone."

HARVEY WARNE TRAIL

From Corte Madera Avenue, Corte Madera, to Corte Madera Ridge Fire Road / .2 miles
Terrain: Heavily wooded, mostly bay and redwood / MCOSD
Elevation: 240' to 380' / very steep
Intersecting Trails: None
Directions: Corte Madera Ave., Corte Madera, to turnout across from #594; limited or no parking

Harvey Warne Trail is little known and little used; it is even misplaced when making its first appearance on the latest Olmsted map. It rises west of Corte Madera Avenue, a couple of hundred yards below the road's summit, from a turnout opposite #594. There is an MCOSD signpost, and parking for just one car.

The first yards are steep. In fifteen yards there is a fork; the "official" route to the right and a locally cut one to the left meet again at .1 mile. Though road noise is audible, the deep forest is appealing. The Trail ends when it meets Corte Madera Ridge F.R., which also rose from Corte Madera Avenue just south of the Harvey Warne trailhead. A few yards above the Trail's end is the important Octopus junction (which see) and access to other Northridge area trails.

Harvey Warne, a longtime Corte Madera resident, was active in the Boy Scouts and a popular hike leader. He died in 1986 in a car crash, on his way to lead a Marin Discoveries outing in the Sierra. The MCOSD dedicated the Trail to him, the first Open Space District trail named for an individual, at a ceremony in May 1987.

HOO-KOO-E-KOO TRAIL & FIRE ROAD

From Southern Marin Line Fire Road to Matt Davis Trail / 4.0 miles
Spur: Between Blithedale Ridge F.R. and Hoo-Koo-E-Koo Trail / .2 miles
Terrain: Part woodland, part chaparral / MCOSD & MMWD
Elevation: From 510' to 1,200' / gradual, short parts steep
Intersecting Trails: Dawn Falls (.5m), Blithedale Ridge F.R. (.9m), Corte Madera (1.5m), Slide Gulch (2.0m), Wheeler (2.3m), connector to Temelpa (2.5m), Temelpa (2.7m), Murray (3.1m), Old Railroad Grade (3.1-3.2m), Old Plane (3.1m), Hogback F.R. (3.9m)
Directions: Southern Marin Line F.R. trailhead, Kent Woodlands

Hoo-Koo-E-Koo (most people emphasize the second syllable, some the third) is among the most colorful of the Mountain's trail names. One version of the name's origin has it that it was purely an invention of Dan Totheroh in his play, "Tamalpa." Others believe a band of Coast Miwok Indians of that name once lived around the base of the Mountain. Harry Allen, president of the TCC when the Trail was started in 1915, named the trail after several Indian middens, or waste sites, were found near the Trail's route. It has also been known as the Kentfield-Ocean Trail since, combined with Matt Davis Trail, it could be taken to the Pacific. In the 1950's, Hoo-Koo-E-Koo's lower, easternmost section was covered during the development of Kent Woodlands, and the middle segment, half its length, was widened to fire road width. Still, Hoo-Koo-E-Koo remains a special and important Mountain route. The trail and fire road designations are used as appropriate.

Hoo-Koo-E-Koo Trail presently begins 100 yards in on the Kentfield end of Southern Marin Line (Crown) Fire Road, rising to the right at a MCOSD sign. The Trail immediately enters woodland, and climbs. In .1 mile a path, actually a former segment of the trail, branches right; veer left.

The Trail runs parallel to, and above, Southern Marin Line F.R., which is occasionally visible. A steep path drops left. Fifty yards beyond, the newly re-cleared Dawn Falls Trail descends to the fire road and Dawn Falls. The rich variety of plants that accompany the Hoo-Koo-E-Koo its whole length is quickly evident. The Trail rises to open chaparral, and offers striking views over Baltimore Canyon. It then meets and crosses Blithedale Ridge Fire Road. The fragrance of ceanothus pervades this intersection in spring.

Across the ridge, the Trail now circles above the head of Blithedale Canyon. Around a quarter-mile past the Blithedale intersection, the Trail encounters, on the right, a massive rock outcropping, Echo Rock. Stand with your back to it and call to hear the echo. Hoo-Koo-E-Koo then enters a redwood grove. At Corte Madera Creek there is an intersection. Corte Madera Trail drops steeply left toward Old Railroad Grade. Clamber right up a few root covered yards to Hoo-Koo-E-Koo Fire Road. To the right is a Spur which runs 400 yards uphill to a junction with Blithedale Ridge F.R. below Knob Hill. We go left.

Hoo-Koo-E-Koo Fire Road crosses over the creek. The uphill is gradual. Open areas alternate with, at stream crossings, groves of redwoods. At one such grove and stream, around 1/2 mile past Corte Madera Creek, look for a culvert pipe bearing "Kaiser Steel" and "USS" logos. It marks the top of the very steep Slide Gulch Trail, which drops to Old Railroad Grade.

In another 1/3 mile is the lower end of Wheeler Trail. A concrete platform, part of the old Slide Gulch water intake, is in the creek bed to the right. Wheeler rises to Eldridge Grade. In another .2 miles, a connector (mistakenly called McKinley Cut Trail on the Olmsted map) drops left to Temelpa Trail. A small tanbark oak guards its easily missed entrance. In 1/8 more miles, Hoo-Koo-E-Koo F.R. itself crosses Temelpa. Left leads down to the paved part of Old Railroad Grade, right to Verna Dunshee Trail near the top of Tam.

Hoo-Koo-E-Koo has now turned from the eastern to the southern flank of the Mountain. The vistas continue to be excellent. The Fire Road meets Murray Trail, which rose from lower on Old Railroad Grade, on the left. A few yards past is the Grade itself. The unmarked Old Plane Trail also rises from this junction. The Grade goes uphill to the right, on its steady climb up Tamalpais. Hoo-Koo-E-Koo continues left, combined with the Grade.

Within less than .1 mile of downhill, Hoo-Koo-E-Koo branches as a Trail again. At this same junction, a connector rises to higher on Railroad Grade. Next is another lovely stretch of Hoo-Koo-E-Koo. It runs in and out of redwood groves, and has sweeping southern panoramas. After .6 miles as a Trail, Hoo-Koo-E-Koo crosses Hogback (Throckmorton) Fire Road. To the left is Mountain Home Inn, which had been visible for a while, and to the right is Old Railroad Grade.

Hoo-Koo-E-Koo has less than .2 miles remaining. Near its end, it crosses a stream over a bridge and passes a magnificent redwood with spiraled bark. Scientists remain uncertain about what causes this spiraling, which is also found in sequoias, cousins of the redwoods. Above to the right are two old outhouses. Hoo-Koo-E-Koo ends at its junction with Matt Davis Trail, by Fern Creek. Matt Davis fulfills the promise of a trip to the ocean. Left on Matt Davis is a return to Hogback F.R. above Mountain Home.

HUCKLEBERRY TRAIL

From Southern Marin Line F.R. to Corte Madera Ridge F.R. / .6 miles
Terrain: Mixed, redwoods and chaparral / MCOSD
Elevation: From 480' to 800' / very steep
Intersecting Trails: None
Directions: Same as Baltimore Canyon trailhead to Magnolia Ave., Larkspur - left on Wiltshire Ave. - right on Marina Vista Ave. - left on Sunrise Lane; no trailhead parking

Huckleberry Trail offers an access to the splendid vistas atop Corte Madera Ridge and also opens up loop possiblities for those coming to the ridge both from Mill Valley and Larkspur-Corte Madera. It is also one of just two or three places in Marin where rhododendron grows.

Huckleberry Trail rises from the eastern (Larkspur) end of Southern Marin Line (Crown) Fire Road. The Trail's start, marked by an MCOSD signpost, is ten yards before the fire road's gate when approaching from Sunrise Lane in Larkspur, ten yards past the gate when coming from Kent Woodlands.

Most of the stiff uphill is in the early going. Huckleberry bushes line the Trail. About a quarter-mile in, by a stand of tanbark oaks and on both sides of the Trail, are several western rhododendron (*Rhododendron macrophyllum*) bushes. They are in the same genus as the more locally abundant western azalea but, unlike the azalea, keep their leaves all year. Rhododendrons are more associated with coastal woodlands north of Marin County. Ben Schmidt, who helped build the Trail in the 1950's, prefers his original name of Rhododendron Trail.

The Trail passes several redwood groves; a couple of times the Trail narrows to squeeze through. In its upper reaches, Huckleberry is more open, through chaparral, with views back of Larkspur. There are short downhill stretches. Except in the driest chaparral, huckleberry remains the dominant shrub.

One last redwood grove and Huckleberry joins Corte Madera Ridge F.R. at a four-way intersection. Left on Corte Madera Ridge goes to Summit Drive in Corte Madera and right to Blithedale Ridge. Be sure to climb a few yards to the right for the glorious Tam view. Glen Fire Road goes straight ahead; it later branches to two forks that descend both sides of Warner Canyon.

Huckleberry is abundant along many of Tam's trails. The three-to-eight foot shrub has toothed leaves and white-to-pink bell-shaped flowers in clusters. In late summer and fall, the small berries make delicious eating; they're sweetest when black.

INDIAN FIRE ROAD

From Phoenix Road, Kent Woodlands, to Eldridge Grade / 1.3 miles
Terrain: Open ridge top; chaparral bordered by madrones; views / MMWD
Elevation: From 560' to 1,400' / lower half very steep and rolling, upper half gradual
Intersecting Trails: Kent F.R. (.4m), Blithedale Ridge F.R. (.8m)
Directions: Northern Crown Road trailhead

Indian Fire Road starts almost 500 feet higher than the nearby Phoenix Lake trailhead, offering quicker access to high on the Mountain. It traverses an exposed ridge top above the deep canyon of Bill Williams Gulch. There are excellent views, particularly of the Tamalpais summit. Sections are as steep as any fire road on the Mountain. To make the going even more tiring, some of the elevation gains are lost in four separate dips, requiring additional uphills.

Indian Fire Road once rose directly from atop Kent Woodlands' Windy Ridge. Its lower part is now paved over as Phoenix Road. Indian F.R. presently starts at an MMWD-signed gate, on the right when going uphill on Phoenix Road. At the end of Phoenix Road is another gate, behind which Harry Allen Trail and Kent Fire Road set off. The shaded Kent F.R. rejoins Indian F.R. for a very short loop possibility.

Indian Fire Road is immediately steep; there's more of the same ahead. The stiff uphills are followed by short level or downhill stretches, earning this stretch the designation of "the roller coaster." (There is another "roller coaster" on Blithedale Ridge F.R.) At the first crest, in 200 yards, is a great Mt. Tamalpais summit scene. A 250,000 gallon water tank is on the left. The Fire Road is criss-crossed with overgrown paths, remnants of a more extensive trail network here before the development of Kent Woodlands. In .2 miles is a short connector down left to Kent Fire Road. In .4 miles, Kent F.R. itself comes in, unsigned, from the far left. It immediately departs, also to the left at the MCOSD signpost a few yards ahead, down to Evergreen Drive.

A stiff up, down, then up again leads to another fire road on the left. This is the northern end of the 2.3 mile long Blithedale Ridge Fire Road; its junction with Hoo-Koo-E-Koo Fire Road is 100 yards below. Continue uphill. An old wood sign points the way to Mill Valley's Baltimore Park, but there is no intersecting trail there.

After another 100 yards of climbing, the now closed Indian Fire Trail sets off to the left. One of the oldest trails on the Mountain (referred to in an 1876 article), it once offered a precipitous trip to near the summit. It is now off-limits, blocked at its several junctions with Eldridge Grade above, to limit erosion and to allow vegetation to cover its prominent slash, so visible on the Mountain's eastern flank.

Indian Fire Road enters some shade, and the uphill finally eases. Look right, over Bill Williams Gulch, to see the part of Indian F.R. you've already climbed. The Fire Road passes through a redwood grove, a sharp contrast from the dry terrain below. After cutting through an even bigger redwood stand, Indian Fire Road ends at its junction with Eldridge Grade. It is 2.4 miles left to the East Peak parking lot; right leads down to the lakes.

Before the arrival of the first Spanish settlers in the Bay Area in the 1770's, Marin's only residents were Coast Miwok Indians. They lived largely off acorns, berries, other natural vegetation, fish, and shellfish. They had settlements around Tam's perimeter and camps on the Mountain. Within seventy-five years, the Coast Miwoks, their lands gone, were decimated. Only a few descendants survive today. Sharp-eyed hikers still can find crushed white shells from their middens, or refuse piles. The native Indians revered Mount Tamalpais, possibly never venturing to its top. Experts debate whether the famous story about a "sleeping maiden" forming the profile of the Mountain's summit ridge is an Indian legend or a later creation.

KENT FIRE ROAD

From Phoenix Road to Evergreen Drive, Kent Woodlands / .7 miles
Terrain: Woodland and chaparral / MMWD
Elevation: 580' to 800' to 620' / steep, parts very steep
Intersecting Trails: Connector to Indian F.R. (.3m), Indian F.R. (.4m)
Directions: Northern Crown Road trailhead

From Phoenix Road, a short street above Crown Road on Windy Ridge in Kent Woodlands, three fire roads depart. The first, to the left at the Phoenix-Crown junction, is a 1/4 mile unpaved section of Crown Road. The second, to the right, is Indian Fire Road. And at the upper end of

Phoenix Road, behind a wood barrier with an MCOSD Blithedale Summit sign, Harry Allen Trail branches left and Kent Fire Road rises straight.

Kent F.R. climbs through tanbark oak-madrone woodland. It briefly narrows to trail width, then broadens again as it meets redwoods. After .3 miles of uphill, a short connector to Indian Fire Road rises to the right. Kent F.R. is again a bit overgrown. The route crests at the intersection with Indian Fire Road. There are excellent Tamalpais views. Indian F.R. goes left up to Eldridge Grade and, to the right, back to Phoenix Road.

Kent F.R. continues left, downhill, at the MCOSD boundary post. It passes a water tank. It then drops very steeply down over rocky, washed-out terrain. The Fire Road ends at the top of Evergreen Drive in Kent Woodlands. It once extended farther down as part of an access route to the Mountain, through Kent family property, from the Northwestern Pacific Railroad line. There is little or no parking at this end. Crown Road is the first intersecting street downhill; left on Crown leads back to Kent's start, right to Southern Marin Line F.R.

Only the part of this Fire Road between Evergreen Drive and Indian F.R. is clearly labelled as "Kent" on Freese and Erickson maps. But since the section between Phoenix Road and Indian F.R. is unnamed, and appears to be a continuation, the whole stretch is here called Kent Fire Road. No family name is more associated with the Mountain than Kent (see Kent Trail). They once owned huge tracts of Mt. Tamalpais; it was once possible to walk on Kent property from Kentfield to Stinson Beach. The preservation of so much of the family's former holdings as open space is a lasting Kent heritage.

SOUTHERN MARIN LINE FIRE ROAD

From Crown Road, Kent Woodlands, to Sunrise Lane, Larkspur / 2.8 miles
Terrain: Lightly wooded hillside; heavily used / MCOSD
Elevation: Around 500' / level
Intersecting Trails: Hoo-Koo-E-Koo (.1m), Dawn Falls (.3), H-Line F.R. (1.2m), Barbara Spring (1.6m)
Directions: Southern Marin Line trailhead, Kent Woodlands

This well used Fire Road is called Crown Road by just about everyone, as most people join it at one end of Kent Woodlands' paved Crown Road. Olmsted and Erickson properly call it Southern Marin Line Road, for the adjacent 24 inch pipeline that brings water from the Bon Tempe treatment plant to southern Marin. In any case, it is the longest completely flat stretch on Mt. Tamalpais. Also contributing to its popularity is its convenience to central Marin population centers. Dog owners find it appealing as dogs are permitted off leash.

Though both ends of the Fire Road are auto-accessible, there is adjacent parking only on the Crown Road-Kent Woodlands side, so we'll start there. (Several "no parking" signs were placed on this end as well in 1989.) Be mindful of nearby residents. The Fire Road begins beyond the gate. French broom has become the dominant vegetation over the last few years. The shrub came to line both sides of the route the entire way until a major broom cut in December 1989; few doubt the broom will return.

In 100 yards, Hoo-Koo-E-Koo Trail rises on the right. It climbs to Blithedale Ridge Fire Road, then continues to Matt Davis Trail. Loops can be made by taking Hoo-Koo-E-Koo, then returning to Southern Marin Line either via Dawn Falls Trail, H-Line Fire Road, or Huckleberry Trail.

In .3 miles, Dawn Falls Trail crosses. To the left is a short, moderately steep descent to the falls. A loop can be made by continuing down Dawn Falls Trail to Baltimore Canyon and returning to Southern Marin Line on the steep Barbara Spring Trail. To the right, Dawn Falls Trail rises to Hoo-Koo-E-Koo. A few yards beyond the Dawn Falls junction is a small suspension bridge nicknamed "the Little Golden Gate." It carries the pipeline over a bend, then back under the Fire Road.

Several great view spots open. The deep canyon immediately to the left is Baltimore Canyon. At 1 1/4 miles, at a pump station, H-Line Fire Road sets off uphill to the right. Branches of the pipeline diverge here to various southern Marin water tanks. Just beyond, on the left, is what appears to be a path down the canyon; it quickly deteriorates.

In another one-third mile, an MCOSD signpost on the left marks the top of Barbara Spring Trail, which leads very steeply down to Baltimore Canyon. Continue winding around the bends. Look back for outstanding views of Tam and the early part of the Fire Road. Both the Erickson and Olmsted maps show an additional trail descending left at around 2.5 miles. This path, still faintly visible at a bend, with an indistinct entrance guarded by a short redwood tree and a manzanita bush, is now too overgrown and steep to be included here.

Southern Marin Line Fire Road ends at a gate. A few steps beyond, on the right, is Huckleberry Trail, which goes uphill to Corte Madera Ridge F.R. The street ahead is Sunrise Lane, off Marina Vista Avenue, in Larkspur. A sign for a private residence at #10 Fire Road gives Southern Marin Line another commonly used alternate name, "Fire Road 10."

The Fire Road, completed in 1951, was built as part of the Bon Tempe Dam project. The Southern Marin pipeline itself continues to the Alto water tanks in Mill Valley. The Fire Road's distance, from gate to gate, was accurately measured as 2.78 miles.

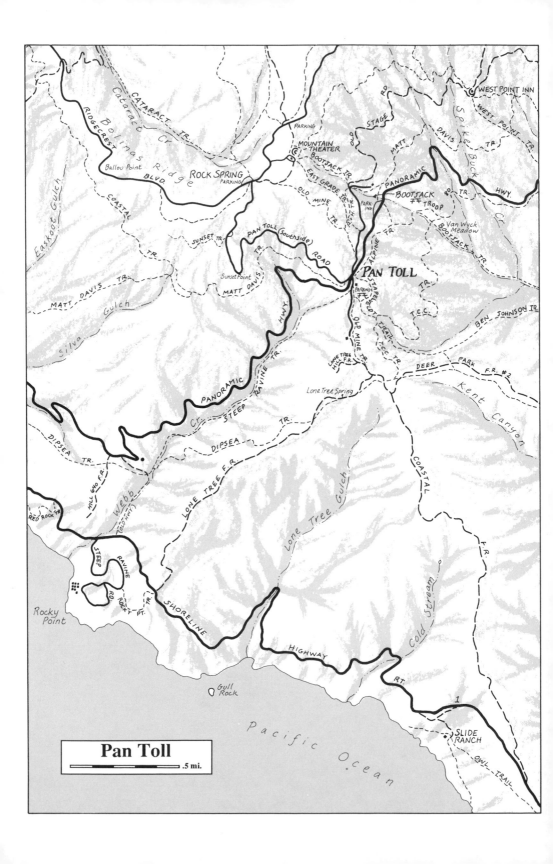

Pan Toll

.5 mi.

PANTOLL TRAILHEAD

Directions to Bootjack and Pantoll:
Highway 101 - Highway 1 - Panoramic Highway

Once there was a toll house on Panoramic Highway here, hence the name Pantoll (or, just as commonly, Pan Toll). Earlier the area was known as Summit Meadow. Two fire roads and six trails meet at Pantoll; Coastal F.R., Old Stage Road, and the Alpine, Easy Grade, Matt Davis, Old Mine, Stapelveldt, and Steep Ravine trails. Also at Pantoll, the Southside (also called Pantoll) Road branches uphill to Rock Spring and the summit from Panoramic Highway. One trail, Sunset Point, departs from Southside Road, about a mile uphill.

Pantoll serves as the headquarters of Mount Tamalpais State Park. By the upper parking area are a fountain, a telephone, and a new bathroom (opened in December 1989 to augment the old one in the campground). Nearby are State Park residences, a ranger station, a maintenance facility, and the Mountain's principal campground. Maps, books, Mt. Tamalpais shirts, campsite assignments, and advice are dispensed at the ranger station. The Mount Tamalpais Interpretive Association begins many of its weekend walks from Pantoll.

Around 1/4 mile east of Pantoll on Panoramic Highway is the Bootjack Picnic Area (formerly Bootjack Camp), another popular trailhead. Bootjack has a large parking lot, bathrooms, water fountains, picnic tables, and a huge outdoor grill. Call 415/456-5218 to make a group reservation. The Matt Davis Trail connects Pantoll to Bootjack.

At press-time, there is a plan to charge a $3 vehicle parking fee at Bootjack and Pantoll. Both Bootjack and Pantoll are served on weekends by Golden Gate Transit buses running between Tam Junction and Stinson Beach.

Suggested loops from Pantoll Ranger Station - elevation 1,500'

*Alpine Trail, .4m, to Bootjack Trail - left, .8m, across Panoramic Highway, through Bootjack Camp, to Mountain Theater - Easy Grade Trail, .6m, to Old Stage Road - right, .1m, to start / **2.0 miles**.*

*Steep Ravine Trail, 1.6m, to Dipsea Trail - left, 1.4m, to Coastal F.R. - left, .2m, to Old Mine Trail - right, .3m, to start / **3.5 miles**.*

*Old Stage Road, .1m, to Old Mine Trail - left, 1.0m, to Mountain Theater Trail - right, .2m, through Mountain Theater to Rock Spring Trail - right, 1.4m, to West Point - right, 1.8m, on Old Stage Road to start / **4.5 miles.***

---

*Matt Davis Trail west, 1.6m, to Coastal Trail - right, 1.4m, to Willow Camp F.R. - right, .1m, across Ridgecrest Blvd. to Laurel Dell F.R. - straight, .5m, to Laurel Dell - right on Cataract Trail, 1.2m, to Rock Spring and across Ridgecrest Blvd. - left, .1m, on Mountain Theater Trail to Old Mine Trail - right, 1.0m, to Old Stage Road - right, .1m, to start / **6.0 miles.***

ALPINE TRAIL

From Pantoll to Bootjack Trail / .4 miles
Terrain: *Redwood forest / MTSP*
Elevation: *From 1,500' to 1,280' / steep*
Intersecting Trails: *None*
Directions: *Pantoll*

Alpine Trail, though short and near the traffic noise of Panoramic Highway, is nonetheless important and well-used because it provides a key connection between Pantoll and both Muir Woods and Mountain Home.

The Trail begins from a sign by the Golden Gate Transit bus stop at Pantoll Ranger Station. Just to the right is the upper end of Stapelveldt Trail. Alpine descends immediately into heavy woodland, with redwoods dominant. Unfortunately, Panoramic Highway, with its accompanying vehicle sounds, runs nearby, 25-100 yards away, across a gully. The Trail becomes more peaceful on its lower end. Several trees are down, victims of a wind storm in the winter of 1989.

Alpine Trail crosses a small bridge. The Trail ends when it meets Bootjack Trail, just beyond a bench. Left on Bootjack leads uphill to Bootjack Camp across the highway. Right goes downhill to Troop 80 Trail, then Van Wyck Meadow, and on to Muir Woods.

The Trail was one of the first projects of the California Alpine Club, and has been called Alpine Club Trail. The venerable club, formed in 1914, has its headquarters at Alpine Lodge on Panoramic Highway near Mountain

Home. The name "Alpine," synonymous with mountain, appears a few other times on Tamalpais. Alpine Dam, creating Alpine Lake, was built at the old Alpine Bridge over Lagunitas Creek.

EASY GRADE TRAIL

From Matt Davis Trail to Bootjack Trail at Mountain Theater / .6 miles
Spur: From Old Stage Road to Easy Grade Trail / .1 mile
Terrain: Tanbark oak woodland / MTSP
Elevation: From 1,540' to 1,980' / steep
Intersecting Trails: Old Stage Road (.1m), Easy Grade Spur (.1m), connector to Riding and Hiking (.2m), Riding and Hiking (.2m)
Directions: Pantoll - Matt Davis east, .1 mile

Easy Grade Trail offers the most direct route from Pantoll to the Mountain Theater. The Trail starts from Matt Davis Trail, though it is more commonly joined 20 yards higher at Old Stage Road. By the Old Stage intersection are a pair of some of the Mountain's oldest, still-in-place signs. They are color-coded to show direction, a system long discarded.

Easy Grade continues uphill into a mostly tanbark oak forest. In a bit over .1 mile of climbing, a brief opening on the right offers a view of Mountain Home and, well beyond, of Mt. Diablo. Easy Grade crosses a rivulet and, twenty-five yards after, there is a T-intersection. Easy Grade Spur comes in on the right from Old Stage Road and the single, united Easy Grade Trail rises to the left. Just beyond is another three-way intersection. Veer right along the fence; left is a short connector to Riding and Hiking Trail. At the end of the fence, Riding and Hiking Trail crosses at a four-way intersection. To the left it goes up to Old Mine Trail, to the right it drops to Old Stage Road. Continue straight and uphill.

Easy Grade re-enters a deep woodland with large, mature trees. A path crosses. A pipeline beside the Trail is visible. There is another opening, with a great shot of West and East peaks. Easy Grade ends when it meets the top of the long Bootjack Trail. A few yards above is an asphalt path leading to the right side (facing the stage) of the Mountain Theater. Look there for the plaque:

MY FEET WILL MARK THE TRAIL OF STARS

dedicated to the memory of longtime play director Dan Totheroh.

The Civilian Conservation Corps built Easy Grade in the late 1930's as an alternate, less steep route than Bootjack Trail to the Mountain Theater.

HILL 640 FIRE ROAD

From Panoramic Highway to Hill 640 / .3 miles
Terrain: Grassland / MTSP
Elevations: Around 640' / almost level
Intersecting Trails: Dipsea (.1m)
Directions: Pantoll - west on Panoramic Highway to mileage marker 7.86

This Fire Road was built to access the military installation that once stood at its end. It sets off southwest of Panoramic Highway, at milepost 7.86, across from a parking area. Enter Hill 640 F.R. through the gate. (Another gate, behind which a connector fire road joins the Dipsea Trail, is 75 yards uphill. Top Dipsea racers, using a legal "shortcut," take that connector and then run on Panoramic Highway for a stretch, completely bypassing Hill 640 F.R.)

In 100 yards, Hill 640 Fire Road crosses the true Dipsea Trail. It is the Dipsea's last intersection when going from Mill Valley to Stinson Beach. The Fire Road continues level. There are lovely views out over Stinson Beach and the ocean. Hill 640 F.R. ends by some isolated trees, where the hill falls off sharply.

By continuing cross-country past a lone eucalyptus tree (though neighboring sprouts are growing at press-time), you'll run into a descending row of now abandoned concrete bunkers. Called "base end stations," they were built during World War II. Triangulation measurements were taken from here and from similar coastal stations, such as those by Muir Beach Overlook, to calculate the distance of any enemy ships. The data would be relayed to the gun batteries lining the Golden Gate.

Since the hill at the Fire Road's end is 640 feet in elevation, the U.S. Geological Survey map calls it Hill 640. The new Golden Gate National Recreation Area "Park Guide" labels it White Gate Ranch Trail, for the old ranch.

LONE TREE HILL FIRE ROAD

From junction of Coastal Fire Road and Old Mine Trail to summit of Lone Tree Hill /
.3 miles
Terrain: Douglas fir forest / MTSP
Elevation: From 1,460' to 1,600' / steep
Intersecting Trails: None
Directions: Pantoll - Old Mine Trail south to end

This Fire Road is not on any maps and is unsigned and officially unnamed. It sets off uphill, directly across Coastal Fire Road, from the lower end of Old Mine Trail. Downed trees from the wind storm of February 1989 force some scrambling. The Fire Road climbs through a deep and haunting Douglas fir forest, passing several immense trees. It's a good area to see or hear owls.

Lone Tree Hill F.R. ends at the top of the hill known both as Bald Hill (the summit was treeless some 75 years ago) and as Lone Tree Hill (for the famous "Lone Tree" below on the south face). Neither name is particularly apt now for the well-wooded hill. The 1,600 foot summit offers one of the Bay Area's most spectacular picnic and view sites. There were once plans to put homes along this road.

Lone Tree Hill forms the "feet" of the summit ridge's Sleeping Maiden profile as seen from many vista points in the East Bay. A separate Lone Tree Fire Road starts from the hill's southeast base and runs down to Highway 1.

OLD STAGE ROAD

From Pantoll to West Point / 1.8 miles
Terrain: Lower part paved, woodland; upper part chaparral; views / MTSP &
MMWD; part of Bay Area Ridge Trail
Elevation: From 1,500' to 1,785' / gradual
Intersecting Trails: Matt Davis (<.1m), Old Mine (.1m), Easy Grade (.1m), Easy
Grade Spur (.3m), Riding and Hiking (.5m), Bootjack (.5m)
Directions: Pantoll

The Old Stage is one of the historic roads in Marin. It was originally graded in 1902 as a wagon road to connect the Mt. Tamalpais Railway at West Point with Stinson Beach (then Willow Camp), Bolinas, and

Olema. There was a daily morning stagecoach departure from the West Point Inn to the Dipsea Inn at Stinson, and a return trip, with up to six horses pulling, in the afternoon. Later a plan surfaced to extend the railway itself to Stinson. The entire proposed rail route lay on lands owned by William Kent. The rail line was never built. Much of the original stage route below Pantoll has been covered by Panoramic Highway. Old Stage Road itself is now paved between Pantoll and Bootjack Trail. Its upper 1.3 miles, however, remain a dirt road, and images of the old stage days can still be conjured.

Across Panoramic Highway from Pantoll Ranger Station, two paved roads rise. The one on the left is Pantoll, or Southside, Road, open to cars heading higher on the Mountain. On the right, behind a gate, is Old Stage Road. The trailhead sign calls it "Old Railroad Grade." Another sign marks part of the route as an equestrian portion of the Bay Area Ridge Trail.

Old Stage is very gently graded throughout. There are several trail intersections in the opening .1 mile. The first, in 50 yards, is with the Matt Davis going west to Stinson Beach. Ten yards later, Matt Davis crosses on the right, going east toward Bootjack. In another 60 yards, Old Mine Trail heads up left to Rock Spring. Twenty yards farther, also to the left, are two entrances to Easy Grade Trail. Between the two entrances, to the right, Easy Grade descends its last few yards to Matt Davis.

Trees line the Road, but there are occasional breaks to outstanding views. Incongruous highway signs dot the Road's edge; they are "spares" from other roads, placed here because some official vehicles pass. There is an entry on the left to a spur of Easy Grade Trail.

In .5 miles is a water chlorination building, beside which is a drinking fountain. Across the Road here, behind a horse trough, is the base of Riding and Hiking Trail. It is the equestrian's continuation of the Bay Area Ridge Trail. A few yards beyond, an asphalt road veers right. It leads to a State Park residence that was originally Matt Davis' cabin. Ten yards down that paved road, Bootjack Trail comes in from Bootjack Camp. Follow Old Stage Road straight ahead. Immediately, Bootjack Trail continues up to the left, on to the Mountain Theater. Old Stage Road becomes dirt-surfaced.

Open chaparral replaces the forest canopy, and the views are superb the rest of the trip. A gate marks the boundary between Mt. Tamalpais State Park, which you are leaving, and MMWD lands. The uphill is so gentle that it's only noticeable when you look back or ahead. One later section is slightly downhill. There are no intersecting trails for 1.3 miles. Relax and enjoy this wonderful stretch of the Mountain.

Old Stage Road crosses over several streams; look for azalea bushes, in bloom and fragrant in May and June, beside them. Sticky monkeyflower, manzanita, chamise, toyon, and chaparral pea are the common shrubs. Be alert for a stagecoach barreling downhill, you never know!

All too soon you're at West Point Inn. Here stage passengers could connect with the Mt. Tamalpais and Muir Woods Railway, dine, or spend the night. The inn still offers overnight lodging and light refreshments. There are restrooms, a fountain, and lovely view sites, some shaded, to rest and picnic. Many trails meet here. In order, clockwise, they are: Rock Spring to the Mountain Theater, Old Railroad Grade uphill, the Grade downhill, Nora to Matt Davis, and the extremely steep West Point Trail to Panoramic Highway.

RIDING AND HIKING TRAIL

From Old Stage Road to Old Mine Trail / .4 miles
Terrain: Mostly woodland, parts grassland; horses permitted / MTSP; equestrian section of Bay Area Ridge Trail
Elevation: From 1,580' to 1,700' / gradual
Intersecting Trails: Easy Grade (.2m), connector to Easy Grade (.2m)
Directions: Bootjack Picnic Area - Bootjack Trail uphill, .2 miles

In 1945, the California State legislature authorized establishment of an equestrian route to wind through 36 counties from the Mexico to the Oregon border. It was to pass through Mt. Tamalpais. After much debate, a decision was made to use existing trails and fire roads on Tam, rather than to build new ones. This Trail, however, was an exception, a connection built specifically for use by horse riders (though hikers, of course, can also take it). Redwood posts painted yellow on the top mark the never-completed project. The posts can still be seen on the Mountain, such as at Double Bow Knot and just to the east of Ridgecrest Boulevard along Bolinas Ridge. In 1989, the Riding and Hiking Trail was designated as an equestrian section of the new Bay Area Ridge Trail.

The Riding and Hiking Trail sets off from the paved section of Old Stage Road a few yards west of the Bootjack Trail crossing. The trailhead is opposite a chlorinator building, where there is a water fountain. Riding and Hiking Trail begins in a woodland of laurel, tanbark oak, and Douglas fir. The uphill is gradual.

In around 1/6 mile, a grassy clearing, an old fence, and a four-way fork are encountered. Easy Grade Trail crosses left down to Old Stage Road and sharply right up to the Mountain Theater. The Riding and Hiking Trail goes straight ahead. In 50 yards, over a slight rise, is another junction. The trail to the left is a short connector back to Easy Grade.

The Riding and Hiking continues up through both grassland and tanbark oak woodland. The Trail ends when it meets Old Mine Trail. Riders are allowed on the Old Mine's remaining uphill to Rock Spring.

STAPELVELDT TRAIL

From Pantoll to Ben Johnson Trail / .9 miles
Terrain: Deep woods; lower half riparian / MTSP
Elevation: From 1,500' to 920' / steep
Intersecting Trails: TCC (twice at .4m)
Directions: Pantoll

Stapelveldt is part of a route between Muir Woods and Pantoll. It is a lovely Trail, largely through a deep, redwood-lined canyon.

The Trail sets off from Pantoll Ranger Station, at the Golden Gate Transit bus stop, just to the right of Alpine Trail. Its opening yards, through the campground, are a bit confusing to follow. Stapelveldt leaves the camp's ridge line and begins its long downhill. Three small footbridges are crossed. Douglas fir is the dominant tree.

In .4 miles, Stapelveldt meets TCC Trail at a bridge. There is a bench, made of an old trail sign, at the three-way intersection. Some old maps indicated a Camp Stapelveldt here. Left, TCC goes 1.4 miles to Bootjack Trail at Van Wyck Meadow. TCC and Stapelveldt descend together for 20 yards to a second three-way junction. Here TCC departs right toward the Dipsea Trail.

Stapelveldt now descends an ever-deepening canyon. Switchbacks, built by the Youth Conservation Corps in 1978, help. The unnamed creek left is heading to Redwood Creek, then on to Muir Woods. Extremely tall redwoods, some branchless for over 100 feet, line the way. One fire-scarred giant can be entered. The downhill eases. Three more feeder rivulets are crossed on bridges.

Stapelveldt drops steeply before its end. The terminus is at its junction with Ben Johnson Trail, which goes straight ahead down to Muir Woods, and right up to Deer Park F.R. and the Dipsea. There is a bench to rest at this lovely, quiet spot.

In July 1989, Fred Sandrock of the Mt. Tamalpais History Project published evidence that the Trail was named for Wilhelm (William) Stapelfeldt (1839-1912). Stapelfeldt apparently was a German-born San Francisco grocer who worked on Mountain trails in the early part of the century. He seems to have been a hiking partner of legendary Tamalpais figures such as Emil Barth, Edward Ziesche, and Alice Eastwood. The Trail has known some half-dozen different spellings.

STEEP RAVINE TRAIL

From Pantoll to Highway 1 / 2.1 miles
Terrain: Riparian; upper 1.7 miles through redwood forest / MTSP
Elevation: From 1,500' to 430' / very steep
Intersecting Trails: Dipsea (1.6m-1.7m)
Directions: Pantoll

Steep Ravine is widely considered to be one of the most beautiful trails on Mt. Tamalpais, if not in all of California. Few who traverse it come away unmoved by its beauty. The Trail follows a spirited creek, through a narrow canyon lined with towering redwoods.

The Trail begins a few yards below Pantoll Ranger Station, to the right off the road leading to the maintenance area. The upper part was recently rerouted, with switchbacks added to lessen the steepness and to help prevent erosion. The woods are less open than what awaits below, and traffic noise from Panoramic Highway can be heard. Huckleberry abounds. There is is a bench, particularly welcome to those ascending the Trail, at .3 miles. Look skyward from above it to see the uppermost redwood in the canyon. It is enormous in girth and towers well over 200 feet, one of the largest trees in Marin.

The Trail crosses a few rivulets, feeders to Webb Creek. In .5 miles, the Trail meets Webb Creek, which began above Panoramic Highway and here flows in from the right. The Trail makes the first of its eight crossings of Webb Creek.

If your attention can be diverted from the creek, from the redwoods, and from the carpets of ferns covering the hillsides, you'll find many other floral treasures. Trillium, or wake-robin, is abundant. Look for its characteristic three broad leaves and, atop a slender stalk, the three-petaled flower. The color varies, with white later fading to pink. Fat and slim Solomon's-seal both have white flowers above the 5-7 "fat" or "slim" leaves. Somewhat similar, but with a reddish stalk and flowers nodding unseen below the leaves, are fairy-lanterns. Still another member of the lily family seen here is Clintonia, with its large glossy leaves, deep rose flowers, and, in early summer, large blue berries. Always special to find is columbine, in the buttercup family. The most abundant shrub along the creek is red elderberry (*Sambucus callicarpa*). It rises to ten feet, with a characteristic five-parted compound leaf. Its clusters of creamy white flowers, in spring, form pyramids. In fall, they bear red berries. Probably the showiest shrub on the Trail is a purple-flowered nightshade, a New Zealand native whose seed "escaped" from a Stinson Beach garden.

Soon after the second Webb Creek crossing is the famous step ladder, which takes the Trail down a precipitous drop beside a waterfall. Proceed down cautiously, facing the steps. The Trail continues ever down, criss-crossing Webb Creek and feeder streams. Fallen redwoods require ducking under; at least one has a "doorway" cut through. You can step inside other redwoods that have fire-wrought openings in their trunks.

Steep Ravine Trail meets the Dipsea Trail by the seventh bridge, over which the Dipsea just made its own first crossing of Webb Creek. The Dipsea offers the easiest, though still strenuous, loop option. Take it, then Old Mine Trail, back to Pantoll for a classic loop. The Dipsea and Steep Ravine trails run together a few score yards beside a small reservoir, part of the Stinson Beach water supply. Interestingly, the earthquake of October 1989 greatly increased the spring flow into the reservoir. A bit uphill, beside a buzzing (when water is being pumped to the storage tank above) power pole, at a marked intersection, Steep Ravine Trail veers left.

This lower stretch of Steep Ravine (sometimes called Webb Creek Trail) is less visited. Many find it as appealing as the more renown upper section. It is quite lush, and may have a greater variety of native plant species than any comparably sized stretch of trail in the Bay Area.

After a slight rise, a short broad path branches right; it reconnects with the Dipsea. The Trail is briefly wide, then narrows again as it descends. A switchback leads to a massive redwood, the last encountered. Delicate blue forget-me-nots, originally garden escapees but now established in redwood forests, dot its base. A bridge provides the last crossing of Webb Creek.

In this tranquil area, Thaddeus Welch, whose landscapes of Tamalpais are considered among the finest ever painted, lived from 1900 to 1905. He and his artist wife Ludmilla built a cabin in a level clearing on the creek's right bank. Only the sharpest eyed observers will find any traces of the Welch's stay, such as some introduced German ivy. It was Welch who coined the name Steep Ravine. Hard as it may be to believe, Highway 1 once came through here; the old roadbed is visible.

Soon after the bridge is a bench, recycled from an old trail sign. There aren't many lovelier settings on the Mountain. The flora here is verdant all year. In fall, berries abound; elderberry, twinberry (*Lonicera involucrata*), strawberry, California blackberry (*Rubus ursinus*), thimbleberry (*R. parviflorus*), salmonberry (*R. spectabilis*), and others. Beyond, the forest opens.

All too soon, Steep Ravine Trail meets today's Highway 1 across from mileage marker 11.00. Just to the right, across the Highway, is the access road into the Steep Ravine Environmental Campground, with its wonderful cabins. Webb Creek empties into the Pacific there.

William Kent purchased the Steep Ravine area in 1904 with the intention of extending the Mt. Tamalpais Railway to Stinson Beach, where he also had extensive holdings. In 1928, on the day before his death, he deeded Steep Ravine to the State of California. One of the Steep Ravine cabins is named for him, another for Welch. The present Steep Ravine Trail was built in 1935-36 by the Civilian Conservation Corps over an earlier route.

SUNSET POINT TRAIL

From Southside Road to White Gate Gulch / .9 miles
Terrain: Grassland, short parts wooded; narrow; views / MTSP
Elevation: From 1,800' to 1,940' / gradual
Intersecting Trails: None
Directions: Pantoll - Southside (Pantoll) Road, 1 mile to Sunset Point parking area

Many unmarked paths lace the grassland in the triangle bounded by Coastal Trail, West Ridgecrest Boulevard, and Southside Road. Sunset Point Trail, while not much more prominent than neighboring routes worn into the hillside, is included here because it sets off from a popular spot and does have a "generic" State Park sign at its start.

Sunset (or Trojan) Point is the splendid view site at a bend in the Southside (Pantoll) Road, about a mile above Pantoll Ranger Station. On sunny weekend days, the parking area 150 yards uphill invariably fills. Visitors fan out over the surrounding hills to select from some of the Mountain's most glorious picnic sites. Sunset Point Trail sets off across the paved road from the parking area.

Sunset Point Trail is the upper (right) of the two options at the trailhead. It sets off across the open grassland. There are spectacular ocean views, even broader than from the more renown Matt Davis and Coastal trails, which run parallel a bit lower. In 100 yards there is a fork; veer left. In another 100 yards, the Trail crosses a seep. Look here in spring for the showy yellow flowers of seep-spring monkeyflower (*Mimulus guttatus*). Sky lupine, blue-dicks, blue-eyed grass, and poppies are among the other flowers adding color to the surrounding grasses.

The Trail begins to narrow and becomes somewhat cambered; fewer people have ventured this far to wear it in. Sunset Point Trail passes through a line of bay trees. The O'Rourke's Bench area is visible above. At .6 miles, the Trail passes an old ranch fence line. A young, colonizing Douglas fir is just to the right. The Trail, now somewhat marginal, enters woodland. Huge rocks protrude on the left. There is another stretch through grassland, then a return to deeper woods. After rains, a stream flows down White Gate Gulch here to Webb Creek in Steep Ravine. This is a special, hidden area. A slide and several downed trees, including a massive Douglas fir, block the Trail here. Paths continue beyond the canyon toward Ballou Point on Ridgecrest Boulevard.

Remember, if you are watching the sunset from the Trail or the trailhead, the gates at both the lower and upper ends of Southside Road are locked after dark.

TCC TRAIL

From Bootjack Trail at Van Wyck Meadow to Dipsea Trail / 1.8 miles
Terrain: Douglas fir forest / MTSP
Elevation: 1,040' to 1,240' / almost level
Intersecting Trails: Stapelveldt (1.4m)
Directions: Bootjack Picnic Area - Bootjack Trail toward Muir Woods, .5 miles

TCC Trail is one of the best designed and loveliest of the Mountain's trails. It crosses some eleven canyons yet remains almost level its whole 1.8 mile length. The Trail is entirely through a forest dominated by Douglas firs.

TCC Trail sets off from Van Wyck Meadow to the right (coming from Bootjack Picnic Area) of the old stone fireplace. It immediately enters deep woodland, where it remains the whole length save for short clearings.

In 25 yards, the first creek is crossed on a bridge. In just over .1 mile is a bench made from an old TCC trail sign.

The Trail winds around canyon after canyon, some with bridges over the creeks, some with only rivulets to step over, some with the stream below trail level. After each bend are masses of huckleberry. The slight uphill is just noticeable.

In 1.4 miles, TCC Trail crosses a bridge and meets Stapelveldt Trail. A signpost and a "sign" bench mark the junction. Straight ahead, Stapelveldt rises to Pantoll. To the left, TCC and Stapelveldt run together for 20 yards to a second junction. Stapelveldt departs to the left, to Ben Johnson Trail. Another bridge is crossed. Redwoods are more abundant, and larger, as they battle the Douglas firs for forest supremacy. The Trail enters Muir Woods National Monument. TCC Trail ends when it hits the Dipsea Trail. One hundred yards uphill to the right is the crest of Cardiac Hill, a stunning view site.

The Tamalpais Conservation Club (TCC) was formed by a band of hikers in 1912 for ". . .the preservation of the scenic beauties and fauna of Mt. Tamalpais and its spurs and slopes." The club's first major activity was a trail cleanup day and they have done more Tam trail building and maintenance than any other volunteer group since. The TCC was a leader in the fight to create Mt. Tamalpais State Park and remains vigilant in living up to its motto, "Guardian of the Mountain." Information on membership can be obtained by writing the TCC at Room 562, 870 Market Street, San Francisco 94102.

This Trail was built during the first World War by TCC trail crews. It was originally named the Houghton Trail for Samuel Monroe Houghton, a founder of the TCC and its president from 1913 to 1914, the year he died. There is a plaque honoring the Tamalpais Conservation Club at the Trail's start in Van Wyck Meadow. It was affixed in February 1989 to the rock out of which an oak tree grows, and from which a fireplace was once crafted. The Trail is also spelled as "T.C.C."

WEST POINT TRAIL

From Panoramic Highway to West Point / .8 miles
Terrain: Chaparral with planted pines; views; loose rock, dangerous to descend;
unimproved / MMWD
Elevation: From 1,000' to 1,780' / extremely steep
Intersecting Trails: Matt Davis (.4m)
Directions: Panoramic Highway to milepost 3.66

West Point Trail rises from a turnout on the north side of Panoramic Highway at milepost marker 3.66. The trail is unsigned as the MMWD considers it too steep and dangerous. The steepness and loose rock certainly do make it hazardous, particularly to descend. Across the highway from the start is the signed top of Sierra Trail.

Ascend a few steps into deep woods. The Trail quickly enters chaparral. There are views of the three Tamalpais summits. Look back for sweeping panoramas to the east, south, and west. Extremely steep sections alternate with somewhat easier stretches.

About halfway up, West Point Trail crosses Matt Davis Trail at an unmarked but evident intersection. Left, Matt Davis goes to Pantoll, right to Hogback F.R. above Mountain Home. Again there are extremely steep segments. The somewhat incongruous line of trees in the chaparral here are mostly pines, not native on Mt. Tamalpais. They were planted here around 1930 and are now a prominent feature of the Mountain when viewed from the south.

West Point Trail forks several times just below its upper end; all branches lead to West Point Inn. The main outlet is below the picnic table area, just left of the bench and of the Nora Trail signpost. The bench carries the plaque :

> IN LOVING MEMORY OF ROBERT SCHNEIDER, WHO TOUCHED OUR LIVES, 10-20-1928, 12-11-1982.

Schneider was a Marin County hiker. The other trails converging at West Point are, clockwise: Old Stage Road, Rock Spring, Old Railroad Grade going up, the Grade going down, and Nora.

West Point Inn was built in 1904 at the westernmost point of the Mount Tamalpais Railway. The first of its cabins was added in 1918, the wonderful lounge in the early 1920's. It was a popular resting, dining, and lodging site for decades. When the railroad went bankrupt in 1930, the MMWD assumed ownership and leased the Inn as a private tavern. By 1942, with the top of the Mountain closed to the public by the military, patronage had declined so significantly that the MMWD was planning to raze the Inn as a fire hazard. When some Tamalpais Conservation Club members learned, reportedly through overhearing a remark by MMWD patrolman Joe Zapella, that the Inn's destruction was imminent, they formed the West Point Club to save it. The Club, now the West Point Inn Association and separate from the TCC, still manages the inn. The association sells light refreshments to visitors. On selected Sundays in spring and summer, they serve justly popular, bounteous pancake breakfasts. Rustic rooms and cabins can still be rented for overnight stays; there is no electricity. The inn's phone number is 415/388-9955.

West Point Trail, which dates from around World War I, originally connected Muir Woods Inn, at the present Camp Eastwood, with West Point Inn. Its lower half, today's Sierra Trail, was cut off by the construction of Panoramic Highway. In the 1930's, the Trail was widened as part of a fire break that stretched from Camp Eastwood to West Peak. The 1898 Sanborn map calls today's Rock Spring Trail the West Point Trail.

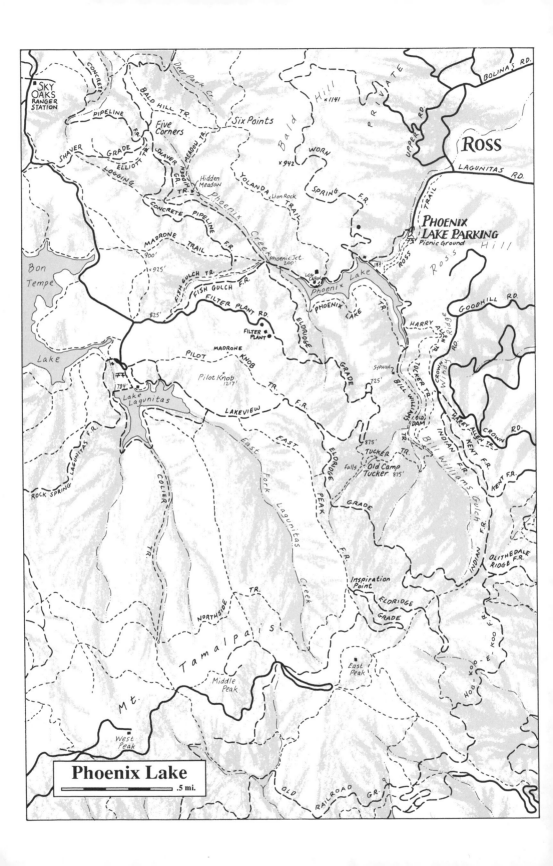

SKY OAKS RANGER STATION

Deer Park Cr.

CONCRETE

PIPELINE F.R.

BALD HILL TR.

Five Corners

Six Points

Bald Hill ×1141

Hill

P R I V A T E

BOLINAS RD.

UPPER RD.

ROSS

SHAVER GRADE

ELLIOTT

LOGGING

SHAVER

PIPELINE

SHAVER GR.

WORN ×942

LAGUNITAS RD.

MEADOW TR.

Hidden Meadow

YOLANDA TRAIL

Lion Rock

SPRING F.R.

PHOENIX LAKE PARKING
Picnic Ground

ROSS TRAIL

Hill

Phoenix Creek

CONCRETE PIPELINE F.R.

MADRONE TRAIL

×900'

×925'

Phoenix Jct. 200'

LOG CABIN

Phoenix Lake

×181

ROSS

Ross

Bon Tempe

825'

FISH GULCH TR.

FISH GULCH F.R.

FILTER PLANT RD.

PHOENIX

LAKE TR.

HARRY ALLEN TR.

ALLEN

CROWN

GOODHILL RD.

Lake

FILTER PLANT

MADRONE

PILOT KNOB TR.

Pilot Knob 1217'

ELDRIDGE GRADE

SYPHON

Windy Ridge

RD.

×784

Lake Lagunitas

LAKEVIEW F.R.

725'

BILL WILLIAM TR.

TUCKER TR.

OLD DAM

Indian Ridge

HARRY ALLEN TR.

KENT F.R.

CROWN RD.

ROCK SPRING

LAGUNITAS F.R.

COLLIER

TR.

East

Fork

EAST

875'

TUCKER TR.

Old Camp Tucker 875'

falls

ELDRIDGE PEAK

GRADE

Bill Williams Gulch

INDIAN F.R.

KENT F.R.

GLITHEDALE RIDGE F.R.

Lagunitas Creek

ELDRIDGE F.R.

Inspiration Point

ELDRIDGE GRADE

HOO-KOO-E-KOO RD.

NORTHSIDE TR.

M t.   T a m a l p a i s

Middle Peak

East Peak

West Peak

Phoenix Lake

.5 mi.

OLD   RAILROAD   GR.

PHOENIX LAKE TRAILHEAD

Directions to Phoenix Lake:
Highway 101 - Sir Francis Drake Boulevard (exit) west, Greenbrae - left on
Lagunitas Road, Ross, to end.

Phoenix Lake has long been the most popular trailhead on the north side of Mt. Tamalpais. Indeed, it has become so popular in recent years that the town of Ross has restricted parking on nearby streets.

Entry to the lake is through Ross' Natalie Coffin Greene Park. Follow Lagunitas Road, here unpaved, past the park's stone entry portals. This stretch, beside Phoenix Creek, is part of the old San Rafael-Bolinas stage route. It bore a sign Dibblee Road until a few years ago. Albert Dibblee bought 78 acres of Ross for $12,000 in the late 1860's. At the end is a small parking lot, often full. A fire road rises to the right, behind a gate, onto Water District land. One-quarter mile above is Phoenix Dam and Phoenix Lake. A second route to the dam is Ross Trail, which runs parallel to, and a few yards south of, Lagunitas Road. There is also a path to the dam from the picnic area. Phoenix Junction, where four fire roads and a trail meet, is at the far, western tip of Phoenix Lake, .6 miles from the dam going counterclockwise.

Greene Park, with its delightful picnic area, was a gift of Ross' Greene family. Natalie Coffin Greene (1885-1966) was a descendant of one of Ross' pioneer families, and very active in civic affairs. Note the telephone in the parking area. It was once regular height until buried by the still quite visible slide. A working phone is at the outhouses by the dam. There are additional outhouses by the parking area. There are fountains at the start of Ross Trail beside the private Lagunitas Country Club, in the picnic area, and 50 yards north from the dam.

To answer a commonly asked question, it is 3.6 miles, accurately measured, to circle Phoenix Lake from the junction of Glenwood Avenue and Lagunitas Road and 2.33 miles around the lake itself.

Suggested loops from Phoenix Dam - elevation 180'

Around Phoenix Lake / 2.3 miles.

Phoenix Lake F.R. counterclockwise, .6m, to Phoenix Junction - right on Shaver Grade, .3m, to Hidden Meadow Trail - right, .7m, to Six Points Junction - right, 1.3m on Yolanda Trail to Phoenix Lake F.R. - left .4m, to start / 3.3 miles.

Phoenix Lake F.R. clockwise, .5m, to Bill Williams Trail - left, .6m, to Tucker Trail - right, 1.1m, to Eldridge Grade - right, 1.6m, to Phoenix Junction - left, .6m, on Phoenix F.R. to start / 4.4 miles.

Phoenix Lake F.R. counterclockwise, .4m, to Yolanda Trail - right, 2.2m, to Worn Spring F.R. - right, 2.2m, to Phoenix Lake F.R. - left, .1m, to start / 4.9 miles.

Phoenix Lake F.R. counterclockwise, .1m, to Worn Spring F.R. - right, 2.5m, to Deer Park Trail - left, .8m, to Deer Park F.R. - left, 1.1m to Shaver Grade - left, 1.2m, to Phoenix Junction - Phoenix Lake F.R. left, .6m (or right, 1.7m), to start / 6.3 (or 7.4) miles.

BILL WILLIAMS TRAIL

From southern tip of Phoenix Lake to Tucker Trail / .6 miles
Terrain: Deep redwood forest; riparian / MMWD
Elevation: From 200' to 380' / gradual
Intersecting Trails: None
Directions: Phoenix Dam - Phoenix Lake F.R., clockwise, .5 miles

Bill Williams Trail starts, at fire road width, from the southern tip of Phoenix Lake. Here too steps connect the fire road and trail sections of the loop around the lake. Bill Williams heads away from the lake shore into deep woodland. In around 200 yards, at a dip in the big water pipeline, Bill Williams narrows. A signpost points the way to Tucker Trail. The pipe is part of the Southern Marin Line, carrying water from the Bon Tempe Treatment Plant. A pump above right, off Eldridge Grade, drives the water up out of Bill Williams Gulch to Kent Woodlands' Crown Road.

Bill Williams follows the hillside through a redwood forest. Bill Williams Creek, one of the sources of Phoenix Lake, is below on the left. This lovely area remains cool on the hottest of summer days, and the creek roars in winter. In a half-mile, the Trail crosses the creek on a bridge. You can see the remains of the old stone Bill Williams Gulch Dam. A wood plaque in a redwood tree beside the bridge dates the small diversion dam to 1886. It played a role in Marin's water supply until Phoenix Lake was filled in 1906.

The Trail crosses back over the creek, now without a bridge. The fording can be a wet one in winter. In summer, you can continue through the dry creekbed. A short, steep uphill leads to a fork. The promising looking path uphill right, taken in error by many, deteriorates. Veer left downhill to the next bridge, which takes the Trail over the creek. Bill Williams Trail then rises a few more yards to meet Tucker Trail. Left leads to Harry Allen Trail, right is a long climb to Eldridge Grade.

Bill Williams lived in a cabin in the gulch in the 1860's. His background is little known; some thought he was a Confederate Army deserter. Alice Eastwood referred to him as "an old wood-chopper." The legend persists that his hidden treasure remains buried somewhere in the gulch. A story relates that laborers building Phoenix Dam in the early years of this century spent more time looking for Bill Williams' gold than working. There was another fruitless treasure hunt when Phoenix Lake was drained in the mid-1980's.

ELDRIDGE GRADE

From Phoenix Junction to Ridgecrest Boulevard / 5.5 miles
Terrain: Lower part forested, upper part mostly chaparral with views; above Indian F.R., bicycles permitted uphill only / MMWD
Elevation: From 200' to 2,250' / gradual
Intersecting Trails: Filter Plant Road (.8m), Tucker (1.6m), Lakeview F.R. (2.0m), connector to East Peak Fire Trail (2.3m), Indian F.R. (3.1m), Wheeler (3.7m), Northside (4.3m), East Peak Fire (5.0m), Redwood Spring (5.3m).
Directions: Phoenix Junction

Eldridge Grade, opened December 13 1884, is the oldest road to the summit of Mt. Tamalpais. It was built as a toll road for horse-drawn wagons; the turnouts were wide enough for six-horse teams. Construction took five months and cost $8,000, with most of the work done by Chinese laborers. The project was spearheaded by John Oscar Eldridge. He had come to California from New York by ship in 1849 at the age of 21. Instead of rushing off to the gold fields, he stayed in San Francisco and became a successful auctioneer. Later, he brought street lighting to San Rafael as founder of the San Rafael Gas Company. His daughter married Sidney Cushing, for whom the Mountain Theater is now named. Eldridge died just two months after his road opened. In the early 1900's, when horse-drawn carriages became obsolete, Eldridge Grade fell into disrepair and plans were advanced to pave the route for auto use. Eldridge Grade remains the principal summit route on the Mountain's north side, a position held on the south side by Old Railroad Grade, which was financed largely by Sidney

Cushing. Like Railroad Grade, Eldridge is never steep, offering a long but steady climb to the summit ridge.

Eldridge is one of three fire roads that rise from Phoenix Junction at the west end of Phoenix Lake. With your back to the lake, Eldridge is to the left or south; to its right is Fish Grade, then Shaver Grade. Eldridge begins under a dense canopy of trees; mostly bay but with redwoods plentiful. There have been serious slide problems in the first 1/2 mile, reducing the Grade to a narrow path in places and sometimes closing it altogether. In .8 miles, Filter Plant Road, which connects to Fish Grade, comes in from the right.

As you continue climbing, the terrain becomes ever drier. Madrones and tanbark oaks become more common; redwoods are found only at stream crossings. Tucker Trail, which rose through dense forest from Phoenix Lake, joins on the left at a right bend in the Grade. Just ahead amidst the redwoods is Bear Wallow Spring, with a seasonal water spigot; there were once both black and grizzly bears on Tam. Views continue to open, particularly to the east.

Lakeview Fire Road, from Lake Lagunitas, joins the Grade on the right. An old trail sign marks the intersection. Just above, chinquapin, a small tree in the oak family, is common. Its spiny bur-like fruit capsules often line the edge of the Grade here. The rest of the ascent is somewhat rocky, as Eldridge is losing much of its topsoil.

In about .3 miles above the Lakeview junction, a wooden post on the right marks a short connector to East Peak Fire Trail. The next fire road to enter is Indian, on the left from Kent Woodlands. Above this junction, bicyclists on Eldridge are restricted to uphill travel only. Continue right. The now closed, extremely steep Indian Fire Trail crosses several times; the intersections have been deliberately blocked by cut branches.

Views to the south, of San Francisco and the San Mateo coastline, expand. To the east it is possible, on the clearest of days, to see the snow capped Sierra, 160 miles away, through the gap in the interior Coast Range north of Mt. Diablo. At a wide horseshoe curve, the signed Wheeler Trail enters on the left. It is a key connection between the north and south side of Tam.

Indian Fire Trail is crossed again. The next big bend to the left is known as Sawtooth Point. Soon after, at a broad horseshoe curve left, an old sign points the way to Northside Trail, which connects all the way to Rifle Camp. Just up Northside is East Peak Fire Trail and scenic Inspiration Point. The next big bend, to the right, is below the formation known as North Knee. Views open to the west. Soon after, East Peak Fire Trail joins on the right.

The Grade now looms over the deep canyon formed by the East Fork of Lagunitas Creek, beginning its long cross-Marin journey to Tomales Bay. Two hundred fifty yards below the end of the Grade, the very steep, unsigned Redwood Spring Trail crosses. Left, it rises as an all-dirt shortcut to the visitor center. Right, it drops to Redwood Spring itself.

Eldridge Grade ends at a gate at Ridgecrest Boulevard. Ridgecrest now covers Eldridge's former route on to West Peak. The Grade originally was 7.3 miles, today it is 5.45 miles. Uphill to the left is East Peak. A few yards to the right are Middle Peak Fire Road and, across Ridgecrest, the top of Old Railroad Grade.

FISH GRADE

From Phoenix Junction to Sky Oaks Road / .8 miles
Terrain: Redwood forest; riparian; upper part paved / MMWD
Elevation: 200' to 720' / very steep
Intersecting Trails: Fish Gulch (.6m)
Directions: Phoenix Junction

Fish Grade and Fish Gulch Trail rise on opposite sides of the the canyon of Fish Gulch. The steepness of the Grade is legendary, intimidating some visitors. Yet people both run and bike up it regularly. It is also quite pretty and is the most direct route between Phoenix Lake and Lakes Lagunitas and Bon Tempe. Since the Grade is well-used by official vehicles, the MMWD suggests that hikers take Fish Gulch Trail.

Fish Grade is the middle of the three fire roads (Eldridge and Shaver grades are the others) that rise from Phoenix Junction. There is no getting lost on the Fish Grade; just keep climbing up, up, up through the cool, quiet forest. Redwoods dominate in the canyon. The creek below is unnamed.

Fish Gulch Trail rejoins Fish Grade. Combined, they immediately meet paved Filter Plant Road, which sets off left to the MMWD's water treatment plant and to Eldridge Grade. There is another 250 yards of stiff uphill on asphalt. The array of water valves to the right, the Bon Tempe Headworks, sends water from Bon Tempe Lake to the treatment (filter) plant and on to southern Marin. The Grade ends at a gate beside Sky Oaks Road. Pumpkin Ridge and Netting trails both rise a few yards away to the right. Bon Tempe Lake is across the road. The line of eucalyptus trees leads to the Lake Lagunitas parking area.

The "Fish" in the name refers to a Mr. Fish who had a camp in the present Lake Lagunitas area in the 1860's. The original grade was built around 1873, when Lagunitas Dam, creating the lake, was completed. That first grade is now the Fish Gulch Trail. The current Fish Grade was carved in 1903 to carry water pipelines down from a new dam, called Tamalpais, which was never completed.

FISH GULCH TRAIL

From Phoenix Junction to Fish Grade | .6 miles
Terrain: Heavily wooded; riparian | MMWD
Elevation: From 200' to 600' | very steep
Intersecting Trails: Concrete Pipeline F.R. (.4m)
Directions: Phoenix Junction

Fish Gulch Trail, originally a broad road, is now the only trail rising from Phoenix Junction. It sets off between the Fish and Shaver grades. The climb, through oak-madrone woodland, is very steep. A water pipeline is visible beside the Trail. The route was cleared in the early 1870's to bring a water line down from the then newly filled Lake Lagunitas. This is actually the original Fish Grade (the present Fish Grade was built in 1903), and is sometimes called Old Fish Grade.

Fish Gulch Trail meets the southern end of Concrete Pipeline F.R., which connects to Five Corners. The remaining ascent is the steepest yet. The fire road (Fish Grade) across the redwood-lined canyon gets steadily closer. In winter, water rushes through the unnamed creek below. There's a last incline past a Water District building known as a baffle chamber.

Fish Gulch Trail veers left to rejoin Fish Grade. A path goes straight ahead. A few yards uphill on Fish Grade is the paved Filter Plant Road, going left to the filter plant and Eldridge Grade. Fish Grade continues steeply up 250 yards to Sky Oaks Road.

In the 1860's, a Mr. Fish lived and worked at the site of the present Lake Lagunitas. The area was called Fish's Camp when Lagunitas Dam was built in 1873.

HARRY ALLEN TRAIL

From Phoenix Lake to Crown Road, Kent Woodlands / 1.3 miles
Terrain: Heavily wooded; .2 miles paved / MMWD & MCOSD
Elevation: From 200' to 580' to 480' / steep
Intersecting Trails: Tucker (.2m), Kent F.R. (.6m)
Directions: Phoenix Dam - Phoenix Lake F.R., clockwise, .4 miles

Harry Allen built this Trail on Sundays over a period of three years in the early 1920's. It connected his home at 55 Olive Avenue in Larkspur's Baltimore Canyon to Phoenix Lake. The development of Kent Woodlands has covered much of it, and diminished the importance of the remaining segments. Today the Trail is in two parts, severed atop Windy Ridge. The less known eastern half, on MCOSD land, was re-cleared and signed in 1987. Though both ends of that segment are accessible by car, most users joins Harry Allen at Phoenix Lake.

The Trail rises from the Phoenix Lake Fire Road at a signpost reading "Allen Trail, to Tucker Trail." The steep initial grade lessens as the Trail enters the forest. Look in winter and spring for the delicate maidenhair fern, with its green, fan-shaped fronds (leaves) branching off slender black stalks. The spores are found under the reflexed outer margins of the fronds. "Adiantum", the fern's genus name, comes from the Greek words "not wet," because the fronds shed water.

Just beyond a creek crossing, the Trail meets the start of Tucker Trail. Most people leave Harry Allen here, taking Tucker either up Eldridge Grade or, with Bill Williams Trail, back to Phoenix. Harry Allen continues up left. Several paths cross. They are remnants of a more extensive trail system here from the days when hikers approached the Mountain from Northwestern Pacific Railroad stops to the east, particularly Baltimore Park near the present Lark Creek Inn. That service was discontinued in 1940.

The Trail climbs out of its forest canopy and passes the introduced garden shrub called Pride of Madeira, a sure sign that homes are near, which indeed they are. The Trail unceremoniously runs into a rusted guard rail opposite 123 Crown Road. A MMWD sign and a lightly etched "Harry" on an old post are the only markings.

To continue on Harry Allen, go right on the pavement along the spine of Windy Ridge. In .1 mile, a fire road goes left. It is the unpaved section of Crown Road. Continue up Phoenix Road. In another .1 mile, an MMWD gate to the right marks the start of Indian Fire Road. A few yards beyond, at the end of the pavement, is a wood barrier with an MCOSD sign. Behind it is Kent Fire Road and, to the left signed "Trail to Crown Road," is Harry Allen.

Squeeze through two redwoods to continue. The narrow Harry Allen Trail passes redwoods and abundant huckleberry. In 1/3 mile there is an MCOSD sign at a fork; veer left. The upper path loops back to near Harry Allen. In another .1 mile, a sign, for the opposite direction, notes "Trail to Windy Ridge." Harry Allen ends 75 yards below this sign, on Crown Road just east of #320. The entry is marked with an MCOSD sign. Crown Road goes right, past Idlewood Road and Evergreen Drive, to the Southern Marin Line (Crown) Fire Road trailhead.

Harris Stearns Allen was president of the Tamalpais Conservation Club in 1916-17. He died in 1947.

HIDDEN MEADOW TRAIL

From Shaver Grade to Six Points / .7 miles
Spur: Between Hidden Meadow Trail and Bald Hill Trail / .1 mile
Terrain: Grassy hillside; lower part riparian; horses permitted / MMWD
Elevation: 270' to 550' / gradual, upper half very steep
Intersecting Trails: Logging (.2m)
Directions: Phoenix Junction - Shaver Grade, .3 miles

Hidden Meadow Trail is barely more than a mile from both the popular Phoenix Lake and the Deer Park trailheads, yet it offers peace and an unspoiled quality reminiscent of early Marin. It passes several inviting picnic sites. The Trail starts to the right when going uphill on Shaver Grade, just under .4 miles above Phoenix Junction, where the grade begins rising steeply.

Hidden Meadow Trail follows Phoenix Creek. In less than .2 miles, the Trail reaches lovely Hidden Meadow. Its grassy knolls are indeed hidden from the rest of the world. The site was formerly known as Marshall Gulch for the Marshall family. They operated a dairy in the area around the turn of the century. Cattle grazed here until 1916. A Mt. Tamalpais History Project walk on the site in April 1988 turned up an old milk bottle from the ranch. (Note that it is unlawful to remove historic artifacts from the Mountain.)

The unsigned Logging Trail enters the meadow from the left. Veer right. If you prefer your picnic sites with views, continue up Hidden Meadow Trail as it climbs the southwest face of Bald Hill. There are level grassy areas higher up with splendid Mt. Tam vistas.

The Trail branches near its top. The left Spur goes to Bald Hill Trail. The main branch, right, rises to, and ends at, Six Points Junction. The continuing options, from left to right, are: Bald Hill Trail to Five Corners, Six Points Trail to Deer Park, Yolanda Trail to Worn Spring F.R., and Yolanda back to Phoenix.

Hidden Meadow Trail was built in the late 1930's.

PHOENIX LAKE FIRE ROAD and TRAIL

Loop around Phoenix Lake / 2.3 miles
Terrain: Riparian; oak-buckeye woodland; half trail, half fire road; horses and bicycles permitted on fire road section only; heavily used / MMWD
Elevation: Around 175' / level to slightly rolling
Intersecting Trails: Clockwise from dam; Ross (at dam), Harry Allen (.4m), Bill Williams (.5m), Eldridge Grade (1.7m), Fish Grade (1.7m), Fish Gulch (1.7m), Shaver Grade (1.7m), Yolanda (1.9m), Worn Spring F.R. (2.2m)
Directions: Phoenix Dam

The loop around Phoenix Lake is one of the most beloved routes on Mt. Tamalpais. Its popularity arises from its accessibility, beauty, safety, access to other trails and to fishing, and the ease of completing the loop. The circle route comprises two distinct parts of almost identical distance; a Fire Road that goes left and right from the dam, and a Trail, sometimes called the Gertrude Ord, on the far side.

Phoenix Lake was formed in 1905 when a dam was constructed in Phoenix Gulch by the Marin County Water Company, a predecessor to the MMWD. Phoenix, with a capacity of 178 million gallons, is the second smallest of the MMWD reservoirs. It is also the lowest in elevation. Because it is several hundred feet below the nearby MMWD filter plant, through which the water must pass to be treated, it is not regularly used as part of the regular County supply. It can, however, be re-activated in an emergency. In early 1989, when there was a threat of drought, a new pump was installed in the center of the lake. Phoenix was most recently drained in 1984, when the current concrete spillway was built to replace the old wooden one, which was deemed unsafe.

Most visitors to Phoenix come from Ross, reaching the dam by climbing either the Ross Trail to the left of Greene Park or the connector fire road to the right. We'll follow the circle route clockwise from where this fire road meets the dam. This offers views of Tam's summit; going the other way affords lovely vistas of Bald Hill.

Cross the dam, passing the several well-placed benches. On the dam's other (southeast) side, narrow Ross Trail joins Phoenix Lake F.R. on the left. The junction is marked with a signpost pointing the way to Ross. Continuing on the Fire Road, you'll notice several paths to the lake's shore. Fishermen, angling for black bass and trout, often line the bank.

In a bit under a half-mile, Harry Allen Trail rises on the left. It connects to Tucker Trail, then continues up to Kent Woodlands. The Fire Road then drops to the lake's southern tip, which is sometimes dry here before the first winter rains. To continue the loop around the lake, go right, up the steps. Straight ahead, into the redwoods, is Bill Williams Trail, which starts at fire road width. It too leads to Tucker Trail.

The loop route continues as a narrow Trail. It has been named Ord Trail by the equestrians who helped build it. Gertrude Ord was a familiar horse rider in the area, and her husband, Eric, was a president of the Tamalpais Trail Riders. Horses are now no longer allowed on this section.

The Trail rolls gently along the lake's south shore. The steepest section is near a bridge, built in the mid-1980's, over an unnamed feeder stream. After a second bridge, installed in 1987 when the Trail was rerouted, forks branch left and right. Both lead back to the Fire Road, with the right fork a 100 yard shortcut. When back on the Fire Road, go right to complete the loop. To the left, at the northwest tip of the lake, is Phoenix Junction, from which the Eldridge, Fish, Old Fish, and Shaver grades rise.

The circuit continues on the old Lagunitas Road. It passes buildings of the former Porteous Ranch. Horses graze behind the fence. A MMWD ranger lives in a house on the site, which is not open to the public. Phoenix Log Cabin, beside the fire road, was built for the Porteous Ranch coachman and foreman, Martin Grant, around 1893. The Water District began restoring it in the summer of 1989.

A few yards later, at a bend, the lovely Yolanda Trail sets off uphill to the left at a marked intersection. The last junction is with Worn Spring Fire Road, which climbs to the top of Bald Hill. A few yards beyond is a water fountain and a trough for horses. Just ahead on the left is another, private MMWD ranger's residence. A memorial plaque on the right honors Clayton Stocking, an MMWD employee who lived there for 42 years (see Stocking Trail). Back at the dam, on the left, are outhouses and a telephone. The distance around Phoenix Lake, avoiding the few shortcuts, has been accurately measured at 2.33 miles.

ROSS TRAIL

From Natalie Coffin Greene Park, Ross, to Phoenix Dam / .6 miles
Terrain: Wooded hillside / Town of Ross & MMWD
Elevation: From 80' to 200' / gradual, parts steep
Intersecting Trails: None
Directions: Same as Phoenix Lake, to intersection of Lagunitas Road and Glenwood
Avenue

Ross Trail bypasses the open-to-autos road approach into Natalie Coffin Greene Park. A well-worn path to the Trail sets off parallel to Lagunitas Road at the Glenwood Avenue intersection. The path follows the fence beside the Lagunitas Country Club, passing a water fountain signed "thirsty joggers." The path then leaves the road's edge, heading left and uphill, to become Ross Trail. It joins Greene Park above the stone portal entrance.

The woods here are rich in vegetation. Spring wildflowers begin blooming early, usually by the first or second week of January. Leading the annual parade, and abundant along the Trail, are milk-maids and fetid-adder's-tongue. The latter, in the lily family, can be recognized by its pair of broad leaves spotted with brown. It displays its three-petaled, purple-striped flowers ever so briefly. The slender flower stalks then droop downward, implanting their own seeds. Later in the year, the fragrant mint yerba buena blossoms abundantly along the Trail.

Ross Trail drops to near the Phoenix Lake parking lot, but remains above it. Ross, or Windy, Hill, 763' high, looms above to the left. A still visible major slide here in 1986 has cut Ross Trail. A short uphill scramble is now required to continue.

The Trail runs above the park's picnic area and Ross Creek. Several steep paths drop to the right. As you approach Phoenix Lake you might, in winter, hear the sound of water rushing down the dam's spillway. Just before the Trail's end, steps bring a path up from Ross Creek. The Trail ends at Phoenix Lake Fire Road on the east side of Phoenix Dam. A MMWD sign, carved "Ross," is at the intersection.

Scotsman James Ross was a pioneer settler who bought much of the Ross Valley in 1857. He died, at age 50, in 1862. Later, his wife Anne had to sell most of the holdings to provide the substantial dowries, as called for in James' will, upon the marriages of the couple's two daughters. The North Pacific Coast Railroad stop of Sunnyside was renamed Ross in 1882. The town of Ross was incorporated in 1908.

SHAVER GRADE

From Phoenix Junction to Sky Oaks Road / 1.7 miles
Terrain: Wooded, parts deeply; lower part riparian / MMWD
Elevation: From 180' to 775' / steep
Intersecting Trails: Hidden Meadow (.3m), Logging (.6m, 1.5m), Concrete Pipeline
F.R. (1.0m-1.1m), Elliott (1.1m, 1.4m, 1.5m), Deer Park F.R. (1.1m), connector fire
road to Bald Hill Trail (1.1m), Sky Oaks-Lagunitas (1.7m)
Directions: Phoenix Junction

Shaver Grade is quite popular with travelers on the north side of Mt. Tamalpais. It is less steep than Fish Grade in going between Phoenix Lake and the upper lakes and is the direct connection between Phoenix and the important Five Corners junction. Though Shaver's upper end is accessible by car, most users join the Grade from Phoenix Lake.

Shaver Grade has a long history. Isaac Shaver (or Shafer or Schaffer) came overland to California from New York in 1852. In 1864 he built a sawmill near the present Alpine Dam and a road to haul the lumber to Ross Landing on Corte Madera Creek, where boats completed the trip to San Francisco. That road was the original Shaver Grade, part of which is today's Logging Trail. The mill closed in 1873. The present Shaver Grade was originally a section of the old county road from San Rafael to Bolinas. Shaver was credited with constructing many of San Rafael's earliest homes. Quite enterprising, he bought the redwood timbers, for $50, when the original San Rafael Mission was torn down. He was the president of San Rafael's first library. Shaver reportedly drowned himself after being accused of wrongdoing in a land transaction.

Shaver Grade is the fire road on the right at Phoenix Junction when your back is to Phoenix Lake. Shaver begins only slightly uphill. It has a timeless, pastoral feel in the woodland beside Phoenix Creek. Hidden Meadow Trail, to nearby Hidden Meadow, branches right at a signpost. The uphill begins in earnest.

In the middle of a horseshoe bend to the right, among redwoods, the easy-to-miss Logging Trail crosses the Grade. To the left, Logging Trail (the old Shaver Grade) goes uphill between a laurel and a madrone. Twenty-five yards farther up the Grade, Logging Trail drops right, down to Hidden Meadow.

Through the trees are views of Bald Hill. The Grade then meets Concrete Pipeline F.R. Left leads to Lake Lagunitas. Shaver and Concrete Pipeline run together uphill, above a tunnel for the water pipeline, for 200 yards to the key junction of Five Corners. Clockwise, the five other spokes (yes, there are six), are: Elliott Trail, Shaver Grade continuing uphill, Concrete Pipeline F.R., Deer Park F.R., and a connector fire road to Bald Hill Trail.

Madrones line the way above Five Corners. Shaver again meets Elliott Trail, crossing left and right. There's a brief, rare downhill. Elliott Trail crosses Shaver a last time. On the left, Elliott continues uphill to Sky Oaks-Lagunitas Trail. From the same junction, marked by a "generic" MMWD sign, Logging Trail sets off downhill.

A final climb leads to Sky Oaks-Lagunitas Trail and, a couple of yards above, paved Sky Oaks Road. Across Sky Oaks Road is both a path and the auto access (also part of the old county road) to the Bon Tempe Dam parking area.

TUCKER TRAIL

From Harry Allen Trail to Eldridge Grade / 1.7 miles
Terrain: Deep forest; riparian / MMWD
Elevation: From 300' to 800' / very steep, parts gradual
Intersecting Trails: Bill Williams (.7m)
Directions: Phoenix Dam - Phoenix Lake F.R. clockwise - Harry Allen Trail, .2 miles

The heavily forested Tucker (or Camp Tucker) Trail is one of the loveliest on the mountain. In summer, it offers a cool respite from summer heat. In winter, rushing creeks and a waterfall are added attractions. The Trail's proximity to Phoenix Lake adds to its popularity. It is steep, however, and does require, after winter rains, some agility in crossing streams.

Tucker Trail branches to the right off Harry Allen Trail at a signed intersection .2 miles up from Phoenix Lake. California buckeyes line Tucker's early yards. Tucker winds through deeper woods. Bill Williams Creek can be heard rushing below. In .7 miles, a few yards after passing an overgrown path on the left (the old Tucker Cut-Off to Windy Ridge), Tucker meets Bill Williams Trail. Bill Williams drops to the bridge below and returns to Phoenix Lake. Some visitors mistake Bill Williams Trail with Tucker.

Veer left to the head of the canyon for the first of the Trail's three crossings of Bill Williams Creek, here of the east fork. A short leap may be required immediately after winter rains. The Trail becomes steeper, rising to a ridge above the canyon of the Creek's middle fork. At 1.1 miles is the second stream crossing. Continue climbing through this peaceful, isolated forest. The third and last crossing is of the Creek's west fork. There's another stiff uphill to a trail sign at 1.5 miles.

This level patch is the site of old Camp Tucker. Here one Mr. Tucker, who did logging in the area in the late 1800's, apparently built and lived in a cabin. Later, the clearing housed picnic tables. A waterfall is visible, and audible, just above, with a very steep path leading to it.

The last .2 miles of Tucker are level. The Trail finally leaves the forest canopy for its first broad views. Tucker ends at a bend in Eldridge Grade. Phoenix Lake is 1.6 miles downhill and Lakeview Fire Road is .4 miles uphill.

Tucker Trail appears on the 1898 Sanborn map.

WORN SPRING FIRE ROAD

From Phoenix Lake to top of Deer Park Trail / 2.5 miles
Terrain: Grassland; views / MMWD & private (public easement)
Elevation: From 200' to 1100' to 510' / very steep
Intersecting Trails: Connector to Yolanda (.1m), Yolanda (2.1m), Buckeye (2.2m, 2.5m), Deer Park (2.5m)
Directions: Phoenix Dam - Phoenix Lake F.R., counterclockwise, .1 mile

Bald Hill occupies a special place for residents of the Ross Valley corridor. Baldy, as it is affectionately called, is visible from many parts of Greenbrae, Kentfield, Ross, San Anselmo, Fairfax and elsewhere. Its open upper slopes have become an integral part of the quality of life for the area. Up close, Baldy is even lovelier, a quintessential California hill, green in the winter and spring, golden in summer and fall. Worn Spring Fire Road traverses the entire west side of Baldy. It offers a splendid trip any time of the year.

Worn Spring is the first fire road rising above Phoenix Lake when going counterclockwise from the dam. The Fire Road is unrelenting, very steeply uphill all the way to the top of Baldy. At the first bend to the right, in less than 100 yards, a steep connector path to Yolanda Trail branches left. Vistas quickly open up; the whole journey is a visual treat.

In less than .4 miles, the Fire Road passes a wooden structure covering the Ross Reservoir. The reservoir dates from 1921 and has a capacity of one million gallons. You can often smell chlorine, added to sterilize the water. Just beyond is a fork. The road right goes the few yards to the reservoir.

Worn Spring's continuation, widened to a fire road after World War II, is to the left.

The trees are mostly madrone, oak, and laurel, watered by Worn Spring. To the right begin vistas of the treeless, upper, grassy slopes of Baldy. In .5 miles the Fire Road drops slightly and crosses over Worn Spring (for the second time). Worn Spring was tapped as an important water source for Marin from 1881 until the completion of Alpine Dam in 1919. Worn Spring was pressed into service again during the drought of 1976-77.

There's a final steep stretch in the woodland, then the trees are left behind. A path goes left; it is the steep, overgrown Burnt Trail (below minimum standards, so not described in this book), heading to Yolanda Trail. The scenery is superb. Mt. Tamalpais rises behind you, Baldy's gentle contours in front. There is no evidence that you are within a mile or two of a population center. And the views, first of the East Bay, then of the San Francisco skyline, then of the greenbelt to the northwest, get ever broader. Near the summit is an MMWD boundary sign. Few visitors realize that much of Baldy, including its summit, is privately held. Though access has long been permitted, it cannot be guaranteed. (A plan to acquire this uppermost 60 acre parcel with public funds is proceeding at press-time.)

The summit, 1.6 miles from the start, is reached via a 50 yard connector to the right. A U.S. Geological Survey post is buried near the peak. As splendid as the views have been, the very top is even more spectacular, as the north opens up as well. It might be windy but, in any case, enjoy the 360 degree panorama, you've earned it!

Return to Worn Spring Fire Road. Across is a second summit of Baldy. If you are not returning directly to Phoenix Lake (and the views on the way back, facing Tam, are among Marin's best) go right. In .1 mile, there is a fork. The unnamed fire road to the right, through private property but long open to all, runs .8 miles to the top of Upper Road West in Ross.

Veer left to stay on Worn Spring F.R. You are descending the north side of Bald Hill, and this stretch was once known as Bald Hill Fire Trail and as Corral Trail. A half mile down from the summit is a residence, the highest on Baldy, with a corral. The Fire Road drops toward a saddle. To the left is one end of Yolanda Trail. To the right is a short connector, on private property and recently closed, to Oak Avenue in San Anselmo. At press-time, there were plans to develop several homesites here.

Worn Spring continues straight ahead. The boundary between Water District (left) and privately held land runs down the center of the Fire Road. Worn Spring drops through oak woodland. At the bottom of the hill,

Buckeye Trail goes left to bypass the next uphill. Worn Spring crests its final uphill, then descends. There are fine views to the northeast.

The Fire Road forks. Right leads to a gate of the privately owned Sky Ranch, from which many equestrians set off. Veer left. The steep downhill drops past the northern end of Buckeye Trail, then the signed top of Deer Park Trail, which goes to Deer Park. A few yards beyond, Worn Spring Fire Road comes to an abrupt end. The precipitous path straight ahead also plummets to Deer Park.

James and Anne Ross bought, in 1857, most of today's Ross Valley. A daughter, also named Anne, married San Franciscan George Worn. James' will called for a large cash dowry for her; most of the land holdings had to be sold to pay it. Worn later recovered much of the acreage. The couple operated a dairy ranch on the Ross slope of Bald Hill. The Worns' residence, called Sunnyside, is the present site of Ross' Marin Art & Garden Center.

YOLANDA TRAIL

From Phoenix Lake to Worn Spring Fire Road | 2.2 miles
Terrain: Woodland, middle part grassy hillside with steep dropoff and views; horses permitted | MMWD
Elevation: 180' to 650' | gradual, southern part steep
Intersecting Trails: Hidden Meadow (1.3m), Bald Hill (1.3m), Six Points (1.3m)
Directions: Phoenix Dam - Phoenix Lake F.R., counterclockwise, .4 miles

Yolanda is one of the most beautiful, and best loved, trails on Tam. Most of the year it captures the early morning sun; in summer, the last light as well. It makes a semicircle around the western side of Bald Hill, with Mt. Tamalpais' summit almost constantly in view. The Trail is among Marin's richest in wildflowers. After the riot of color in spring, pink willow-herbs bloom after mid-summer and California fuchsias add red into November. Yolanda's proximity to the Phoenix Lake and Deer Park trailheads also contributes to its popularity.

The Trail rises from Phoenix Lake at a marked signpost just before the old log cabin when going counterclockwise around the lake. An alternate entry to Yolanda, closer to the dam but steeper, is just up Worn Spring Fire Road from Phoenix.

Yolanda starts uphill through oak-madrone woodland. There is an MMWD residence and a corral in the fenced-in, off-limits enclosure just below. It was part of the old Hippolyte Dairy Ranch. The Porteous family bought 1,100 acres here in 1883, and renamed the property Porteous Ranch. The alternate entry from Worn Spring enters on the right, by a "no horses" sign. In spring, this part of the Trail is lined with irises. After a good climb, the bulk of the Trail's total rise, you leave the trees for another special part of Yolanda.

The Trail, carved onto the steep southwest slope of Bald Hill by the Civilian Conservation Corps in the 1930's, offers a stunning Mt. Tam vista, and an equally stunning drop down the hillside if you're inattentive! Though but a mile as the crow flies from the heavily populated Ross Valley, the Yolanda here appears tranquil and timeless. Only 50 yards into the open area, the Trail passes a few entrances on the right to Burnt Trail, which appears on both the Erickson and Olmsted maps but is now too steep and overgrown to be included here. Yolanda winds its way, rolling, around Bald Hill. It becomes more wooded as it approaches Six Points.

At Six Points Junction (which see), Yolanda bends to the right. This last section of Yolanda (called Yolanda North on Erickson, as opposed to the Yolanda South just covered) is along Baldy's north face. Except for one open stretch, it is well wooded; only Baldy's sun-dried south face doesn't support trees. The Trail is every bit as peaceful as before. A path goes up, right, to Worn Spring Fire Road. Occasionally visible below on the left is the old Deer Park School. There are some muddy patches in winter as the Trail is used by horseback riders from the nearby Sky Ranch and Marin Stables. The views back toward Tam are superb.

Yolanda re-emerges into the open at its terminus at Worn Spring Fire Road. At press-time, there were plans to build several homes near this intersection. Both left on the fire road, toward Deer Park, and right, to the top of Baldy, border private property. The fire road straight ahead, to Oak Avenue in San Anselmo, is also on private property and is presently closed.

The name Yolanda comes from an area, now part of San Anselmo, that was the first stop west of the Hub on the old Northwestern Pacific rail line. The Trail originally started from the station. An attractive San Anselmo street still carries the name.

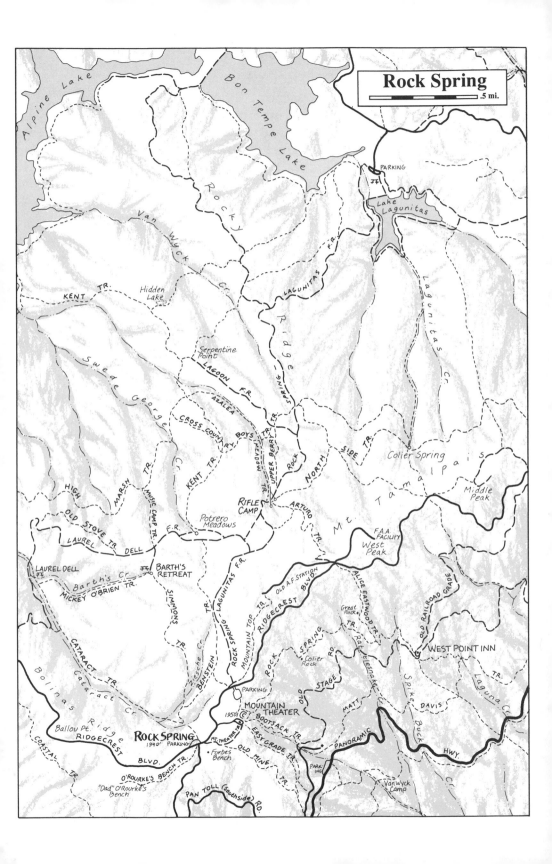

Rock Spring

.5 mi.

Alpine Lake

Bon Tempe Lake

PARKING

Lake Lagunitas

Rocky

Van Wyck Cr.

KENT TR.

Hidden Lake

LAGUNITAS F.R.

Lagunitas Cr.

Ridge

Serpentine Point

LAGOON F.R.

Swede George

AZALEA

CROSS COUNTRY

BOYS TR.

MEADOW

UPPER BERRY TR.

ROCK

SPRING TR.

NORTH SIDE TR.

Colier Spring

Mt Tamalpais

Middle Peak

MARSH TR.

KENT TR.

Cr.

HIGH

RIFLE CAMP

ARTURO TR.

OLD STOVE TR.

LAUREL DELL

MUSIC CAMP F.R.

Potrero Meadows

F.A.A. FACILITY
West Peak

LAUREL DELL

Barth's Cr.

BARTH'S RETREAT

SIMMONS TR.

LAGUNITAS F.R.

Old A.F. Station BLVD

RIDGECREST BLVD.

Alice Eastwood TR.

OLD RAILROAD GRADE

MICKEY O'BRIEN TR.

CATARACT TR.

BENSTEIN TR.

ROCK SPRING TR.

MOUNTAIN TOP TR.

ROCK SPRING TR.

Great Rock

TR.

WEST POINT INN

Zische Cr.

Colier Rock

SPRING RD.

Rattlesnake Cr.

Spike Buck

DAVIS TR.

Laguna Cr.

Bolinas Ridge

Cataract Cr.

Parking

MOUNTAIN THEATER

1950

OLD STAGE RD.

MATT TR.

Ballou Pt.

ROCK SPRING
1940'

Parking

BOOTJACK TR.

PANORAMIC

COASTAL TR.

RIDGECREST BLVD.

MT. THEATER TR.

Forbes Bench

EASY GRADE TR.

OLD MINE TR.

PARKING

HWY.

O'ROURKE'S BENCH TR.

"Dad" O'Rourke's Bench

PAN TOLL (Southside) RD.

Van Wyck Camp

Cr.

ROCK SPRING TRAILHEAD

Directions to Rock Spring:
Highway 101 - Highway 1 - Panoramic Highway - Southside (Pantoll) Road to Ridgecrest Boulevard junction

This trailhead is invariably called Rock Springs, but purists correctly point out that there is only one spring. It is popular for the stunning views in the area, and for access to trails high on the west slope of the Mountain. The trailhead's large parking area is at the junction of Ridgecrest Boulevard and Southside (Pantoll) Road. Gates at Pantoll and on Ridgecrest Boulevard near Fairfax-Bolinas Road bar automobile access to Rock Spring from around an hour after sunset until morning. During exceptionally hot and dry weather, or during rare snowfalls, vehicular access to the summit may be blocked at Rock Spring. There are outhouses by the parking lot. There is no fountain but many drink the untreated water from Rock Spring itself, which flows into a stone enclosure just down Cataract Trail.

Directly across Ridgecrest Boulevard from the parking lot, a steep path climbs to the top of the prominent knoll. There, behind the trees, is the Forbes Bench, commanding a wonderful view. It honors Mountain veteran John Franklin Forbes. He and other members of the Cross Country Boys Club used to gather nearby and read and tell stories. Alice Eastwood read Sherlock Holmes installments from Collier's Magazine. The bench was placed by Forbes' son, John Douglas Forbes, in 1981.

Rock Spring has been a named feature of Mt. Tamalpais for over 100 years.

Suggested loops from Rock Spring - elevation 1,940'

*Cataract Trail, 1.1m, to Mickey O'Brien Trail - right, .7m, to Barth's Retreat - connector fire road, .1m, to Laurel Dell F.R. - right, .2m, to Benstein Trail - right, 1.2m, to Cataract Trail - left, .1m, to start / **3.4 miles.***

*Rock Spring Trail, .1m, to Ridgecrest Blvd. - left, .1m, to Rock Spring-Lagunitas F.R. - left, .8m, to Potrero Meadow - left, 1.6m, on Laurel Dell F.R. to Cataract Trail - left, 1.2m, to start / **3.8 miles.***

*Cataract Trail, .1m, to Simmons Trail - right, 1.0m, to Barth's Retreat - connector fire road, .1m, to Music Stand Trail - straight, .5m, to High Marsh Trail - left, 1.5m, to Cataract Trail - left, 1.5m, to start / **4.7 miles.***

BENSTEIN TRAIL

From Simmons Trail to Laurel Dell F.R. / 1.2 miles
Spur: From Benstein Trail to Ridgecrest Blvd. / .1 mile
Terrain: Deep woodland / MMWD
Elevation: 1,920' to 2,250' to 1,980' / steep
Intersecting Trails: Rock Spring-Lagunitas F.R. (.6m-.7m), connector to Barth's Retreat (.9m)
Directions: Rock Spring trailhead - Cataract Trail - Simmons Trail, .1 mile

Benstein Trail is part of the most direct route from Rock Spring to Potrero Meadow. It also is a good place to see one of Mt. Tamalpais' most beloved flowers, the Calypso orchid.

The start of Benstein Trail was rerouted in the mid-1980's to minimize erosion damage to the meadow below Rock Spring. Benstein now sets off farther north of the parking lot than previously. To reach Benstein, take Cataract Trail 100 yards downhill to Simmons Trail, which is signed. In .1 mile, Benstein sets off to the right from Simmons at a marked fork.

Benstein climbs, with occasional help from stone and wood steps, at the edge of a Douglas-fir forest. The main entrance area to the Mountain Theater can be glimpsed to the right. In .3 miles, a marked spur (sometimes called Benstein Extension) to Ridgecrest Boulevard and the theater branches right. Veer left for a bit more uphill. The Trail crosses a rivulet and goes over a serpentine rock outcrop. Steve Petterle, formerly of the Marin Municipal Water District, dubbed this area "Serpentine Swale."

In .6 miles, Benstein meets and joins Rock Spring-Lagunitas Fire Road. Go left, toward Rifle Camp. In 100 yards, Benstein departs from the Fire Road to the left at a signpost. The Trail heads into deeper woods and crests at 2,250'. The downhill is steep, again with steps helping. At a clearing in the forest is a giant, isolated Douglas-fir. Soon after, on a serpentine outcrop, there are splendid views north. Mt. St. Helena, and even higher peaks in Mendocino County, can be seen on clear days. The nearby trees are Sargent cypress. A path goes left from here to near Barth's Retreat; veer right.

There is then a steady downhill to Benstein's end at Laurel Dell F.R. Nearby to the right is the main Potrero Meadow, and to the left is Barth's Retreat. Straight ahead, just below, is Potrero Camp, a picnic site.

And what of the orchid, *Calypso bulbosa*? Enjoy the search for these jewels, here at their southernmost limit in California. I'll not pinpoint their locations; look carefully under Douglas firs in early spring. Never pick, or even risk trampling, any wildflower on the Mountain.

Henry Benstein, or Bernstein, (the two names, both of which have appeared on maps and signposts, provide a lively source of debate, with some of the most respected of the Mountain's historians on opposite sides) was an inveterate Mountain hiker, TCC member, and a "regular" at Potrero Camp. He died in 1938, and this former Potrero Camp Trail, which he helped build in 1921-22, was renamed in his memory.

CATARACT TRAIL

From Rock Spring to Alpine Lake / 2.9 miles
Terrain: Heavily wooded; riparian; parts rocky / MMWD
Elevation: From 1,970' to 650' / very steep, parts extremely steep
Intersecting Trails: Simmons (.1m), connector to Laurel Dell F.R. (1.0m), Mickey O'Brien (1.2m), Laurel Dell F.R. (1.2m-1.3m), High Marsh (1.5m), Helen Markt (2.3m)
Directions: Rock Spring

Cataract Trail is always listed near the top of favorite Tamalpais trails. It is lovely at any time of year but really comes into its own in winter, particularly after a storm. Cataract Creek, which the Trail parallels, is then a torrent, cascading down over waterfall after waterfall amidst deep woods. Since Cataract Trail is accessible on both ends by road, and because it is so steep and has only very strenuous loop possibilities, a car shuttle is ideal for those wishing to cover its full length. Leave one car at the turnout where the Fairfax-Bolinas Road bends sharply uphill past Alpine Dam (8 miles from Fairfax), and drive to Rock Spring. You'll then have an all-downhill, nearly three-mile walk back.

The Trail begins downhill directly north from the gate at the Rock Spring parking lot. There are outhouses to the left. To the right, in a rocky, shaded groved, is a picnic area. Below the rocks is the source of Rock Spring. Cataract Creek begins its flow to Alpine Lake from the area farther to the right, called Serpentine Swale. In about 100 yards, the combined Simmons and rerouted Benstein trails branch right. Just beyond, Rock Spring is fed, untreated, into a stone pool from a storage tank. In a few more yards, Cataract Trail crosses Ziesche Creek, here joining Cataract Creek.

The Trail enters the forest, where it remains, with few exceptions, the rest of the way. Within twenty yards, a sign points the Trail to Laurel Dell.

Planks across Cataract Creek lead to a short path to Ridgecrest Boulevard. Cataract continues gradually downhill. Cataract Creek is to the left, and will be for the next two miles. The Trail crosses over several feeder rivulets.

In just over .5 miles, the Trail meets a grassy clearing on the right. A common flower here is false lupine. To the left are azalea bushes. More are encountered lower along the creek. Cataract Trail reenters woodland. Huckleberry and wood rose are common shrubs. In one mile, a bridge, unofficially called Ray Murphy Bridge for the ranger who built it (without authorization), goes left over Cataract Creek. It offers a shortcut to Laurel Dell Fire Road, which runs on the opposite bank of the creek. There is no other bridge over the creek for 1.3 miles.

Next is the wonderful meadow known as Laurel Dell. Just to the right, at the very start of the clearing, is Mickey O'Brien Trail, heading to Barth's Retreat. After winter rains, the crossing of Barth's Creek here can be extremely wet, even unpassable except in waterproof boots. There is a small bridge on the right. Past the creek is the junction with Laurel Dell F.R. Veer left off the fire road, into the delightful, shaded Laurel Dell picnic area, to continue on the Cataract Trail. Here are tables, a fountain (untreated), trash receptacles, and, across the meadow, outhouses.

Across the creek and a few yards downstream of the picnic area is a path known as Old Stove Extension; it is now in poor condition. Cataract Trail, and the adjacent creek, now begin plunging more steeply. After some switchbacks, the Trail meets one end of High Marsh Trail, which goes to Kent Trail. The junction is signed, and has a bench. Other paths to High Marsh branch off Cataract just below. At a steel railing along some stone steps is a particularly fine view of one of the creek's waterfalls. You can get right next to the water; it's a great place to pause.

The descent continues moderately steeply. The redwoods and Douglas-firs beside the creek are extemely tall, among the most impressive on the Mountain. Far from any road, this is a magical stretch.

At 2.3 miles, Cataract meets one end of Helen Markt Trail, which goes right, to Kent Trail. A sign affixed to a Douglas-fir marks the junction. Cataract Trail descends very steeply left (avoid the even steeper shortcut). In about 100 yards it crosses the creek, after having spent over two miles on the right bank. The angled bridge is an old one; countless photographs have been taken from it. Few cover the Trail without wanting to linger here above the torrent. The pool above was once a water source. The trunk of a bigleaf maple forces you to duck as you cross.

The Trail continues down, often extremely steeply. Rocks and roots make extra demands for caution. Some new wooden steps and a bridge were added in 1989. There are turnouts to get special views of falls. A couple of the rivulet crossings can be a bit tricky, involving short leaps, after winter rains.

The Trail and Cataract Creek meet Alpine Lake. Anglers often line the bank below. The creek's journey is over but the Trail continues a bit farther. This broader stretch was once part of the San Rafael-Bolinas stagecoach road. Cataract Trail ends at Fairfax-Bolinas Road at a big bend near milepost 8.09. Alpine Dam is a couple of hundred yards to the right.

Cataract Trail appeared on the 1898 Sanborn map. The Civilian Conservation Corps rebuilt the Trail in the 1930's.

MICKEY O'BRIEN TRAIL

From Laurel Dell to Barth's Retreat / .8 miles
Terrain: Deep woodland; riparian / MMWD
Elevation: From 1,680' to 1,960' / steep
Intersecting Trails: Connector to Laurel Dell F.R. (.6m)
Directions: Rock Spring - Cataract Trail, 1.1 miles

Mickey O'Brien is a lovely trail, through deep forest beside a stream in one of the quietest parts of the Mountain. Since it connects two of Tam's landmarks, Laurel Dell and Barth's Retreat, it is part of many north side loop walks.

Mickey O'Brien (misspelled "O'Brian" on the trailhead signpost) begins just where Cataract Trail hits the open meadow of Laurel Dell. Look for the trailhead on the right if you are coming from Rock Spring, to the left at the end of the meadow when coming from Laurel Dell picnic area. Mickey O'Brien immediately plunges into a forest dominated by Douglas-firs. Barth's Creek, a companion the whole way, is to the left. It joins Cataract Creek at Laurel Dell.

In .2 miles is the Trail's only clearing, a grassy hillside to the right. Just before the start of this clearing look left, toward the stream, to see what is recognized as one of the world's two largest Sargent cypress trees. It is 85 feet high, with a circumference of 10 feet, 2 inches. Its size and presence here are unusual. The tree is usually found, stunted and shrublike, on dry, exposed serpentine ridges. Several tree guides describe the Sargent cypress' height limit as 40 or 50 feet. The tree can be told from surrounding Douglas-firs by its less furrowed bark. The cypress' needles and rounded cones, also diagnostic, are too high to see without binoculars. This particular tree has two equally prominent forks splitting from the main trunk about 15 feet up, and many low branches. The tree's preeminence was only recognized in 1980, by the late Thomas Harris. The second giant, 96 feet high but with a smaller circumference, is just downstream. Many Sargent cypress trees are fallen here, not a good sign for their future.

To the right at the clearing, a couple of hundred yards up the creek bed, is the wreckage of a Navy Corsair fighter. It was involved in a two plane collision in 1945. Both pilots parachuted to safety.

Mickey O'Brien crosses some rivulets. Then the Trail passes between some boulders. Just on the other side, a .2 mile connector heads left across the creek to Laurel Dell Fire Road. A signpost was placed here in the summer of 1989. Continue uphill without crossing the creek. A marked path leads up right to an outhouse.

The Trail terminates at a bridge over Barth's Creek. The bridge is dedicated to the memory of veteran Mountain worker and hiker Harold Atkinson, who built the Mickey O'Brien in 1930 and rerouted it in 1971. Few people worked harder on the Mountain's trails than Atkinson. On the bridge's near side, Simmons Trail begins its journey to Rock Spring. Across the bridge is Barth's Retreat (see Simmons Trail). Laurel Dell Fire Road is 100 yards uphill atop the connector fire road.

Michael Francis "Mickey" O'Brien was a native San Franciscan who devoted himself to the Mountain. He was a charter member of the Tamalpais Conservation Club, served as its president in 1925-26, edited its newsletter, "California Out of Doors," for 8 years, and served on the executive committee for 30 years. In 1947, at age 69, he suffered a heart attack after a session of trail work on Hoo-Koo-E-Koo. Returning to the Mountain just three weeks later to continue his work, he died at Alpine Lodge, beside Panoramic Highway. It was the perfect way to go for a Mountain veteran. This Trail, once called Barth's Creek Trail, then K.C. Trail, was dedicated to him in 1948.

MOUNTAIN THEATER FIRE TRAIL

From Rock Spring to Mountain Theater / .2 miles
Terrain: Grassland; horses permitted to Old Mine Trail / MTSP
Elevation: From 1,980' to 2,020' / gradual
Intersecting Trails: Old Mine (.1m)
Directions: Rock Spring

A few yards east of the Rock Spring trailhead, and across Ridgecrest Boulevard, a Trail rises behind a gate. State Park signs at its start and end identify it as Mountain Theater Fire Trail. It is well-used during Sundays in May and June by visitors exiting the annual Mountain Play.

The Trail climbs a grassy hillside. At a spectacular view site, Old Mine Trail branches off right. Veer left. Mountain Theater Fire Trail skirts a hill, with more excellent vistas. The Trail ends at the Madrone Grove, also called Sherwood Forest, a picnic area just west of the amphitheater itself.

The first Mountain Play, "Abraham and Isaac," drew 1,200 spectators in 1912. William Kent donated the theater site to the Mountain Play Association in 1915 as a memorial to his friend and business partner Sidney Cushing. Cushing, for whom the theater is named, was the prime mover behind the Mt. Tamalpais Railway. The present stone amphitheater was constructed by the Civilian Conservation Corps in the 1930's.

MUSIC CAMP TRAIL

From Laurel Dell Fire Road to High Marsh Trail / .5 miles
Terrain: Wooded; riparian; parts rocky / MMWD
Elevation: From 2,000' to 1,760' / steep, lower section very steep and rocky
Intersecting Trails: None
Directions: Rock Spring - Cataract Trail - Simmons Trail to Barth's Retreat - connector to Laurel Dell Fire Road

The Music Camp, one of the hidden treasures of Mt. Tamalpais, never fails to enchant first-time visitors. They are invariably drawn to visit again. The camp's presence, so unexpected in the deep woods, is one of the reasons Mt. Tamalpais is so beloved. The little known, unmarked Trail leading near it is called, with equal appropriateness, Music Camp by Olmsted and Music Stand by Erickson.

Many people walk by the upper end of the Trail without noticing it as it is unsigned and all but invisible. Look for it on the north side of Laurel Dell Fire Road opposite from the signed connector fire road to Barth's Retreat. Descend 30 or 40 yards through the rocks and chamise in the clearing toward the trees. A creek bed, which doubles as the upper end of the Trail, comes into view. The Trail branches left of the creek bed in a few more yards, and is then relatively easy to follow.

The downhill, through forest, is gradual to steep. The adjacent creek, dry much of the year, is the uppermost reaches of the West Fork of Swede George Creek, heading to Alpine Lake. The Trail crosses to the right bank of the creek, then crosses back to the left bank (creek again to the right). Thirty yards from this re-crossing, by a double-trunked Douglas fir tree and a spring, an easily missed path departs left. It leads, in 50 yards, to the Music Camp itself.

There, in a sylvan setting, is an old rusted music stand. Visitors leave coins where the sheet music would rest. An equally battered chair, a table, and wood plank benches complete the camp's furnishings. Sing as loud as you want here for it is, after all, the Music Camp. A path continues from the other side of the camp back to Laurel Dell F.R.

Return to the Trail and go left to continue the descent. The Trail becomes more open, and rockier and steeper. Be careful. A path branches right to High Marsh Trail. There are more crossings of the creek bed. This is a particularly lovely, isolated area. Music Camp Trail ends when it hits High Marsh Trail, which goes left 1.5 miles to Cataract Trail and right .6 miles to Kent Trail.

Though it is nice to think of it as older, the Music Camp Trail was carved in the 1950's by Ben Schmidt, a music lover and one of the most important Mountain trail builders of the post-World War II era. Schmidt, raised on Tam in a cabin near the Tourist Club, still hikes regularly as he approaches his 80th birthday. The Trail has also been called the Frank Meraglia, for a Mountain veteran who died in the mid-1970's.

OLD MINE TRAIL

From Mountain Theater Trail to Coastal (Old Mine) Fire Road | 1.5 miles
Terrain: Upper part grassland with sweeping views, middle .2 miles paved, lower part tanbark oak woodland; horses permitted; views | MTSP; part of Bay Area Ridge Trail
Elevation: From 2,000' to 1,460' | middle part steep
Intersecting Trails: Riding and Hiking (.6m), Old Stage Road (1.0m)
Directions: Rock Spring - Mountain Theater Trail, .1m

The upper section of Old Mine Trail passes some of the Mountain's best view sites. To pick up Old Mine, cross Ridgecrest Boulevard from Rock Spring and follow Mountain Theater Trail. In around 100 yards, there is a signed junction. Mountain Theater Trail continues left to the theater and Old Mine Trail branches right. To the right of the intersection, atop the tree covered hill, is Forbes Bench. This upper part of Old Mine, to Riding and Hiking Trail, is an equestrian section of the new 400 mile, multi-use Bay Area Ridge Trail.

Shortly, a path departs left toward the theater. Old Mine goes over a serpentine outcropping. There is a path to the top of the hill on the left. Take it to get even more stunning views than Old Mine itself offers. On clear days, the snow-capped Sierra may be visible, along with Mt. Diablo, the San Francisco skyline, both towers of the Golden Gate Bridge, and the Pacific. The hill is popular as a wedding site, and as a place to fly kites.

Old Mine begins dropping steeply. It passes beside and through a woodland. Tanbark oaks are the most common tree. At .4 miles, a massive Douglas-fir, with huge lower limbs, sits aside the Trail's left margin. Pantoll, the Trail's destination, briefly comes into view.

After some switchbacks, Old Mine meets Riding and Hiking Trail, which goes left to Easy Grade Trail and to Old Stage Road. Veer right, back into the forest. A shortcut to Pantoll branches right; stay off it as there are erosion problems below. Old Mine swings left and meets the asphalt Old Stage Road. The junction is signed, and there is an old reflector signpost from Highway 1 alongside.

The original Old Mine Trail is now split by Old Stage Road and Panoramic Highway. To pick up the Trail again, go to Pantoll by turning right, then crossing Panoramic. Follow the paved road (part of the original Old Mine Fire Road) downhill from the ranger station. Forty yards past the Steep Ravine Trail turnoff, Old Mine Trail resumes, well marked, on the left. This fairly level lower section is a pedestrian route of the Bay Area Ridge Trail.

A quarter-mile into the Douglas-fir forest is the old mine, just above on the right, that gave the Trail its name. A re-done sign, copying the original filing, dates this "Denos Claim" to May 1863. There was a modest gold rush on Tam then with over a dozen claims, probably none profitable, filed. There are traces of gold in some Tam quartz outcroppings. This mine site was uncovered in 1952.

The Trail ends shortly after, when it again meets Coastal (Old Mine) Fire Road, at a four-way intersection. Coastal goes left to the Dipsea and to Deer Park Fire Road, which is the southern continuation of the Bay Area Ridge Trail. Right is a return to Pantoll through the State Park's maintenance yard. Straight across is the bottom of unsigned Lone Tree Hill Fire Road.

O'ROURKE'S BENCH TRAIL

From Rock Spring to O'Rourke's Bench / .3 miles
Terrain: Grassland; views / MTSP
Elevation: From 1,980' to 2,070' / gradual
Intersecting Trails: None
Directions: Rock Spring

This Trail leads to the stunning view knoll on which O'Rourke's Bench sits. Actually, many paths fan out across the grassy hills in this area just west of Ridgecrest Boulevard; the most direct route from Rock Spring to the Bench is called O'Rourke's Bench Trail here.

Pick up the Trail across Ridgecrest Boulevard from the Rock Spring parking area, 10 yards north (right) of the gate that closes the road each night. The splendid, open area that O'Rourke's Bench Trail enters was only added to Mt. Tamalpais State Park in 1953. The 265 acre addition was due to the generosity of, among others, William Kent, Jr. and John I. Miller, for whom Miller Trail is named.

In 50 yards, O'Rourke's Bench Trail passes a clump of laurels clinging to the rocks; one is fallen and dead. Douglas firs are beginning to invade. Soon after, the Trail passes along the right edge of an almost bare serpentine rock outcropping. Next is another isolated stand of trees, this one of oaks. The soil, derived from greenstone rock, is a rich red. Veer left and circle the next stand of laurels to spot O'Rourke's Bench.

This treasure, carved out of the stone rocks and sheltered by the laurels, commands a spectacular view to the southwest. The plaque on the bench reads:

'GIVE ME THESE HILLS AND THE FRIENDS I LOVE, I ASK NO OTHER HEAVEN.' TO OUR DAD O'ROURKE, IN JOYOUS CELEBRATION OF HIS 76TH. BIRTHDAY, FEB. 25TH. 1927. FROM THE FRIENDS TO WHOM HE SHOWED THIS HEAVEN.

You'll surely want to stay a while, even if the area's notorious winds and fog are swirling. Paths continue beyond the Bench.

Richard Festus "Dad" O'Rourke was an impeccably dressed Mountain veteran who led his wife and four daughters, and legions of others, on hikes on Tamalpais. He is credited with being a catalyst for both the founding of the Tamalpais Conservation Club and the building of the Mountain Theater. Much beloved, he was honored by this bench at his favorite resting place, which he called "edge of the world." There is a splendid picture of O'Rourke and his wife, sitting on the bench on the day of its dedication, in Lincoln Fairley's "Mount Tamalpais, A History."

ROCK SPRING TRAIL

From Rock Spring to West Point / 1.7 miles
Terrain: Chaparral, parts wooded; short part on asphalt; views / MTSP & MMWD
Elevation: 1,970' to 1,780' / almost level
Intersecting Trails: Eastwood (1.3m)
Directions: Rock Spring

Few of the Mountain's trails have such consistently breathtaking views as Rock Spring. It is also popular because it is fairly level, and connects three of the Mountain's special places; Rock Spring, Mountain Theater, and West Point.

Rock Spring Trail sets off just 10 yards north of the Rock Spring parking lot, to the right (east) at the Cataract Trail sign. The Trail passes below huge oaks and picnic tables. Calypso orchids are found here in spring. Beneath the rocks here is the source of Rock Spring itself. Work was done on the spring in 1933 to keep it flowing all year. In 1972, the spring's outlet was relocated to its present site, just down Cataract Trail. In .1 mile, the Trail hits Ridgecrest Boulevard directly across from the main entrance to the Sidney B. Cushing Memorial (Mountain) Theater. Cross the pavement and enter the theater; it is open year round.

The next section is on an asphalt path. In 40 yards, at a fork, is a plaque. Placed in 1986, it honors the Civilian Conservation Corps for constructing the amphitheater 50 years earlier. Hauling, shaping, and placing the heavy serpentine rocks to make the seats was an extraordinary undertaking. Veer left. This approach to the upper seats of the theater, taken by thousands on Sunday play dates in May and June, seems oddly quiet any other time.

A second plaque, dating from 1983, is passed. It honors three men: ex-Congressman William Kent, who donated the theater's land; Sidney Cushing, the driving force behind the Mt. Tamalpais Railway; and Alfred Pinther, a past president of the Mountain Play Association, the California Alpine Club, and the Tamalpais Conservation Club. A few yards past, a trail sign points the way, right, to the upper ends of the Bootjack and Easy Grade trails. Rock Spring Trail goes straight ahead, across the upper aisle of the amphitheater. This is a special place, during the splendid productions or when it is deserted the rest of the year. Sit and enjoy the views over to the East Bay. Maybe there'll be a wedding under way.

The Trail continues on the other side of the theater, past a pair of drinking fountains. It immediately encounters, on the left, massive Pohli Rock, which commands a stunning view site. Salem Rice, the leading authority of Mt. Tamalpais' geology, dates the Rock's greenstone to a sea floor lava flow some 400 million years ago. Pohli Rock has long been intimately connected to the Mountain Play. It has been used as a prop in several productions, people still watch the play from atop it, and there are two very moving plaques affixed to it. The one on the left, somewhat hidden, says:

I LINGERED ON THE HILL WHERE WE HAD PLAYED, GARNETT HOLME, 1873-1929.

Holme, a drama instructor at the University of California, was one of the prime movers behind the creation of the Mountain Play, and served as its first director. He died in 1929, after a fall on the Mountain. His ashes are embedded in the rock.

The other plaque reads:

TO AUSTIN RAMON POHLI, A LOVER OF THIS MOUNTAIN, WHO DIED MAY 20, 1913, AGED 20 YEARS, THIS ROCK IS DEDICATED.

Pohli was the son of Emil and Kate Pohli. Mrs. Pohli was one of the founders of the Mill Valley Outdoor Art Club and chairwoman, in 1904, of a committee that was fighting to save Muir Woods (then called Sequoia Canyon). Ramon Pohli was a student at Cal when he met Holme, who appointed him the Mountain Play's first business manager. Pohli fell to his death while climbing near Snow Creek Falls in Yosemite just 20 days after the triumphal opening of the very first Mountain Play, the success for which he was given large credit. Pohli's ashes were scattered on the Mountain. The rock was formally dedicated to him on May 17, 1914.

In a few more yards, at a boundary post, the Trail leaves Mt. Tamalpais State Park into the Water District. A path heads off left to a Mountain Theater parking lot. Continue right through the woodland. The downhill is just noticeable. Rock Spring Trail runs through both light forest and chaparral.

At .9 miles, the Trail passes through a prominent serpentine rock band, with exceptional views. Look on the right for Colier Rock, a serpentine boulder commanding a great vista. It bears a patina-covered bronze plaque:

TO JOHN M. COLIER, A LOVER OF NATURE.

This is the same Colier of Colier Spring and Colier Trail (which see) and this was his favorite vista point.

Another serpentine band is passed. A bridge crosses the headwaters of Rattlesnake Creek. About .1 mile farther, a new signpost marks the lower end of Eastwood Trail, which rises very steeply to Ridgecrest Boulevard. Continue straight ahead. You can begin to see glimpses of West Point Inn. Evidence of a burn remains on the left. The Trail crosses Spike Buck Creek.

Rock Spring Trail passes posts, once part of a stile to keep horses out. In another 100 yards, the Trail ends at Old Railroad Grade, here circling around West Point Inn. The Nora and West Point trails also meet at the inn.

Rock Spring has been a named feature on Mt. Tamalpais for over 100 years. Rock Spring Trail was shown on the 1898 Sanborn map as the West Point Trail. Since West Point was a name added to Tamalpais in 1896 during construction of the rail line, the Trail probably dates to 1896-98.

SIMMONS TRAIL

From Cataract Trail to Barth's Retreat | 1.1 miles
Terrain: Mixed forest and open serpentine; parts rocky | MMWD
Elevation: 1,960' to 2,210' to 1,960' | very steep
Intersecting Trails: Benstein (.1m)
Directions: Rock Spring - Cataract Trail, .1 mile

Simmons Trail often plays a part in loop trips north from Rock Spring. It is also the direct route to two of the Mountain's treasures, Barth's Retreat and the Music Camp. The Trail offers splendid vistas as it passes over the western edge of Tam's summit ridge.

The Simmons trailhead is around 100 yards north of the Rock Spring parking area. The Trail branches to the right off Cataract Trail at a signpost. Another access is a few yards lower, just past the stone enclosure into which the untreated water of Rock Spring is carried. The area is currently a bit confusing as the Benstein Trail has been rerouted, for erosion control purposes, onto the Simmons Trail for the first .1 mile of each.

In just 50 feet, Simmons crosses Cataract Creek, here only a trickle. Benstein departs to the right, on its way to Laurel Dell F.R. The two trails end only .1 mile apart as the crow flies. They offer an attractive loop opportunity. Simmons veers left to follow the left bank of Ziesche Creek. Pioneer Tam hiker Edward Ziesche built a cabin here between 1880 and 1890. It was razed around 1935. The exact site was only rediscovered in 1988 by Sausalitan Phil Frank, creator of the cartoon "Farley" and an avid Tam explorer. The area is criss-crossed with faint, old paths, including an earlier routing of the Simmons.

The Trail crosses the creek over a bridge. There is a stand of introduced redwoods. This was the site of old Camp Norway. Two forks present themselves; they soon unite. The Trail begins to climb. The ascent is first through a forest of mostly bay and very tall Douglas-firs. A replica of an old sign pointing the way to Barth's Retreat has been affixed to a dead fir. The original is in the Lucretia Little History Room of the Mill Valley Public Library.

Simmons then enters an open serpentine rock area. The Trail is lined with chaparral shrubs. A faint path, known to some as Perkins Pass Trail (not separately described), crosses. To the right, it joins Rock Spring-Lagunitas F.R. between the two forks of Benstein. To the left, it goes, even fainter, to the splendid rock "throne." The view when seated in the "throne," one of Tam's many hidden treasures, is spectacular.

In .5 miles, the Trail levels at its crest of just over 2,200'. This starkly lovely area is the western edge of the Mt. Tamalpais summit ridge. There is nothing higher to the west until Hawaii. The trees found amidst the rocks are Sargent cypress. Howell's description of the Sargent cypress may well have been inspired here: "These gray-green trees blend with the gray-green rock of the serpentine barrens to form a picturesque and memorable part of the Mount Tamalpais scene." Look carefully at the trees and, on many, you'll see mistletoe (*Phoradendron densum*). It is a parasitic plant, robbing the trees of nutrients; "phoradendron" means tree-thief in Greek.

The Trail passes briefly through another forest, then opens in an area once known as Buck Meadows. There is a welcome bench. Simmons hits a second crest. Though a bit lower than the first, the shorter surrounding vegetation permits just as dramatic views. Simmons then descends steadily along the edge of, and through, a predominantly Douglas-fir forest.

Simmons Trail ends at its junction with Mickey O'Brien Trail, which goes left to Laurel Dell. At this junction a bridge, dedicated to the memory of Harold Allen Atkinson (1903-1983), crosses Barth's Creek. Atkinson was an active member of the Tamalpais Conservation Club for decades; his name appears on an April 21, 1912 trail cleanup assignment list.

Barth's Retreat, a popular picnic site among hikers for generations, is on the other side of the bridge. There are old tables and a water fountain. Professor Emil Barth was a versatile musician and music teacher. He was associated with the Mountain from 1886, when he arrived from Germany. He built a cabin here, named Casa Escondida, that he lived in, part-time, until his death in 1926. The obituary for him in the TCC newsletter, *California Out of Doors*, of January 1927 said: "No one knew the trails and unfrequented paths as he did, no one loved them more, and few have done as much as he to find beauty spots and build trails to reach them." His extensive music collection was donated to the San Francisco Public Library by his wife in 1937.

A fire road connector to Laurel Dell F.R. rises from Barth's Retreat. Half-way up it, on the left, is a plaque to long-time MMWD patrolman Joe Zapella. Across Laurel Dell F.R. from the connector's junction is the unmarked upper end of Music Camp (Stand) Trail.

The Trail dates from around World War I. Fred Sandrock of the Mt. Tamalpais History Project speculates the Trail may be named for Colonel Charles A. Simmons, who made a film promoting the virtues of California and who was an early donor to the Tamalpais Conservation Club.

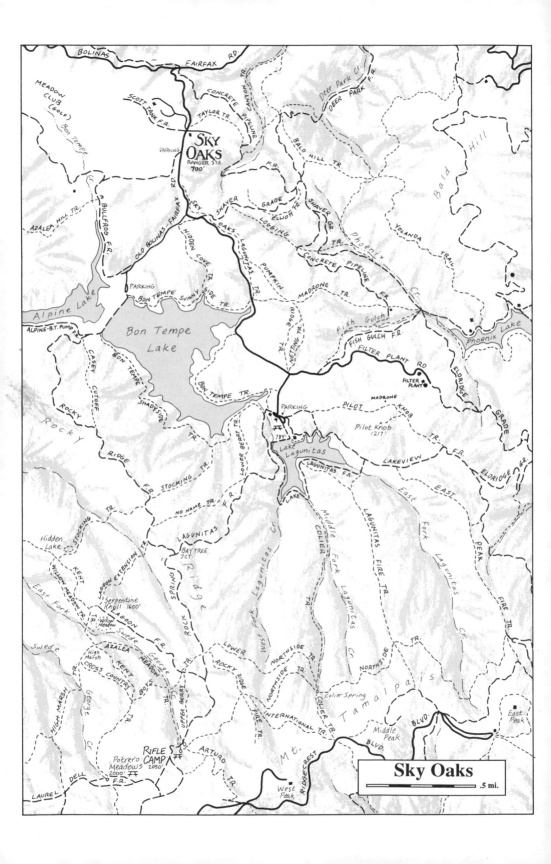

Sky Oaks

.5 mi.

SKY OAKS TRAILHEAD

Directions to Sky Oaks Road:
Highway 101 - Sir Francis Drake Boulevard (exit) west, Greenbrae, to San Anselmo -
left on Center Boulevard, which becomes Broadway in Fairfax - left on Bolinas Road
to Lake Lagunitas sign opposite #700 Bolinas Road

Sky Oaks Road provides access to Lakes Lagunitas, Bon Tempe, and Alpine. These "upper lakes," as they are sometimes called, are immensely appealing to a wide range of users. A vehicle use fee, currently $3 a day, is collected at the toll booth opposite the MMWD Sky Oaks Ranger Station. Annual passes costing $25 ($10 for senior citizens) are sold at the station or at MMWD headquarters on Nellen Avenue beside Highway 101 in Corte Madera. The following trail junctions (with mileage from the ranger station) are encountered along Sky Oaks Road: Taylor (at the station), Scott Tank F.R. (at the station), Bullfrog F.R. (.1m), Sky Oaks-Lagunitas (.1m), Shaver Grade (.4m), Pumpkin Ridge (.7m and 1.5m), Bon Tempe (1.0m), Madrone (1.0m), Netting (1.5m), and Fish Grade (1.5m).

Bon Tempe Dam is reached by the only right turn off Sky Oaks Road, .6 miles from the Ranger Station down an unpaved road that once was part of the San Rafael-Bolinas stagecoach route. There are portable outhouses on both sides of the dam, but no other facilities. There is a wheelchair-accessible entry ramp to Bon Tempe Lake at Redwood Cove off Sky Oaks Road.

The Lake Lagunitas parking lot, at the end of Sky Oaks Road 1.6 miles from the Ranger Station, has outhouses, water, a telephone, and an attractive picnic area with tables and grills. The lake itself is reached by going uphill a couple of hundred yards on the fire roads to the left or right of the picnic area. Sky Oaks, by the present ranger station, was the site, from 1924 to the early 1940's, of Camp California, a University of California summer training camp for engineering students. After World War II, the University did not renew its lease and the area became the Sky Oaks Girl Scout Camp. Today, it is headquarters for rangers of the Marin Municipal Water District. Just on the other side of the present toll booth was the site of a Civilian Conservation Corps camp, built in 1935. On December 9, 1941, two days after Pearl Harbor, National Guard troops moved in, and the area was used for military training during World War II.

Suggested loops from Lake Lagunitas parking area - elevation 730'

*To Lake Lagunitas F.R., .1m - left or right, 1.6m, around Lake Lagunitas - to start, .1m / **1.8 miles**.*

*Left or right on Bon Tempe Trail around Bon Tempe Lake / **4.0 miles**.*

*To Lake Lagunitas F.R., .1m, - right (counterclockwise), .6m, to Colier Trail - right, 1.1m, to Lower Northside Trail - right, .9m, to Rocky Ridge Fire Trail - right, .1m, to Rock Spring-Lagunitas F.R. - left, .2m, to Lagoon F.R. - right, .8m, to Lagoon Extension Trail - right (straight), .4m, to Rocky Ridge F.R. - left, .2m, to Stocking Trail - right, .6m, to Bon Tempe (Shadyside) Trail - right, .3m, to start / **5.3 miles**.*

*Bon Tempe (Shadyside) Trail, .3m, to Lower Berry Trail - left, .4m, to No Name Trail - right, .5m, to Rocky Ridge F.R. - right, .1m, to Stocking Trail - left, .6m, to Kent Trail - right, 2.3m, to Alpine-Bon Tempe Pump F.R. - straight, .5m, to Bon Tempe (Shadyside) Trail - right, 1.3m, to start / **6.0 miles**.*

Circuit of Mt. Tamalpais

*To Lake Lagunitas F.R., .1m, - left (clockwise), .5m, to Lakeview F.R. - left (straight), .8m, to Eldridge Grade - right (straight), 3.5m, across Ridgecrest Blvd. to Old Railroad Grade - left, 1.5m, to West Point - right on Rock Spring Trail, .4m, to Eastwood Trail - right, .6m, across Ridgecrest Blvd. to Arturo Trail - left, .5m, to Rifle Camp - right, 2.4m, on Rock Spring-Lagunitas F.R. to start / **10.3 miles**.*

ALPINE-BON TEMPE PUMP FIRE ROAD

From Bon Tempe Dam to Kent Trail / .5 miles
Terrain: Riparian; lightly wooded / MMWD
Elevation: From 720' to 650' / gradual
Intersecting Trails: Rocky Ridge F.R. (<.1m)
Directions: Across Bon Tempe Dam from parking lot

This Fire Road is the main access to Kent Trail. It sets off from Bon Tempe Dam on the far side from the spillway and parking area. Here too, by an outhouse, are also the starts of the Bon Tempe (Shadyside) and Casey Cutoff trails.

In 20 yards, Rocky Ridge F.R. departs to the left, beginning a long, stiff uphill. Alpine-Bon Tempe Pump Fire Road descends toward Alpine Lake. This was the area where the Tamalpais Dam was to be built. Work was started in 1903 but never completed. Instead, Phoenix Dam was built, in 1905, then Alpine Dam, in 1917-19. The Tamalpais Dam foundations are still visible across the lake when Alpine is low.

The Fire Road meets Alpine Lake by the pump house, which dates to 1956. The Fire Road was built to provide MMWD personnel with access to the pump. From here, water is pumped up to Bon Tempe Lake, then on through the treatment plant to Marin consumers. To the left at the Fire Road's end is the signed start of Kent Trail, which winds its way four miles to Potrero Camp. The Fire Road is also called Pumphouse F.R.

AZALEA HILL TRAIL

From Fairfax-Bolinas Road to Bon Tempe Creek / .8 miles
Terrain: *Part grassland, part woodland; short parts rocky and slippery; views; horses permitted / MMWD*
Elevation: *From 1,080' to 1,180' to 650' / very steep*
Intersecting Trails: *None*
Directions: *Same as Sky Oaks but continue on Fairfax-Bolinas Road to parking turnout by milepost 3.76*

Azalea Hill Trail sets off from a gate on the east (left coming from Fairfax) side of Fairfax-Bolinas Road, at a parking area about a mile beyond the Meadow Club golf course. Across the paved road is the start of Pine Mountain Fire Road into the drainages of the Little and Big Carson creeks, a huge area of Water District land outside this book's coverage but well worth exploring.

Azalea Hill Trail begins climbing at fire road width; this broad section is open to cyclists. In around 200 yards there is a first glimpse of Mt. Tamalpais' summit. The views get ever better, among the finest of the Mountain to be found. In .2 miles, a path to the 1,217' summit of Azalea Hill branches to the right. The side trip is worth making. Wade through the shrubby leather oak (*Quercus durata*) and the manzanita, over the serpentine rocks, to check out the outstanding views.

Azalea Hill Trail continues to the left of a wonderful meadow, which is covered with colorful wildflowers in spring and early summer. At the far side of the meadow, the now narrow Trail begins a short but very steep and dangerous descent over serpentine rock. The route is so indistinct that early editions of the Olmsted map showed the Trail ending here. Carefully follow the Trail downhill. There are some intersecting paths; keep heading toward the Bon Tempe spillway. The views can be distracting. It is beside the Trail at the base of the steepest section that the dense mass of azalea bushes, which gave the hill and Trail their names, is found.

The Trail then resumes in reasonable condition, though it is still slippery, into a grove of black oaks and stately madrones. One of the madrones is particularly enormous. Isolated rest and picnic sites, with views of Mt. Tamalpais across Bon Tempe Lake, beckon in this idyllic area. There is some poison oak as well, however.

After descending a hillside covered with bracken fern, Azalea Hill Trail meets a path just above Bon Tempe Creek. The path goes right, to the shore of Alpine Lake. Follow it to Liberty Gulch Trail for a loop option. Or take the path left to find the driest crossing of Bon Tempe Creek to Bullfrog Fire Road; a leap may still be required. Bullfrog goes left to Sky Oaks Ranger Station and right to Bon Tempe Dam.

AZALEA MEADOW TRAIL

From Rock Spring-Lagunitas Fire Road at Rifle Camp to junction of Kent and High Marsh trails / .9 miles
Terrain: Riparian; heavily wooded; passes two meadows / MMWD
Elevation: 2,000' to 1,500' / steep, short parts very steep
Intersecting Trails: Cross Country Boys (.3m)
Directions: Ridgecrest Boulevard at FAA gate - Arturo Trail

The unsigned Azalea Meadow Trail is not on the Erickson, MMWD, TCC, or Charette maps and was only added to later editions of Olmsted (where it is called Willow). Azalea Meadow Trail's isolation insures its quietude. Many visitors rate it among the Mountain's lovelier trails. And perhaps nowhere on the Mountain is there a greater concentration of azaleas.

The Trail begins off Rock Spring-Lagunitas F.R. directly across (north) from the metal backpack rack at Rifle Camp. A MMWD sign once here is now gone and the opening couple of yards are somewhat obscure. The Trail descends through a deep woodland of mostly Douglas fir and madrone. The nearby stream, followed closely throughout but never crossed, is the East Fork of Swede George Creek. At .3 miles, as you duck beneath a madrone, look to the right for a large huckleberry patch.

By the clearing known as Azalea Meadow, there are two tricky three-way intersections. At the first, Cross Country Boys Trail forks left to Kent Trail. Cross Country Boys and Azalea Meadow then run downhill together for 15 yards to a second junction. Here Cross Country departs to the right, to Lagoon Fire Road.

Directly ahead is Azalea Meadow (called Azalea Flat on Olmsted). Western azaleas are usually in full bloom here in May and June. The creamy white flowers, with their intoxicatingly sweet scent, are a delight to the senses. Bees often swarm above the meadow, creating a steady hum as they pollinate the next generation of azaleas.

Continue left, downhill, besides the creek. Swede George flows all year. Azaleas line the creek and Trail. This little traveled part of the Mountain is a delight. Boulders offer places to rest.

About .3 miles down from Azalea Meadow is a second, even larger clearing, Willow Meadow. It too has many azalea bushes. Ripe blue elderberries are a favorite of birds here in summer. The Trail runs left, along the clearing's perimeter. It then drops another .1 mile to its end at a four-way intersection. Left and right is Kent Trail. Straight across is the eastern end of High Marsh Trail, with High Marsh itself some 200 yards ahead.

BON TEMPE TRAIL

Around Bon Tempe Lake / 4.0 miles
Terrain: Half woodland, half grassland; riparian; .1 mile paved; horses permitted except around Pine Point / MMWD
Elevation: Around 730' / almost level
Intersecting Trails: Clockwise from Bon Tempe Dam; Hidden Cove (.5m), Madrone (1.0m), Sky Oaks-Lagunitas (1.0m), Rock Spring-Lagunitas F.R. (2.5m), Lower Berry (2.8m), Stocking (2.8m), Casey Cutoff (3.8m), Alpine-Bon Tempe Pump F.R. (3.8m)
Directions: Bon Tempe Dam parking lot

It is possible to circle the shore of Bon Tempe Lake by trail, save for a short section around Redwood Cove. The loop is often viewed as being in two segments; the southern, wooded "Shadyside," and the northern, largely open "Sunnyside." I use these designations as well. The circuit is described clockwise from Bon Tempe Dam, though the Trail is just as commonly joined from the Lake Lagunitas parking lot. The circle distance of just under 4.0 miles is based on hugging the shore on the Sunnyside part, avoiding the several well-worn shortcuts.

Both a fire road and a narrow path rise from the Bon Tempe Dam parking area. Start with either, they quickly meet. Just about 75 yards from the start, the fire road drops to the right and narrows to trail width after passing an MMWD building. A shortcut path goes left. The next inlet is Hamburger Cove, a popular fishing spot. Several deer trails and shortcuts come in from the left; stick to the gently rolling path beside the lake. It can be quite hot here in summer.

The next secluded inlet is aptly called Hidden Cove. A path comes in from the left and, ten feet later, Hidden Cove Trail sets off uphill. About a mile in, at Redwood Cove, Bon Tempe Trail is routed onto Sky Oaks Road at a marked crosswalk. Go right. Across the pavement here is an entry to Madrone Trail and to Sky Oaks-Lagunitas Trail. In less than a hundred yards, at the bend, is the splendid redwood that gives the cove its name. Beside it is a wheelchair-accessible outhouse. In the cove is a ramp that offers a place to fish for those in wheelchairs. Soon after, the Trail drops off the road back to the lake shore.

Paths that parallel Sky Oaks Road offer shortcuts. Veer right, towards the shore, to circle lovely, wooded Pine Point. This section is sometimes called Pine Point Trail. The Trail approaches the tip of this charming peninsula. Introduced pines provide shade for picnickers and for the fishermen who often line the shore. The area presents a pastoral tranquility.

The Trail runs into a junction of dirt roads at the lake's southeast tip. Continue right, around the lake. You immediately pass an important array of valves. They regulate the flow of water from Bon Tempe to the nearby treatment plant. In summer, cooler water from the bottom of the lake is drawn. In winter, when the bottom of the lake is clouded by sediment raised from the overflow of Lake Lagunitas, the clearer water from the top of the lake is released.

The now broad Trail then meets the Lake Lagunitas parking lot. Nearby are water fountains, a lovely picnic area, outhouses, and a phone. Cross the bridge over Lagunitas Creek. The Shadyside of Bon Tempe Trail continues around the lake to the right, up a short rise.

After hugging the shore of an inlet at the lake's southeast corner, Shadyside emerges into an open area. Beyond a small stream is the unmarked bottom of Lower Berry Trail, rising on the left to Rock Spring-Lagunitas F.R. You re-enter the forest and reach the first of

Shadyside's three bridges. On the far side of the bridge, the unmarked Stocking Trail climbs steeply to the left toward Rocky Ridge F.R.

The next mile is very gently rolling, and peaceful. Horses sometimes cause short muddy patches in winter. There are lovely views out over the lake through the trees. Around 1/2 mile past the third bridge, the Trail descends a few steps onto Bon Tempe Dam. Casey Cutoff Trail, to Rocky Ridge, rises uphill to the left before the last step. Alpine-Bon Tempe Pump F.R., on the left past the outhouse, leads to the starts of both Rocky Ridge F.R. and Kent Trail.

Cross the dam to complete the loop. To the left is the eastern tip of long, thin, Alpine Lake. To the right is one of the most beautiful sights in the Bay Area; Mt. Tamalpais reflected in the waters of Bon Tempe Lake.

Bon Tempe is an Americanized version of the Swiss-Italian surname Bautunpi. Two brothers, Guiseppi and Pasquale Bautunpi, leased 1,180 acres here in 1868 to run a dairy ranch. In 1874, they had 88 cows on the ranch and produced 115 pounds of butter a day. The main ranch buildings, just downstream of Bon Tempe Dam, were removed in 1918 before Alpine Lake was filled.

Bon Tempe Lake was formed in 1949 upon completion of the dam on Lagunitas Creek. It has a capacity of 1.3 billion gallons, ten times larger than Lake Lagunitas upstream but significantly smaller than Alpine and Kent lakes downstream. The loop Trail was built, largely by the Tamalpais Trail Riders, just after the lake was filled.

BRIDLE PATH FIRE ROAD

From Lake Lagunitas parking area to Lake Lagunitas / .3 miles
Terrain: Woodland / MMWD
Elevation: 730' to 840' to 790' / very steep
Intersecting Trails: Pilot Knob (.2m)
Directions: Lake Lagunitas parking area

Two fire roads rise from near the outhouses at the Lake Lagunitas parking lot. The one to the right is the direct pedestrian route to Lake Lagunitas. The one to the left, used by MMWD vehicles and equestrians heading to the lake's east shore, is Bridle Path Fire Road. It also offers access to Pilot Knob Trail.

The Fire Road sets off steeply uphill. A sign, "bridle path," gives the broad road its unofficial name. Another fire road immediately branches to the right. It leads to the MMWD lakekeeper's private residence, and is not open to the public.

At the summit of the Fire Road, Pilot Knob Trail, marked by an old sign, sets off to the left. It leads to the famous large madrone tree, the summit of Pilot Knob, and Lakeview Fire Road. Bridle Path F.R. then drops to the shore of Lake Lagunitas.

The Fire Road was built over the lower part of Pilot Knob Trail so that MMWD vehicles would not have to go directly past the lakekeeper's house.

BULLFROG FIRE ROAD

From Sky Oaks Road to western tip of Alpine Lake / .8 miles
Terrain: Meadow with boggy sections; part riparian / MMWD
Elevation: Around 680' / almost level
Intersecting Trails: None
Directions: Sky Oaks Road, 100 yards past toll booth

Bullfrog Fire Road is a level alternative to Sky Oaks Road in going from the Ranger Station to Alpine and Bon Tempe lakes. Bullfrog, however, can be quite muddy in its first half in winter; passable, but messy.

Bullfrog begins at the parking turnout on the right 100 yards past the Sky Oaks toll booth. Just beyond the entrance gate is a fork. The option right (not described) heads into the private Meadow Club golf course; Bullfrog goes left. Paths branch left off Bullfrog to the top of the tree-lined ridge south. At 1/3 mile, a path branches right, rejoining the route to the Meadow Club.

In winter, the area is a virtual bog, ideal for frogs. Bullfrogs (*Rana catesbeiana*) were introduced west of the Rockies but are now widespread. This largest of western frogs, up to 8 inches, breeds in early spring. Males are territorial. Females select their mates, then lay as many as 20,000 eggs.

The Fire Road leaves the meadow near a service road, which veers right onto the golf course. Bullfrog swings south. A short rise brings the Fire Road to an old quarry site. From here were taken the rocks used to build Bon Tempe Dam. Across from the quarry is the driest, but still not necessarily easy, crossing of the northeast inlet of Alpine Lake. Take it to reach the Liberty Gulch and Azalea Hill trails.

Bullfrog Road ends at a gate. The eastern tip of Alpine Lake is to the right. A flock of domestic geese often congregates here. The dirt road beyond, which is open to autos and is part of the old San Rafael-Bolinas stage route, forks just uphill. The right branch leads to Bon Tempe Dam, the left up to Sky Oaks Road.

CASEY CUTOFF TRAIL

From Bon Tempe Dam to Rocky Ridge Fire Road / .5 miles
Terrain: Oak woodland; unimproved / MMWD
Elevation: From 730' to 1,200' / extremely steep
Intersecting Trails: None
Directions: Bon Tempe Dam parking lot - cross dam

Casey Cutoff Trail "cuts off" around .3 miles of Rocky Ridge Fire Road in climbing from, or descending to, Bon Tempe Dam. The drawback is a trip even steeper than the fire road, with at least one section that some may find unacceptably precipitous going downhill.

At the far end of Bon Tempe Dam from the parking area, Alpine-Bon Tempe Pump F.R. branches right, Bon Tempe (Shadyside) Trail goes left, and the unsigned Casey Cutoff Trail rises between them. The first yards right of the steps are a bit confusing, with a few forks. Follow any of them up and the main Trail quickly becomes evident.

The Trail passes into a short clearing, going over serpentine rock. Then comes the steepest section, lasting almost 100 yards. Use particular care if you're descending. There is a second tough haul soon after, amidst tanbark oaks. Near the top, views open behind.

There is an MMWD sign on the Trail around 15 yards before it meets Rocky Ridge F.R. It is of some help when looking for the otherwise unmarked Cutoff when descending Rocky Ridge. At the junction, it is .8 miles downhill right to the dam and .6 miles uphill left to Stocking Trail.

Casey May is presently the chief ranger for the Marin Municipal Water District. The Trail was named for him when MMWD workers grew tired of talking about "that trail with no name from Bon Tempe Dam."

COLIER TRAIL

From Lake Lagunitas to International Trail / 1.5 miles
Terrain: Riparian; deep woodland; rocky / MMWD
Elevation: 790' to 2,280' / extremely steep
Intersecting Trails: Northside (1.1m), Lower Northside (1.1m)
Directions: Lagunitas Dam - Lake Lagunitas F.R. to second bridge

Colier (or Colier Spring) Trail follows the middle fork of Lagunitas Creek up from Lake Lagunitas to Colier Spring, and continues to just below the saddle between West and Middle peaks. For riparian, woodland beauty, it rivals the more famous Cataract Trail, but is even steeper. Indeed, its middle part is as steep as any Trail on the Mountain. Those prepared to tackle it will be well rewarded.

The Trail rises at a signpost beside the middle of the three bridges around Lake Lagunitas. It starts gently enough beside the right bank of the Middle Fork of Lagunitas Creek, which is flowing unfettered for the last time in its long journey to Tomales Bay. Below, the creek is dammed to form Lake Lagunitas, and then Bon Tempe, Alpine, and Kent lakes.

Colier crosses the creek three times in the first .3 miles. None of the crossings are marked or have bridges, so expect to do some rock hopping after a winter rain. Colier then becomes extremely steep. It climbs the divide between two branches of the Middle Fork, and then follows the western branch. Because the Trail is infrequently cleared and used, it is often lined with fallen limbs. The steepness forces rest stops. Enjoy the serenity of one of the most peaceful parts of Marin. Ramrod straight redwoods mix with madrones and tanbark oaks.

There is some relief in the uphill after around .9 miles. Then, at 1.1 miles, the Trail meets Colier Spring at a five-way intersection. Huge redwoods tower above the site. The spring, once known as Butterfly Spring, has long been a favorite resting spot among veteran Mt. Tam visitors. Cool, refreshing water used to be directed out of the pipe, but storms in the early 1980's have shifted the spring and cut the flow. A rough-hewn bench, beside a huckleberry bush, offers a place to sit. Northside Trail comes in from the left. It leaves to the right, now split as Northside (or Upper Northside) and Lower Northside. Colier Trail continues uphill.

The Trail is above the headwaters of the Middle Fork. A shortcut path branches right in .1 mile; continue uphill to the left. An old TCC marker pointing the way to West Point is fastened to a tree. Colier ends at International Trail. Go left 100 yards to the start of International on

Ridgecrest Boulevard to enjoy one of the best views on Mt. Tamalpais. Or, if you don't want the solitude broken, take International right and downhill back to Upper Northside.

Louise Teather, in her book "Place Names of Marin," describes the man behind the Trail's and spring's name: "John Munro Colier (or Collier) was a Scot, described as a lovable and wealthy eccentric who sometimes pretended to be a tramp and went about asking for handouts. He hiked Mt. Tamalpais and worked on the trails for many years, and when he died in 1916 a marker was placed [at his favorite view site on Rock Spring Trail] in his memory." Colier was a vice-president of the Cross Country Club, and a charter member of the TCC. Harold Atkinson, in his unpublished "History of the Tamalpais Conservation Club," said, "(Colier) was the original conservationist. . .He knew every shady nook and spot, every water course, every pool on Tamalpais." Besides this Trail, Colier is credited with building Eastwood Trail. Colier, a bachelor, left a sizable bequest to Children's Hospital in San Francisco.

The Trail was rerouted in the mid-1960's, which accounts for several of the faint alternate routes that appear. The section above Colier Spring was a later addition to the original route.

CONCRETE PIPELINE FIRE ROAD

From Fairfax-Bolinas Road at junction with Sky Oaks Road to Fish Gulch Trail / 2.8 miles
Terrain: Light woodland / MMWD
Elevation: Around 500' / almost level
Intersecting Trails: Taylor (.6m), Canyon (.7m), Deer Park F.R. (1.3m), connector fire road to Bald Hill Trail (1.3m), Shaver Grade (1.3m-1.4m), Elliott (1.3m), Logging (1.7m), Madrone (2.5)
Directions: Same as Sky Oaks to the junction of Sky Oaks and Fairfax-Bolinas roads; limited roadside parking

Concrete Pipeline Fire Road is second only to Southern Marin Line F.R. as the longest near level stretch on Mt. Tamalpais. It would be the longest if its 1.3 mile continuation north of Fairfax-Bolinas Road (so just outside this book's boundary) to Happersberger Point is considered. The Pipeline is also popular because there is free parking at its trailhead; driving up Sky Oaks Road requires paying a fee. And Concrete Pipeline has an excellent variety of wildflowers due to its varying habitats and the vigilance of passersby who pull out the invasive brooms.

The Fire Road sets off from a gate opposite #700 Bolinas Road, a few yards below Sky Oaks Road and the "Lake Lagunitas" sign. The current trailhead sign is in error; it is 1.3, not 1.9, miles to Five Corners. The opening yards are downhill to a pair of green Water District pump stations, called the Jory Gatehouse for the former Jory ranch here. Then the Fire Road levels.

Concrete Pipeline does indeed follow a pair of water pipelines, visible particularly at the turns. They are graded downhill at a uniform one foot per thousand feet, though the Fire Road itself has some undulations. Some traffic can be heard on Sky Oaks Road above, but that soon disappears and the area is lovely and peaceful. There are nice views through the trees. The first intersection, on the right, is with Taylor Trail, which goes up to the ranger headquarters on Sky Oaks Road. There's a dip and then a rise around a sweeping bend. This area is particularly rich in wildflowers during spring.

The Fire Road rises as it approaches the key junction of Five Corners (which see). The pipeline itself goes under Five Corners through what is called the Porteous Tunnel; the area was once part of the Porteous Ranch. At Five Corners, Shaver Grade and Concrete Pipeline briefly combine as they descend to the right. At the next junction, .1 mile below, Shaver Grade splits off downhill to the left.

It is just under one mile on Concrete Pipeline from this junction to the Madrone Trail intersection, which makes it popular with runners doing timed workouts. A sign here warns bicyclists that there is no outlet at the far end of the Fire Road. There are some occasionally muddy patches just ahead. At the first big horseshoe curve, unsigned Logging Trail crosses. The first junction is to the left and down; the second, 20 yards later, is right and up. Both halves later meet Shaver Grade.

The Fire Road passes two MMWD buildings, the Phoenix gate house and pump station. Between them, Madrone Trail rises uphill on the right, heading to Bon Tempe Lake. Concrete Pipeline then drops to, and ends at, its junction with Fish Gulch Trail, which comes in from the left. The uphill continuation, part of the original Fish Grade, is considered as Fish Gulch Trail.

Concrete Pipeline Fire Road was built in 1918 as part of the Alpine Dam project. The adjacent pipeline, which originally was concrete, takes water from Alpine Lake through the Pine Mountain Tunnel (which ends at Happersberger Point) then on to the main distribution network. A second, parallel steel pipeline was added in 1926.

CROSS COUNTRY BOYS TRAIL

From Upper Berry Trail to High Marsh Trail at High Marsh / 1.1 mile
Terrain: Heavily wooded, parts chaparral; parts overgrown / MMWD
Elevation: From 1,760' to 1,520' / upper part gradual, lower half very steep
Intersecting Trails: Lagoon F.R. (.1m), connector to Upper Berry (.2m), Azalea Meadow (twice at .4m), Kent (.7m)
Directions: Lake Lagunitas parking area - Rock Spring-Lagunitas F.R. - first junction with Upper Berry Trail

Cross Country Boys is one of the trickiest Trails on the Mountain to follow. There are no signs at its remote start or end, or at its five intersections. It runs largely in deep woods, without obvious landmarks. And several popular maps have shown it, and its intersections, inaccurately.

Across Rock Spring-Lagunitas F.R. from the bottom of Rocky Ridge Fire Trail, the unsigned Upper Berry Trail heads off into woodland. In .1 mile, a few yards above a rivulet, Upper Berry forks. The branch to the right is the start of Cross Country Boys Trail. In less than 100 yards, Cross Country meets and crosses, at an MMWD "no horses" sign, Lagoon Fire Road.

Cross Country Boys heads into deep forest. In another .1 mile, it hits a three-way intersection. Left is a 50 yard connector back to Upper Berry Trail. Veer right. A couple of hundred yards beyond, Cross Country meets Azalea Meadow. In May and June, fragrance from the blossoming azaleas pervades this special area.

Continue around the meadow to another three-way intersection. Right is Azalea Meadow Trail, rising from Kent Trail. Left, Cross Country Boys and Azalea Meadow trails are combined for 15 yards to yet another three-pronged intersection. Here Azalea Meadow Trail splits uphill left to Rifle Camp while Cross Country Boys continues to the right.

At .7 miles, Cross Country meets Kent Trail at a four-way junction by the forest's edge. This is near the site of the the old Cross Country Boys Club Camp, remnants of which are still to be found. Kent goes left up to Potrero Camp and right down to High Marsh Trail.

The steeper, more rugged continuation of Cross Country Boys Trail is a later addition. It goes straight, immediately into the chaparral. Rattlesnakes have been known to nest here, below the Kent junction. Shrubs overgrow the Trail; some ducking is required. Be careful not to brush the sharp-pointed chaparral pea. Outstanding views open. A splendid isolated, multi-trunked oak tree is passed. The Trail keeps descending, sometimes very steeply. Chinquapin trees, then madrones, become more common. A path branches left. Just before the Trail's end is an azalea.

Cross Country Boys Trail meets High Marsh Trail directly across from High Marsh. The marsh is gradually receding, becoming a meadow in the natural order of succession. Regular observers note how much smaller the marsh is now than years ago. High Marsh Trail goes left to Cataract Trail, and right some 200 yards to Kent Trail.

The Cross Country Boys Club was formed in 1891 as an offshoot for "fast hiking men" of the Sightseers Club, itself founded three years earlier. Only a handful of women, one being Alice Eastwood, were admitted as associate members. Lincoln Fairley reprints ("Mount Tamalpais, A History," page 68) a delightful account of a splinter group of the club, called the "Hill Tribe," that was written in 1905: "(They) prowled these hills year after year. . .over the endless trails, light of pack and light of heart. . .Their sole object seemed to be the hills, and for wide views from them, and the silent places."

EAST PEAK FIRE TRAIL

From Lakeview Fire Road to Eldridge Grade / 1.2 miles
Terrain: Chaparral, overgrown with shrubs; dangerous loose rock; views; unimproved / MMWD
Elevation: From 830' to 2,080' / extremely steep
Intersecting Trails: Connector to Eldridge Grade (.4m), Northside (1.1m)
Directions: Lake Lagunitas Dam - clockwise on Lake Lagunitas F.R. - Lakeview F.R., .2 miles

East Peak Fire Trail is one of the steepest trails on Mt. Tamalpais. Loose rock makes it very dangerous to descend; don't attempt it unless you're a "mountain goat" type. The Trail's steepness, loose rocks, overgrown shrubs, and the lack of signs puts it at the edge of this book's minimum standards. The Water District considers the Trail as closed, and no longer maintains it.

The lower end of East Peak Fire Trail is hard to spot. Look for it around 300 yards up Lakeview Fire Road from Lake Lagunitas. Just past a 15 foot tall oak tree, East Peak Fire Trail sets off to the right. It passes through the meadow, crosses a creek bed, then becomes easier to follow.

The Trail climbs steeply. The three-needled pine trees are Coulters. Look on the ground for their massive cones, the heaviest pine cones in the world, weighing up to five pounds. Chaparral replaces the grassland. The Trail has several forks; just keep going up toward the crest of the hill. There are stunning Mt. Tamalpais views, as there are throughout the Trail. Enjoy the brief, and only, downhill. At the bottom, a short connector goes left, meeting Eldridge Grade at a post. East Peak Fire Trail goes straight ahead, and straight up.

The Trail gains 600 feet in elevation over the next precipitous half-mile as it climbs the ridge line toward East Peak. To the right is the deep canyon of the East Fork of Lagunitas Creek. Across the canyon, the almost equally steep Lagunitas Fire Trail tops the next ridge. Shrubs and stunted trees intrude onto the Trail. Common are chinquapin, chaparral pea, yerba santa, ceanothus, madrone, and manzanita.

At elevation 2,000 feet, the Fire Trail meets Northside Trail at the splendid view site called Inspiration Point. Just to the left is Eldridge Grade. To the right, Northside goes to Colier Spring and Rifle Camp.

East Peak Fire Trail is less overgrown in its remaining climb, but barely less steep. Near its upper end is a huge rock whose flat top offers a perfect place to rest and enjoy one of the Mountain's best vista points. Virtually all of Marin north of Tamalpais is visible. The Trail ends a few more yards up when it meets Eldridge Grade. The Grade, here making a bend, goes a half-mile uphill to Ridgecrest Boulevard and three miles downhill back to Lakeview F.R. for a loop option.

The Trail was originally a fire break, cut by the Civilian Conservation Corps in the early 1930's to a width of 200 feet. There were four such fire trails (Indian, Lagunitas, and Rocky Ridge were the others) on Water District lands on the north side of Tam.

FILTER PLANT ROAD

From Fish Grade to Eldridge Grade / 1.0 mile
Terrain: Wooded, mostly with redwoods; western half paved / MMWD
Elevation: From 620' to 520' / west part almost level, east part gradual
Intersecting Trails: None
Directions: Sky Oaks Road - Fish Grade, .1 mile

Though paved most of its exactly one mile length, Filter Plant Road is used in many loops in the lakes area. To reach Filter Plant Road's western end, follow Sky Oaks Road to the row of eucalyptus trees. To the left at this bend is the paved upper portion of Fish Grade (and the starts of the Pumpkin Ridge and Netting trails). Follow Fish Grade down 1/6 mile past the Bon Tempe Headworks. Asphalt-topped Filter Plant Road splits off to the right while Fish Grade, now dirt, continues downhill. The Road is basically level. It passes in and out of stands of redwoods. Water District employees drive on the Road, so be alert.

In .6 miles the route meets the filter plant, properly called the Bon Tempe Water Treatment Plant. The structures, built in 1959, are painted green, to minimize their visual impact. Much of southern Marin's drinking water, some 20 million gallons a day from Bon Tempe Lake, flows through the plant. Chemicals, particularly aluminum sulfate, are introduced here to gather foreign matter into "floc" particles. The water is slowly mixed, building up the size of the "floc" particles until they settle out. The water is then passed through filter beds of graduated gravel, sand, and anthracite coal to remove further impurities. Lime, to reduce corrosion, and chlorine, to kill bacteria, are also added to the water before it moves along. The District's one other treatment plant, built in 1962 and somewhat larger, is in the San Geronimo Valley.

Veer left around the huge tank to continue. The waste water recovery pond is to the left. There is a unique perspective down to Phoenix Lake. A steep service road heads uphill as the pavement gives way to dirt. A pleasant, gradual, tree lined descent brings the Road to its end at Eldridge Grade. To the right, the Grade rises to the top of Tam, to the left it drops to Phoenix Junction.

The Erickson and MMWD maps, and Water District personnel, call this Road the Southern Marin Line, which indeed it is a part. But since there is a gap in the Line Road over Bill Williams Gulch to the east, I, like Olmsted, reserve the designation Southern Marin Line F.R. only for the section between Kentfield's Crown Road and Larkspur's Sunrise Lane. Many users call it Filter, or Treatment, Plant Road.

HIDDEN COVE TRAIL

From old San Rafael-Bolinas Road to Bon Tempe Lake at Hidden Cove / .3 miles
Terrain: Grassland; horses permitted / MMWD
Elevation: From 750' to 840' to 720' / steep
Intersecting Trails: None
Directions: Sky Oaks Road - connector fire road to Bon Tempe, 50 yards

Almost a half-mile in on Sky Oaks Road from the toll booth, an unpaved road, the vehicle access to Bon Tempe Dam, branches right.

It is part of the old San Rafael-Bolinas stage road. Follow it a few yards and, as it begins to drop, look left to spot a wood post and an opening. Hidden Cove Trail sets off straight ahead, and a path (called Dam Trail on Erickson but not separately described in this book) drops to the right, parallel to the road.

Within a few yards, Hidden Cove Trail forks. The path to the left climbs to the top of a lovely hill. Veer right. Continue uphill through the grassland. Poppies and lupine contribute to spring color. Coyote bush is the dominant shrub. The Trail crests at a saddle. Paths lead up the hills to the left (Cross Bar Knoll) and right. Here, and on the whole descent, are splendid views of the Mountain across Bon Tempe Lake.

The trees encountered on the way down are Coulter pines. They were introduced in the lakes area during a planting project in the 1930's. Coulters bear the heaviest cones of any pine in the world, weighing up to five pounds, and the specimens here certainly live up to the reputation. A bit lower are oaks. The Trail ends when it hits Bon Tempe (Sunnyside) Trail at Bon Tempe's shore. The remote, quiet inlet is aptly called Hidden Cove. It is a bit under a half-mile to the right to Bon Tempe Dam.

KENT TRAIL

From Alpine Lake to Potrero Camp / 3.9 miles
Terrain: Deep woods, some chaparral; lower part riparian / MMWD
Elevation: From 650' to 1,980' / steep, parts very steep
Intersecting Trails: Helen Markt (1.5m), Willow Meadow (2.3m, 2.8m), Stocking (2.3m), connector to Serpentine Point (2.7m), High Marsh (2.9m), Azalea Meadow (2.9m), Cross Country Boys (3.5m).
Directions: Bon Tempe Dam - Alpine-Bon Tempe Pump F.R.

Few, if any, Mt. Tamalpais trails offer a better wilderness experience than Kent Trail. Throughout its length, from its early part beside Alpine Lake, to its middle section amidst one of the Mountain's deepest forests, through its upper reaches with sweeping northern vistas, Kent Trail offers solitude, variety, and beauty.

Kent Trail begins from the shore of Alpine Lake at the foot of the fire road down from Bon Tempe Dam. The pump station that lifts Alpine Lake water to Bon Tempe is on the right and Kent Trail is to the left. An MMWD sign indicates that it is 4.2 miles to Potrero Meadow.

Within 50 yards on Kent, the first of several narrow paths come in from the left. None are maintained, so stay on Kent. The Trail arcs around several coves of Alpine Lake. Huge Douglas firs line the shore. The site of Kent Cabin, used by the Kent family for fishing retreats, now sits offshore under Alpine Lake. In winter, when the water level is high, sections of the now abandoned power lines across the lake are under water. When the water is low, what some call Cheda Island emerges just offshore.

The rolling Trail crosses several streams, some requiring a bit of rock hopping to cross in winter. Azaleas, delightfully fragrant in May and June, grow beside them. A promising looking path forks left, uphill. It soon deteriorates deep in the forest. The biggest stream crossing, of Van Wyck Creek, is at 1.1 mile. The varying height of the water level here has led to several different options for Kent being worn in around the cove.

Kent encounters a short, steep uphill, then resumes rolling gently. It crosses a couple more rivulets. Kent leaves the lake shore at a signed junction with Helen Markt Trail. Helen Markt continues near the shore, toward Cataract Trail, while Kent veers left, uphill. A small TCC sign is affixed to a Douglas fir 15 feet up Kent. A second entrance to Kent, which quickly meets the first, is 75 yards ahead on Helen Markt.

Kent, now climbing steeply, follows an old water pipeline, part of the former Swede George Line that was in service until 1956. This is one of the loveliest, quietest parts of the Mountain. No signs or sounds of civilization intrude within this forest. During the week you can pass a whole day here without seeing anyone. Huckleberry is abundant.

After .3 miles of uphill, you begin to hear the waters of the East Fork of Swede George Creek, then arrive directly beside the creek without crossing. A concrete rubble diversion dam on the East Fork was built in 1888 and a 6" steel pipeline laid to Fish Grade. Swede George water was an important addition to the County supply, particularly before Alpine dam was built in 1919. Swede George himself, who died in 1875, was a woodcutter in the area.

Next up, on the right, is the standing water of Foul Pool. A large fallen madrone crosses the Trail here. Then the Trail enters a magnificent redwood grove. The older giants still show black scars from the 1945 fire. Younger redwoods circle the fallen "mother" trees from which they sprouted. Spend some time here; let the solitude work its wonders.

After just under .9 miles of climbing from Alpine Lake, Kent Trail meets Stocking Trail at an intersection presently marked only by logs on the ground. Stocking goes left, passing Hidden Lake in around 100 yards. Kent continues uphill, rising steeply above the redwoods. Five yards below the

Kent-Stocking intersection is the unmarked Willow Meadow Trail. Its start and first yards, through tanbark oak, are hard to see. Willow Meadow Trail will meet Kent again, higher.

The climbing remains steep. Later, wood steps help. In .4 miles from Stocking, just after leaving the tree canopy, a seeming path branches left, quickly to deadend. One hundred yards later, at the rock crest, is an important fork. To the left is a short connector to the vista point of Serpentine Knoll and to routes back to Bon Tempe and Lagunitas lakes. Kent veers right. After a descent, Kent again meets, and crosses, Willow Meadow Trail. To the left is Willow Meadow itself.

Fifteen yards later, Kent Trail crosses the East Fork of Swede George Creek, which flows all year here, over a bridge. One hundred yards later is a four-way intersection. To the left is Azalea Meadow Trail. Kent continues straight. To the right is High Marsh Trail, with High Marsh itself .1 mile away.

After another half-mile of steep uphill, Kent crosses Cross Country Boys Trail. To the right, downhill into the chaparral, Cross Country Boys drops to High Marsh; to the left it goes to Azalea Meadow. Kent enters chaparral. There are splendid views north and west, including of the Point Reyes peninsula. After some stone steps, Kent Trail crests at just over 2,000 feet in elevation. The Trail drops a bit as it returns to woodland.

Just beyond, Kent ends at Potrero Camp at the edge of lower Potrero Meadow. Tables, outhouses, azalea blossoms, the meadow, and choice of sun or shade make this a favorite resting spot. The larger, upper Potrero Meadow is 400 yards to the left along the path. The 100-yard connector fire road up from the camp leads to Laurel Dell F.R.

No family name is more closely associated with Mt. Tamalpais than Kent. With wealth derived from their Chicago packing company, Albert Kent, the family scion who died in 1901, and his son William amassed huge land holdings. There was a time when it was possible to walk from the present Kentfield to the ocean at Stinson Beach entirely on their property. William Kent, an independent United States Congressman from 1910-1916 who helped author the legislation to create the National Park Service, made many land donations to the public. On Tamalpais, these included Muir Woods National Monument, much of Mt. Tamalpais State Park (including Steep Ravine the day before his death in 1928), and the Mountain Theater site. The family remains a benefactor to the County. William's son Thomas Kent, for whom Kent Lake was named, was on the MMWD Board of Directors for 39 years until his death in 1959. In 1988 the family helped save a historic building adjacent to the Adaline Kent School (formerly Kent property), in Kentfield, from the wrecker's ball.

The often realigned Kent Trail appears on the 1898 Sanborn map.

LAGOON EXTENSION TRAIL

From Lagoon Fire Road to Rocky Ridge Fire Road | .4 miles
Terrain: *Wooded; short part in chaparral and rocky | MMWD*
Elevation: *From 1,500' to 1,320' | steep*
Intersecting Trails: *None*
Directions: *Lake Lagunitas parking area - Rock Spring-Lagunitas F.R. - Lagoon F.R. to lower end*

No trail on Mt. Tamalpais evokes more confusion over its name than this one. Today's Stocking Trail, which does pass Hidden Lake, was called Swede George Fire Trail on the 1934 Water District map, and Hidden Lake Trail on the W.P.A.-Federal Writer's Project map of three years later. After World War II, that trail was improved to accomodate horses, and the trail workers renamed it Stocking Trail, to honor Clayton Stocking. Then, through a series of errors, the name Hidden Lake Trail became attached to a then unnamed parallel trail to the south (the one described in this section), which doesn't pass Hidden Lake. This illogical name, which now causes confusion among visitors to the area, has come to be widely accepted and appears on the Olmsted, TCC, and Charette maps. Erickson retains a better name, Lagoon Extension Trail, since the Trail sets off where Lagoon Fire Road deadends. To make matters even worse, there is a second "Lagoon Extension-Hidden Lake" trail, illegally built and not on any map, that runs roughly parallel to, and never more than 100 feet below, the "main" one. Both are unsigned. Lagoon Extension Trail is described downhill because its lower end is presently very hard to spot.

Lagoon Fire Road goes up, over, then down behind Serpentine Knoll when taken from Rock Spring-Lagunitas F.R. Then, after some 250 yards of downhill, it narrows to become Lagoon Extension Trail. A few yards before the narrowing, two paths branch left. The first is a now overgrown route to Kent Trail. The second is the parallel, alternative Lagoon Extension Trail. It immediately bends right, enters deep woodland, crosses a creek by a slide, then rejoins the upper Trail.

The upper, "true" Trail also goes directly into forest. It passes through an enchanting stand of dense, fire scarred, slender redwood trees. The next section is lined with tall manzanita shrubs, which form a canopy over the Trail. Just beyond, look for remnants of an old tree house, occasionally occupied not many years ago. The "alternative" Lagoon Extension Trail comes in from the left.

The Trail continues dropping. It then meets, and crosses, a fork of Van Wyck Creek. Fifteen yards above the crossing is a fork; veer left. Five yards farther is another fork; veer right. The route is now indistinct. Work your way over the rocks and chaparral. Lagoon Extension Trail hits Rocky Ridge F.R. at a small turnout presently only marked by a couple of rocks. Three young Douglas-firs, 10' tall at the start of 1990, stand by the junction. The west end of No Name Trail is 100 yards to the left. Just beyond it, Stocking Trail (the original Hidden Lake Trail, which passes Hidden Lake) crosses Rocky Ridge. Got it?

LAGOON FIRE ROAD

From Rock Spring-Lagunitas Fire Road to Lagoon Extension Trail / .8 miles
Terrain: Mostly chaparral; views / MMWD
Elevation: From 2,040' to 1,500' / very steep
Intersecting Trails: Upper Berry (.1m), Cross Country Boys (.1m), connector to Kent Trail (.6m)
Directions: Lake Lagunitas parking area - Rock Spring-Lagunitas F.R., 1.9 miles

Lagoon Fire Road was originally one of several broad fire trails cut across Water District lands in the early 1930's. It ended up playing a key role as a supply route in the battle against the huge fire of 1945. Because Lagoon Fire Road's upper end is easier to locate, and is barely farther from a trailhead than the lower end, the trip will be described downhill.

Lagoon Fire Road starts, well-signed, from Rock Spring-Lagunitas F.R. nearly two miles up from the Lake Lagunitas parking area. Its upper reaches are wooded. Just 100 yards down, Upper Berry Trail crosses. Both left, uphill, and right, downhill, lead back to Rock Spring-Lagunitas F.R. In another 60 yards, a second trail, Cross Country Boys, crosses. To the left is Azalea Meadow; to the right, a union with Upper Berry.

The Fire Road leaves the woods for open views above the chaparral. Lagoon's surface is distinctive; iron-rich red clays mingle with the blue-green serpentine rocks. The prominent large outcropping of Serpentine Knoll (or Point), the Fire Road's destination, is plainly visible.

Before reaching it, to the left, have been several pig traps, including perhaps the largest on the Mountain. Traps are being removed at press-time, as the feral pig eradication program seems to have succeeded.

Lagoon hits Serpentine Knoll. The views are outstanding in all directions. At the crest, a short but important connector to Kent Trail departs left. The Fire Road continues down over the crest another 250 yards. It ends when it narrows to trail size. The continuation to Rocky Ridge F.R. is Lagoon Extension Trail. A few yards before, two other unmarked options branch off to the left. The first is a path to Kent Trail. The second is a lower, parallel branch of Lagoon Extension Trail.

There is some debate over which "lagoon" is referred to in the Fire Road's name. Some think it is Hidden Lake, as there once were plans to extend the Fire Road to the lake. Others feel it refers to the seasonally wet area by the Fire Road just south of Cross Country Boys Trail.

LAGUNITAS FIRE TRAIL

From Lake Lagunitas to Middle Peak Fire Road | 1.4 miles
Terrain: Mixed chaparral and light forest; overgrown; parts with loose rocks; views; unimproved | MMWD
Elevation: From 800' to 2,250' | extremely steep
Intersecting Trails: Northside (1.2m)
Directions: Lagunitas Dam - Lake Lagunitas F.R., either direction, .8 miles

Lagunitas Fire Trail is unsigned, unmaintained, extremely steep, and dangerous to take downhill for the loose rock. Yet it does appear on most maps, though not the MMWD's; they abandoned the Trail in 1985. It offers a direct route from Lake Lagunitas to the Mt. Tamalpais summit area, with splendid vistas along the way.

The bottom entrance to the Trail is easy to miss. It lies roughly equidistant from the dam whether circling Lake Lagunitas clockwise or counterclockwise. Clockwise, look for the Trail at the end of the straightaway after crossing the first of the three bridges. There are two entrances, 20 yards apart, at the bend. Counterclockwise, cross two bridges and look right.

The Trail rises steeply through a mostly madrone woodland. Lake Lagunitas is visible through the trees. You can also glimpse Pilot Knob across the water. Here Pilot Knob towers above. As you climb you see it gradually decreasing in importance, until, near the top of the Trail, it appears only as a "bump" in the broad panorama. Paths lead back to the lake left and right, but the Trail is reasonably clear.

There are occasional level spots, even short downhills, but the going is definitely up. Irises are abundant in spring. The Trail emerges from the tree canopy into chaparral. The shrubs manzanita, chamise, chinquapin, chaparral pea, and yerba santa prevail most all the rest of the way. They grow close to the unmaintained Trail; don't go sleeveless or you may get cut scraping the pea or manzanita. The views expand as the Trail climbs the long ridge.

After seemingly endless climbing, Lagunitas Fire Trail hits a band of loose rock below and beside a huge rock outcropping. Carefully clamber up the rock on a tiny path to enjoy a rest site with great views, and no chance of disturbance. Soon after the rock band, which is hard to ascend and dangerous to descend, the only intersecting trail, Northside, is crossed. Left leads to East Peak Fire Trail, a "sister" trail on the next ridge east, and to Eldridge Grade. To the right, Northside goes to Colier Spring and Rifle Camp.

Lagunitas Fire Trail is rather overgrown just above the intersection, but only briefly. A second loose rock band, and large rock, is passed. The Trail reenters woodland. A common tree here is California nutmeg, which is not related to the famous spice. Its 1-to-2 inch evergreen needle-leaves end in sharp points. The green fruits are also distinctive. Their thin fleshy covering, with a fragrant juice, peels away to reveal a hard seed case.

Some metal and wood fragments are visible to the right. They are remnants of a once rather substantial dwelling in these quiet, little visited woods. The site still carries its name, "Kisban Hermitage," for Ben Kisban, who had a camp here. He was a pharmacist who fled his native Hungary after the 1956 uprising there.

The Trail ends when it hits Middle Peak Fire Road. To the left is Ridgecrest Boulevard, near the top of both Old Railroad and Eldridge grades, while right leads to Lakeview Trail and the summit of Middle Peak.

This route up the ridge line is an old one. It was widened to a broad fire break, some 200 feet across, by the Civilian Conservation Corps in 1933-34. Advancing vegetation has narrowed it again.

LAKE LAGUNITAS FIRE ROAD

Around Lake Lagunitas | 1.6 miles
Terrain: *Riparian; tanbark oak-madrone woodland; heavily used | MMWD*
Elevation: *Around 800' | almost level*
Intersecting Trails: *Clockwise from east side of dam; Bridle Path F.R. (.1m), Lakeview F.R. (.5m), Lagunitas Fire (.8m), Colier (1.0m), Rock Spring-Lagunitas F.R. (1.4m)*
Directions: *Lagunitas Dam*

A fire road (trail width in a few spots) circles Lake Lagunitas. It was opened in 1879 as a scenic coach drive. Today the circuit provides one of the most delightful short walks the Mountain has to offer.

The easiest access to Lake Lagunitas is from the parking area at the end of Sky Oaks Road. Follow the 150-yard connector fire road that rises to the left of the picnic area. It meets the east end of Lagunitas Dam at a lovely view site; Mt. Tamalpais both rising above the lake and reflected in the water. The loop will be described clockwise from the dam. Bicyclists and equestrians can begin the loop by taking Bridle Path F.R. up from the parking lot.

Go left up a few stone steps. To the left is a private MMWD residence, the home of the lakekeeper. In 1877 the first telephone line in Marin County was laid to the lakekeeper's residence here. To the right are paths down to the lake's shore. In .1 mile, Bridle Path F.R. comes in on the left. It rises to the start of Pilot Knob Trail. The circuit continues, passing accesses to some lovely peninsulas jutting into the lake. There is an outhouse to the left. Above, the grassy face of Pilot Knob looms.

At .5 miles, Lakeview F.R. separates, going straight to Eldridge Grade. Lake Lagunitas F.R. veers right and crosses the East Fork of Lagunitas Creek over a bridge. It is the three forks, all of which are crossed on the loop, of this important creek that are impounded to form Lake Lagunitas. Bon Tempe, Alpine, and Kent lakes are also formed by dams lower on Lagunitas Creek's course.

The view across the lake here, with fishermen often lining the far shore, is idyllic. At the end of the straightaway are two entries to the extremely steep, unsigned Lagunitas Fire Trail. It ascends to Middle Peak. Just before the next bridge, over the Middle Fork, Colier Trail sets off on a precipitous climb to Colier Spring.

After the third bridge (across West Fork), the Fire Road passes a pump station sitting on a pier over the lake. Shortly past, Rock Spring-Lagunitas

Fire Road departs sharply left on its long uphill to Potrero Meadow and Ridgecrest Boulevard. Past the outhouse, Rock Spring-Lagunitas F.R. continues straight down to the parking lot. To complete the loop, cross the dam. A plaque on the near end acknowledges the role of the San Francisco Foundation (which then administered the Buck trust) in restoration work after the big 1982 storm. Check the logs in the water below the dam for western pond turtles sunning themselves. The distance around the lake has been accurately measured at 1.59 miles.

Lake Lagunitas ("lagunitas" means "little lakes" in Spanish) is the oldest and highest in elevation of the five man-made reservoirs on the north side of Mt. Tamalpais. The lake is in one of the wettest areas of Marin; over 90 inches of rain fell in the 1982-83 season. Its dam, completed in 1873, was constructed largely by Chinese laborers working for the fledgling Marin County Water Company, a predecessor to the MMWD. The founder of the company was William T. Coleman, a one time prominent San Francisco vigilante. Coleman owned a large San Rafael housing tract which received the lake's water. Water also went to San Quentin prison. It was Coleman who planted the eucalyptus trees that line the last stretch of paved road before the Lagunitas parking area.

In 1988, a program to make the lake, long a fishing oasis (Coleman released 20,000 trout into the lake as early as 1875), self-sustaining with trout began. The pump in the water near the dam oxygenates the water when temperatures rise in summer. There are remnants of the lake's old fish hatchery in the picnic area beside the spillway.

LAKEVIEW FIRE ROAD

From Lake Lagunitas Fire Road to Eldridge Grade / .8 miles
Terrain: Lightly wooded / MMWD
Elevation: From 800' to 980' / lower part almost level, upper part steep
Intersecting Trails: East Peak Fire (.2m), Pilot Knob (.5m)
Directions: Lagunitas Dam - Lake Lagunitas F.R. clockwise, .5 miles

To reach Lakeview Fire Road, follow Lagunitas F.R. clockwise from Lagunitas Dam. In a half-mile, at the junction at the easternmost edge of the lake, Lakeview Fire Road continues straight (east) while Lake Lagunitas F.R. veers right.

The almost treeless southern wall of Pilot Knob towers above on the left. A meadow opens on the right. At an oak tree, the barely discernible, unsigned East Peak Fire Trail sets off to the right. Lakeview then enters an area until recently dominated by Coulter pines. Coulters, which have the heaviest cones, weighing up to five pounds, of any pine, were originally planted here in the 1930's. They are native to California (the nearest natural stand is on Mt. Diablo), but not to Mt. Tamalpais. The MMWD began cutting the Coulters in 1987 to restore the area's native vegetation after the trees showed signs of disease. Several Coulters still stand here, and on nearby trails.

Lakeview bends right, rising steeply. Pilot Knob Trail, which skirts the hill's northern flank, departs left at a signed junction. The Fire Road enters madrone woodland. A path sets off to the left. Lakeview continues to climb until its end at Eldridge Grade. Left on Eldridge leads down to Phoenix Lake, right up to East Peak.

Lakeview Fire Road first appears as a fire trail on the 1925 Northwestern Pacific Railroad map. Trees, both introduced and naturally expanding, have blocked the "lake view" since. There is a completely separate Lakeview Trail on the north face of Middle Peak.

LIBERTY GULCH TRAIL

From northern shore of Alpine Lake to Fairfax-Bolinas Road / 1.3 miles
Terrain: Lightly wooded; parts muddy / MMWD
Elevation: From 645' to 940' / gradual
Intersecting Trails: None
Directions: Sky Oaks Road - Bullfrog F.R.

A stagecoach road from San Rafael to Bolinas was built, largely by Chinese laborers, in 1878. One section ran through the valley now covered by Alpine Lake. Around the turn of the century, when plans for Tamalpais Dam, which would have flooded that part of the road, were proceeding, a bypass was constructed. The bypass is today's Liberty Gulch Trail; slides and vegetation have narrowed it to trail-width in many places.

To reach Liberty Gulch Trail, take the first right turn off Sky Oaks Road after the ranger station. This dirt road, the auto access to Bon Tempe Dam, is the end of a shortcut, built in 1884 from Ross, of the original stage route. At the bottom of the downhill, the continuation of the old road is evident; getting there in winter and spring is another matter. The driest crossing of this northeastern arm of Alpine Lake will likely be to the right, off Bullfrog Fire Road. Retrace your steps back to Alpine's shore. The exact location of the start of Liberty Gulch Trail depends on the height of the lake, which varies by season. A path always remains above high water.

The concrete foundations for the never completed Tamalpais Dam are visible on both banks of Alpine, and in the lake bed when the water is low. Liberty Gulch Trail begins climbing when opposite the Alpine-Bon Tempe Pump Station across the lake. It passes under supports for the power lines, now abandoned, that cross the lake. The Trail rises gradually through woodland. It passes several seeps, which are sometimes quite muddy. At the seeps are horsetails, yellow seep-spring monkeyflowers (*Diplacus guttatus*), fragrant azaleas, and, in fall, hedge nettle (*Stachys pycnantha*).

The Trail veers above the arm of Alpine Lake that covers Liberty Gulch. Samuel Vincent Liberty and his wife operated a dairy ranch in the gulch from 1876, and, after the stage road was built, a roadhouse offering meals. The ranch house burned in 1885, was rebuilt, then abandoned in the 1890's. Later, the Lagunitas Rod and Gun Club had their headquarters there. The building site is now under water.

As the Trail rises into the open chaparral, you'll notice debris thoughtlessly tossed down from Fairfax-Bolinas Road above. The trail ends at a gully. The continuation to the paved road has been blocked by slides. Only a dangerous, narrow path traverses the hillside, meeting the road by a parking turnout at milepost 4.18. Fairfax-Bolinas Road then follows the original stage route toward Bolinas.

LOGGING TRAIL

From Shaver Grade to Hidden Meadow / .7 miles
Terrain: Oak woodland; riparian / MMWD
Elevation: From 700' to 350' / steep
Intersecting Trails: Concrete Pipeline F.R. (.4m), Shaver Grade (.6m)
Directions: Sky Oaks Road - Shaver Grade, .2 miles

Around .2 miles down Shaver Grade from Sky Oaks Road, two trails branch to the right by a MMWD sign. The upper one is Elliott Trail. The lower, on the left, is the start of Logging Trail.

Logging Trail begins in grassland. It passes between an oak and a madrone, then drops toward a wooded canyon. This is a pleasant, quiet, little-traveled area. Farther along, the stream canyon is lined with redwoods. In just under a half-mile, the Trail meets Concrete Pipeline F.R. at a bend. The unsigned Logging Trail continues across the Fire Road around 20 yards to the left, beyond the two prominent pipelines. It drops another 250 yards to once again meet Shaver Grade. This also unmarked junction is between a laurel and a madrone at a bend in the Grade.

Go 25 yards uphill (left) on Shaver to continue on Logging Trail. The Trail ends when it descends to Hidden Meadow Trail in the lovely grass clearing of Hidden Meadow.

Logging Trail actually was the first Shaver Grade, and some call it Old Shaver Grade. In the 1860's, lumber was brought down it from Isaac Shaver's sawmill operation near the present Alpine Dam. The wood was hauled to Corte Madera Creek at Ross Landing, by the junction of today's Sir Francis Drake Boulevard and College Avenue. There it was loaded onto boats bound for San Francisco.

LOWER BERRY TRAIL

From Bon Tempe Trail to Rock Spring-Lagunitas Fire Road / .4 miles
Terrain: Oak-madrone woodland, part grassland; horses permitted / MMWD
Elevation: From 730' to 980' / steep
Intersecting Trails: None
Directions: Lake Lagunitas parking lot - Bon Tempe (Shadyside) Trail, .3m

The historic and once popular Berry Trail was split apart by the construction of Rock Spring-Lagunitas Fire Road in the mid-1930's. The lower part, now called Lower Berry Trail, has been restored and signed while the top part, Upper Berry Trail (which see), is also maintained. The middle section, which largely ran to the west of Rock Spring-Lagunitas F.R., fell into disrepair after water pipelines were laid over it to the Air Force station atop West Peak. It is now heavily overgrown, so is not described.

Lower Berry rises from the southeast corner of Bon Tempe Lake, in the one open, grassy area on the Shadyside portion of the loop around the lake. Look for the Berry trailhead after the crossing of a rivulet and just before the re-entry into woods. The uphill is immediately very steep. Turn around to get some lovely perspectives of Bon Tempe.

The Trail enters a woodland with large madrones. Lower Berry climbs steadily in the shade. The Trail ends when it hits Rock Spring-Lagunitas Fire Road. The junction is marked by a new MMWD signpost. Barely noticeable and unsigned, No Name Trail, not on Erickson or Olmsted, heads right here, from the same side of the fire road. It goes to Rocky Ridge Fire Road.

Berry Trail, perhaps originally an Indian path, was said to have been rediscovered by Mountain veteran S. Lucien Berry around the turn of the century. Berry and his friend Emil Barth then worked on the Trail. Berry's ashes were scattered along the Trail by his widow, his son, and his father, accompanied by Alice Eastwood and John Forbes. Old Freese maps of the Trail carried the words "no berries" to forewarn those seeking edible berries.

MADRONE TRAIL

From Sky Oaks Road to Concrete Pipeline Fire Road / .9 miles
Terrain: *Madrone woodland; horses permitted / MMWD*
Elevation: *From 730' to 850' to 500' / steep*
Intersecting Trails: *Pumpkin Ridge (.2m)*
Directions: *Sky Oaks Road, .9 miles past Ranger Station*

Madrone Trail is aptly named. For almost its entire length it passes through a woodland dominated by madrones. Madrone is a characteristic tree on much of Tamalpais — John Thomas Howell pictures a madrone on the frontispiece of his "Marin Flora" — but here, north of Bon Tempe and Lagunitas lakes, they really hold forth. Willis Jepson, who compiled a definitive California flora in the early 1900's, said of madrone, "A tree than which none other in the western woods is more marked by sylvan beauty." Its most distinctive feature is its peeling bark, revealing the smooth, cool terra cotta-colored wood beneath. The leaves are thick and leathery, green above, grayer below. The trees bear orange-red fruits in fall.

Madrone Trail starts uphill opposite where Bon Tempe (Sunnyside) Trail joins Sky Oaks Road. The unsigned trailhead is at an equestrian crossing marked by white road bumps. A second entry is by the wheelchair-accessible outhouse at Redwood Cove. One hundred feet up, Madrone meets Sky Oaks-Lagunitas Trail. The two run together to the right for 60 yards. Veer left at the next fork. Just above, both Madrone access routes merge to continue, a bit indistinct, up the hillside.

At the top of Pumpkin Ridge, Pumpkin Ridge Trail crosses. Both left and right lead to Sky Oaks Road. Two Madrone Trail options, which join in twenty yards, continue on the other side of the ridge. Madrone Trail rolls, though it is generally downhill. The Trail is surrounded by twisted madrones. This is a peaceful area, abounding in deer. In another .4 miles there is a somewhat tricky fork. Veer left; the path straight ahead deteriorates.

There are a few yards of uphill, then a steady, moderately steep descent. Madrones remain constant companions. The Trail ends at Concrete Pipeline F.R., by a Madrone Trail sign. The two Water District buildings across the fire road are the Phoenix gate house and pump station. Shaver Grade is one mile to the left, Fish Gulch Trail .2 miles to the right.

NETTING TRAIL

From Sky Oaks Road to Pumpkin Ridge Trail / .3 miles
Terrain: Half grassland, half oak-madrone woodland / MMWD
Elevation: From 730' to 860' / steep
Intersecting Trails: None
Directions: Sky Oaks Road, 1.5 miles past Ranger Station

Sky Oaks Road bends right, when coming from the Ranger Station, at a line of eucalyptus trees. On the north (left) side of the road at the bend, two trails rise from a common start. The more prominent one, with a "generic" MMWD sign, veers left uphill; it is Pumpkin Ridge Trail. The somewhat indistinct Netting Trail sets off to its right.

After passing a few oaks, Netting traverses a grassy hillside. Look to the right for some particularly beautiful views of Mt. Tamalpais towering above Pilot Knob. The Trail passes into woodland, with tanbark oak dominant, as it rises to Pumpkin Ridge. Netting ends when it reconnects to Pumpkin Ridge Trail. Less than .1 mile ahead is Madrone Trail.

The name comes from protective netting placed by the MMWD over the Trail route during a re-planting project. Parts of the netting remain visible.

NO NAME TRAIL

From Rock Spring-Lagunitas F.R. at Lower Berry Trail to Rocky Ridge F.R. / .5 miles
Terrain: Part wooded and riparian, part chaparral on serpentine; unimproved /
MMWD
Elevation: From 980' to 1,260' / steep, parts very steep
Intersecting Trails: None
Directions: Lake Lagunitas parking lot - Rock Spring-Lagunitas F.R., .6 miles

This Trail has been dubbed No Name by its few users because it hasn't appeared on a published map. It passes through an otherwise untouched part of the Mountain, and has some outstanding view sites. Though it is not maintained, No Name is in relatively good shape and is fairly easy to follow.

No Name Trail's unmarked start is next to the signpost by the top of Lower Berry Trail at Rock Spring-Lagunitas F.R. No Name appears to be a continuation of Lower Berry, but the now overgrown middle section of Berry actually runs on the other side of the Fire Road.

After a short drop at the start, veer left. The uphill begins, and is then occasionally very steep. The Trail climbs through deep woodland, crossing several rivulets. A slide makes for a narrow couple of yards. At the last, and largest, creek crossing, before the Trail leaves the forest, look for the many azaleas.

The Trail levels somewhat when it hits the open, serpentine rock. There are splendid views of the lakes and beyond to the north, and of the summit of Mt. Tamalpais to the south. The Trail is briefly hard to follow; veer left to re-enter the woodland.

No Name Trail ends when it meets Rocky Ridge Fire Road in a level clearing. There used to be a pig trap beside the Trail in these last yards. The trap's removal is a sign that the MMWD has won the battle against the feral pigs. Uphill to the left are a horse trough and hitching post. There once was a water tank here. Stocking Trail is less than .1 mile to the right and Lagoon Extension Trail is 100 yards to the left.

PILOT KNOB TRAIL

From Lake Lagunitas to Lakeview Fire Road | .8 miles
Terrain: Madrone woodland | MMWD
Elevation: From 850' to 1,000' to 900' | gradual
Intersecting Trails: None
Directions: Lake Lagunitas parking lot - Bridle Path F.R., .2 miles

Pilot Knob is a prominent 1,187' hill looming above Lake Lagunitas. The Knob's distinctive summit, where the grassy south slope meets the tree-covered north slope in a sharp line, is visible from much of Tam and from many parts of the Ross Valley. Pilot Knob Trail goes near the hill's summit; a side branch leads to the very top. The Trail also passes Marin's largest madrone tree.

Two fire roads rise near the outhouses at the Lake Lagunitas parking lot. The connector to the right goes to Lagunitas Dam. The other, once the foot of Pilot Knob Trail but now widened as Bridle Path Fire Road, climbs .2 miles to a crest. From there, Pilot Knob Trail sets off east while Bridle Path drops to Lake Lagunitas. An old trail sign marks Pilot Knob's start.

The early part of the Trail passes through both open and lightly wooded stretches. In the openings are great views of Tam towering above the lake. In around 1/3 mile, in a cleared area to the left, is a massive old madrone. It takes the outstretched arms of five or six people to circle its trunk. The tree shows signs of stress, and has received special care by Water District personnel trying to save it. The Window Trail that both the Olmsted and Erickson maps show as leading to just west of the tree is now overgrown.

Pilot Knob Trail continues climbing through a mixed woodland. At the route's highest point, a half-mile from the start and before a steady drop down, a path goes right. It leads to the top of Pilot Knob itself. Definitely make this steep, extra 200 yard climb. The open summit is special, a great place to pass a few minutes or a few hours. Lake Lagunitas glistens below, Tam dominates above. Pilot Knob's south slope is largely treeless because the direct sun keeps it too dry to support the trees so abundant on the north slope.

Returning to Pilot Knob Trail, now go right. Descend through a forest containing representatives of each of the Mountain's most common trees. A massive double-trunked redwood is known as "Supertree." The madrone, though, remains king. Pilot Knob Trail ends at a signed junction with Lakeview Fire Road. To the right is Lake Lagunitas and to the left, uphill, is Eldridge Grade.

The Trail was built in 1955 by the Tamalpais Trail Riders. They originally named it the Doris Schmiedell Trail, for one of the group's co-founders. The Trail has since been closed to horses. Pilot Knob is said to have been named after a similar-looking hill in Vermont.

PUMPKIN RIDGE TRAIL

Between Sky Oaks Road / .7 miles
Terrain: *Madrone woodland; horses permitted / MMWD*
Elevation: *From 730' to 900' to 800' / steep*
Intersecting Trails: *Netting (.3m), Madrone (.4m), Sky Oaks-Lagunitas (.7m)*
Directions: *Sky Oaks Road, 1.5 miles past Ranger Station*

There are few, if any, places on Mt. Tamalpais where deer are seen more regularly than on Pumpkin Ridge. A Trail runs on the top of this madrone-covered ridge. With its lovely views of Bon Tempe Lake and the Mountain, some choice picnic sites, and ease of access, Pumpkin Ridge Trail makes for pleasant hiking. Particularly inviting are the balmy summer evenings (though remember that MMWD lands close to the public around an hour after sunset) the area enjoys.

Pumpkin Ridge Trail starts and ends on Sky Oaks Road; I'll describe it from the easier-to-locate trailhead atop Fish Grade. Look for the trailhead on the left, just before Sky Oaks Road bends at the line of eucalyptus trees leading into the Lake Lagunitas parking area. A pair of trails branch off a few yards up the hill; Netting Trail to the right and Pumpkin Ridge Trail to the left.

Pumpkin Ridge Trail climbs the grassy hill. Steps made from railroad ties were added to this opening section in spring 1989. At .1 mile, the Trail reaches the ridge line, dominated by madrone trees. Soon after, look right for a great shot of Pilot Knob and, beyond, Mt. Tamalpais.

At .3 miles, Netting Trail rejoins on the right. One hundred yards later, Madrone Trail crosses the spine of Pumpkin Ridge. On the right, Madrone (in two forks that immediately merge) drops to Concrete Pipeline F.R. Left, Madrone descends to Sky Oaks Road. Pumpkin Ridge Trail continues, fairly level, along the top of Pumpkin Ridge. A few redwoods break the madrone's near-monopoly. Iris are abundant here in spring; long-time Mountain hike leader and historian Nancy Skinner calls the trail, "Iris Trail."

You are likely to see or hear deer. The Mountain's natives are mule (blacktail) deer, with a distinctive black-tipped tail. They browse on shrubs, twigs, grasses, and flowers, generally in the morning and evening. Their mating season is in the fall. The males then shed their antlers, soon to begin growing a new set. In early spring, the pregnant does find a hidden site to bear their usually two young. Seeing the spotted, frisky fawns is always a special treat. They can walk within minutes of birth.

In .5 miles, the Trail passes an open grassy slope, a nice picnic spot. An alternate route forks right; it stays in the forest a bit longer before rejoining the Trail. Pumpkin Ridge Trail descends to Sky Oaks-Lagunitas Trail and Sky Oaks Road, and ends. A small parking turnout and a MMWD "dogs-on-leash, no bikes" sign mark the junction.

Doris Vitek, a veteran Mountain equestrienne and the wife of long-time MMWD employee Jim Vitek, is the "pumpkin" for whom the ridge and Trail are named. Actually, her nickname is "punkin"; "pumpkin" originally appeared as a misspelling on a map. The wood and berries of the madrones do add an orange-red, pumpkin hue to the ridge. An earlier name was Nebraska Ridge. The Trail covers an old Water District road across the ridge line.

ROCK SPRING-LAGUNITAS FIRE ROAD

From Lake Lagunitas parking area to Ridgecrest Boulevard / 3.4 miles
Terrain: Half wooded, half open with views / MMWD
Elevation: From 730' to 2,080' / gradual, lower 1.9 miles steep to very steep
Intersecting Trails: Lake Lagunitas F.R. (.2m-.3m), Lower Berry (.7m), No Name (.7m), Rocky Ridge F.R. (1.2m), Rocky Ridge Trail (1.7m), Upper Berry (1.7m, 2.2m), Lagoon F.R. (1.9m), Azalea Meadow (2.3m), Arturo (2.3m), Northside (2.3m), Laurel Dell F.R. (2.6m), Benstein (2.9m-3.0m), Mountain Top (3.4m)
Directions: Lake Lagunitas parking area

Rock Spring-Lagunitas Fire Road (or, just as commonly, Lagunitas-Rock Spring F.R.) plays a role in many trips high onto the Mountain from the upper lakes. It intersects over a dozen north side trails. It is also one of the very few routes that crosses Tamalpais' east-west summit ridge, thereby connecting the north and south faces of the Mountain. Though both the Fire Road's ends are accessible by car, and the views downhill are even better than those going up, it is described uphill because the Lake Lagunitas trailhead is so popular a starting point.

The Fire Road begins from the far right side (as you drive in) of the Lake Lagunitas parking area, across the bridge over Lagunitas Creek. At the start, to the right, is one end of Bon Tempe (Shadyside) Trail. Rock Spring-Lagunitas F.R. rises to the left, beside Lagunitas Creek. Here is a reminder of how lovely the whole length of the creek, which has been dammed to form Lagunitas, Bon Tempe, Alpine, and Kent lakes, once looked. At the crest of the first hill is Lake Lagunitas, with the dam just to the left. Look carefully at the row of logs in the water and you might see western pond turtles warming in the sunshine.

Rock Spring-Lagunitas F.R. runs together with Lake Lagunitas F.R. for 150 yards before veering right and uphill away from the lake. The next 1 1/2 miles are very steep. The climb is first through forest. In .4 miles above Lagunitas, Lower Berry Trail comes in on the right from Bon Tempe Lake. The Berry Trail once went on to Potrero Meadow before the Fire Road, cutting the route, was built. Berry's middle section on the other side of Rock Spring-Lagunitas F.R. is now overgrown; it would provide a shortcut if cleared. Also at the Lower Berry junction, unsigned No Name Trail sets off west to Rocky Ridge Fire Road.

The tree cover thins and largely disappears, opening views. At 1.2 miles, the upper end of Rocky Ridge F.R. joins on the right. It drops to near Bon Tempe Dam, and offers a loop possibility back. The bay beside the new signpost at the intersection accounts for the name Bay Tree Junction. An older sign is affixed to a Douglas fir, now the prevalent tree here.

Continuing up, a point is passed where all three of Tam's summits can be seen. The climbing begins to ease, but it doesn't end. At 1.7 miles, an old sign on the left marks the bottom of steep Rocky Ridge Trail. It leads to the Lower Northside and Northside trails. On the right side of the Fire Road here, unsigned, is the start of Upper Berry Trail.

In another .2 miles, back in the Douglas fir forest, is the upper end of Lagoon Fire Road. It descends to Serpentine Knoll. Six hundred yards beyond, Upper Berry Trail re-enters on the right, the spot marked only by a MMWD "no horses" sign. A new concrete water tank is to the left. Shortly beyond, also to the left, is a water trough and, up some stone steps, an old water spigot. The fountain carries a well-worn TCC plaque:

OUR APPRECIATION OF THE KINDNESS OF THE OWNERS OF THIS WONDERLAND IN PERMITTING US TO ENJOY IT, WITHOUT CHARGE, CAN BEST BE SHOWN BY GATHERING ALL PAPER, BOTTLES, AND LITTER AND DEPOSITING SAME IN RECEPTACLES. . .

A "non-potable water" sign has been placed here as well, since the water is untreated. The water actually now flows from a valve behind the spigot.

In a few more yards is historic Rifle Camp, once a hub of several camps in the area. The origin of its name is obscure; one often told story says that a dog named Schneider, owned by Dick Maurer, president of the Down & Outer's Club, dug up a rifle here. It is officially called Rifle Picnic Area now, and there are picnic tables and outhouses. The unusual tree by the farthest table is what may be the Mountain's largest service berry (*Amelanchier pallida*). A few yards below Rifle Camp are the lower end of Arturo Trail, which climbs toward West Peak, and the west end of Northside Trail, which goes all the way to Eldridge Grade. Across the Fire Road from the camp's metal backpack rack is the unmarked upper end of Azalea Meadow Trail, which descends to Kent Trail.

A few yards of uphill lead to the main Potrero Meadow, one of the Mountain's treasures. "Potrero" means "fenced-in pasture land" in Spanish, and the meadow was once leased for grazing purposes. A .3 mile path across it on the far right leads to the lower Potrero Meadow and to Potrero Camp. Keep off the delicate meadow proper. The now abandoned buildings of the old Air Force Station are quite prominent on the ridge above.

Rock Spring-Lagunitas F.R. continues left around the meadow. In spring, madrones in bloom stand out across the way, lending a yellow tint to the evergreens. A path (the old Potrero Cutoff Trail, not separately described) goes left back to Arturo Trail. Before leaving the meadow, the Fire Road meets, on the right, one end of Laurel Dell F.R. There is a second access a few yards beyond.

After a bit more uphill, Rock Spring-Lagunitas F.R. encounters, on the right, Benstein Trail. From this intersection Benstein heads to Potrero Camp. The Fire Road and Benstein run together for 100 yards, then the latter splits off toward Rock Spring.

A crest is reached; there is a glimpse of southern vistas. Paths depart to the right. Then a second crest is hit and, suddenly and dramatically, even broader southern views open. This is the very divide of the north and south side sides of Mt. Tamalpais. The Fire Road ends as it drops to Ridgecrest Boulevard at a gate across from a Mountain Theater parking lot. An old sign says the Fire Road leads to Ross. Rock Spring is nearby to the right (west), accounting for the Fire Road's name. The presently unmarked and unmaintained Mountain Top Trail goes left, up toward West Peak, from the same gate.

Rock Spring-Lagunitas Fire Road was built in the early 1930's by the Civilian Conservation Corps.

ROCKY RIDGE FIRE ROAD

From Alpine-Bon Tempe Pump F.R. to Rock Spring-Lagunitas F.R. / 1.8 miles
Terrain: Chaparral; exposed; rocky; views / MMWD
Elevation: From 720' to 1,410' / steep, parts very steep
Intersecting Trails: Casey Cutoff (.8m), Stocking (1.4m), No Name (1.5m), Lagoon Extension (1.6m)
Directions: Bon Tempe Dam - Alpine-Bon Tempe Pump F.R., 200 feet

Rocky Ridge is a prominent, almost treeless rib on Tam's north side. A fire road tops it, offering access from Bon Tempe to several remote north side trails. The exposed terrain of Rocky Ridge Fire Road can be blustery in winter winds and hot in summer, but, in return, the views are excellent.

To reach Rocky Ridge, cross Bon Tempe Dam from the parking area, then veer right on Alpine-Bon Tempe Pump Fire Road. In 200 feet, Rocky Ridge Fire Road sets off uphill to the left. A signpost points the way to Potrero Meadow. The most common trees on Mt. Tamalpais; bay, Douglas fir, madrone, tanbark oak, coast live oak, redwood, and buckeye, are all found within Rocky Ridge's first quarter-mile. Higher, the trees, save for a few isolated individuals and groves, are left behind.

The views are immediately sweeping. Gulls regularly fly overhead on their way to and from Bon Tempe, where they go to dip in the fresh water. The prominent green, greasy-appearing rocks on the Fire Road are serpentine, designated as California's state rock in 1965. Serpentine, a metamorphic rock thrust up from the deepest levels of the earth's crust, is common on Mt. Tamalpais. Because its soils are heavy in magnesium, and deficient in essential minerals potassium and aluminum, serpentine supports only a specialized, low-growing plant community. The abundant loose rocks and prominent rock outcroppings undoubtedly account for the ridge's and the Fire Road's name.

In .8 miles, currently barely noticeable on the left (there is a MMWD sign 15 yards in), is Casey Cutoff Trail. It drops even more steeply, as a shortcut, back to Bon Tempe Dam. The grueling uphill eases after about a mile and there are actually three brief downhill stretches. At the third, just past a prominent tree grove, Stocking Trail enters on the left from Bon Tempe

Lake. The junction is nearly invisible amidst the rocks and manzanita. The continuation of Stocking, to Hidden Lake, is 75 yards farther up Rocky Ridge on the right. A line of logs marks the entrance. The area is ablaze with blue from ceanothus in early spring.

In another .1 mile there is a clearing on the left. The unsigned No Name Trail sets off through it on its trip to the top of Lower Berry Trail. There is more uphill, then the Fire Road re-enters shade. Four hundred feet above No Name is the unmarked, hard to spot, entry to Lagoon Extension Trail. Look on the right, at a small turnout before a bend to the left; it is sometimes marked with a cairn.

Rocky Ridge Fire Road ends at Rock Spring-Lagunitas Fire Road. The signpost points the way left to Lake Lagunitas, right to Potrero Meadow. The intersection is called Bay Tree Junction for the bay (laurel) overlooking it. Rocky Ridge itself continues higher, topped now by Rock Spring-Lagunitas F.R., then, higher still, by Rocky Ridge Fire Trail (which see) to near West Peak.

The route up Rocky Ridge is one of the oldest on Mt. Tamalpais, dating to the 1860's or earlier. The present Fire Road was built around 1932.

ROCKY RIDGE FIRE TRAIL

From Rock Spring-Lagunitas Fire Road to near West Peak | .7 miles
Terrain: Lightly wooded, parts open; loose rock; views | MMWD
Elevation: From 1,760' to 2,260' | very steep
Intersecting Trails: Lower Northside (.1m), Northside (.3m)
Directions: Lake Lagunitas parking area - Rock Spring-Lagunitas F.R., 1.7 miles

Rocky Ridge Fire Trail does not appear at all on the MMWD map, and only its lower half is shown, unnamed, on the Erickson and Olmsted maps. It is wide, but too steep and rocky to be called a fire road.

The Fire Trail begins uphill off Rock Spring-Lagunitas F.R. at an old wood sign pointing the way to Northside Trail. Across Rock Spring-Lagunitas here is the base of Upper Berry Trail. Seventy-five yards up Rocky Ridge, at a signpost, Lower Northside Trail goes left to Colier Spring. Continue climbing. The views really open behind, to Point Reyes and Mt. St. Helena. In .3 miles, Northside Trail crosses. It goes left to International Trail, Colier Spring, and Eldridge Grade; right to Rifle Camp.

The remaining section of Rocky Ridge Fire Trail is little visited because it meets a deadend. Continue up the rocky terrain. Water pipelines, originally laid to serve the former Air Force station on West Peak, are visible beside the Trail. Sargent cypress trees, in their element on these serpentine outcrops high on the Mountain, dot the area. Turn around to see the spectacular views, or wait for the return.

The public part of Rocky Ridge ends at a fence. The Trail does rise farther toward the white domes of the off-limits Federal Aviation Administration tracking facility atop West Peak. The MMWD trail sign here seems curious as there is no access from above, though hikers are beating a path to the right, along the fence line, to Arturo Trail.

Rocky Ridge Fire Trail was cut in the 1920's as a long, broad, continuous fire break from Alpine Lake to West Peak. Construction of Rock Spring-Lagunitas F.R. cut the Fire Trail in two, and separated the two sections by a half-mile. The surviving, rerouted lower half is called Rocky Ridge Fire Road in this book. The prominent rib of Rocky Ridge itself is one of the oldest routes on the Mountain. Lincoln Fairley noted ("Mount Tamalpais, A History," page 55) that the ridge was followed by surveyor William Brewer in 1862 in the first documented ascent, though others had undoubtedly gone up earlier, of Mt. Tamalpais.

SCOTT TANK FIRE ROAD

From Sky Oaks Ranger Station to Scott Tanks | .3 miles
Terrain: Grassland and oak woodland; short part paved | MMWD
Elevation: From 700' to 800' | gradual
Intersecting Trails: None
Directions: Across Sky Oaks Road from Ranger Station

This little-used fire road, not on the Olmsted or MMWD maps, ends at a private property line without any loop possibilities. It does offer a visit through a pastoral part of the Mountain and, particularly on the return, fine views.

Directly across from Sky Oaks Ranger Station, a few yards before the toll booth, two paved roads depart. One forks right and leads to the private Crest Farm. The other is Scott Tank Fire Road. In fifty yards, it too forks. Right is the driveway of a private MMWD ranger residence. Scott Tank F.R., now dirt, continues straight ahead. A sign informs bikers that there is no through access.

The Fire Road rises above Bon Tempe Meadow. Ahead on the left is the private Meadow Club golf course, built in 1926. Deer are a common sight here, particularly in evening. The oak woodland evokes images of an earlier, quieter California. A few invading Douglas fir trees, which may one day replace the oaks, remind us that the natural world changes too. The land over the ridge to the right (and ahead and to the left as well) is private property, and a residence is visible. The Boy Scout's Camp Lilienthal was just to the north; the scouts have since moved to Camp Tamarancho.

The Fire Road ends at a pair of green water tanks called the Scott Tanks. The Fire Road was graded to service them. Harry S. Scott built the adjacent Crest Farm. An avid equestrian, he was a founder and the first president, in 1939, of the Tamalpais Trail Riders. On the way back, enjoy the excellent view of the north wall of Mt. Tamalpais.

The Erickson and Olmsted maps show a trail (called Scott Tank on the former) going through the north edge of Bon Tempe Meadow and the golf course to Fairfax-Bolinas Road. That trail passes through private property so is not described here. The Meadow Club once leased their 162 acres of land from the Water District. In 1977, as part of a negotiated settlement, Club members put up $2,500 each to purchase a 2,200 acre parcel in the Kent Lake watershed. They then exchanged that parcel with the MMWD for ownership of the golf course property.

SKY OAKS-LAGUNITAS TRAIL

Between Sky Oaks Road / 1.1 miles
Terrain: *Grassland, parts wooded; sometimes muddy; horses permitted / MMWD*
Elevation: *Around 750' / almost level, rolling*
Intersecting Trails: *Shaver Grade (.2m), Elliott (.3m), Pumpkin Ridge (.5m), Madrone (.7m-.8m)*
Directions: *Sky Oaks Road, .1 mile past Ranger Station*

Sky Oaks-Lagunitas Trail (sometimes simply called Sky Oaks Trail) runs alongside Sky Oaks Road, providing an alternative to the pavement. It is popular with horse riders, so is occasionally muddy in winter. The Trail begins about 100 yards past the Sky Oaks toll booth, to the left and just beyond the short protection road. Sky Oaks-Lagunitas Trail bends right, onto a grassy hillside that is rich with wildflowers in spring. Poppies, Chinese-houses, larkspurs, cream-cups, farewell-to-springs, and blue and white brodiaeas are just some of the more colorful blossoms.

The Trail enters shade, alongside a creekbed. The route goes in and out of light woodland throughout. In 1/4 mile, Sky Oaks Trail crosses the top of Shaver Grade just a few feet below the paved road. Soon after, Sky Oaks-Lagunitas meets the top of Elliott Trail, which drops left to Shaver Grade. Veer right. The Trail re-enters woodland, then rises to a clearing. There are views of Bald Hill and the North Bay. Just beyond, Sky Oaks-Lagunitas meets Pumpkin Ridge Trail, coming down from the left. Again veer right, to within a few feet of the paved road.

In this open area are striking vistas of Mt. Tamalpais. Also look left up Pumpkin Ridge; it's unusual not to see deer grazing on the hillside. The Trail again approaches the road. A "horse crosing" of Sky Oaks Road, marked by white road bumps, leads to Bon Tempe Trail. Here too is one end of Madrone Trail; it runs together with Sky Oaks Trail for 60 yards before splitting off left uphill. Continue through the baccharis, mindful of the pervasive poison oak.

Sky Oaks-Lagunitas Trail passes a new wheelchair-accessible outhouse beside the huge redwood of Redwood Cove. The Trail continues up, into woodland, as it rounds the cove. The terrain opens again, with more fine views. A final drop to the paved road brings the Trail to its end. There are "horse," "dog-on-leash," and "no-bike" MMWD signs here. Across the road is Pine Point peninsula and an entry to the trail around Bon Tempe.

Sky Oaks was the name of the 1930's Civilian Conservation Corps camp by the Trail's start, of the girl scout camp there after World War II, and of the present Marin Municipal Water District Ranger Station.

STOCKING TRAIL

From Bon Tempe Lake to Kent Trail / 1.2 miles
Terrain: Lower half lightly wooded and rocky, upper half wooded / MMWD
Elevation: From 730' to 1,250' / lower half very steep, upper half gradual
Intersecting Trails: Rocky Ridge F.R. (.5m)
Directions: Lake Lagunitas parking area - Bon Tempe (Shadyside) Trail to first bridge

Stocking Trail has two distinct halves. The lower part, rising from Bon Tempe Lake, is quite steep, unmarked, poorly maintained, and passes mostly through open, rocky terrain. The half west of Rocky Ridge is gentler in slope, all in forest, maintained, and is now signed (maybe, more on this below). Stocking offers a direct route to the deep, quiet forests of northwest Tamalpais, and also passes one of the Mountain's treasures, Hidden Lake.

Stocking begins off the Bon Tempe (Shadyside) Trail, .4 miles from the Lake Lagunitas parking lot on the far side of the first footbridge. Stocking rises left, unsigned and somewhat indistinct. A creek, dry in summer, is to the left. The first clearing uphill, a grassy area with boulders on the right, was the site of the old Camp Handy. Emil Barth reportedly named it because is was "handy" to Fairfax and Ross. In late summer and early fall, it is filled with the sticky, fragrant, yellow flowers of madia.

The going gets even steeper. Azaleas add color and fragrance in May and June. The Trail emerges from the trees to serpentine chaparral. Look back to get a vista of Pilot Knob, Bald Hill, and the East Bay. There is no clear trail through the rocky terrain. Just keep climbing through the manzanita and you will reach Rocky Ridge F.R. No sign marks the intersection.

Stocking continues across Rocky Ridge some 50 yards to the left (south). The MMWD kept setting wood signposts here and someone kept maliciously cutting them. Now, good-sized logs line the entry. Just in, the sharply spiked, six-foot-high shrub lining the Trail is chaparral pea. Its lovely rose-purple flowers are in bloom in late spring. Laurels mark the Stocking's re-entrance into forest.

In .2 miles from Rocky Ridge, Stocking descends to cross Van Wyck Creek. The Trail passes through a cut in a huge, old, fallen redwood. It is believed to be the fabled Hogan Tree. The plaque which dedicated this grove of giant redwoods to veteran Mountain hiker John Hogan, who once had his Camp Hogan here, is said to still be on the tree's underside. A few yards ahead, the Trail goes straight through a clump of chain ferns. The area is sometimes quite wet in winter. Then, .6 miles in from Rocky Ridge, is the treasure of Hidden Lake.

Approach Hidden Lake quietly, you never know what unusual animal or animal behavior you'll encounter. Mt. Tamalpais is rich in many things but natural lakes are not among them. This duckweed-covered pond, shrinking in size and drying up in the natural succession of the Mountain's terrain, is unique habitat, and the wildlife know it. It was once known as Wildcat Lake; wildcats, or bobcats, still live on Tam. You'll want to linger here.

Stocking continues another 100 yards to its unsigned junction with Kent Trail. This deep forest is one of the loveliest, quietest parts of Mt. Tamalpais, if not the whole Bay Area. Redwoods, Douglas-firs, tanbark oaks, and madrones rise high to compete for sunlight. Downhill on Kent about five yards is the barely visible lower end of unsigned Willow Meadow

Trail. Kent descends to Alpine Lake. Left up Kent, between a redwood and a huge tanbark oak, leads to Serpentine Knoll and Potrero Camp.

Clayton Stocking was a long-time employee and foreman for the Marin Municipal Water District. He retired in 1962 and died in 1969. He is also honored by a plaque by Phoenix Dam, where he lived for 42 years. For an explanation of how the Trail came to be called Stocking, see the Lagoon Extension Trail. Earlier names included Swede George Fire Trail, Hidden Lake Trail, and, for the part below Rocky Ridge, Camp Handy Trail.

TAYLOR TRAIL

From Sky Oaks Ranger Station to Concrete Pipeline Fire Road | .5 miles
Terrain: Tanbark oak-madrone woodland; horses permitted | MMWD
Elevation: 700' to 525' | steep
Intersecting Trails: None
Directions: Sky Oaks Ranger Station

Taylor Trail offers a pleasant connection between Sky Oaks Ranger Station and Concrete Pipeline Fire Road, avoiding paved, open-to-cars Sky Oaks Road. The Trail descends from the fence to the left (facing the building from the road) of the ranger station. This is the former site, from 1924 to 1941, of a University of California summer camp at which engineering students were taught surveying skills. During World War II, there was military housing here. After the war, the area was the Girl Scouts' Sky Oaks Camp.

The Trail drops steadily its whole length. Trees line the route, making the Trail quite pretty. Taylor ends at its junction with Concrete Pipeline F.R. To the left, in .6 miles, is Fairfax-Bolinas Road; to the right, in 3/4 miles, is Five Corners. Also to the right, in about 75 yards, is the unsigned upper end of Canyon Trail.

Taylor Trail was built in the early 1930's. It was named for Lawrence B. Taylor, the superintendent of the Civilian Conservation Corps Camp that stood near Sky Oaks in the 1930's. He oversaw many of Tam's major trail-building projects. He also was an avid equestrian.

UPPER BERRY TRAIL

Between Rock Spring-Lagunitas Fire Road / .5 miles
Terrain: Deep forest / MMWD
Elevation: From 1,760' to 1,920' / gradual, parts steep
Intersecting Trails: Cross Country Boys (.1m), Lagoon F.R. (.1m)
Directions: Lake Lagunitas - Rock Spring-Lagunitas F.R., 1.7 miles

U pper Berry is the restored top section of the old Berry Trail (see Lower Berry Trail), an old route up the north side of Tamalpais. It starts, unsigned, directly across Rock Spring-Lagunitas F.R. (to the right when coming from Lake Lagunitas) from the Northside Trail sign at the base of Rocky Ridge Fire Trail.

Upper Berry immediately enters woodland. In .1 mile, the Trail forks. Veer left; the right fork is the east end of Cross Country Boys Trail. Upper Berry then crosses Lagoon Fire Road. Less than .1 mile to the left is Lagoon's junction with Rock Spring-Lagunitas F.R., while right leads down to Serpentine Knoll.

Upper Berry is slightly overgrown as it descends into deep woods. It meets a connector back to Cross Country Boys and Azalea Meadow. A few yards of steep uphill leads to the East Fork of Swede George Creek and the former site of Ted Cooper's Bridge. Crossing the creek in winter can be tricky without a bridge; a replacement of Ted Cooper's original was itself a victim of a fallen tree and has yet to be rebuilt. After crossing, look back to see, affixed to a laurel, an old sign dating the bridge to 1928. The "D.&O.C." refers to the Down & Outer's Club, a small group of hikers who frequented the area. Just upstream is a remnant of a now murky old swimming hole, fed by an underground spring. Cooper lived in a camp just downstream from here, and did significant work on the Trail. He died in an auto accident on the Mountain in 1932, on the way to a vacation in Steep Ravine. His ashes were scattered by his camp.

Upper Berry continues through the woods. It rises steeply over root-covered terrain to meet Rock Spring-Lagunitas F.R. across from a new water tank. The junction is presently marked only with a "no horses" sign. Less than 100 yards to the right is Rifle Camp and the Northside, Arturo, and Azalea Meadow trails.

WILLOW MEADOW TRAIL

From junction of Kent and Stocking trails to Willow Meadow / .6 miles
Terrain: Deep woods; riparian; unimproved / MMWD
Elevation: From 1,240' to 1,500' / steep, parts very steep
Intersecting Trails: Kent (.5m)
Directions: Bon Tempe Dam - Rocky Ridge F.R. - right on Stocking Trail to intersection with Kent Trail

This unsigned Trail has only recently appeared, unnamed, on maps. Since it goes to Willow Meadow, I'll use the unofficial name Willow Meadow Trail.

The Trail's lower end, in one of the loveliest woodlands on Tam, is very difficult to spot. From the unmarked junction of the Kent and Stocking trails, go downhill on Kent about 15 feet. Willow Meadow Trail starts uphill to the left. It is overgrown with tanbark oak its first 25 yards or so, then becomes clear to follow. In around 100 yards, just past a huge Douglas fir, a path branches right; stay left.

Willow Meadow Trail rises steadily, with some very steep parts. Because the Trail is little known, and is already in one of the quietest parts of the Mountain, serenity is assured. The East Fork of Swede George Creek becomes audible and visible in the deep canyon to the right. The creek runs surprisingly strongly even in fall before the winter rains.

The Trail levels when it meets the creek for a short but delightful stretch. Azaleas are abundant. It's a great place to sit and relax. The Trail skirts the creek's right bank. It then meets Kent Trail again. Left, Kent heads toward Alpine Lake. To the right, within 15 yards, Kent crosses Swede George on its way to the High Marsh and Azalea Meadow trails. Willow Meadow Trail continues across Kent.

In around 75 yards, the Trail ends at Willow Meadow. This large, flat, sometimes wet, grassy area is also skirted, to the south, by the Azalea Meadow and the Cross Country Boys trails. Willows are found in the moister parts. A rest stop here in this remote, peaceful clearing is all but mandatory.

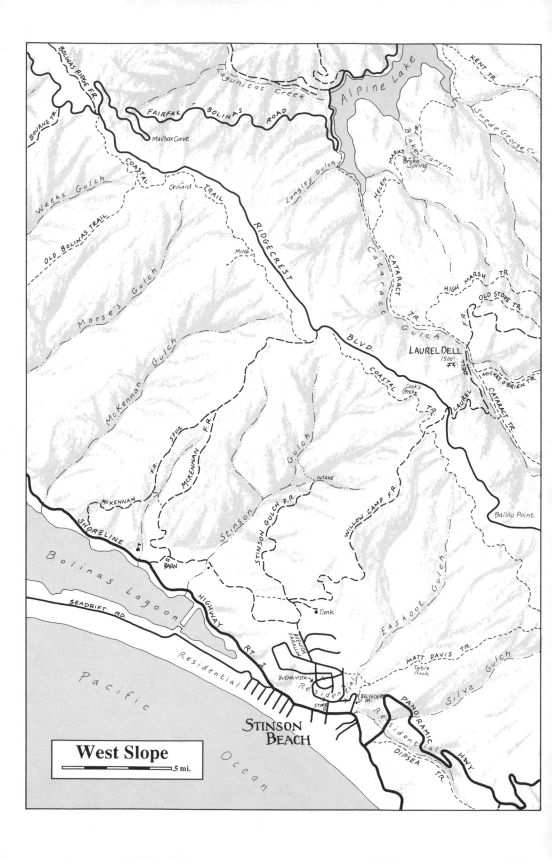

West Slope

|———————| .5 mi.

WEST SLOPE TRAILHEAD

Directions to Stinson Beach:
Highway 101 - Highway 1 or
Highway 101 - Highway 1 - Panoramic Highway to end

Directions to West Ridgecrest Boulevard:
Highway 101 - Highway 1 - Panoramic Highway - Southside Road or
Fairfax-Bolinas Road, from either central Fairfax (where it is known as Bolinas Road) or from Highway 1 at north edge of Bolinas Lagoon

The trails described in this section do not focus around a single trailhead. Rather, they are reached from several access points along the western slope of Mt. Tamalpais, either along Highway 1 near the ocean or along West Ridgecrest Boulevard atop Bolinas Ridge.

Willow Camp and McKennan fire roads run between Bolinas Ridge and Highway 1 at Stinson Beach. Both are accessible by car at either end. Stinson Gulch Fire Road can be reached from the parking area at the end of Stinson Beach's Avenida Farralone. Going south from Stinson Beach, in order, Red Rock Trail, Steep Ravine Road, Rocky Point Trail, Lone Tree Fire Road, Coastal Fire Road, and Owl Trail depart from Highway 1. Lone Tree and Coastal rise to high on the Mountain, the others drop toward the ocean. The Dipsea and Matt Davis trails both have a trailhead in Stinson Beach, but are described in the Mill Valley and Mountain Home sections, respectively.

Several other trails and fire roads depart from scenic West Ridgecrest Boulevard. Heading northwest on the boulevard from Rock Spring (which is treated as a separate trailhead), they are: Willow Camp, Laurel Dell, and McKennan fire roads, and Old Bolinas-San Rafael Trail. All but Laurel Dell run on the west side of the road.

Two more trails, Old Stove and High Marsh, are most easily reached from West Ridgecrest so are included here. Helen Markt Trail is also described in this section. Its closest access is from Fairfax-Bolinas Road near Alpine Dam.

Suggested loop from Highway 1 - elevation 420'

Mileage marker 10.67 - Lone Tree F.R., 1.8m, to Coastal F.R. - left, .3m, to Steep Ravine Trail - left, 2.1m, to Highway 1 - left, .3m, to start / 4.5 miles.

Suggested loop from Alpine Dam - elevation 650'

Cataract Trail, 1.2m, to High Marsh Trail - left, 2.1m, to Kent Trail - left, 1.5m, to Helen Markt - left, 2.0m, to Cataract Trail - right, .6m, to start | 7.4 miles.

Suggested loop from Stinson Beach - elevation 60'

Matt Davis Trail, 2.4m, to Coastal Trail - left, 2.4m, to McKennan F.R. - left, 2.2m to Willow Camp F.R. - left, 1.5m, to Avenida Farralone and start | 8.5 miles.

COASTAL TRAIL and FIRE ROAD

From Highway 1, Muir Beach, to junction of Fairfax-Bolinas Road and Ridgecrest Boulevard | 8.9 miles
Terrain: *Almost entirely coastal grassland; short forested sections; views; part of Bay Area Ridge Trail | MTSP & GGNRA*
Elevation: *From 460' to 1,800' to 1,450' | southern section very steep, then gradual and rolling*
Intersecting Trails: *Heather Cutoff (.2m), Deer Park F.R. (2.3m), Dipsea (2.4m), Lone Tree F.R. (2.5m), Old Mine (2.6m, 2.9m), Lone Tree Hill F.R. (2.6m), Steep Ravine (2.9m), Matt Davis (2.9m-4.5m), Willow Camp F.R. (5.9m), McKennan F.R. (6.9m), Old Bolinas-San Rafael (8.5m)*
Directions: *Highway 1 to milepost 7.35*

Coastal Trail is the longest single route in Marin. It can be taken, except for short discontinuities, from the Golden Gate Bridge to the Fairfax-Bolinas Road, a distance of over 17 miles. From there, the long-distance traveler can continue by following Bolinas Ridge Fire Road to near Olema, then joining the extensive Point Reyes National Seashore trail network. Much of the route is at fire road width; those sections are called Coastal Fire Road here. Coastal Trail is also called the Coast, and the Pacific Coast, Trail. There is a separate Coast Trail in Point Reyes, running above the ocean from Palomarin trailhead to Limantour Road.

The Mt. Tamalpais section of Coastal starts as a fire road east off Highway 1, across from milepost 7.35. On the ocean side of the highway is a view turnout with a "Dangerous Cliffs" warning sign. Coastal Fire Road parallels Highway 1 for .2 miles. It runs through Heather Farm, which grows flowers for commercial sale. Though the farm is leased to the Banducci family, the land is part of Golden Gate National Recreation Area and the Trail itself is open to passage. There are fine ocean views.

At the boundary sign and fence, Coastal F.R. enters Mount Tamalpais State Park. Heather Cutoff Trail branches right here, descending 21 switchbacks to Frank Valley and the Muir Woods Road. Coastal F.R. goes straight ahead, beginning its very steep climb. Some maps label this section of Coastal to Pantoll as Old Mine Fire Road.

Coastal is the only route through this large southwest corner of Mt. Tamalpais; right and left are large, rarely-visited tracts. The ever-broadening vistas are outstanding. A common flower in summer along the grass margin is gumweed, readily recognizable by the creamy, sticky fluid sitting atop it. After a half-mile of stiff uphill, the Fire Road levels. Just ahead is the grove of Monterey pines, visible from so many south side trails, that shelters Shansky Backpack Camp.

The pines were planted beginning in 1959 by previous landowner Tony Brazil and his friend Roane Sias. They envisioned growing 5,000 three-to-six-foot Christmas trees, sales of which would finance their children's college educations. The site was called the Brazil-Sais (or B.S.) Christmas Tree Farm. But the property was purchased a few years later by, and added to, Mount Tamalpais State Park. In 1979, Hillsborough resident Albert Shansky donated funds for construction of the present camp. It was named for his son, Lee, an avid hiker on Tam before his premature death. There are four campsites, available by reservation only, including an isolated, view one called "the honeymoon suite," an outhouse, and some tables. There is no water, and fires are not permitted. In February 1989, a wind storm decimated the camp. Scores of trees were toppled, noticeably thinning the grove. The camp remains closed in early 1990.

There is a short, welcome dip but then Coastal resumes climbing. Trees line Kent Canyon to the right. Cold Stream Canyon is to the left. After just over two miles without an intersection, Coastal F.R. meets Deer Park F.R., coming in on the right. This next section of Coastal, straight ahead and uphill, was formally dedicated as part of the 400 mile long Bay Area Ridge Trail on September 23, 1989.

In another .1 mile, the Dipsea Trail crosses Coastal. The junction is at the top of Cardiac Hill. Dipsea runners treasure the site, for the views, for the water station here on race day, and, most of all, for the prospect of all the downhill to Stinson Beach ahead. After another .1 mile of uphill, Coastal meets the upper end of Lone Tree F.R. The latter descends west (left) all the way to Highway 1. Look back for one of the loveliest vistas on Tam.

Coastal now enters a Douglas-fir forest. Just ahead is the signed Old Mine Trail, which goes right, parallel to Coastal, to Pantoll. To the left at the junction is the unsigned Lone Tree Hill Fire Road. It climbs 1/4 mile to the top of the hill.

Coastal's rise is gentler than earlier. It passes just above an old mine site; a sign marking the spot is visible from Old Mine Trail a few yards below. Coastal then passes a gate and, paved, enters the Pantoll maintenance yard. Beyond are State Park employee residences. Old Mine Trail rejoins on the right, and then Steep Ravine Trail sets off to the left. Coastal meets the important trailhead of Pantoll (which see). The ranger station here is the headquarters for Mount Tamalpais State Park.

From the parking area cross Panoramic Highway and climb a few steps. Coastal continues left (west) as part of Matt Davis Trail; the two are combined for 1.6 miles. Coastal's remaining six miles, between Pantoll and Fairfax-Bolinas Road, are a pedestrian section of the Bay Area Ridge Trail.

The going is now fairly level. The united Coastal and Matt Davis pass through a deep Douglas-fir forest. Then, after a mile, the route enters grassland and one of the Mountain's best-loved stretches. At a signed fork in the grassland, just past a grove of bay trees, Coastal Trail resumes its separate identity. Matt Davis goes left for its descent to Stinson Beach. Coastal Trail continues straight. A sign designates the next 4.3 miles of Coastal Trail as the Bob Cook Memorial Section, and it is often called Bob Cook Trail.

On a fogless day the views from this long, open section rival any to be found in Marin. The sweeping panoramas, as the towering west wall of Tamalpais plunges toward the Pacific, are breathtaking. And the visual feast goes on for miles. Paths lace the area. The Trail begins rising to near its high point at 1,800'. Look for hang gliders, launched from designated sites off Ridgecrest Boulevard, floating toward Stinson Beach. In .8 miles from the Matt Davis Trail split, a rusted old vehicle lies beneath a laurel tree, a remaining bald tire perhaps a clue to its arrival here. The Trail passes through other isolated laurel groves, and meanders around the gulches of Tam's west face.

Around 1.6 miles from the Matt Davis split, the Trail crosses Willow Camp Fire Road. It's a stiff .1 mile uphill to Ridgecrest Boulevard, or a steep, beautiful 1.7 mile drop left to Stinson Beach. Coastal Trail gently descends from this high point. One of several old cattle drinking tubs to be seen on the Trail, and a clump of planted calla lilies, are reminders of when the area was privately owned and used for grazing.

One-quarter mile from Willow Camp F.R., just past a laurel tree, is the stone Cook Memorial Bench. A plaque tells the story:

ROBERT B. COOK 1959-1979

THIS SCENIC 4.3 MILES SECTION OF PACIFIC COAST TRAIL, BETWEEN THE MATT DAVIS AND LAUREL TRAILS, IS DEDICATED TO THE MEMORY OF BOB COOK. IT WAS CONCEIVED AS HIS EAGLE SCOUT PROJECT AND, THROUGH HIS PERSISTANCE AND DETERMINATION, WAS BUILT WITH VOLUNTEER LABOR OVER A TWO YEAR PERIOD.

Cook died in an airplane crash on his way to do trail work in Idaho. The plaque was unveiled in a ceremony on June 1, 1980. Rest and enjoy the wonderful view.

In another .1 mile, the Trail enters a sizable grove atop Stinson Gulch. A plaque dedicates the bridge:

IN MEMORY OF MIKE AMOROSO, MILL VALLEY LIONS CLUB 1978.

Amoroso was a Mill Valley liquor store owner involved in many civic projects.

Coastal approaches Ridgecrest Boulevard, then merges with it for 50 yards. There are views of the north side of the Mountain. Leave the pavement at the gate which marks the top of McKennan Fire Road. It too drops to Stinson and offers, with Willow Camp F.R., a very strenuous but lovely loop option.

Coastal Trail approaches the pig fence. It was erected in late 1987 to keep a then growing feral pig population from moving to Point Reyes National Seashore. The hardy pigs were proving a menace to vegetation, particularly bulbous plants such as the Mountain's orchids. Hunting and trapping have reduced the pigs' numbers.

When the Trail comes to the edge of the fence, look carefully to spot remnants of the McKennan Gulch Copper Prospect. The brownish soil of the Trail changes to gray-black. A test cut is still visible as a depression five yards to the right. To the left, ten yards below the pig fence, is the now filled tunnel entrance to the mine itself. The area was worked in the 1930's; copper tracings are still to be found. At an opening in the pig fence around 100 yards farther north, an overgrown path drops to the left.

Around 1.2 miles from the McKennan F.R. crossing, Coastal Trail passes above an old orchard which still yields a few apples. It was once known as Fountainhead Orchard, for the spring a few yards to the southwest. The continuing Trail, completed in 1976 as the Laurel Trail, then veers left away from the road, crossing through the pig fence. The Douglas firs here are huge. Coastal circles a hill separating it from Ridgecrest Boulevard. This is a lovely, peaceful stretch. The Trail leaves the forest and recaptures ocean views. Aromatic sages line the way.

Coastal reenters woodland and drops. At the bottom of the switchbacks, at a potentially tricky intersection, the unsigned Old San Rafael-Bolinas Trail branches left. It is one of the oldest trails on the Mountain, and descends a half-mile before disappearing in grassland. Coastal Trail continues uphill to the right. The Trail recrosses the pig fence and spends its last yards beside Ridgecrest Boulevard, in deep woodland.

Coastal Trail ends where Ridgecrest Boulevard makes a T-intersection with Fairfax-Bolinas Road. This junction has historically been known as Ridge Crest. It was the site of a lodge, variously called Summit House (for it was at the highest point of the old San Rafael-Bolinas stage route), and Larsen's, Consy's, and Wright's (for successive owners). The lodge was a resting place for stage travelers. It burned in 1945, several years after it had been abandoned. The trailhead sign is inviting, indicating, for example, that it is 19.0 kilometers back to Tennessee Valley. Also inviting is the 11.3 mile long Bolinas Ridge Fire Road across the pavement. It is a combined use (pedestrian, biker, equestrian) section of the Bay Area Ridge Trail, dropping to Sir Francis Drake Boulevard near Olema. Like Coastal Trail, it offers another of Marin's special wilderness experiences.

HELEN MARKT TRAIL

From Cataract Trail to Kent Trail / 2.0 miles
Terrain: Redwood forest / MMWD
Elevation: From 1,080' to 800' / rolling, parts steep
Intersecting Trails: None
Directions: Fairfax-Bolinas Road to milepost 8.09 (six miles west of Sky Oaks Road, .2 miles past Alpine Dam) - Cataract Trail, .6 miles

Helen Markt (the "t" is silent) is one of the Mountain's lovelier trails. It winds above the cool, wet, remote southwest shore of Alpine Lake. Since it takes some effort to reach either end, and even its easiest loop possibility is strenuous, Helen Markt remains little-visited. Reaching a trailhead involves either a 2.3 mile walk from the Bon Tempe Dam parking area or a very steep .6 mile uphill on Cataract Trail from Alpine Dam. I'll describe the latter approach, as it is shorter.

Climb Cataract Trail and cross the angled bridge over Cataract Creek. About 25 yards above the bridge, a sign, affixed to a Douglas-fir, indicates the start, to the left, of Helen Markt Trail. Cataract Trail continues uphill right.

Helen Markt begins downhill. It crosses a prominent fallen Douglas-fir, cut for easier passage. The tree's huge size assures that it will continue to remain (as it has for years) a landmark of the Trail, though the work of wood-decaying fungi will ultimately prevail. Helen Markt winds and rolls through this relatively untouched woodland. The area above (south) is one of the largest on Tam without a regular trail, only an occasional deer path.

In .6 miles, in a grove of redwoods after a downhill, look carefully at the left margin of the Trail, and listen, for Broko Spring. It emerges from the ground here through the clay and is a safe source of cool water most all the year. "Broko" was a nickname for Joe Vitek, brother of the Trail's builder and a volunteer trail worker himself. The stream just ahead cuts through Blake Canyon, named for Arthur H. Blake, a long-time Bay Area hiker and environmentalist who died in 1957.

Ahead are masses of huckleberry shrubs, covered with tasty berries in late summer and fall. At 1.3 miles, the Trail crosses Swede George Creek, one of the strongest streams on the Mountain, on a wonderful bridge. The near end is secured to a Douglas-fir, the far end to a redwood. A path right leads to the edge of the creek.

The Trail climbs steeply and hits a short clearing at the edge of chaparral. Look left over the manzanita to see Alpine Dam at the far end of the lake. Helen Markt descends back into the woods. It then touches the shore of Alpine Lake, a fine place to rest. A path right is a shortcut when climbing Kent Trail. In another 75 yards Helen Markt ends when it meets Kent Trail, which goes straight ahead toward Bon Tempe Dam and uphill to Serpentine Point, High Marsh and Potrero Camp.

Jim Vitek, who knows the north side of Tamalpais probably better than anyone after 60 years of hiking over it and a career with the MMWD, constructed the Trail in the early 1950's. It was built to provide a new long loop possibility from Bon Tempe. Frank and Helen Markt were toll takers on Ridgecrest Boulevard in the 1930's, when it was still a toll road. They lived in a house (destroyed in the 1945 fire) at the junction of Ridgecrest and Fairfax-Bolinas Road. The couple later resided beside Lake Lagunitas, where Frank served as lakekeeper from 1940 until his retirement in 1965. Helen Markt died while Vitek was working on this Trail, so it was named in her honor.

HIGH MARSH TRAIL

From Cataract Trail to junction of Kent and Azalea Meadow trails / 2.1 miles
Terrain: Heavily wooded with some grassland, chaparral / MMWD
Elevation: From 1,400' to 1,500' / rolling, short parts steep
Intersecting Trails: Connector fire road to Laurel Dell F.R. (.2m), connector to Laurel Dell F.R. (.6m), Spur of Old Stove (.8m), Music Camp (1.5m), Cross Country Boys (2.0m)
Directions: Rock Spring - West Ridgecrest Boulevard - Laurel Dell F.R. - Cataract Trail downhill, .3 miles

It takes an effort to hike the full length of High Marsh Trail; at least six miles roundtrip, more for a loop, from any place reachable by car. This assures that the Trail, already in one of the remotest parts of the Mountain, will be peaceful and quiet, even on the busiest summer weekends. The Trail is mildly rolling by Mt. Tamalpais standards, covers a variety of terrain, has several splendid view sights, and, of course, passes wonderful High Marsh itself.

High Marsh Trail leaves Cataract Trail at a well-marked junction .3 miles below Laurel Dell. In around 1/6 mile, after passing a couple of shortcut paths back to Cataract, the Trail emerges from the forest to a grassy hillside. This is one of the loveliest places on Mt. Tamalpais, with gently contoured hills, wonderful views, and a riot of wildflowers in spring. You'll find orange poppies and fiddlenecks, yellow creamcups and buttercups, white woodland-stars and wild cucumbers, blue-eyed-grass, baby-blue-eyes, and blue lupines, and pink and reds from geraniums and scarlet pimpernels.

At .2 miles is the somewhat indistinct end of a connector fire road (shown as not going all the way through to here on the Olmsted map) from Laurel Dell F.R.. The Trail reenters woodland. At the top of an uphill, a signpost marks a 75 yard connector, right and uphill, to Laurel Dell F. R. High Marsh levels, and passes through a stretch of manzanita.

A Spur to Old Stove Trail enters on the right at .9 miles. The unmarked junction is easy to miss, particularly going in this direction. Look for it at the end of an uphill (the top of which is the divide between the drainages of Cataract and Swede George creeks) in a clearing. If you hit the wood steps downhill, you've gone 50 yards too far. Old Stove also leads to Laurel Dell F.R.

The views just beyond are outstanding, to Mt. St. Helena and beyond. The Trail drops, and returns to a forest canopy. The roller coaster rises to another clearing in the chaparral, again offering great vistas. A path, which could cause some problems, branches sharply left; veer right downhill. The next junction, unsigned and on the near side (left bank) of the West Fork of Swede George Creek, is with Music Camp Trail. There is a prominent rock to the left here. Music Camp Trail rises to near the hidden Music Camp, then on to Laurel Dell F.R.

Few, if any, parts of the Mountain are farther from a road than this next section. The deep forest, in which no signs of civilization are heard or seen, takes the sense of wilderness still further. A downhill path forks left to Willow Meadow Trail. Around .1 mile beyond, unexpectedly, High Marsh appears.

The marsh, like Hidden Lake, is a drainage-collecting slump that resulted from the huge Potrero landslide on the north side of West Peak. High Marsh is smaller than it was but a few decades ago as the surrounding vegetation advances, and can be completely dry in fall. It remains a most appealing resting place. At the marsh, Cross Country Boys Trail, unsigned, rises steeply uphill to the right. High Marsh Trail is somewhat indistinct as it hugs the fluctuating water line. The Trail soon becomes clear again.

It's a level .1 mile to the Trail's end at a four-way intersection. Kent Trail goes left to Alpine Lake and right to Potrero Camp. The trail directly across is the Azalea Meadow, heading to Rifle Camp. The lack of signposts, the presence of more trails than on most maps, and the lack of landmarks in the forest make this one of the easiest areas on the Mountain to get lost.

High Marsh Trail was built without authorization from the Water District in the 1960's by a single individual. It was first called the Gracie Trail.

LAUREL DELL FIRE ROAD

From Ridgecrest Boulevard to Potrero Meadow / 2.1 miles
Terrain: Grassland, forest, and chaparral; part riparian / MMWD
Elevation: From 1,920' to 1,640' to 2,020' / gradual, rolling
Intersecting Trails: Connector to Cataract Trail (.3m), Cataract (.6m), connector fire road to High Marsh Trail (.8m), connector to High Marsh Trail (.8m), Old Stove (.9m, 1.3m), connector to Mickey O'Brien (1.4m), connector fire road to Barth's Retreat (1.6m), Music Camp (1.6m), connector fire road to Potrero Camp (1.7m), Benstein (1.8m)
Directions: Rock Spring - West Ridgecrest Boulevard, 1.4 miles

Laurel Dell Fire Road provides access to some of the famous sites on the north side of the Mountain, including Laurel Dell itself, Barth's Retreat, the Music Camp, the two Potrero Meadows, and Rifle Camp. It is well graded, and passes through several different habitats. There are also some exceptional vista points.

The Fire Road sets off east of Ridgecrest Boulevard, at a gate beside a sizable parking turnout. When coming from Rock Spring, the Laurel Dell trailhead is around 100 yards past, and across Ridgecrest from, the top of Willow Camp Fire Road. There were tank traps on the ridge here during World War II.

Laurel Dell F.R. descends in a sweeping arc through the open grassland. It soon enters woodland. In 1/3 mile, a signed path forks to the right. It crosses Cataract Creek over a bridge, and is a shortcut to Cataract Trail. Just before the Fire Road itself drops to the creek, look left, at the edge of the woodland, for an old fenced enclosure. It was built to protect Laurel Dell's water source from the cattle that used to graze here.

The Fire Road crosses the creek at the edge of Laurel Dell Meadow. The crossing can be quite wet, even unpassable except with high boots, after winter rains and there is no easy way to skirt it. Mickey O'Brien Trail rising to Barth's Retreat, and Cataract Trail climbing to Rock Spring, are both a few yards to the right. A new horse trough and hitching post were added late in 1989.

The tree-ringed meadow at Laurel Dell is immensely appealing. The picnic area is just ahead; go left opposite the outhouses. Laurel Dell has been, justifiably, a favorite destination for generations. Tables are set beneath the laurels, beside Cataract Creek. The water fountain, fed by Peter Bourne Spring, is now signed as non-potable because the water is untreated, though many still use it. Cataract Trail, to High Marsh Trail and Alpine Dam, continues downhill from the picnic area.

Laurel Dell F.R. now heads uphill, into a forest of Douglas-firs. Around .1 mile from Laurel Dell, a connector fire road climbs left to what are known as the "Bare Knolls," then on to High Marsh Trail. In a couple of hundred feet is a signed 75-yard-long connector, once part of the Dead End Trail, that also ends at High Marsh Trail. Just beyond, Laurel Dell F.R. makes a big bend. In the bend, unmarked on the left, is Old Stove Trail. It is recognizable by a few wooden steps. One fork of Old Stove goes to High Marsh Trail, another reconnects to Laurel Dell Fire Road.

As the route climbs, the tree cover opens. You can look back to the gate at Ridgecrest Boulevard where the Fire Road began. On a level section in the chaparral, Old Stove Trail, even less easy to spot than before, rejoins Laurel Dell F.R. The junction is directly across from a small clearing, which harbors remnants of an old camp site. Beyond, just before the tree line, a .2 mile connector (once part of Old Stove Trail) to Mickey O'Brien Trail leaves to the right.

The Fire Road rises into forest again, then drops back into chaparral. At the bottom of the dip, a sign atop a connector fire road points the way down to Barth's Retreat and to the Simmons and Mickey O'Brien trails. The latter offers a loop option. To the left, opposite the sign, is the unmarked and indistinct top of Music Camp Trail.

Laurel Dell Fire Road crests just ahead. The views to the north are outstanding. On the clearest of winter days, snow-capped mountains, 100 miles away in Mendocino County, are visible from here. Closer sights include the Point Reyes peninsula and Alpine Lake. The Fire Road returns to woodland. It passes a short connector on the left which drops to Potrero Camp, lower Potrero Meadow, and the top of Kent Trail. In another 50 yards, to the right at a signed intersection, Benstein Trail begins its journey to Rock Spring.

Part of lower Potrero Meadow is visible to the left. Then the larger upper Potrero Meadow, one of the treasures of Mt. Tamalpais, is met. Laurel Dell F.R. bends right. There is an old sign at what used to be a crossing, now closed, of the meadow. A path to Rock Spring-Lagunitas F. R. branches right. In a few more yards, Laurel Dell Fire Road ends when it meets Rock Spring-Lagunitas F.R. To the left is Rifle Camp and an over two mile descent to Lake Lagunitas. To the right is Rock Spring.

Laurel Dell was earlier known as Old Stove Camp, for a stove once found there. It was reportedly renamed Laurel Dell by J. H. Cutter, first president of the Tamalpais Conservation Club. The laurel, or bay, may be the most common tree on Tamalpais. Laurel Dell Fire Road was built by the Civilian Conservation Corps in the 1930's over parts of Old Stove Trail.

LONE TREE FIRE ROAD

From Highway 1 to Coastal Fire Road / 1.8 miles
Terrain: Grassland; views / MTSP
Elevation: From 420' to 1,380' / very steep
Intersecting Trails: Dipsea (1.1m, 1.2m, 1.3m, 1.4m, 1.5m, 1.6m)
Directions: Highway 1 by the south side of mileage marker 10.67

Though the ocean views are continuous and spectacular when following Lone Tree Fire Road downhill, it is described uphill because the bottom is accessible by car. Climbing Lone Tree also permits a descent on its closest loop partners, the Dipsea and Steep Ravine trails. The views going uphill are outstanding as well and, given the route's steepness, there will be reason to rest and enjoy them.

Lone Tree F.R. starts from a gate on the east side of Highway 1 by mile signpost 10.67. Across the highway is a parking turnout and the top of Rocky Point Trail, which goes to the Steep Ravine cabins. The State Park trailhead signs at both ends call the Fire Road the Dipsea Fire Trail, but the name Dipsea is firmly tied to the separate, famous Dipsea Trail. Other maps (Olmsted and the State Park one, for example) use the name Lone Tree. To confuse matters a bit more, the present Dipsea Trail was originally called Lone Tree Trail before the Dipsea Inn was built in 1904.

The climb begins very steeply, and rarely relents the whole way. Baccharis is the common shrub alongside the Fire Road. Otherwise grassland, dotted with wildflowers, dominates. No trails cross the large area to the right, above and through the canyons of Lone Tree Gulch and Cold Stream, until Coastal Fire Road. This whole southwest face of Tamalpais remains little visited and little explored.

Older maps show now overgrown paths heading left to Webb Creek. At 1.1 miles, a sign marks where the Dipsea Trail departs left to Stinson Beach. The Dipsea Trail then criss-crosses and runs together with Lone Tree F.R. the rest of the ascent.

There is a brief downhill, a welcome respite from the steady grind. Lone Tree F.R. rises to the edge of a hill covered with Douglas-firs. The Dipsea Trail goes right, bypassing an uphill. The hill above was bare − even sometimes called Bald Hill − around the turn of the century, save for a single redwood, the famous "lone tree." That redwood is still alive and visible on the lower, right edge of the tree line. A short path to the left of Lone Tree F.R. circles behind the redwood and passes the Lone Tree fountain. The fountain was built by the Tamalpais Conservation Club in 1917 by tapping Lone Tree Spring. Dipsea runners and other passers-by still use it. A storm in the winter of 1989, however, has narrowed the flow to a trickle. The fountain area offers a lovely, sheltered picnic site on hot or windy days.

The Dipsea Trail departs right at its last intersection with Lone Tree F.R. The Fire Road ends just above, when it meets Coastal Fire Road at a three-way intersection. Left leads to Old Mine Trail, the separate Lone Tree Hill F.R., and to Pantoll. Right on Coastal F.R. leads to the Dipsea Trail at Cardiac Hill, the top of Deer Park F.R., Camp Shansky, and Highway 1.

Part of Lone Tree Fire Road, below the first Dipsea junction, has been known as Warm Spring Trail because it once continued (before construction of Highway 1) to the hot spring at the mouth of Webb Creek. The whole historic route was widened to a fire road, separate from the Dipsea, in the 1950's.

McKENNAN FIRE ROAD

From Ridgecrest Boulevard to Willow Camp Fire Road / 2.2 miles
Spur: Between McKennan F.R. and Highway 1 / .7 miles
Terrain: Open grassland; views / MTSP & GGNRA
Elevation: From 1,680' to 20' / very steep, parts extremely steep
Intersecting Trails: None
Directions: Rock Spring - West Ridgecrest Blvd., 2.2 miles

McKennan Fire Road is long and steep, one of the toughest uphills on Tam. Since both its ends are accessible by car, a one way, downhill trek with a shuttle is more pleasant, and that is how it will be described. A difficult but lovely loop with Coastal Trail and Willow Camp Fire Road is another candidate.

McKennan sets off to the west from Ridgecrest Boulevard at a gate. The trailhead is at the northern end of Coastal Trail's short stretch on Ridgecrest Boulevard, around 1.5 miles from Fairfax-Bolinas Road. Immediately the panorama, which includes the San Francisco skyline, is breathtaking. The ocean is in view nearly the whole way down. After a relatively level start, the Fire Road meets a magnificent, old, solitary Douglas fir, battered by lightning but still alive in a rocky outcrop. The downhill steepens considerably, the first of three such precipitous stretches.

A brief uphill is encountered before McKennan enters a grove of bay and Douglas fir. Beyond, ceanothus, its blue blossoms intoxicatingly fragrant in late winter and early spring, lines the Fire Road. There is an old fence line beside a level stretch. Dairy ranches once covered this face of Bolinas Ridge; there are still several north of Fairfax-Bolinas Road. Another level stretch is through a second Douglas fir grove. The next downhill is again quite steep.

At a prominent fork, a GGNRA hiker's symbol sign points the way left. The .7 mile long route to the right fork is considered as a Spur of McKennan here. It is an old ranch road, now unmaintained but still in good shape, that runs north as it gently descends. In about a half-mile it seems to disappear at a line of goldcup oak trees. Cut left ten yards through the grass to pick up the Spur again. Isolated, colonizing Douglas-firs, which may one day cover the whole hillside now that grazing has ended, become more common. The Spur ends at a gate beside Highway 1 next to milepost 14.06. There is no trail sign there, though the land is part of Golden Gate National Recreation Area. McKennan Gulch, which forms the northern boundary of this book, and Audubon Canyon Ranch are to the right (north).

The main McKennan Fire Road continues downhill to the left. Bolinas Lagoon and Stinson Beach appear ever closer. The grassland has been disturbed from the many years of grazing; the grasses are now virtually all non-native Eurasian species. The Fire Road here is becoming overgrown. The long descent ends by several ranch buildings, now part of GGNRA but some are still used as residences.

McKennan then meets Willow Camp Fire Road at a signed fork. Left lead to Stinson Beach's Avenida de Farralone, then back up to Bolinas Ridge. Around .1 mile to the right is Highway 1 at milepost 13.69, by the Bolinas-Stinson School. Across the highway is Bolinas Lagoon, one of the Bay Area's finest birdwatching sites.

Hugh McKennan, who came to California from Ireland during the Gold Rush, raised ducks on his ranch here. He shipped up to 1,000 eggs a day from Bolinas to San Francisco by schooner, and also ran a ferry across the lagoon. The Fire Road appears on the 1898 Sanborn map. Its name has been spelled at least half a dozen ways on maps over the years since.

OLD BOLINAS-SAN RAFAEL TRAIL

From Coastal Trail west toward Highway 1 / .5 miles
Terrain: Upper part heavily wooded, lower part grassland; unimproved / GGNRA
Elevation: From 1,320' to around 900' / very steep
Intersecting Trails: None
Directions: Junction of Ridgecrest Blvd. and Fairfax-Bolinas Road - Coastal Trail, .4 miles

This unnamed Trail is a remnant of one of the oldest routes, connecting San Rafael to Bolinas, in Marin. Padres at the San Rafael Mission used it when traveling to the Bolinas area. It appears as Tam's only trail on an 1860 map. The sections of the old route east of Bolinas Ridge are now either overgrown, covered by Fairfax-Bolinas Road, or under Alpine Lake. This surviving segment, not found on recent maps, runs down the ridge that separates Volunteer Canyon to the north from Morse's Gulch to the south. To reach it, follow Coastal Trail from Fairfax-Bolinas Road. At the bottom of a significant dip, beside a creek bed, Old San Rafael-Bolinas Trail sets off to the right. The Trail descends on the left bank of this creek, which cuts through Volunteer Canyon to Bolinas Lagoon.

The early going, through a deep woodland in one of the Mountain's more remote corners, is only slightly downhill. In around 1/6 mile, the Trail meets an old fence. The land north (right) is private, part of Audubon Canyon Ranch. It is open to the public only on weekends from mid-March to mid-July, otherwise by appointment. The forest thins, offering some outstanding views.

The Trail, ever steepening, cuts through a meadow. After a brief return to forest, the Trail reaches a grassy hillside. Morse's Gulch is the canyon to the left. Stinson Beach beckons below. The Trail deteriorates to a barely visible path through the grass, below this book's minimum standards. The remaining descent of some 900 vertical feet is therefore not described.

OLD STOVE TRAIL

Between Laurel Dell Fire Road | .3 miles
Spur: Between Old Stove Trail and High Marsh Trail | .1 mile
Terrain: Chaparral | MMWD
Elevation: From 1,780' to 1,960' | steep
Intersecting Trails: None
Directions: Rock Spring - West Ridgecrest Boulevard - Laurel Dell F.R., .9 miles

Old Stove Trail is unmarked and easy to miss at both its ends. To reach the trailhead, descend Laurel Dell Fire Road from Ridgecrest Boulevard. One-third mile beyond Laurel Dell itself, at the far end of a sweeping bend, Old Stove sets off up a few wood steps to the left.

Old Stove leaves the forest and enters chaparral. The Trail peaks at a splendid, isolated, rocky view site. A short Spur drops left to High Marsh Trail. The main Old Stove continues right another .1 mile, into chamise. It ends upon rejoining Laurel Dell Fire Road. Directly across the fire road here is a prominent clearing in the trees that housed an old camp site, remnants of which are still visible. Potrero Meadow is less than a mile to the left.

Old Stove Trail dates to around 1910. It once connected Laurel Dell to Potrero Meadow. Laurel Dell Fire Road subsequently covered most of the original route. There was also an Old Stove Extension, which ran from across Cataract Creek at Laurel Dell up to Bolinas Ridge. Already somewhat faint, it was largely obliterated after a storm in December 1987. Laurel Dell was originally called Old Stove Camp, for an old stove that lay there for years. Parts of an old stove were unearthed there in 1990.

OWL TRAIL

From Highway 1 to Slide Ranch | .9 miles
Terrain: Coastal scrub; ocean views | GGNRA
Elevation: From 440' to 160' | gradual
Intersecting Trails: None
Directions: Highway 1 to Muir Beach Overlook, between mileposts 6.96 and 7.00

Owl Trail sets off from the parking lot of Muir Beach Overlook, a dramatic vista point high above sheer cliffs. A GGNRA hiker's sign points the way to the Trail, heading north. In 100 yards the Trail meets a parking turnout and continues just to the left of four wooden posts.

The Trail skirts the hillside toward a prominent lone Monterey cypress tree. Owl Trail, periodically maintained by Slide Ranch residents, is usually clear to follow. Several paths drop to the ocean or climb to Highway 1. Occasionally, baccharis, lupine, or blackberry must be brushed aside. The Pacific is in constant view and within hearing. In 1/3 mile, the Trail passes a clump of eucalyptus.

In .4 miles, a well-worn path crosses left and right. It connects a turnout on Highway 1 above to the rocky shore below. Other paths cross shortly after. One passes the introduced cypress, drops to a dome-shaped structure owned by Slide Ranch, and continues on to the ranch.

Owl Trail becomes a bit less distinct. It continues to descend gradually to a row of tall cypress and eucalyptus. Several great horned owls spend their days in these trees, but you'll need to look very carefully to spot them. The Trail skirts the right edge of the east-west tree line, then the left edge of the north-south row. The path back toward the dome comes in on the left.

Just past a metal sculpture of a bird, Owl Trail ends at the access road into and out of Slide Ranch. About 75 yards uphill to the right is the public parking area. The road continues down to a PG&E station. Also, paths descend from the ranch to the boulder-strewn shoreline.

Slide Ranch, a delightful blend of spectacular scenery, domesticated animals, and old farm buildings, covers 134 acres. The Nature Conservancy bought the former dairy ranch in the late 1960's when plans to develop it were emerging. The property later became part of the Golden Gate National Recreation Area. The non-profit Frontier Arts Institute at the ranch offers very well received tours for school groups; call the ranch manager at 415/381-6155 for details. Several of the buildings are used as private residences.

Great horned owls, the largest of several owl species to be found on the Mountain, are effective nocturnal predators. They kill rodents, birds, and other prey as large as skunks. The great horned's large size (nearly 2 feet in height), ear tufts, and the noiseless flight characteristic of owls distinguish them.

RED ROCK TRAIL

From Highway 1 to Red Rock Beach / .3 miles
Terrain: Coastal scrub / MTSP
Elevation: From 230' to sea level / very steep
Intersecting Trails: None
Directions: Highway 1 to milepost 11.43 (south of Stinson Beach)

This short, deadend Trail is the principal, and usually only, access to Red Rock Beach. The trailhead is on Highway 1, about a mile south of central Stinson Beach. There is a sizable parking area atop the Trail, and additional parking across Highway 1.

Red Rock Trail winds its way steeply downhill. Views of Red Rock and of the beach open around a bend. The Trail descends a set of steps, then leaves the coastal scrub. The rocks are indeed reddish. A second set of steps leads directly to the beach, which is a favorite of sunbathers. Look back. A faded carving in the top step reads:

> IN MEMORY OF WENDY STOYKA, THE WOMAN I LOVE – LOST AT SEA IN SEED.

It is possible to walk to Stinson Beach, to the north, during low tides.

ROCKY POINT TRAIL

From Highway 1 to Steep Ravine Road / .3 miles
Terrain: Coastal scrub / MTSP
Elevation: From 420' to 220' / very steep
Intersecting Trails: None
Directions: Highway 1 to milepost 10.67

Rocky Point Trail offers a shorter and steeper route down to the Steep Ravine cabins and campground than paved Steep Ravine Road (which see). It is, however, heavily lined with poison-oak, which can be avoided only with caution. Since the spectacular ocean views are so engrossing, the chances of brushing against the poison-oak are even greater.

The Trail descends from a turnout off Highway 1 just south of mileage marker 10.67. Across the highway is the Lone Tree Fire Road entry gate. Immediately veer right. The narrow Trail descends steeply. Baccharis and sage are the dominant shrubs, with poison-oak mingling freely. Coastal wildflowers abound in spring.

The Trail ends at the paved road, which continues down to the campground. A path, also laced with poison-oak, skirts the edge of the bluff aptly known as Rocky Point.

STEEP RAVINE ROAD

From Highway 1 to Steep Ravine cabins / 1.1 miles
Terrain: Mostly asphalt, lower part dirt; views / MTSP
Elevation: From 380' to 50' / gradual
Intersecting Trails: Rocky Point (.5m)
Directions: Highway 1 to mileage marker 11.04

A road leads down from Highway 1 to the Steep Ravine cabins and campground. A gate blocks cars — only overnight guests are given the lock's combination — so the road, though largely paved, is included in this book. The road is not named, but, since it leads to the Steep Ravine cabins and campground, is called Steep Ravine Road here. Rocky Point Road would be just as appropriate. The separate, famous Steep Ravine Trail climbs to Pantoll from across the highway.

The descent to the cabins is gradual, and glorious, even in fog. The views of the Pacific are continuous, as is the sound of the surf. Along the way, two unmarked paths branch back up to the left. The second is Rocky Point Trail, which meets Highway 1 about one-third mile south of Steep Ravine Road. At a gate, a dirt fire road comes in on the left. It arcs down to again meet the paved road, making the lower half of Steep Ravine Road into a loop.

The pavement continues lower to the parking lot, and outhouses, for the Steep Ravine cabins. The cabins, perched just above the breaking surf, were long a private retreat for the Kent family and their friends. Now they have been repaired and opened to the public on a reservation basis. Call the California State Park reservation service, MISTIX, at 800/444-PARK. The current fee is $25 a night. There is no electricity, water, or bathrooms in the cabins themselves. The names of the ten cabins: William Kent, Dipsea, Thaddeus Welch, Rocky Point, Willow Camp, Webb Creek, Hot Spring, San Andreas, Farallon, and Whale Watchers, reflect features or history of the area. There are also six campsites, with equally special settings, just to the south.

A path leads down to the mouth of Webb Creek, site of a once popular hot spring. It is now accessible only in fall, at very low tides, below -.7'. Then it is possible to dig in the sand to reach the spring's warm water. Another path, lined with poison-oak, skirts just above the surf at Rocky Point.

STINSON GULCH FIRE ROAD

From Willow Camp Fire Road to Stinson Gulch / .6 miles
Terrain: Coastal grassland, parts wooded / GGNRA
Elevation: From 320' to 380' / almost level
Intersecting Trails: None
Directions: Parking lot at north end of Avenida Farralone in Stinson Beach - Willow Camp F.R. uphill, .2 miles

This Fire Road is unsigned and has no recognized name. I use Stinson Gulch Fire Road because it ends near Stinson Gulch. To reach the trailhead, follow Willow Camp Fire Road uphill from the gate and sign at the north end of Stinson Beach's Avenida Farralone. In .2 miles, there is a fork. The connector fire road to the right goes to the water tank. Bear left. Twenty yards beyond is still another fork. To the right, Willow Camp F.R. heads steeply uphill. On the left is a path, marked with a small hiker symbol sign, that connects to lower on Willow Camp. Straight ahead is the start of Stinson Gulch Fire Road.

Follow Stinson Gulch F.R. through the coastal grassland. There are fine views of the ocean, Seadrift, and Bolinas Lagoon. A water pipeline skirts the Fire Road's right edge; the Fire Road was likely built to service the line. In a quarter-mile, the Fire Road enters its first wooded area, a forest of mostly laurel. The last tree before the return to open terrain is a bigleaf maple. Unlike the laurels, it loses its leaves in winter.

The Fire Road winds in and out of woodland. Then, a large, fallen laurel blocks the way. It isn't worth scrambling over since the Fire Road ends just a few yards beyond in the stream canyon, where the pipeline begins. Only a narrow path continues.

WILLOW CAMP FIRE ROAD

From Ridgecrest Boulevard to Highway 1 / 3.0 miles
Terrain: Coastal scrub and grassland; views / MTSP & GGNRA
Elevation: From 1,900' to 10' / very steep
Intersecting Trails: Coastal (.1m), Stinson Gulch F.R. (1.7 miles), McKennan F.R. (2.9m)
Directions: Rock Spring - West Ridgecrest Blvd., 1.3 miles

Willow Camp is the southernmost of several very steep fire roads that descend west from the 15-mile-long, almost 2,000' high Bolinas Ridge. It can be covered as a loop in combination with Coastal Trail and either McKennan Fire Road or Matt Davis Trail. A shuttle makes a one way downhill trip also possible, as both ends of Willow Camp are accessible by car.

Willow Camp F.R. departs from Ridgecrest Boulevard just south of, and across the pavement from, the parking turnout atop Laurel Dell F.R. There is some road shoulder parking at the marked trailhead. Both a fire road and trail descend towards the ocean; they merge in less than .1 mile as the single broad Willow Camp Fire Road. In another few yards, Willow Camp reaches a four-way intersection. Coastal Trail departs left to Matt Davis Trail and right to McKennan F.R. Continue downhill to Stinson Beach. The sweeping vistas of ocean and coastline are spectacular. Indeed, for views, Willow Camp holds its place with any route on Mt. Tamalpais.

At .4 miles, the Fire Road enters a grove of bays, oaks, and massive, lichen-covered Douglas-firs. The irises found here are a different species from the irises abounding on the grasslands just a few yards ahead, offering an excellent opportunity to distinguish between them. Amidst the trees in spring are Douglas, or Marin, Iris. In the clearing beyond are clumps of ground iris. Marin iris is taller, with stems of 8 inches or more. Their arching leaves are shiny above, dull below. They are much admired for their variable, delicate color shadings. Ground iris grows close to the ground, has similar upper and lower leaf surfaces, and a lovely fragrance.

You can begin to hear the surf at Stinson Beach. The Fire Road bends right and skirts the hillside, with a precipitous drop left. A conspicuous plant the rest of the way is wild cucumber, or manroot. Check out the trail pattern visible below to avoid getting confused later. Willow Camp Fire Road leaves Mount Tamalpais State Park and enters Golden Gate National Recreation Area.

Just beneath the level of the prominent water tanks, a four-way junction is reached. To the right is the start of Stinson Gulch F.R., which ends in .6 miles in a canyon. The path to its left, marked by a hiker's sign, offers a quarter-mile shortcut in the descent of Willow Camp F.R. Continue left. In twenty yards there is another fork; the short fire road to the left goes up to the water tanks. It's then some 300 yards downhill to a large GGNRA sign headed "Willow Camp Fire Trail." To the left, next to the fence line, is a broad path; it ends in 1/4 mile. Beyond the gate is a small parking area at the end of Avenida Farralone in Stinson Beach. Veer right to continue.

Willow Camp now drops more gently. It meets the bottom of the shortcut path. It then descends through a cool wooded stretch, rich with coastal vegetation. The Fire Road cuts through an old ranch, now part of the GGNRA; please respect the residents' privacy. A connector fire road to the right leads to a water tank and ends. Continue straight. At a marked junction, beside a cactus and an old barn, McKennan Fire Road sets off to the right on its long climb to Ridgecrest Boulevard.

Willow Camp Fire Road ends in another hundred yards, at milepost sign 13.69 on Highway 1. Bolinas Lagoon, one of the finest birdwatching spots in the Bay Area, is across the road. Bolinas-Stinson School borders on the right, and downtown Stinson Beach is 1.2 miles to the left.

Willow Camp was the original name of Stinson Beach. The town was renamed in 1920 for Nathan Stinson, who had bought land in the area in 1870 and then developed a resort called Willow Camp. Willows still line Easkoot Creek beside the main entry into the popular beach. This Fire Road appears only on post-World War II maps.

KEY JUNCTIONS

There are many important trail junctions on Mt. Tamalpais. Those accessible by car are designated as trailheads. Other key junctions, where four or more trails or fire roads meet, are presented below to avoid repetition in the text. The elevation of the junction, and the nearest trailhead(s), are also given.

BOY SCOUT JUNCTION, *380' (Deer Park)*

This big junction has seven spokes. Clockwise from Deer Park Fire Road with your back to Deer Park, they are: Bald Hill Trail to Six Points, Deer Park F.R. rising to Five Corners, a connector fire road dropping to Canyon Trail, Moore Trail, Ridge Trail, Junction Trail, and Deer Park F.R. downhill. Camp Lilienthal, once a half-mile to the west, was long used by the boy scouts. The scouts since have moved to Camp Tamarancho on the slopes of White's Hill.

CAMP ALICE EASTWOOD, *600' (Mountain Home, Muir Woods)*

This historic area was the site of the first Muir Woods Inn, from 1907 to 1913, and of a large Civilian Conservation Corps camp in the 1930's. Alice Eastwood was curator of botany at the California Academy of Sciences for 56 years and a life long hiker and naturalist on the Mountain. She was present when the current group camp was named in her honor in 1949 on her 90th birthday. Meeting the paved, level clearing of the camp, clockwise with your back to the asphalt section of Camp Eastwood Road, are: Fern Canyon Trail to Muir Woods, Plevin Cut Trail, Camp Eastwood Road descending to Muir Woods, Sierra Trail rising to Panoramic Highway, and paved Camp Eastwood Road to Mountain Home.

FIVE CORNERS, *520' (Phoenix Lake, Deer Park)*

There are actually six options at Five Corners; a short, connector fire road was added after the junction's name was well established. The six choices, clockwise from the top of Deer Park F.R. with you back to Deer Park, are: the .1 mile connector to Bald Hill Trail, the combined Shaver Grade and Concrete Pipeline F.R. going downhill, Elliott, Shaver Grade going uphill, and Concrete Pipeline F.R. toward Fairfax-Bolinas Road. In February 1989, Harrison Ford and Sean Connery were at Five Corners to film a chase scene for the film "Indiana Jones and the Last Crusade."

MOUNTAIN THEATER, *1,990' (Rock Spring)*

The Mountain Theater, formally called the Sidney B. Cushing Memorial Theater, is one of the Mountain's star attractions. The first Mountain Play was presented there in 1913, and the stone seats added in the 1930's. Five trail options directly meet the theater. They are: Rock Spring, across the upper row of seats, heading west to Ridgecrest Boulevard and east to West Point; Bootjack and Easy Grade trails coming in from the south; and Mountain Theater Trail going west to Old Mine Trail.

OCTOPUS, *390' (Old Highway 101)*

Marin County Open Space rangers have dubbed this eight-way intersection (five fire roads and three paths) "the Octopus." It is most easily reached via Corte Madera Ridge F.R., a couple of hundred yards uphill from Corte Madera Avenue. There is a water pump station building at the intersection. The junction's other intersecting fire roads, clockwise when reached uphill on Corte Madera Ridge F.R., are: Escalon-Lower Summit F.R. heading to Escalon Drive in Mill Valley, the upper end of Mill Valley's Sarah Drive, Corte Madera Ridge F.R. continuing up toward Blithedale Ridge, and Escalon-Lower Summit F.R. going north to Summit Drive in Corte Madera. The top of Harvey Warne Trail is a few yards below the junction. A separate, four-way junction, dubbed the "Escalon Octopus," is .6 miles to the south on Escalon-Lower Summit F.R.

PHOENIX JUNCTION, *200' (Phoenix Lake)*

This is the important junction at the western tip of Phoenix Lake. The choices, clockwise from Phoenix Lake Fire Road with your back to the lake, are: Eldridge Grade beginning its climb to the top of Tam, Fish Grade to the Sky Oaks Road, Fish Gulch Trail, and Shaver Grade to Five Corners.

RIFLE CAMP, *2,000' (Ridgecrest Boulevard)*

Less than 50 yards east of the main Potrero Meadow is Rifle Camp (now called Rifle Picnic Area by the MMWD). This historic gathering and resting spot has outhouses and picnic tables. It supposedly got its name after a dog dug up a rifle at the site. The intersecting trails and fire roads are: Rock Spring-Lagunitas F.R. going north and south, the base of Arturo Trail, the west end of Northside Trail, and the upper end of Azalea Meadow Trail.

SIX POINTS, *550' (Deer Park, Phoenix Lake)*

There are presently only five options at Six Points; a trail climbing higher up Bald Hill is now overgrown. The choices, clockwise from Yolanda Trail with your back to Phoenix Lake, are: Hidden Meadow Trail, Bald Hill Trail toward Five Corners, Six Points Trail down to Deer Park F.R., and Yolanda continuing to Worn Spring F.R.

WEST POINT, *1,780' (East Ridgecrest Boulevard, Pantoll)*

West Point refers to the westernmost point of the Mt. Tamalpais Railway, "the crookedest railroad in the world." The West Point Inn, still standing and still offering accommodations (by reservation only), was built at the site in 1904. From here, travelers could rest before transferring to or from the Bolinas stagecoach. West Point, with its splendid views, picnic tables, fountain, and inn offering light refreshments and bathrooms, remains a favorite stopping place for Mountain visitors. The intersecting trails and fire roads, clockwise from Old Railroad Grade with your back facing downhill, are: Nora Trail dropping to Matt Davis Trail, West Point Trail also dropping to Matt Davis, Old Stage Road to Pantoll, Rock Spring Trail to the Mountain Theater, and Old Railroad Grade continuing around the inn to the summit.

ROCKS

The geologic history of Mt. Tamalpais is far from well understood. Some authorities show the Tam region under water as recently as a couple of million years ago, as most of the rest of the Bay Area clearly was. Other authorities point to Tam's complete absence of marine fossils, which are found on other Bay Area hills that were submerged, as evidence that the Mountain has been above water, perhaps as an island, for tens of millions of years.

To better comprehend what is known about Tam geologically, some background on plate tectonics is in order. The Earth's crust is composed of several plates, which move in relation to another. It is this motion which causes mountain building, and earthquakes. Mt. Tamalpais lies at the western edge of the North American Plate. Just to its west, across the San Andreas Fault (partly covered by Bolinas Lagoon), lies the Pacific Plate, on which the Pt. Reyes peninsula sits. At one time another plate, the Farallon, lay between the North American and Pacific plates. The Pacific Plate is creeping northwest at an average rate of nearly two inches a year along the San Andreas Fault, but the movement is occasionally more dramatic — some 20 feet in seconds during the 1906 earthquake.

The rocks that comprise Mt. Tamalpais are mostly 80-150 million years old. They largely formed from sediments that were eroded and carried westward off the then young Sierra Nevada to the ocean basin which covered western California. These sediments were deposited atop volcanic rock that lay beneath the sea. Some of this volcanic rock intruded upward. The North American plate then rode over the Farallon plate, scraping off, jumbling, and thrusting upward these rocks as today's Coast Range, of which Tamalpais is a part. This tangled association of rocks, whose chronology is so difficult to unravel, is called the Franciscan Complex (or Assemblage or Formation).

Erosion then began its relentless task. Less resistant rock was washed away, and the combination of earthquakes and water-logged soil helped trigger landslides. Salem Rice, who has studied the geology of the Mountain probably more closely than anyone, speculates that Tam has been roughly its present height for millions of years, that its present three-peaked profile became recognizable around 100-150,000 years ago, and that further erosion and slides will someday turn the highly resistant rock core of East Peak into more of a spire.

Mt. Tamalpais is active geologically. It has evolved to the topographic feature it now is and, sitting beside the active San Andreas Fault, is subject to further pressures. It is also worth emphasizing that though some its rocks are of volcanic origin, Tamalpais itself was never a volcano.

All three of the basic rock classes — igneous, metamorphic, and sedimentary — are represented on Mt. Tamalpais, with sedimentary rocks much the most common. Some of the more abundant rock types, which account for over 95% of the Mountain, are described below.

SANDSTONE, MUDSTONE, SHALE

These sedimentary rocks form the bulk of Mt. Tamalpais. Sandstone, mudstone, and shale are composed of, in decreasing order of particle size, compressed and bound sand, mud, and clay. The original particles were eroded off the Sierra Nevada, dropped into an ocean trench at the site of the present Coast Range, then compressed into rock about 80 to 150 million years ago. Graywacke is a dark-gray compact type of sandstone dominant on the Mountain. It is made up of medium-sized, angular sand grains between which are mud and clay-sized particles. Because these rocks readily weather to soil, which is in turn covered by vegetation, they are not generally seen exposed. Much of the sandstone, mudstone, and shale has been well fractured and sheared, forming, with other rocks, what is called "melange."

GREENSTONE

Greenstone is igneous rock of volcanic origin; occasionally pieces can be found showing the holes, called vesicules, from which gases escaped as the lava cooled. It is green, from the presence of the mineral chlorite, only when fresh. Though highly resistant, when fractured greenstone weathers to a thick, iron-rich soil which oxidizes to a reddish brown. This soil holds moisture well and supports both heavy forests and grasslands. Fifteen mile long Bolinas Ridge, on the western side of Tamalpais and the most coherent rock mass on the Mountain, is greenstone. Pilot Knob and most of Bald Hill are also blocks of greenstone.

SERPENTINE

Serpentine (also called serpentinite) is probably the most distinctive rock on Mt. Tamalpais. Its boulder-size masses of varying grays, greens, and blues are familiar to most visitors. Serpentine is a metamorphic rock formed deep in the earth, below the floor of the Pacific, from peridotite, the most abundant rock of the earth's mantle. Because serpentine lacks aluminum, a main ingredient of clay soils, it does not weather to soil and thus remains largely exposed. It is also deficient in the important plant nutrients potassium, calcium, and sodium, and has a very high level of magnesium, toxic to some plants. It thus supports a plant life that is quite distinctive; some plants grow only on serpentine, others take different forms or exist out of their normal ranges on it.

West Peak is composed of serpentine. The seats of the Mountain Theater are blocks of serpentine, most of which had to be hauled to the site from elsewhere on Tam. Serpentine is the state rock of California.

CHERT

Chert is a very hard sedimentary rock composed almost entirely of the mineral quartz. Quartz, also called silica, is crystallized silicon dioxide. Because chert resists erosion, and appears in several, sometimes dramatic colors (though white is the most common form), its few outcropppings, such as East Peak, boldly stand out.

CREEKS

Scores of creeks, streams, and rivulets lace Mt. Tamalpais. A few flow the year-round, many dry up in summer before being replenished by fall rains. The major creeks on the Mountain, all crossed by trails, are described below. Note that creeks have an unambiguous right and left bank, as determined by facing downstream (the direction the water flows).

BILL WILLIAMS CREEK

Fed by several forks (which are crossed by Tucker Trail), Bill Williams Creek flows through Bill Williams Gulch into Phoenix Lake. It, and Phoenix Creek, are the lake's major sources. A still evident dam on Bill Williams Creek, dating back over 100 years, provided an early water source for the Ross Valley. Bill Williams, reputedly a deserter from the Confederate army, lived by the creek in the 1860's.

CATARACT CREEK

Cataract Creek starts just east of Rock Spring, in an area called Serpentine Swale, at around 2,000 feet in elevation. The creek, followed for just about its whole length by Cataract Trail, descends relatively gently to Laurel Dell. Then it begins dropping precipitously. The creek's strong flow, and numerous waterfalls, make it a favorite of Mountain visitors. Cataract Creek once met Lagunitas Creek near the present Alpine Dam. Today it flows into Alpine Lake.

CORTE MADERA CREEK

This Corte Madera Creek, not to be confused with one of the same name that runs through the Ross Valley, flows down Tamalpais' southeast flank. Its highest feeder is near 2,000 feet, east of East Peak. The old Mt. Tamalpais Railway followed the creek upstream for a couple of miles from downtown Mill Valley. Corte Madera Creek empties into Richardson Bay. Corte Madera means "cut wood" in Spanish; the redwoods along the creek's drainage were important sources of lumber before Gold Rush days.

FERN CREEK

The higher of Fern Creek's two feeder forks starts from near the top of Old Railroad Grade, at just over 2,200'. Fern Creek drops some 2,000' down the Mountain's south side to Redwood Creek in Muir Woods National Monument. Fern Creek Trail passes beside its upper reaches, Fern Canyon Trail beside its lower course. Fern Creek was once tapped as a water source for Mill Valley, Tiburon, and Belvedere. Remnants of the pipeline and intakes are still visible on the Mountain.

LAGUNITAS CREEK

Lagunitas is probably the most important creek on the Mountain and in Marin. Four dams have been placed along its course to store much of the county's water supply. The creek forms from three forks high on the Mountain's north face, the East Fork being the highest at near 2,300 feet. The three forks merge at Lake Lagunitas, at an elevation of 783'. Lower in elevation along Lagunitas Creek are the dams impounding Bon Tempe Lake, Alpine Lake, and, just outside this book's boundary, Kent Lake. Lagunitas Creek then continues through Samuel P. Taylor State Park, where it is sometimes called Papermill Creek. Beyond, it flows to the town of Point Reyes Station, then empties into Tomales Bay. Salmon and steelhead trout still work their way upstream on the creek in winter to spawn.

LARKSPUR CREEK

The headwaters of Larkspur Creek, on the Mountain's east slope, are below Blithedale Ridge. Two feeders meet at Dawn Falls, below which the creek flows through Baltimore Canyon. After crossing under Larkspur's Magnolia Avenue the creek meanders towards Corte Madera Creek. Larkspur is a common Tamalpais wildflower.

REDWOOD CREEK

Redwood Creek is well known because it flows through the heart of Muir Woods National Monument. Redwood Creek descends Redwood Canyon into the Monument. It then winds through Frank Valley, and meets the ocean at Muir Beach. Redwood Creek also still supports a salmon and steelhead run. The adult salmon struggle upstream in winter to lay and fertilize their eggs, then die. The young swim downstream to the ocean after the fall rains, there to spend several years before returning to the very same creek to complete their life cycle. The aptly named creek supports some of Marin's tallest redwoods.

SWEDE GEORGE CREEK

Swede George Creek has three forks that flow through a largely trail-less area on the Mountain's deeply wooded northwest face. High Marsh Trail crosses all three forks. The East Fork starts the highest, at around 2,000 feet by Rifle Camp. The three forks briefly unite before they flow into Alpine Lake. Swede George Creek was used as a water source until the 1950's; the pipeline is still visible. Swede George was a woodcutter who lived on the Mountain in the late 1800's.

VAN WYCK CREEK

Van Wyck Creek lies between the drainages of Swede George Creek to the west and Lagunitas Creek to the east. Its headwaters are at around 1,600 feet. Several trails (Lagoon Extension, Stocking, Kent) cross the creek before it empties into Alpine Lake. Sidney Van Wyck was a lawyer who volunteered his services to the Tamalpais Conservation Club during their legal battles in the 1920's to form Mt. Tamalpais State Park.

WEBB CREEK

Webb Creek starts above Panoramic Highway, west of Pantoll, and flows to the ocean. Its course is down lovely Steep Ravine, with the Steep Ravine Trail crossing it eight times and the Dipsea Trail once. The creek flows under Highway 1 to end at the Pacific a few yards north of the Steep Ravine cabins. The mouth of the creek is by a hot spring, now accessible only during minus tides in fall. Jonathan Webb was president of the Tamalpais Conservation Club in 1915-16 and long an aide to William Kent, who once owned the whole drainage of the creek. Webb died in 1944.

OTHERS

Other important creeks on the south side of Mt. Tamalpais include Laguna, Old Mill, Cascade, Spike Buck, and Rattlesnake. On the north side are Phoenix, Bon Tempe, Deer Park, and Tamalpais creeks. Table Creek is a significant one on the west face, Warner Creek on the east slope.

LAKES

There are five man-made lakes; Alpine, Bon Tempe, Kent (just outside this book's boundary), Lagunitas, and Phoenix, in the Mt. Tamalpais watershed. All are on the Mountain's north side, all were built as reservoirs, and all but Phoenix are in the drainage of Lagunitas Creek. Fishing is permitted in all the lakes. Boating, permitted before World War II, is now strictly prohibited, as is swimming. Other natural sites on Tam that carry the designation "lake," such as Hidden Lake and Lily Lake, are quite small and shallow.

ALPINE LAKE

Alpine is much the largest of the Mountain's four lakes; its storage capacity of 2.9 billion gallons exceeds the other three combined. The lake has a surface area of 219 acres, a shoreline of 10.4 miles, and a mean depth of 103 feet. Alpine Lake was formed in 1919 upon completion of Alpine

Dam, at the site of the former Alpine Bridge over Lagunitas Creek. The dam, now crossed by Fairfax-Bolinas Road, was raised in 1924 and again in 1941. It now stands at 636 feet elevation. When Alpine overflows, a mighty waterfall cascades down the dam's west face. Water from Alpine is pumped up to Bon Tempe, or flows into Kent Lake. The Kent and Helen Markt trails traverse the lake's south shore but there are no all-trail loop options.

BON TEMPE LAKE

Bon Tempe Lake, at 718 feet above sea level, was created in 1949 by Bon Tempe Dam. The lake flooded part of the old Swiss Bautunpi (of which Bon Tempe is a corruption) Brothers' dairy ranch. The lake has a capacity of 1.3 billion gallons and a surface area of 144 acres. Water from the lake is pumped directly to the nearby Bon Tempe treatment plant, then distributed to southern Marin County customers via the Southern Marin Line. The lake is readily accessible from Sky Oaks Road. A four mile trail circles Bon Tempe's shore.

LAKE LAGUNITAS

Lagunitas was the first of the Mountain's man-made lakes, formed in 1873. It is also the highest, at 784 feet, and the smallest, with a capacity of 127 million gallons and a surface area of 23 acres. The lake was originally built by developer William Coleman to supply water to his new housing tract in San Rafael and to San Quentin Prison. Water flows from Lagunitas to Bon Tempe. Lagunitas was drained in 1986 to prepare to make it self-sustaining with trout. The other lakes are periodically stocked with bass and trout. Lagunitas is reached by going uphill from the parking and picnic area at the end of Sky Oaks Road. A 1.6 mile fire road circles Lagunitas.

PHOENIX LAKE

Phoenix Lake is the most visited of the lakes, as it is the closest to population centers. Both because Phoenix is so popular as a recreation destination and because its surface is several hundred feet lower in elevation than the MMWD treatment plant, its water is pumped out and distributed only in emergencies, as in the drought of 1975-76. A new pump was put in place in 1989 in the middle of the lake to prepare for a then emerging shortage. Otherwise, overflow above Phoenix' 172 million gallon capacity passes out of the reservoir system. Phoenix Dam was erected in 1905 and raised in 1908. Phoenix Lake was drained in 1985, when its wooden spillway, deemed unsafe, was replaced by a concrete one. Phoenix is reached through Ross' Natalie Coffin Greene Park at the end of Lagunitas Road. A well-used 2.33 mile loop, half trail and half fire road, circles the 25 acre lake.

WEATHER

Mount Tamalpais, and most of coastal California, has a Mediterranean climate characterized by mild temperatures, dry summers, and winter rains. There are four other such Mediterranean climates in the world; the coast of Chile, the west coasts of Australia and South Africa, and the Mediterranean basin itself. While there is rarely a day when the sun doesn't shine somewhere on Tam, fog and rain are two other key components of the Mountain's weather.

Fog is a common occurrence, particularly on the Mountain's western and southern slopes from May through August. The summer fog cycle begins with prevailing winds that flow roughly parallel to the northern California coast. They push surface water of the Pacific southward and, ultimately, away from the land. The surface water is replaced by upwelling water, 10 to 15 degrees colder, from deeper in the ocean. This cold water is well known to anyone trying to swim off the Northern California coast. Inshore winds, moisture laden after a long trip over the ocean, comes into contact with the cold coastal waters. Cooler air holds less moisture so the excess water condenses, much of it on salt spray particles, as fog. When the hot inland air rises, as it does most every summer afternoon, it forms a low pressure area that "sucks" in the coastal fog bank.

The Mountain's west slope, nearest the ocean, is naturally most affected by summer fog. August average temperatures are among the coolest in North America. Fog can be an almost daily occurrence; Point Reyes, just northwest of Tam, is many years the foggiest place in the lower 48 states. Usually, though, the warming mid-day sun burns the fog off for a few hours. Fog also penetrates to Tam's southern flanks through the gaps of Frank Valley and Tennessee Valley. The eastern slopes are less affected, though fog drawn into San Francisco Bay often covers the area early and late during summer days. The north side, protected by the wall of Tamalpais, is virtually fog-free in summer, with sunny skies daily and temperatures often reaching 90 degrees. The sight of Tam's summit ridge blocking the advancing fog is a common, but always dramatic, summer spectacle.

Some time in September, the southern-retreating sun cuts the difference between inland and offshore temperatures sufficiently to turn off the main fog-producing mechanism. The entire Mountain is generally sunny all day and, without the fog's cooling influence, temperatures are often warmer than in mid-summer. By October, the Pacific High has retreated far enough south, with the jet stream following, to open the Tam region to storms moving across the ocean. The first rains may be warm ones from off Mexico. Later, generally by the end of November, the winter rain pattern begins, with storms blown in from off Hawaii or Alaska.

In winter, a different type of fog, known as "radiation" fog, occasionally covers parts of the Mountain, particularly on the north side. Air near the ground absorbs moisture from the damp earth. In early morning, temperatures have dropped so low, sometimes below freezing in the valleys, that the moisture condenses as fog. The hilltops may be sunny. This fog usually burns off by mid-morning.

. Annual rainfall has averaged 52 inches at Lake Lagunitas over the past 100 years. This is more than double the average for San Francisco. January is usually the wettest month followed, in roughly equal pairs, by December-February, November-March, and October-April. But exceptions are commonplace; December of 1989 had no rain at all, a first for at least 100 years. The most annual rainfall was 109 inches in 1889-90 and the least was 20 inches in 1923-24. The last major drought occurred in 1975-77, when there were two consecutive years with under 25 inches of rain. The almost 90 inches that fell in 1982-83 was the high this century and resulted, particularly after a storm in early January, in devastating floods. Kentfield has been among the wettest populated weather stations in the country.

Warmer, spring-like days are often commonplace by February. Indeed, over 100 Tamalpais plant species may be blooming in January. The grasslands generally appear greenest in March. The Pacific High begins drifting back north, blocking the rains. By the end of May, the grasses are brown. The rainless period, sometimes six months long, starts; by late summer dry grasses will be a major fire danger on Tam. The fog cycle is born anew.

The upper part of the Mountain often has its own weather. Winds reached 107 miles per hour on December 1, 1951. An all-time Tam low temperature of 19 degrees was recorded on January 19, 1922. On May 14, 1921, the aurora borealis, or northern lights, was plainly visible. There is, every few years, enough snow to cross-country ski. The largest snowstorm in modern times was in January, 1922; a poster of Tam blanketed in white has been widely distributed. There was a separate weather station near East Peak from 1898 into the 1920's.

Another weather factor worth noting is the existence of "micro-climates" on Tam. The shape of the valleys and ridges creates pockets differing in rain, fog, and temperature conditions. "Banana belts" mix with fog-bound areas. Redwood trees, which require abundant year-round moisture, grow yards away from dry chaparral shrubs like chamise. To paraphrase an old expression, "If you don't like the weather on Tam, just keep walking!"

FLORA

John Thomas Howell, in his definitive book, "Marin Flora," describes some 1,400 species of vascular plants (the most evolutionarily advanced, including ferns, coniferous trees, and flowering plants), over 800 of which are found on Mt. Tamalpais. Clearly, only a sampling of the Mountain's rich flora can be presented here. A familiarity with these species, representing most of the plants regularly encountered, should serve the needs of most Tamalpais visitors, or form a base for further study.

Beside each plant's common name is the botanical (scientific) name. These may appear intimidating at first, but are essential. Many plants have no, or several, common names, and some common names are applied to more than one species. Besides, the botanic names are often lovely and descriptive in their own right. Botanic names are given in the trail descriptions only for those plants not listed below.

PLANT COMMUNITIES

The Mountain's flora forms several plant communities, or associations. Four communities, frequently referred to in the text, are introduced below. These associations serve only as guides. Disparate communities such as redwood forest and chaparral are frequently found just yards apart, the communities' boundaries and makeup are themselves in transition, and many plants can be found in more than one habitat.

Redwood-Douglas Fir (Coniferous) Forest

Redwoods and Douglas firs, in pure stands and intermingled with one another and with other trees, form the Mountain's tallest and deepest forests. Both are conifers; the seeds are borne in cones. Two other less common native conifers on Tamalpais are California nutmeg and Sargent cypress. Pines, a type of conifer, are not naturally found on the Mountain.

Redwoods were once more common on Tamalpais and throughout the Bay Area. Virtually all the virgin stands were logged between 1850 and 1900; the Bay Area was literally built of redwood. To cite one example, Corte Madera, which means "cut wood" in Spanish, was covered with redwoods down to the shore of San Francisco Bay. Muir Woods reminds us of the treasures we have lost.

Second-growth redwoods, some now over 100 years old and reaching the 200 foot heights of the original monarchs, are now found on many of the wettest parts of the Mountain. Redwoods require a great deal of year-round moisture, so favor stream canyons in the summer fog belt (which provides drip water during the rainless summers). The correlation between redwoods and creek canyons soon becomes obvious to anyone walking the Mountain's trails. Laurel and tanbark oak, which can survive in the shade, are associated with the redwood forest.

Competing directly for sunlight with the redwoods, and therefore often just as tall, are Douglas firs. They are vigorous colonizers, and have successfully invaded many former hardwood forests and grasslands in just the last several decades.

Broad-leaved (Hardwood) Forest

The other type of woodland on Mt. Tamalpais consists of trees whose seeds are found in fruits. Those trees, also called hardwoods, have broad leaves as opposed to conifers' needles. Five trees; laurel (bay), madrone, tanbark oak, coast live oak, and buckeye, make up most of this forest on Mt. Tamalpais. Of the five, all but the buckeye retain their leaves throughout the year. This forest tends to occur between the wetter redwood-Douglas fir forests and the drier chaparral and grasslands. There is, however, much intermingling. Excellent examples of this woodland occur around Lake Lagunitas and Phoenix Lake.

Chaparral

Howell says, "It is the chaparral that gives to Mt. Tamalpais its distinctive texture. . .From a distance, there is a velvety quality that characterizes it and gives depth to the blues and purples that pervade the slopes; from near at hand there is still that seeming smoothness and a lawnlike quality that belie the tough and rugged character of the plant cover. Up steep slopes, over rolling summits, and across broad flats spreads the unbroken array of shrubs, dense, erect, stiff − the pile in the fabric of the mountain's mantle."

Chaparral is distinctive of coastal California and of the world's four other Mediterranean climates (coastal Chile, the west coasts of South Africa and Australia, and the Mediterranean Basin). Chaparral is dominated by shrubs, whose impenetrable nature becomes known to every Mt. Tamalpais visitor wandering off trail. Chaparral covers the Mountain's drier, exposed slopes and ridges, where the soils lack humus or the rocks don't hold much soil. Early pictures, for example, of the upper 1,200 feet or so of the south side of Mt. Tamalpais show an all but unbroken mat of chaparral. Subsequent tree plantings and natural expansion has altered that image somewhat, but chaparral remains dominant.

Grassland

The Mountain's grasslands are now comprised largely of non-native grasses. The native perennial grasses usually lost in competition with the more vigorous introduced annual grasses. These Old World grasses were imported both deliberately, as better livestock feed, and accidentally, such as on hooves of cattle and horses. Native grasses, which do not brown as quickly in summer as the alien grasses, do retain footholds throughout Tam, particularly at woodland margins.

The Mountain's grasslands are presently shrinking as control of fire and elimination of grazing has permitted invasion by bracken fern, chaparral shrubs such as baccharis, and trees (particularly Douglas fir). Large expanses remain, among other places, along Bolinas Ridge, on Bald Hill, and in the Potrero Meadows.

TREES

While there are more than a million trees on Mt. Tamalpais, five or six species account for over 90% of them, and the short list below covers over 99%. Thus, even infrequent visitors to Tam can learn to distinguish the trees and gain a richer understanding and appreciation of the natural history of the Mountain. The trees are presented here in, very roughly (based on my own observations, not on any scientific census), descending order of their abundance on Mt. Tamalpais.

DOUGLAS FIR *(Pseudotsuga menziesii)*

It would be difficult to even occasionally visit Mt. Tamalpais and not come away with respect for the Douglas firs, perhaps, in total biomass, the most abundant living thing on the Mountain. They grow to huge height and girth, rivaling and often surpassing their more famous neighbors, the redwoods, with whom they often compete for sunlight. For years the ancient Kent Tree, a Douglas fir still standing in Muir Woods, was the tallest tree in Marin.

Douglas firs (or Douglas-firs) are found along most all trails, and are often dominant. They are actively colonizing areas of the Mountain's grasslands, converting them to forests. A dramatic example is at Lone Tree Hill. Where just a single tree, a redwood, stood on its south facing slope early in this century, it is today covered with Douglas firs.

Pseudotsuga means "false hemlock" as the trees display some characteristics of hemlocks and some of the true firs. The cones, 2-3 inches, are distinctive for their three-pointed bracts. The flexible evergreen needles - singly in rows, not in sheathed bundles like the pines — are 3/4 to 1 inch long. Douglas firs have thick, deeply furrowed bark that feels harder to the touch than redwood's. The trunks can be branchless for great heights or, when the tree originally grew without competition for sunlight, may be circled with low, drooping branches. The heavily branched specimens are known as "wolf trees," for they often kill their understory vegetation. Douglas fir is today the most important lumber tree of the Pacific northwest, though, of course, it is no longer logged on Tam.

LAUREL *(Umbellularia californica)*

Laurel (interchangeably called "bay" in this book) contends with the Douglas fir as the most common tree on the Mountain. Their eliptical evergreen leaves, 2-5" long and shiny dark-green above, are unmistakeable for their pleasing, pungent fragrance. Their oil is so much more potent than the bay-leaf of commerce that some recipes call for substituting it in a strength of 1 part to 10. The laurel's shape varies tremendously according to environmental conditions, ranging from thick-trunked 80-foot-tall, fully crowned specimens in protected valleys to thin, bent, six foot specimens on the windiest, exposed ridges. Bays often grow in circles, root sprouting from a dead "mother" tree. Also a common sight are multiple shoots sent straight up from a fallen or bent tree.

The nut of the laurel was eaten, after roasting, by local Indians. Our bay is in the same family as its Mediterranean cousin of the laurel wreath, but of a different genus.

REDWOOD *(Sequoia sempervirens)*

Redwoods are the tallest trees in the world, with specimens over 360 feet in Humboldt County and over 250 feet on Mt. Tamalpais. They are also among the longest living of all things, some over 2,000 years old. And, of course, redwoods are among the world's best loved trees, attracting nearly 2 million visitors annually to Muir Woods, which has the Mountain's finest stands.

Besides the redwood's height and age, also distinctive is the very thick, reddish-brown bark. Redwoods often survive fires because of this thick bark and its lack of flammable resins. Scientists can unravel much of the fire history of Tam by studying redwoods. The bark is also resistant to insect and fungus infestation.

The tree's evergreen needles vary in appearance between the lower and topmost branches. The exposed top story needles are shorter to conserve water. The cones are remarkably small for so large a tree, 1/2" to 1 1/8".

They hold the tiny redwood seeds which, though they weigh only 1/8,000th of an ounce, contain all the genetic information needed to sustain the tree for centuries. Most reproduction is, however, vegetative. Younger trees, sprouting from the "mother" tree's surprisingly shallow roots, commonly encircle dead monarchs.

Redwoods were once wide ranging over the Pacific rim but global climatic changes, such as the Ice Ages, have reduced them to a narrow coastal band from just south of Big Sur to southern Oregon. They were far more widespread on Mt. Tamalpais before virtually all were logged. There are also on the Mountain several dense groves of thin, relatively short redwoods, as along Sierra Trail. Some of these stands sprang up after fires and have not yet thinned out; others represent redwoods struggling at the drier limits of their range.

The coast, or California, redwood is related to, but a different genus from, the more massive in girth giant sequoia *(Sequoiadendron giganteum),* which grows in a small number of groves in the Sierra.

MADRONE *(Arbutus menziesii)*

The madrone is well known to Mountain visitors for its highly distinctive bark, which peels back in strong light to reveal the smooth reddish wood. This wood remains cool to the touch on the hottest of summer days. The trunk and branches are often twisted. The 2-6" long evergreen leaves are thick and leathery, elliptic in shape, dark green and shiny above. Madrones lend a distinctive feel to areas they dominate, such as the ridges just north of Lakes Lagunitas and Bon Tempe. There, alongside the Pilot Knob and Madrone trails, are to be found Marin's largest madrones.

W. L. Jepson, author of the landmark "Manual of the Flowering Plants of California," wrote of the madrone, "No other of our trees. . .makes so strong an appeal to man's imagination − to his love of color, of joyful bearing, of sense of magic, of surprise and change." Howell adds, "(Madrone's) flowers and fruits (are) beyond compare − the former like sculptured ivory urns, the latter like etched carnelian globes."

The madrone is in the same family (heath) as the shrub manzanita. Both display peeling bark, and a small madrone can be the same size as a large manzanita. The bigger leaves of madrone are a good distinguishing feature. Local Indians ate the madrone's fruits both heated and raw.

TANBARK OAK *(Lithocarpus densiflorus)*

Though in the same beech family as the oaks, the tanbark oak, or tanoak, is not a true oak (genus *Quercus*). One difference is that the male flowers are in erect catkins, as opposed to the drooping catkins of oaks. Though rarely dominant in any one area of Mt. Tamalpais, tanbark oaks are nonetheless abundant, as on the south shore of Lake Lagunitas and on Old Mine Trail above Pantoll. Tanbark oaks are generally associated with madrones at the drier borders of redwood forests. They range in size from over 100 feet, as by the junction of Simmons and Kent trails, to shrubs at the edge of chaparral. Their leaves are most distinctive; oblong, thick, leathery, light green above and lighter below, with wavy-toothed borders. The leaves vary tremendously in length, from 2 to 8 inches depending on habitat.

The acorns of tanbark oaks were a principal source of flour for Indians of Marin. Later, the bark was the main source in California of tannin, used for tanning leather, dyeing, and for making ink; tanoaks were commercially harvested on Mt. Tamalpais.

OAK *(Quercus* spp.*)*

There are around 10 species of oak growing on Mt. Tamalpais. The oaks are not always easy to tell apart as they often have different leaves on the same tree and hybridize with one another. All have alternate leaves, separate male and female flowers on the same twig, and hard-shelled acorns. Coast live oak *(Q. agrifolia)* may be the Mountain's most common oak tree. Its leaves are convex above, and the midribs on the lower side have small hairs. The large, usually 7-lobed deciduous leaves of the black oak *(Q. kelloggii)* are distinctive. Canyon live, or goldcup, oaks *(Q. chrysolepis)* have a golden (turning to gray) pubescence on the underside of their young leaves. They are common in the Mountain Theater area.

Oak seedlings are a favorite food of deer, whose unchecked population on the Mountain may have adversely effected oak's ability to compete.

TOYON *(Heteromeles arbutifolia)*

This member of the rose family is usually a shrub on Tamalpais, but often a tree, depending on growing conditions. Its shiny, evergreen leaves are sharply saw-toothed. Most distinctive are the clusters of small red berries, similar to the Christmas berries of the eastern holly, that mature in fall and persist into winter.

CALIFORNIA BUCKEYE *(Aesculus californica)*

These members of the horse chestnut family may be the most variable in appearance of all the Mountain's trees. In winter their smooth, light gray branches are bare. In early spring, fresh, distinctive 5-parted palmate leaves emerge. In late spring, pinkish, fragrant candle-like flower clusters rise. In summer, the pear-like fruit capsules (buckeyes) form. The leaves begin yellowing and dropping. In fall the capsules darken. They linger on otherwise bare limbs before dropping to sprout new trees.

Buckeye seeds are poisonous. Local Indians leeched out the toxin (which they used to stupefy fish), then turned the residue to flour. The buckeyes' nectar and pollen are said to be poisonous to bees. Buckeyes are found throughout Tamalpais; there is a short Buckeye Trail on the northwest slope of Bald Hill. Our species is different from the buckeye that is the state tree of Ohio.

CALIFORNIA NUTMEG *(Torreya californica)*

The California nutmeg is usually found high on the Mountain's north side, as along Northside Trail. The sharp-pointed needles, with two whitish lines below, are diagnostic; accidentally squeeze a row and you'll not soon forget the nutmeg. The tree and seeds are aromatic. Male and female reproductive parts are found on separate trees. Nutmegs bear an elliptical fruit with a fleshy outer green layer around a very hard shelled seed. Though nutmegs are often little more than shrub height, Howell reported an 86-foot specimen fallen in Cataract Creek. Marin's nutmegs are botanically unrelated to the true nutmegs from which the spice is made; the name arose because the fruits look somewhat similar.

SARGENT CYPRESS *(Cupressus sargentii)*

Sargent cypress forms striking stands high on the Mountain, almost always on exposed serpentine rock. Distinctive are the small round cones, sectioned into 6 or 8 parts. The short, scalelike leaves differ from those on the other conifers on Tam. Sargent cypresses are often stunted, their trunks twisted. However, the two largest Sargent cypresses in the world (the tree only grows in California) are on the Mickey O'Brien Trail. One is 96' tall, the other 85'. The Audubon Society "Field Guide to North American Trees" lists the species height limit as 50 feet!

BIGLEAF MAPLE *(Acer macrophyllum)*

This is an aptly named tree; it has among the largest leaves of any of the world's some 125 species of maples. Most people recognize the deeply lobed, 5-parted maple leaf. The leaves add fall color to the Mountain as they turn yellow before dropping off. Single seeds are found in each of the paired "wings" of the fruit, called a samara. Look for the maples along streams, such as by Corte Madera Creek on the lower part of Old Railroad Grade.

ALDER *(Alnus* spp.)

There are two species of alder on the Mountain, white alder *(A. rhombifolia)* and red alder *(A. rubra)*. The latter is found only near the coast, and has the very edge of its leaf rolled inward. Alders grow almost exclusively along stream banks, where they can be fairly abundant, as on the lower part of the Steep Ravine Trail. Howell writes of the white alder, "To see the green-gold of their blossoming crowns in January is one of the floral treats of the year."

CHINQUAPIN *(Castanopsis chrysophylla)*

Though often shrub-like, chinquapins can reach over 50 feet tall, as on Benstein Trail. Most distinctive are the spiny, bur-like fruit capsules, often abundant on the ground beneath the trees. The folded, lance-shaped leaves, shiny green above and yellow below, are also diagnostic. Chinquapins are in the same beech family as the oaks, but are of a different genus, and bear erect catkins.

WILLOW *(Salix* **spp.)**

At least six species of willows grow naturally on Mt. Tamalpais. The arroyo willow *(S. lasiolepis)* is perhaps the most abundant. Willows are found in wet soils, such as along coastal stream beds.

INTRODUCED TREES

There are no pines native to Mt. Tamalpais but at least four species, Monterey *(Pinus radiata)*, Coulter *(P. coulteri)*, Knobcone *(P. attenuata)*, and Bishop *(P. muricata)*, have been planted and become locally naturalized. Monterey has needles in clusters of 3 and closed cones whorled around the limbs and trunk. Many were planted along the old rail line, such as at Mesa Station, West Point, and today's East Peak parking lot. Coulters, which have the heaviest pine cones in the world, up to 5 pounds, were planted in the Bon Tempe and Lake Lagunitas area around 1930. They are now gradually being removed, as along Lakeview Fire Road. Bishop pines also have closed cones in rings or whorls but with needles in bunches of two. They are native on the west side of the San Andreas Fault, though with some natural stands on the east side, just north of Tam. There is a large, planted row on Old Plane (Vic Haun) Trail. Knobcones, which have slender cones and three needles per bunch, are found on Laurel Dell Fire Road between Laurel Dell and Potrero Meadow.

Eucalyptus and acacia are two Australian natives that were introduced to Tamalpais. There is a very distinctive row of eucalyptus, planted over 100 years ago, on Sky Oaks Road near the Lake Lagunitas parking lot. Acacias are found near Mountain Home on Panoramic Trail and Gravity Car Grade. Both species are invasive of the Mountain's native vegetation.

SHRUBS

Shrubs are generally considered to be plants with woody stems, less than 10 feet tall, and without a single main axis or trunk. There is, however, a great deal of overlapping between shrubs and trees. Several species appear on Mt. Tamalpais as both trees and shrubs, depending on growing conditions. Sargent cypress, for example, is a tree that grows to over 90 feet on the Mickey O'Brien Trail but can appear a shrub-like two feet tall by the intersection of the Northside and Rocky Ridge trails.

Shrubs are an important component of the flora of Mt. Tamalpais, dominating huge areas, notably the chaparral, and rarely absent anywhere. As with the trees, though less dramatically, fewer than 25 species account for most of the shrubs on the Mountain. Below are the most common of Mt. Tamalpais' shrubs. They are grouped within the plant community in which they are most likely to be found and presented alphabetically.

CHAPARRAL

California sagebrush *(Artemesia californica)*

The shrub's gray foliage has a distinctive sage fragrance. The leaves are divided into thread-like segments

Ceanothus, California lilac *(Ceanothus spp.)*

There are over 40 species of ceanothus in California, some six on Mt. Tamalpais. Blue-blossom *(C. thyrsiflorus)* is the most common here. Its branchlets are ridged and its glossy leaves are prominently 3-veined. But most distinctive is the sweet, pervasive fragrance exuded from its clusters of blue flowers in early spring. One reliable spot, among many, to enjoy this intoxicating aroma is the intersection of Hoo-Koo-E-Koo Trail and Corte Madera Ridge Fire Road. Indigobrush *(C. foliosus),* buckbrush *(C. ramulosus),* and muskbrush *(C. jepsonii)* are other common Tamalpais ceanothus species.

Chamise *(Adenostoma fasciculatum)*

This member of the rose family rivals poison oak as the single most common shrub species on the Mountain, particularly on the driest slopes. Its short evergreen needles are in bunches (fascicles). The stems are stiff. Chamise's cream-colored, stalkless flowers bloom in crowded, pyramidal clusters in late spring. They linger and turn purplish, giving Tamalpais' south face its characteristic tint in fall. The plant is also known as greasewood.

Chaparral pea *(Pickeringia montana)*

This shrub has lovely pink-purple, pea-like flowers, a few of which linger into fall. It also has sharp, spiny stem tips that can be painful when brushed.

Golden-fleece *(Haplopappus arborescens)*

The branches of this shrub in the sunflower family stand erect and closely bunched. Atop are clusters of yellow flowers, blooming into early fall, wrapped in bracts. The narrow leaves are fragrant.

Manzanita *(Arctostaphylos* **spp.)**

There are some six species of manzanita on the Mountain, not always readily distinguishable from one another. "Manzanita" means "little apple" in Spanish and that certainly describes the appearance of the fruit, which begins to appear in summer. The often pinkish-tinged, delicate, urn-shaped flowers are a common sight in late winter and early spring. Fallen blossoms sometimes cover sections of trails. Also distinctive is the bark, which peels, like that of the related madrone, to reveal a reddish trunk. Two of the manzanita species have burl-like bases. Another, *A. montana,* or Tamalpais manzanita, is found only in Marin County, on serpentine, and was named by Alice Eastwood for Tamalpais. It is the latest blooming of our manzanitas.

Oaks *(Quercus* **spp.)**

Oaks are generally trees but one variety of the interior live oak, (*Q. wislizeni* var. *frutescens*) and one species, leather oak, (*Q. durata*), are important shrubs on Tamalpais. The former, more common, has uncurved leaves. The latter has tough leaves that are convex above, with the margins rolled inward. Leather oak is restricted to serpentine outcrops.

Sticky (Bush) monkeyflower *(Mimulus aurantiacus)*

Most every Tam visitor can recognize the funnel-shaped, orange-buff flowers of this widespread shrub. It is in bloom from February through August, sometimes even later. The bottom sides of the opposite leaves have a sticky-to-the-touch coating, hence the common name.

Tree (Bush) poppy *(Dendromecon rigida)*

Though not as abundant as other of the shrubs listed here, tree poppies are prominent when their large, brilliant, four-petaled yellow flowers are in bloom.

Yerba santa *(Eriodictyon californicum)*

The leathery, willow-shaped leaves of yerba santa are sticky above, woolly below. They are sometimes spotted with a black mold. Yerba santa has purplish-white trumpet-shaped flowers. It was used, either smoked or as a tea, by local Indians and early settlers to ease respiratory ailments.

GRASSLAND

Brooms (*Cytisus* spp.)

Brooms, not native to Marin, form thick borders to many trail and road cuts, particularly on the east side of the Mountain. When unchecked, they have completely overrun and obscured several old routes. Because brooms are so invasive and hardy, and crowd out native flowers, organized broom pulls are becoming an increasingly common activity. The shrubs do have striking yellow blossoms through much of the year. Contrary to what is often said, French broom (*C. monspessulanus*) is the more common broom on Tam. Scotch broom (*C. scoparius*) has larger flowers and smaller, almost needle-like leaves.

Coyote-bush *(Baccharis pilularis)*

Coyote bush, or baccharis, is extremely common alongside Tamalpais grassland trails, such as Lone Tree Fire Road and the open sections of the Dipsea. It is an important colonizer of grassland after livestock grazing ceases. Each shrub contains either male or female flowers. In winter, the seeds are dispersed by white tufts of hair, which top the seeds on the female plants, and give the shrub another common name, fuzzy-wuzzy. In spring and summer, spittle-bugs tend to favor the coyote-bush, covering the leaf axils with their foam.

Lupine *(Lupinus* spp.*)*

There are some 10 lupine species on Mt. Tamalpais, several of them shrubs and not easy to tell apart. Lupines are in the pea family and have the characteristic flowers, usually blue, and seed pods. Their palmate leaves are also distinctive. Howell calls the low-growing, grayish-leaved Tamalpais lupine (*L. douglasii* var. *fallax)* "one of the most beautiful flowering shrubs."

WOODLAND

California hazel *(Corylus californica)*

This is a large shrub, occasionally a small tree. It is common along stream-side trails throughout the Mountain. Its round leaves are very soft to the touch. The drooping male catkins begin appearing in January; the tiny, female catkins, with bright red stigmas, are separate and erect. The nuts, resembling the related filberts of the east coast, were eaten by local Indians and are important to squirrels and chipmunks.

Huckleberry *(Vaccinium ovatum)*

Huckleberry lines long sections of many forest trails, such as Sierra, the Kent above Alpine Lake, and, of course, the Huckleberry. The berries are small, but sweet and tasty when black and ripe in fall. The alternate leaves are shiny above, with saw-toothed margins. The pinkish-white flowers are urn-shaped like the manzanita's and madrone's; all are members of the heath family.

Western azalea *(Rhododendron occidentale)*

Azaleas are found in wet areas; along stream banks, springs, and marshes. Their showy, fragrant, creamy-white flowers make them one of the Mountain's favorites. Azaleas are usually in peak bloom in May and June. The smooth green leaves sprout each spring. Azaleas are perhaps most abundant on Tam along the East Fork of Swede George Creek, site of one of the Mountain's Azalea Meadows.

Elk-clover *(Aralia californica)*

Elk-clover (also called spikenard) is found in wet places, its roots always near flowing water. The huge leaves, as large as any to be found on the Mountain, are diagnostic. Amazingly, they die back each year, to grow anew full size in the spring. One of the last shrubs to blossom, elk-clover sends up clusters of tiny white flowers in mid-summer. They form purple-black berries, which are poisonous, in fall.

California honeysuckle *(Lonicera hispidula)*

Honeysuckle is a vine that entwines itself around other plants, and is often seen overhanging woodland trails. The uppermost of the opposite leaves are fused around the stem. It produces pinkish flowers in spring and red berries in late summer. Other berry-producing members of the honeysuckle family on Tamalpais are the red and blue elderberry, two species of snowberry, and twinberry.

MULTI-HABITAT

Poison oak *(Toxicodendron diversiloba)*

Unfortunately, what may be the Mountain's most common shrub, poison oak, causes an allergic reaction in many people. Anyone who has had a bad case of the itchy rash learns to identify the plant's usually distinctive (but varied, hence the "diverse-lobed" species name) lobed, three-part leaves. The leaves vary in color from green to, later in the year, red. In fall, this red colors many a hillside. Poison oak (or poison-oak) can be an isolated plant a few inches high, grow as mats on coastal hills, form a several foot tall thicket, or even appear to be a small tree as it climbs as a woody vine. It is related to poison ivy and poison sumac, but not to the true oaks.

Coffeeberry *(Rhamnus californica)*

In fall, the black berries of this shrub resemble coffee beans. Otherwise there is no relation between the two plants. Coffeeberry, commonly 3-5 feet tall, is common in light woodland and chaparral.

FERNS

There are some 20 species of ferns on Mt. Tamalpais. Ferns differ from the evolutionarily more advanced flowering plants in that they reproduce by spores, not seeds, and have two distinct, alternate generations. The sporophyte generation, the one commonly seen, bears and drops the spores. The spores germinate into the smaller gametophyte generation, which produces sperm and egg cells. Sperm, dependent on moisture for mobility, fertilize the eggs, which then develop into the sporophytes. The commonest ferns on Mt. Tamalpais are listed below.

Bracken fern *(Pteridium aquilinum)*

Bracken, one of the more widely distributed plants in the world, is probably the most abundant fern on Tamalpais. It is found in many habitats, but is most prominent when it is colonizing grasslands, as along the Hogsback section of the Dipsea. Bracken's young, still rounded shoots are considered a delicacy (called "fiddleneck") in the Orient, but mature fronds have been known to poison cattle.

Western sword fern *(Polystichum munitum)*

This large fern is so named because its leaflets have serrated edges and hilt-like bases. It is very common in redwood forests, such as in Steep Ravine, and other deep woodlands.

Western (Giant) chain fern *(Woodwardia fimbriata)*

Chain ferns are generally the largest ferns found on the Mountain, sometimes rising to six feet or more in height. They are found only in the wettest places, in seeps and along stream beds. Howell cites the stand on Stocking Trail at Van Wyck Creek as containing "the largest and most luxurious specimens."

Goldback fern *(Pityrogramma triangularis)*

Goldbacks are found in shaded areas that are somewhat drier than those favored by the above two species. The leaflets curl up and dry in summer. This fern is well known for leaving a tracing of golden green powder when its underside is pressed against a dark object, like blue jeans.

Maidenhair fern *(Adiantum jordani)*

The much admired maidenhair, with its delicate, rounded segments, is common in shaded, rocky canyons. A close relative, *A. pedatum*, with divided stalks, is known as the five-finger fern.

WILDFLOWERS

M t. Tamalpais is exceptionally rich in wildflowers in both numbers and varieties of species. Many species grow here at either their northern or southern geographic limit. Also, there are several flowers that grow only on or near the Mountain.

Presented below is a selection of around fifty of the Mountain's most abundant, or most showy, native species. They are grouped by color of the floral leaves; the petals and sepals. Be aware that color can vary among flowers of the same species, and that nature's colors rarely fit neatly into groupings. After the brief description, the flower's principal habitat, its peak blossoming months, and its family are given. Habitat and period of bloom are only guides and approximations. The peak bloom, for example, depends on weather, the flower's location on the Mountain, and other factors. Expect to find all the species a bit before and after the months given.

There is floral color on Tam all year. Alice Eastwood, the grand lady of the Mountain's flora, once said, "There have been years when a hundred native plants could be found in bloom on and around Mt. Tamalpais in early January" (California Out of Doors, 1915). The season is generally at its peak from mid-March to mid-May. Remember, do not pick any flowers. It is not only illegal, it robs others of the chance to enjoy them and prevents the plants from forming the seeds for next year's flowers. Also, some species are very rare and local. Further, picked wildflowers generally wither quite quickly.

WHITE

Soap-plant *(Chlorogalum pomeridianum)* - The spider-like flowers are tightly shut through the day, only opening in late afternoon to attract

vespertine (evening active) insects. The up to two-foot-long, wavy-edged, narrow leaves, forming a cluster around the base, are distinctive any time of the day.
*Grassland * May-June * Lily family*

Western trillium, Wake-robin *(Trillium ovatum)* - Trillium is closely associated with redwoods. It has three broad, pointed leaves, whorled around the stem. The single white flower atop the stalk (pedicel) fades to pink. A second Mountain trillium species (*C. chloropetalum*) is stalkless.
*Redwoods * February-March * Lily family*

Fairy-bells *(Disporum hookeri)* and **Fairy-lanterns** *(D. smithii)* - These similar species both have drooping flowers and orange-red berries that are only visible when the upper leaves are lifted. The pale green-tinged petals of the fairy-bells, the commoner of the two species, are more curved back than those of the whiter fairy-lanterns.
*Coniferous forest * March-April * Lily family*

Fat- *(Smilacina racemosa)* and **Slim-** *(S. stellata)* **Solomon's-seal** - Both species have clusters of tiny flowers. In the former they are arranged in a panicle (loosely branched), in the latter in a raceme (single flower stalks around a stem). Both species have long, alternate, clasping leaves; they are thinner in slim-Solomon.
*Coniferous forest *February-March * Lily family*

Miner's-lettuce *(Claytonia perfoliata)* - This well known plant is easily identified by the round, leafy disk that clasps the flower stalk. It is found in wet places. The flowers are tiny. The fleshy, basal leaves were a source of greens for local Indians and early settlers.
*Woodland * February-April * Purslane family*

California strawberry *(Fragaria californica)* - The very small but tasty berries are unmistakeable. Also distinctive are the serrated, three-parted leaves.
*Woodland borders * May-June * Rose family*

Milk-maids *(Cardamine californica)* - These very common flowers are often the first, or almost first, to bloom on the Mountain, usually by January. They persist into June. The four small petals frequently have a pinkish tinge.
*Broad-leaved forest * January-March * Mustard family*

Morning-glory *(Calystegia purpurata)* - This is the most common of the several morning-glory species on Tam. The long stem trails along the ground or entwines around shrubs. The outer edge of the united petals usually have a pinkish, then later purplish, tinge.
*Coastal grassland * April-June * Morning-glory family*

Yerba buena *(Satureja douglasii)* - Yerba buena trails low on the ground in woodlands. It has one small, five-petaled, two-lipped flower at each leaf. The fragrance of its glossy leaves, long used in teas, makes it a worthwhile find. San Francisco's first name was Yerba Buena, "good herb."
*Broad-leaved forest * May-June * Mint family*

Woodland-star *(Lithophragma affine)* - There are two *Lithophragma* species on the Mountain. They are not as abundant as some of the other flowers here but the five white petals, each cleft into three parts at the top, are quite showy and distinctive.
*Forest and Grassland * March-April * Saxifrage family*

Wild cucumber, Manroot *(Marah fabaceus)* - The five-petaled flowers grow along entangling vines that can reach 30 feet in length. The roots are huge, accounting for the common name. The large 5-7 pointed leaves have a U-shaped base. The globe-shaped melon, each containing four seeds, is covered with spines. A different species grows along the coast.
*Grassland * March-May * Cucumber family*

Yarrow *(Achillea millefolium)* - The small white flowers are found in flat-topped clusters above 1-3 foot stalks. The "thousand leaves" of the species name refers to the fine divisions. The plant was named for Achilles, in myth the first of many to use it medicinally.
*Grassland * April-June * Sunflower family*

Rosinweed *(Calycadenia multiglandulosa)* - The small irregular flowers stand out because they are in bloom in late summer and fall. The roughly one-foot-tall stems have short leaves covered with a sticky, fragrant, glandular secretion.
Grassland August-October * Sunflower family*

YELLOW-CREAM

Star lily *(Zigadenus fremonti)* - These are among the first "spring" bloomers, sometimes showing color in late December. The 6 cream-colored flower segments form a star pattern.
*All but deep forest * January-March * Lily family*

Yellow mariposa-lily, Gold-nuggets *(Calochortus luteus)* - This is a striking flower, its three brilliant yellow petals marked with red-brown blotches on their inner surfaces. They are often found with poppies on grassy hillsides. There are other showy *Calochortus* species on Tam as well.
*Grassland * May-June * Lily family*

California-buttercup *(Ranunculus californicus)* - This well-known flower has many petals (9 to 16) with shiny upper surfaces. Local Indians ate the seeds.
*Moist areas * February-May * Buttercup family*

Cream-cups *(Platystemon californicus)* - Each of the 6 cream-colored petals has a yellow spot at the base. The long single stem, 3-12 inches tall, is very hairy.
*All but deep forest * March-April * Poppy family*

Redwood violet *(Viola sempervirens)* - The lower of the five asymmetrical petals has a V-shaped point. The rounded, evergreen leaves rise from creeping stalks. These violets are found under redwood trees. There are several other violet species on the Mountain.
*Redwoods * March-April * Violet family*

Footsteps-of-spring *(Sanicula arctopoides)* - The plant's flat rosette of three-parted, toothed leaves is yellowish, as are the clusters of tiny flowers. It is indeed a harbinger of spring. There are several other common sanicles on Tam.
*Grassland * February-March * Parsley family*

False lupine *(Thermopsis macrophylla)* - This plant can be told from true lupines by the 3 palmate leaflets; lupines have 4 or more leaflets. The hairy stalks rise to 3 feet. These plants are often found in dense clusters.
*Grassland * March-April * Pea family*

Narrow-leaved mule-ears *(Wyethia angustifolia)* - The long, lance-shaped basal leaves resemble mules' ears. The flower heads look like the true sunflowers. A second Tamalpais species is found in more shaded areas.
*Grassland * March-April * Sunflower family*

Tarweed *(Hemizonia lutescens)* - One of the latest flowers to bloom, tarweed provides yellow color and a pleasing, characteristic fragrance to otherwise dry grasslands in summer and fall. The 2-4 foot stalks are hairy and sticky. There are other Tamalpais tarweeds, in both the *Hemizonia* and *Madia* genera.
*Grassland * July-November * Sunflower family*

Gumweed *(Grindelia hirsutula)* - This is a rather unmistakable plant for the milky, gummy resinous fluid exuded at the top of the buds. The showy flower heads brighten summer's brown grasslands.
*Grassland * May-June * Sunflower family*

Goldfields *(Lasthenia californica)* - Goldfields' golden-yellow flower heads are often found in large carpets, coloring grasslands. The hairy stems are 1-10 inches tall.
*Grassland * February-May* Sunflower family*

ORANGE

California poppy *(Eschscholzia californica)* - This is the state flower of California. It is not a true poppy (genus *Papaver,* of which there is one species on the Mountain, blooming only after fires). The petals close in the

evening. Poppies can be found into fall. Howell says, "No poet has yet sung the full beauty of our poppy, no painter has successfully portrayed the satiny sheen of its lustrous petals, no scientist has satisfactorily diagnosed the vagaries of its variations and adaptability. . .Cherish it and be ever thankful that so rare a flower is common!"
*Grassland * March-April * Poppy family*

BROWN, GREEN

Mission-bells *(Fritillaria lanceolata)* - The brown, mottled, nodding, bowl-shaped flowers are often missed in deep woodland. Mission-bells send up large leaves their first year to gather energy for blossoming the next year. The plant was first discovered in Corte Madera.
*Woodland * March-April * Lily family*

Fetid-adder's-tongue, Slink-pod *(Scoliopus bigelovii)* - In January, the two large, glossy, mottled leaves of the slink-pod appear abundantly in redwood forests. The three-petaled, purple-striped flowers are harder to see. The slender, sinewy flower stalks droop to the ground after fertilization, self-planting the seeds.
*Coniferous forest * January-February * Lily family*

RED, PINK

Red clintonia *(Clintonia andrewsiana)* - The plant's large, glossy, basal leaves stand out in redwood forests as they manufacture the nutrients needed to send out the rosy clusters of flowers. After fertilization, clintonia produces blue berries.
*Redwoods * April-May * Lily family*

Calypso orchid *(Calypso bulbosa)* - Though not common in Marin, the calypso is too notable to be omitted. Each plant has a single oval leaf and flower, the slipper-like lower sixth petal of which is speckled. They are generally found only beneath Douglas firs. There are several other orchids, perhaps the largest plant family in the world, on Tamalpais, but all are uncommon or rare.
*Douglas fir forest * March-May * Orchid family*

California fuchsia *(Zauschneria californica)* - Fuchsias are not that common, but they are quite noticeable because they provide color in fall, and can even linger into December. The woody plants have red tube-shaped flowers, beyond which the stamens and pistils extend. They are found in rocky areas.
*Chaparral * August-October * Evening primrose family*

Indian-pink *(Silene californica)* - Indian-pink is also not common, but is a visual treat when spotted. Each of the flower's scarlet-red petals are lobed into 4 parts. The opposite leaves clasp the 6-18 inch stalks.
*Chaparral * May-July * Pink family*

Starflower *(Trientalis latifolia)* - The starflower's stalk (pedicel) is remarkably thin and delicate. It supports pink, star-shaped flowers. The number of petals, usually 6, can vary.
*Woodland * April-May * Primrose family*

Indian warrior *(Pedicularis densiflora)* - The finely cut leaves of the Indian warrior are often colored red-purple. The tubular flowers have an upper beak and a shorter lower lip. It is one of the first flowers to bloom.
*Chaparral * January-March * Figwort family*

Indian paintbrush *(Castilleja franciscana)* - Paintbrush is very distinctive, with brilliant red tubular flowers projecting at right angles from, and atop, two-foot-tall stems. Each flower has two protruding yellow, joining petals.
*Woodland & Chaparral * February-April * Figwort family*

Farewell-to-spring *(Clarkia amoena)* - The four pink-red petals have a darker red blotch in the center. The plant is one to three feet tall. It is in bloom as spring ends. There are some five other clarkias on Tamalpais. Perhaps most striking is red-ribbons, or lovely clarkia (*C. concinna*). Three of its four petals point up, one down, and each is three-lobed. Helen Sharsmith, in her "Spring Wildflowers of the San Francisco Bay Region," says of it, "flowers of bizarre beauty."
*Grassland * April-May * Evening primrose family*

Wild buckwheat *(Eriogonum nudum* **and** *E. vimineum)* - Though the tiny, clustered flowers are hardly showy, the buckwheats are noticeable because they are in bloom in summer and fall.
*Chaparral * July-September * Buckwheat family*

Redwood sorrel *(Oxalis oregana)* - The three-parted leaves, which fold up at night, resemble clover. Each 4-7 inch stalk produces a single, funnel-shaped, white, pink, or lavender flower.
*Redwoods * February-March * Pink family*

Checkerbloom *(Sidalcea malvaeflora)* - These large, colorful flowers stand out in grasslands atop their 1-2 foot stalks. The species produces two types of flowers; a larger, pale mauve one that has pistils and stamens, and a smaller, deep rose one that has only female parts.
*Grassland * March-May * Mallow family*

Columbine *(Aquilegia formosa)* - Columbine is one of the Mountain's more striking flowers. The 5 scarlet petals form nectar tubes, yellow on the inside, that project upward on the nodding stalk.
*Woodland * March-May * Buttercup family*

Milkwort *(Polygala californica)* - Not that showy or abundant, milkweed is noticed because it provides late color in woodland areas. Its 3 low-lying, rose-purple petals are shaped like flowers in the pea family.
*Woodland * May-June * Milkwort family*

Venus (Red) thistle *(Cirsium proteanum)* - This is one of some half-dozen Tamalpais thistles. The reddish to purplish flowers project prominently high among white, cobweb-like hairs. The plant stands 1 to 5 feet tall.
*Chaparral * May-June * Sunflower family*

BLUE-PURPLE

Shooting-star *(Dodecatheon hendersonii* var. *cruciatum)* - Shooting-stars are very distinctive, much admired early bloomers in light woodland. The 4 petals, usually pink to purple, are bent downward. They are separated from the dark, pointed anther tube by a white to yellow band.
*Woodland * February-March * Primrose family*

Tamalpais jewelflower *(Streptanthus glandulosus* var. *pulchellus)* - This plant is one of a handful that grows only on Mt. Tamalpais and nowhere else. It is found high on the Mountain, generally in serpentine. The flask-shaped flower has 4 purple petals overhanging the purple sepals. The 1-2 foot stem is hairy.
*Chaparral * May-June * Mustard family*

Hound's-tongue *(Cynoglossum grande)* - This is one of the first wildflowers to bloom each year. In 1989, I saw some in full color on December 14 along Concrete Pipeline Fire Road. It already displays its round, prickled, fruit by March or April. The large, long-stalked leaves give hound's tongue its name. The blue flowers are coiled on the 1-3 foot stem. They have a white ring in their center, as do the similar, but smaller-leaved, forget-me-nots. Forget-me-nots, introduced from Europe, are now naturalized on Tam.
*Broad-leaved woodland * January-February * Borage family*

Marin (Douglas) iris *(Iris douglasiana* var. *major)* - The iris, with the poppy, is perhaps the best loved of the Mountain's flowers. It displays an infinite variety of shadings. Indeed, "iris" means rainbow in Greek. It has a 3-parted, petal-like style that can be lifted to reveal the hidden stamens. All parts of the iris are poisonous. A second iris species, ground iris *(I. macrosiphon)*, has a fragrance. Its leaves are the same green color above and below; Marin iris' are duller on the underside.
*Broad-leaved woodland * February-May * Iris family*

Blue-eyed-grass *(Sisyrinchium bellum)* - Many consider this among the Mountain's loveliest flowers. The 6 flower segments surround a yellowish center.
*Grassland * February-May * Iris family*

Bluedicks, Brodiaea (*Dichelostemma capitatum*) - There are some 7 brodiaeas on Mt. Tamalpais, all with leafless stems and underground bulbs. Bluedicks are among the first to bloom, with a tight cluster of flowers. The later blooming Ithuriel's-spear, or grass-nut, has flowers on longer stalks that spread at the tips. Later blossoming still, into July, is harvest brodiaea. It has 3 stamens, unlike the 6 of the previous two species.
*Grassland * February-March * Lily family*

Baby-blue-eyes *(Nemophila menziesii)* - Howell says, "Certainly this is one of the most beautiful and best-loved wildflowers of the spring, a high favorite with everyone." The 5 united petals, above a sprawling stem, are generally a sky blue, though the color can vary. Also common is *N. heterophylla*, with smaller, paler, bowl-shaped flowers. It is found more in shaded areas.
*Grassland * February-March * Waterleaf family*

Western larkspur *(Delphinium hesperium)* - The spurred upper sepal makes larkspurs distinctive. There are 5 small petals. The town on the Mountain's east slope is named for this flower. Red larkspur (*D. nudicaule*) is also common, in more shaded areas.
*Grassland * May-June * Buttercup family*

Sky lupine *(Lupinus nanus)* - There are some 10 lupine species, not easy to distinguish from one another, on Mt. Tamalpais. Some are shrubs. Of the annual, sky lupine, Howell writes, "It is this lupine which in the spring obscures the green of grassy hills and valleys with mantles and sheets of blue. . ."
*Grassland * March-April * Pea family*

FAUNA

Mt. Tamalpais is also home to a richly diversified animal world. Some of the largest species once here, such as black and brown bear, elk, coyote, mountain lion, condor, are completely gone (though reports of mountain lion and coyote sightings occasionally surface). Yet many other animals survive, even thrive, on the Mountain. Presented below are some of the birds, mammals, reptiles, and fish to be found by the patient Tam observer.

BIRDS

More than 300 species of birds have been seen on or above Mt. Tamalpais. Over 70 species breed on the Mountain. Some birds spend their whole lives on the Mountain, many just the winters, a smaller number just the summers, and a sizable number only pass through during migration. For example, the raptor (bird of prey) migration south over Tam each fall is perhaps the most spectacular of its kind in the United States. Described below are some of the more numerous birds that reside on Mt. Tamalpais all year.

Double-crested cormorant *(Phalacrocorax auritus)*

Cormorants are common on the north side lakes as they compete with anglers (invariably more successfully, so thus a source of some annoyance) for the fish. They have a long, dark, slender body with an orange throat pouch. Cormorants are often seen drying their outstretched wings.

Great blue heron *(Ardea herodias)*

Herons are tall (4-5 feet), graceful, gray-blue birds. They stand motionless in shallow water, patiently waiting to spear fish and crustaceans. Great blues nest in redwood trees at Audubon Canyon Ranch in the northwest corner of Tam. The herons begin arriving in late January. Thousands of visitors come to the Ranch to observe the annual nesting cycle.

Great egret *(Casmerodius albus)*

These all-white plumaged birds, with yellow bills and black legs, also nest on the Mountain at Audubon Canyon Ranch. They start arriving in March, then proceed to outnumber the neighboring great blue herons. A smaller, all-white egret, the snowy *(Egretta thula),* with a black bill and yellow legs, has also recently begun to nest at the Ranch. The great egret is the symbol of the National Audubon Society, one of whose initial missions was to stop their slaughter for the plumes (aigrettes) that were used in women's hats.

Mallard *(Anas platyrhynchos)*

Hundreds of ducks, representing ten or more species, are found on the Mountain's lakes during winter. Most are migrants that raise their broods farther north. Only the mallard regularly breeds here. Male mallards have a glossy green head, white collar, and chestnut breast. The females, as with many ducks, are plainer; a mottled brown.

Gulls *(Larus* spp.*)*

Gulls are regularly seen flying over the Mountain, or floating on the lakes. The most numerous local gull species are California *(L. californicus)*, ring-billed *(L. delawarensis)*, and western *(L. occidentalis)*. The latter is the only gull common the year around. Of the three, westerns are the largest, ring-billeds the smallest. The gulls take three to four years to reach the clean, full adult plumage. Adult westerns have pink legs, California gulls have greenish-yellow legs, and ring-billeds have yellowish legs. Ring-billed gulls bear a black ring near the tip of their bill.

Turkey vulture *(Cathartes aura)*

With a wingspan of nearly six feet, turkey vultures are the largest birds seen on Tam, save for the roughly equal sized ospreys and the rare eagle. Vultures are a familiar sight on the Mountain as they soar silently on the thermals, rarely flapping their wings, in search of carrion. They are distinguishable from hawks by the black and white pattern under their wings, the somewhat V-shape (dihedral) in which they hold their wings, and their small, naked, red head. Turkey vultures nest on the Mountain in hollow stumps and rotting logs, laying two eggs. If you come across a turkey vulture flying up from the ground, there's more than likely to be a dead deer or other mammal nearby.

Red-tailed hawk *(Buteo jamaicensis)*

The piercing, descending cry of the red-tailed hawk, described as "keeeer-r-r," is one of the most vivid of the wild sounds on Tamalpais. The call is sometimes well imitated, though always a trifle feebly, by Steller's jays. Red-tails are commonly seen soaring, circling, and sometimes "stilling" − floating motionless against the wind − in search of rodents. They are the largest local hawk, with a wing span of over 4 feet. Very distinctive is the chocolate-brown head. Only the adults have the distinctive red tail.

American kestrel *(Falco sparverius)*

Kestrels are the smallest of the area's falcons, a family of fast-flying raptors distinguished by their long, narrow, pointed wings. Kestrels commonly hover over a single spot as they seek reptiles, small mammals and insects. Their two larger cousins, the merlin and the peregrine falcon, can also occasionally be sighted.

California quail *(Callipepla californica)*

This is the state bird of California. Quail are often heard giving their distinctive "chi-ca-go" call, or rustling through brush, or seen scurrying across trails. In summer, adults may have 10 or more young trailing behind. The plume atop the head is diagnostic.

Mourning dove *(Zenaida macroura)*

Mourning doves are ground feeders that rise with an explosive start when startled, and their wings whistle in flight. Their pointed tails have white outer feathers. The dove's "mournful" cooing can sometimes be mistaken for an owl's call. They are the most abundant and widespread of America's doves. In the same family are band-tailed pigeons *(Columba fasciata)*, which fly in flocks between the tops of trees.

Great horned owl *(Bubo virginianus)*

Owls, being nocturnal hunters and well camouflaged when they perch in trees by day, are not readily seen. The great horned owl, common on the Mountain, is the likeliest to be noticed, particularly if it is being "mobbed" by smaller birds trying to force its departure. The great horned's large size (to 25 inches in length), ear tufts and its distinctive hoots are characteristic. Like all owls, they fly silently and have immobile eyes.

Anna's hummingbird *(Calypte anna)*

The Anna's is the only hummingbird to winter on the Mountain. They go into a torpor at nights to preserve body heat. Anna's have all-green backs. In summer, they are joined by two other species, Allen's and the uncommon rufous hummingbird. Mature males of both these species have a rufous color on their back. The males of the three species do a splendid mating flight; arcing, climbing, then ending with a rapid dive that produces a distinctive sound with their tail feathers.

Acorn woodpecker *(Melanerpes formicivorus)*

The acorn woodpecker, with its red cap, white forehead and cheeks, black chin, and white wing patches, is quite noticeable. These gregarious woodpeckers store acorns, often in Douglas firs, in tight fitting holes so that squirrels cannot pry them out. Downy, hairy, and Nuttall's are three other local black-backed woodpeckers. They too hammer away at trees searching for insects, building nests, or signaling territorial claims.

Northern flicker *(Colaptes auratus)*

Flickers are large (12-14 inches) woodpeckers that are just as likely to be found feeding on the ground (if they haven't been startled first) as in a tree. The white rump is quite prominent in flight on the otherwise barred back.

Scrub jay *(Aphelocoma coerulescens)*

There are two species of jays present, if not seemingly omnipresent, on Mt. Tamalpais; scrub jay and Steller's jay *(Cyanocitta stelleri)*. Both are blue, but are different species from the blue jay of the east. Scrub jays are more common in the Mountain's drier chaparral and oak woodland regions. Steller's, distinguished by their black crests, are more likely found in the cool, coniferous forests. A famous sign at Van Wyck Meadow indicate that three Steller's jays live there. Jays are opportunistic food gatherers.

Common raven *(Corvus corax)*

Ravens are considered perhaps the most intelligent of all birds, and are one of the widest ranging. They figured prominently in the mythology of the native Miwok Indians, and still hold a special appeal as they soar over the wildest places. Ravens are larger than Tamalpais' other large all-black bird, the American crow *(Corvus brachyrhynchos)*. Ravens have a wedge-shaped tail, as opposed to the fan shape of the crow, and a more nasal call.

Chestnut-backed chickadee *(Parus rufescens)*

These tiny, 4 3/4" birds are among the most approachable on the Mountain; they often come within a foot or two as they dart among tree limbs. Their black cap and throat, white cheeks, and rufous back, plus the call that sounds like "chick-a-dee," also identify them.

Bushtit *(Psaltriparus minimus)*

Often associated with chickadees, but even smaller, are the plain, gray, bushtits. Indeed, they are Tam's smallest birds outside the hummingbirds. Bushtits are often seen in small flocks moving between shrubs or trees.

Wrentit *(Chamaea fasciata)*

The call of the male wrentit — accelerating, single-pitched stacatto notes ending with a descending trill (the trill is absent from females' calls) — is heard throughout the year in chaparral. Spotting the common, 6 1/2" brown bird in the thick shrubbery is less easy. Wrentits are renown for spending their whole lives in very small areas.

American robin *(Turdus migratorius)*

The robin needs no introduction. There are several other members of the same thrush family on Tamalpais. In winter, the varied thrush *(Ixoreus naevius)*, similar in appearace to the robin but with a dark "necklace" across its breast, winters in deep woods. Hermit thrushes *(Catharus guttatus)* have spotted breasts, white eye rings, and a particularly lovely, flutelike song. Swainson's thrushes *(C. ustulatus)* are summer nesters that head for Central and South America in winter.

Western bluebird *(Sialia mexicana)*

Bluebirds are not quite as common as some of the other birds listed here, but are always a pleasing sight. The males are a deep blue-purple on the head, throat, and wings. Both males and females have chestnut breasts. Bluebirds catch insects in open meadows.

Western meadowlark *(Sturnella neglecta)*

Meadowlarks wear a distinctive V-shaped black "necklace" across their yellow breasts and have white outer tail feathers. They sing a flute-like, gurgling song. They are found most commonly in grassland.

Red-winged blackbird *(Agelaius phoeniceus)*

Among the most abundant birds in America, red-winged blackbirds are found in marshes and grasslands on Tamalpais. The brilliant red on the adult male's black wing, when caught in the right light, is a visual treat. The males of the also common Brewer's blackbird *(Euphagus cyanocephalus)* are all black, with a purplish gloss on the head and neck.

Pine siskin *(Carduelis pinus)*

Pine siskins are finches, a family of sparrow-sized, thick-billed seedeaters that have a characteristic undulating flight. Siskins can be found in most Tam habitats, but usually in coniferous woodland or atop thistles. When flying, often in large groups, siskins display yellow in their tail and wings on otherwise brown, streaked bodies. Other common Tamalpais finches include: purple finch *(Carpodacus purpureus)*, a woodland denizen that is actually rose-red; house finch *(C. mexicanus)*, a native of the west that was introduced to the east coast in the 1940's; and the bright yellow, black, and white patterned American *(Carduelis tristis)* and lesser *(C. psaltria)* goldfinches, commonly seen darting among thistles.

California towhee *(Pipilo fuscus)*

Two species of towhees live and breed on Tamalpais. Both have long tails and forage on the ground, scratching up food with their feet. The California (formerly the brown) towhee is notable for its very lack of distinguishing marks; it is plain brown, rusty beneath the tail. The rufous-sided towhee *(P. erythrophtalmus),* on the other hand, is strikingly patterned. Its black wings have white spots and its black tail has white outer edges. The white belly is bordered with rufous, and the eyes are red.

Dark-eyed junco *(Junco hyemalis)*

Juncos may be the most common birds on Mt. Tamalpais; it would be a rare walk in which many aren't seen. They are sparrow size with a dark head, white belly, and white outer tail feathers which are visible in flight. Juncos forage on the ground, and build their nest on the forest floor.

White-crowned sparrow *(Zonotrichia leucophrys)*

White-crowned sparrows migrate, but many are present all year on Tam. Adults have white and black striped caps. They are seen scratching for food on trails, often with the similar golden-crowned sparrows *(Z. atricapilla),* then darting into shrubs or grassland when approached. Their songs display dialects, and experts can distinguish where a particular white-crowned was raised.

Song sparrow *(Melospiza melodia)*

Song sparrows are often seen perching, and singing, atop shrubs. They have a distinctive brown spot on the upper-center of their streaked breasts. Their specific name, "melodia," is accurate; their song is among the loveliest of Tam's birds.

MAMMALS

Seeing a mammal (other than man!) in the wild is always a special experience. Around 35 species of mammals, ten of them bats, survive on Tam. The larger of the remaining mammals to be found on the Mountain are presented below.

Mule (Black-tailed) Deer *(Odocoileus hemionus)*

The black-tailed is the native, and only, deer species on Mt. Tamalpais. With several of their predators gone, and hunting long forbidden, deer are now abundant on Tam.

In fall, male bucks spar with their antlers of hardened cartilage for mating rights. After breeding, the antlers are shed. A new set, likely larger than the previous year's, begins to form in winter. In spring the antlers are covered with short hairs, "velvet," which then are scraped off. In early spring, pregnant females seek hidden shelters to bear their usually two fawns. The spotted fawns are able to walk within minutes of birth.

Deer are most active in early morning and at dusk. These are their favorite times for browsing on shrubs, berries, sprouting trees, and other plants. Deer have an average lifespan in the wild of around 16 years.

Squirrel, Chipmunk

The bushy-tailed western gray squirrel *(Scirius grisius)* is a familiar sight on the Mountain as it scurries up trees and leaps across branches. Gray squirrels make barking sounds, deeper than birds' calls. They feed mainly on acorns; many are stored and never found again. They nest in trees and bear a litter of 3-5 young in spring. Gray squirrels were almost wiped off the Mountain in the 1930's by a rabies epidemic.

California ground squirrels *(Citellus beecheyi)* are less common on Tam. Ground squirrels build long burrows in grassland. They lack the gray squirrel's light underbelly, have a dark patch between their shoulders, and a less bushy tail. They can have two litters a year.

Sonoma chipmunks *(Eutamias sonomae)* are seen dashing among the rocks and shrubs high on the Mountain. They jerk their tail each time they chirp. They pack their fur-lined cheek pouches with seeds, often burying them to be re-dug later. The light striping on the back provides excellent comouflage. These chipmunks nest around logs, and give birth to 4-6 young. Tam's chipmunk was once regarded as a separate species, *Eutamias alleni.*

Rabbit, Hare

Its long ears make the black-tailed hare *(Lepus californicus)*, or jackrabbit, unmistakable. Hares startle potential predators by using their long hind limbs to make a sudden initial leap, then bound and zig-zag at up to 35 miles per hour. Females scrape the barest of nests, or none at all, and give birth to 1-3 litters a year, each with from 2-4 furry young.

Brush rabbits *(Sylvilagus bachmani)*, or cottontails, are smaller and less swift than jackrabbits. They stick to dense vegetative cover to avoid predators. Their young, like all true rabbits, are born blind, without fur, and helpless; the young of hares are born fully furred and capable of hopping.

Bobcat *(Lynx rufus)*

Bobcats, though not rare on the Mountain, are seen only infrequently because they are largely nocturnal and their fur provides excellent camouflage. They can be mistaken for an escaped house cat but are bigger, weighing 15-30 pounds, have tufted ears, and a short, bobbed tail. The usually two young are born helpless in spring and are cared for by the mother until fall. As with all cats, they leave no claw marks on their tracks. Bobcats capture rodents, rabbits, and birds, and sometimes eat carrion.

A handful of an even larger cat, the mountain lion *(Felis concolor),* or cougar, likely still roam on Tamalpais, though many life-long hikers have never seen one. These long-tailed cats require large territories to survive.

Skunk

There are two species of skunk found on Mt. Tamalpais, the striped *(Mephitis mephitis),* and the spotted *(Spilogale putorius).* Striped skunks have two white stripes lining their black backs. They are found in deeper woods. The smaller spotted skunks have four broken stripes and a white-tipped tail. Skunks are omnivorous, feeding on insects, berries, rodents, eggs, and carrion. Their powerful scent gland spray keeps them relatively free of natural enemies. In spring, 2-6 helpless young are born. They remain in the mother's care, often trailing single file, throughout the summer. Skunks are usually nocturnal; if you see one roaming during the day it may be rabid and should be given an even wider berth than usual.

Long-tailed weasel (*Mustela frenata*)

The slender weasel is able to invade mouse and rat burrows; rodents are its primary prey. Weasels weigh only eight ounces or so, averaging nine inches in body length plus a 3-6 inch tail. Weasels are golden-brown above, whitish-yellow below. Weasels raise a single litter of 4-8 young each year. They dig dens under rock slides and woodpiles, or use the burrows of other animals. Though rarely seen, weasels are not uncommon, particularly on Tam's grassy west slopes.

Raccoon *(Procyon lotor)*

Raccoons are nocturnal and omnivorous. Raccoons have extremely agile and sensitive fingers, which are believed to contain more sensory nerves than any other mammal. They tend to dunk their food in water before eating it. Female raccoons bear 2-7 young in early spring, then rear them for a couple of months. Raccoon scat is often seen atop small rocks along fire roads and trails. Raccoons are fearless night raiders of trash containers alongside homes on the Mountain's slopes.

Gray fox *(Urocyon cinereoargenteus)*

You have to be sharp, and lucky, to see a fox on Mt. Tamalpais, as they are nocturnal, wary, and their rusty and gray coat blends in with chaparral. Gray foxes have a black-tipped tail. They are omnivorous, eating rodents, insects, grasses, berries, and other plants. They climb trees when seeking birds' eggs. Gray foxes mate in winter. Both parents share in raising the 2-5 young.

Sightings in Marin of another canine, the coyote *(Canis latrans)*, began again in 1981 after a 40 year hiatus. The coyote may yet return to Mt. Tamalpais.

Feral pigs *(Sus scrofa)*

Pigs, descendants both from domestic escapees and from stock introduced for game hunting elsewhere in Marin, established a wild (feral) population on Mt. Tamalpais. Their burgeoning numbers, perhaps 200 at the peak, became a problem in the mid-1980's. They uprooted bulbs and other vegetation. Professional hunters were brought in and pig traps were set out and stocked; the meat was donated to dining halls for the needy. One boar was six feet, seven inches from tail to snout and weighed 330 pounds. Also, a fence was built along Bolinas Ridge, just west of Ridgecrest Boulevard, to keep pigs from roaming down into Point Reyes National Seashore. These measures have sharply reduced the feral pig population.

FISH

Silver salmon *(Oncorhynchys kisutch)*

Silver (also called coho) salmon spawn on Tam in Redwood Creek, which flows through Muir Woods. The 18-30 inch long, silver-to-brick-red adults swim upstream from the Pacific after the onset of winter rains. The females deposit 2,000-3,500 eggs each in shallow depressions at the creek's edges. The males, sometimes fighting for the privilege, fertilize the eggs. The females then cover the eggs. Soon after, all the adults die.

In 40-60 days, the young emerge and spend the summer in the creek. The first significant fall rains allow Redwood Creek to breach the sand bar that forms each summer at its mouth by Muir Beach. The young fingerlings, around 2 1/2" long, can then complete their downstream migration. They reach the ocean, adapting to the salt water. After one to three years (usually two) in the open water, they gather once again offshore outside Redwood Creek. Only some six salmon out of every 10,000 eggs laid complete the whole life cycle.

Steelhead trout *(Salmo gairdnerii)*

Steelhead have a life cycle similar to the closely related silver salmon. The 26" long silver adults, which develop a red lateral band in fresh water, also swim up Redwood Creek each winter to spawn. The young head to the ocean each fall. A significant difference is that steelhead adults are able to survive the spawning season. Those that do swim back to the Pacific, and, if they survive the winter, return to Tam to spawn again.

REPTILES

Lizards

Lizards, of several species, are common on Mt. Tamalpais. Western fence lizards *(Sceloporus occidentalis)* are in the iguana family. They bask in the sun atop rocks, logs, or fence posts. Males have blue throat patches and blue on the underside of the belly; a common name is "blue-belly." Western skinks *(Eumeces skiltonianus)* are sleeker and shinier, more snake-like. They have a brown stripe, edged with light and black stripes, down their backs. Skinks hunt insects under leaves, logs, and rocks. Juveniles have bright blue tails. One theory is that the striking color diverts predators' attention to the tail, which is replaceable. Alligator lizards *(Gerrhonotus* spp.) spend much time under rocks and logs, but are also good climbers. They have short limbs and a fold on the side of their bodies.

Snakes

Several species of snakes live on Mt. Tamalpais. Best known, and the only poisonous one, is the western rattlesnake *(Crotalus viridis)*. They are two to five feet in length. Rattlers are distinguished by their broad, triangular head and the rattles at the tip of the tail. A rattle segment is added each time the snake sheds its skin, which can be 3-4 times annually for young snakes, once a year or less for older rattlers. Rattlesnakes eat small mammals and birds, as well as other reptiles.

The rubber boa *(Charina bottae)* is a shiny plain brown above, lighter below. The tail is shaped somewhat like its head. They are 14-29 inches in length, and prefer moist, wooded areas. Like their relatives, the pythons, boas kill by constriction.

The gopher snake *(Pituophis melanoleucus)* can grow to eight feet in length. It resembles the rattlesnake in appearance, though without the rattlers. When aroused, they sometimes hiss, flatten their head, and vibrate their tail, giving them an even more rattlesnake-like appearance. Gopher snakes kill rodents, rabbits, and birds by constriction.

The common, or California, kingsnake *(Lampropeltis getulus)* is also large; three to seven feet in length. The alternating bands of black or brown with white or yellow are distinctive. They too can hiss and vibrate their tail like the rattlesnake. Actually, rattlers are one of their dietary items.

The western yellow-bellied racer *(Coluber constrictor)* can reach 6 feet in length. They are sleek, with large eyes. Racers are good climbers.

Garter snakes *(Thamnophis* spp.*)* are the most aquatic of local snakes. They are slender, around 2-3 feet long, and are stiped on the back and sides.

The ringneck snake *(Diadophis punctatus)* is slender and about 2 feet long. It usually has a diagnostic orange neck ring. The belly and underside of the tail are also orange-red; the bright side of the tail is coiled and flashed when the snake is alarmed.

JURISDICTIONS

At the turn of this century, all of Mt. Tamalpais was privately owned. The original Mexican grants of Mountain land had been carved up for dairy ranches, railroads, stage roads, logging operations, hunting clubs, water resource developments, homesites, mines, and other ventures. In 1908, to save one of the last stands of uncut redwood trees in the Bay Area, William Kent donated the initial acreage of Muir Woods National Monument to the federal government. That marked the start of a trend that has continued to this day, and most of Mt. Tamalpais is now publicly owned. The principal managers of Mt. Tamalpais land arc described below.

MARIN MUNICIPAL WATER DISTRICT (MMWD)

The Marin Municipal Water District (abbreviated throughout this book as MMWD) manages the largest part of Mt. Tamalpais. It was created by a general election in 1912 as the first public water district in California. It supplanted two private water companies already operating on the Mountain.

The MMWD manages virtually all the north side of Mt. Tamalpais. Its holdings continue north across the Fairfax-Bolinas Road (this book's boundary) onto Pine Mountain and San Geronimo Ridge. On the Mountain's south face, Water District boundaries cut through Rock Spring, the Mountain Theater, Panoramic Highway, and Mountain Home. To the east, the MMWD extends to Old Railroad Grade, Blithedale Ridge, and Windy Ridge. On the west, the MMWD boundary runs roughly along the spine of Bolinas Ridge.

The MMWD provides water to over 55,000 service connections, 90% of them residences, in southern and central Marin. It maintains seven reservoirs (four — Alpine, Bon Tempe, Lagunitas, and Phoenix — within this book's boundaries) with a total storage capacity of 26 billion gallons; 822 miles of pipeline; 139 storage tanks; 107 pump stations; and two water treatment plants. These reservoirs and structures are now prominent features of the Mountain.

As population pressures in Marin intensify, the Water District has increasingly recognized its alternate role as manager of watershed lands for open space and recreation purposes. Their current visitor's brochure states, "Mount Tamalpais holds a spiritual significance for the San Francisco Bay Area. It is a beacon for the community; a guardian of things that are wild and wonderful; a friend; an experience. . .it is truly a place to be revered and respected. Marin Municipal Water District is steward of this land, protecting it for water supply and preserving it for future generations. Enjoy the watershed experience. It is a legacy that we pass to our children."

The MMWD ranger station is at Sky Oaks, on Sky Oaks Road off Fairfax' Bolinas Road. The phone number is 415/459-5267. There are MMWD ranger residences on the Mountain near there, and at lakes Lagunitas, Alpine (scheduled), and Phoenix. All district lands are open to the public from sunrise to sunset, without charge, except for a vehicle fee (presently $3 daily, or $25 for an annual pass) to use Sky Oaks Road. Large group activities require permits. No overnight camping or use is allowed. The administrative headquarters of the Marin Municipal Water District is at 220 Nellen Avenue in Corte Madera (415/924-4600).

MOUNT TAMALPAIS STATE PARK (MTSP)

Mount Tamalpais State Park (abbreviated MTSP) is the second largest land unit on the Mountain. The park comprises much of the south side of Tamalpais, south of the MMWD lands but excluding Muir Woods. The park also extends south of the Muir Woods Road, this book's southern boundary, to Highway 1. On the west, the park goes to the Pacific between, roughly, the mouths of Cold Stream and Webb creeks. To the east, Panoramic Highway defines the park's boundary.

Mount Tamalpais State Park was one of the first of now some 250 California state parks. A proposal in 1926 to build a road between Mountain Home and Stinson Beach stirred the TCC and other outdoors groups into action. They feared the road would lead to development of the private 500+ acre Newlands-Magee property, which lay between Mountain Home and Bootjack. A legislative bill authorized the state to contribute $1 for every $2 collected to buy the parcel. When James Newlands and William Magee refused to sell, condemnation proceedings fixed the value of their land at $52,000. The money was raised and the purchase completed in 1928. The Newlands-Magee property, plus 138 acres south of it to Muir Woods and 200+ acres in Steep Ravine, the latter two parcels donated by William Kent, became the park's initial nucleus. Since then, the park has grown to 6,400 acres.

Today, Mount Tamalpais State Park is one of the most popular in the State system, with over one million visitors annually. Park headquarters are at the Pantoll ranger station (415/388-2070), where there are several employee residences. The park operates four overnight fee campgrounds, the only ones on Mt. Tamalpais (see Recreation section). Mount Tamalpais State Park is open every day without charge. Note that State Park trail signs indicate the trail name on top, in smaller letters, and the destination below, in larger letters.

MUIR WOODS NATIONAL MONUMENT (MWNM)

Muir Woods is the most visited part of Mt. Tamalpais. Indeed, with nearly two million visitors annually, Muir Woods is one of the most popular attractions in the nation's park system. Most visitors see little more of the Monument than the level stretch along Redwood Creek north of the main entrance. Actually, the Monument covers 560 acres, mostly north and west of the main entrance, and rises to 1,300 feet in elevation at Cardiac Hill near the crest of the Dipsea Trail. Another boot-shaped parcel lies south of Muir Woods Road.

The preservation of Muir Woods from loggers and developers was a key event in this country's then fledgling environmental movement. Towering stands of virgin redwoods once lined many Bay Area creek canyons before they were felled to provide the wood used in the post-Gold Rush building boom. By 1900, few uncut groves remained. A 1903 meeting to create a park on Tamalpais failed but it helped prompt William Kent, who already owned huge tracts of the Mountain, to purchase, two years later, 295 acres of uncut redwoods along Redwood Creek. The seller, Lovell White, reportedly had offers of over twice the $45,000 price, but knew Kent would protect the land. In 1908, partly to thwart an attempt by the North Coast Water Company to condemn 57 of the acres and build a dam on Redwood Creek, Kent donated the whole parcel to the federal government. Kent later donated over 180 additional acres to the monument.

Muir Woods is open daily without charge (though contributions are welcomed) from 8 a.m. to sunset. The monument is now part of the Golden Gate National Recreation Area. It retains its own resident site management staff, which can be reached at 415/388-2595.

MARIN COUNTY OPEN SPACE DISTRICT (MCOSD)

The Marin County Open Space District (MCOSD) was formed as a tax-supported public agency in the general election of 1972. Their nearly 1,000 acres of Tamalpais acquisitions since then have been concentrated in the Baltimore Canyon area and along Blithedale and Corte Madera ridges, all on the Mountain's east side. The District has been the most active agency in recent years in purchasing additional Tamalpais land, helped in part because it administers the open space funds donated by the Marin Community (Buck) Foundation.

MCOSD preserves on Tamalpais usually do not have water fountains, toilets, or other amenities. Parking at access points is often very limited. Many of the trails and fire roads are not signed and few are named. Rangers do patrol the lands. The District's headquarters are at the Marin County Civic Center in San Rafael. The phone number is 415/499-6387.

AUDUBON CANYON RANCH (ACR)

Audubon Canyon Ranch occupies a sizable parcel on the northwest corner of Mt. Tamalpais, north of Volunteer Canyon and west of Bolinas Ridge. The Ranch was founded in the early 1970's as a joint effort of the Golden Gate and Redwood chapters of the Audubon Society to protect a nesting site for great blue herons and great egrets. The Ranch has become an important nature preserve and education center. Because ACR lands are open to the public only on weekends during the nesting season of March to mid-July, none of the several trails through the Ranch are included in this book. Permission to enter at other times should be obtained from Audubon Canyon Ranch, 4900 Shoreline Highway, Stinson Beach, Ca. 94970 (415/868-9244).

PRIVATE

Though one of the key criteria used in selecting trails to include in this book was that they be on public land, a handful presented do pass through private property. They are included because they have long been traveled without hindrance, or because there is a public easement through the land, or because only a small fraction of the trail's total length is private. I urge the reader to be particularly courteous when passing through any of these private sections, not only because it is proper, but because future access could later be denied.

BAY AREA RIDGE TRAIL

The approximately 400 mile long Bay Area Ridge Trail is scheduled to be completed in the early 1990's. It will provide pedestrians, bikers, and equestrians with a public access route around San Francisco Bay. Some parts of the Ridge Trail will accommodate all three types of user; in other areas there will be parallel routes. The Ridge Trail passes north to south through Mt. Tamalpais on existing trails and fire roads (a possible exception, not settled at press-time, is an equestrian route on the east side of Ridgecrest Boulevard along Bolinas Ridge). Most of the Tam sections were formally dedicated as part of the Ridge Trail on September 23, 1989. New blue signs were placed. Trails that are part of the Bay Area Ridge Trail are noted as such in the text. It is important to point out that the Bay Area Ridge Trail is not a separate jurisdiction; rules of the land managers through which the Ridge Trail passes prevail.

The largely volunteer Bay Area Ridge Trail Council, which has spearheaded this huge undertaking, is headquartered at 116 New Montgomery Street, Suite 640, San Francisco, 94105. Their phone number is (415) 543-4291.

RECREATION

HIKING

Hiking has long been the principal "raison d'etre" for visiting Mt. Tamalpais. All trails in this book are open to hikers; indeed, most were built by hikers. That anyone can, at any time and without any reservation or fee, take a walk through the beautiful, varied, and vast open spaces of the Mountain is a privilege long cherished, and zealously guarded.

No group leads more hikes, over 200 annually, on the Mountain, than the Sierra Club. Their first Tam hike was in 1902, not long after the club was co-founded by John Muir here in the Bay Area. Hikes are open to members and non-members alike without charge. Membership information, and the club's Activities Schedule, can be obtained from the Bay Chapter office at 6014 College Avenue, Oakland 94618 (415/653-6127), or from the Sierra Club's national headquarters at 730 Polk Street, San Francisco 94109 (415/776-2211). The Sierra Club also continues to play a major role in trail maintenance.

Another group that regularly offers walks, presently every Saturday and Sunday out of either Pantoll, Bootjack, or Rock Spring, is the Mt. Tamalpais Interpretive Association. It was founded as a volunteer arm of the State Park in 1983 in response to post-Proposition 13 budget problems. The association is expanding its selection of activities, all free of charge. Members staff, on a volunteer basis, the Visitor Center (which they refurbished) by the East Peak parking area. The association can be reached at 801 Panoramic Highway, Mill Valley, CA 94941 (415/388-2070).

There are regularly scheduled, almost hourly on busy summer weekends, docent or ranger led walks in Muir Woods National Monument. Call (415) 388-2595 for more information. In spring, during the egret and heron nesting season, docents lead walks through Audubon Canyon Ranch. The Ranch is at 4900 State Route (Highway) 1, just north of Stinson Beach. The phone number is (415) 868-9244.

Many other other hiking and social clubs have been associated with Mt. Tamalpais. Some, such as the Tourist Club and the California Alpine Club, both of which have clubhouses on the Mountain, and the Contra Costa Hills Club, are still active. Others, such as the Cross Country Boys Club and the Down & Outer's Club, have passed into Mountain lore.

RUNNING

Running has a colorful history on the Mountain. The Dipsea Race, now one of the most famous trail runs in the world, was first held in 1905. High school cross-country meets have been held on Tam for decades. A hardy band of runners has gathered by Mountain Home every Saturday morning since the 1960's to begin their long runs. Virtually every local distance runner trains on the Mountain's trails.

To some runners, no trail is too steep, narrow, or rocky. However, trails noted as "very steep," "extremely steep," and/or "rocky" in the text headings will prove unrunnable, uphill or downhill, for most people. Some trails, shared with horses, can be quite muddy after rains, and are so noted. Otherwise, Mt. Tamalpais' fire roads and trails offer some of the best running to be found anywhere in the world.

Much the largest running club in Marin is the Tamalpa Runners. Membership information can be obtained by writing them at P.O. Box 701, Corte Madera 94925.

MOUNTAIN BIKING

Mountain bikes were literally invented in the shadow of Mt. Tamalpais, in small shops near the San Anselmo-Fairfax border in the 1970's. The pioneers first tested their fat-tired, multi-geared, durable bikes on Tam. Even the "mountain" in "mountain bike" refers to Tamalpais. The popularity of mountain (off-road) biking has proved phenomenal, and it is easily the fastest growing recreational activity on Tamalpais.

The mountain biking boom has generated a spirited debate on the Mountain between cycling advocates and those who wish to restrict their use. The present policy, in all jurisdictions, is that mountain biking is permitted on, and only on, Tamalpais' fire roads and paved roads. I specifically labelled each route in this book as either a trail or a fire road (or a grade, the same as a fire road for biking purposes) to make this distinction clear. Speed limits are presently 15 miles per hour and 5 on curves or when passing. CHECK SIGNS AND THE LATEST JURISDICTION REGULATIONS because all rules are subject to change.

The Bicycle Trails Council of Marin (415/972-BIKE) represents many mountain cyclists on local issues.

HORSE RIDING

The horse was the chief mode of transportation on Tamalpais for nearly a hundred years after the arrival of the first non-native settlers. Horse-drawn stagecoaches plied routes up and over the Mountain, until motor vehicles rendered them obsolete. However, riding horses remains a popular activity on the Mountain.

Horses are permitted on the Mountain's fire roads and on some trails. Trails open to horses are noted with "horses permitted" in their heading description. Trails on Tamalpais in the State Park, except for Riding and Hiking and Heather Cutoff, are closed to horses. Trails through Marin County Open Space District and Golden Gate National Recreation Area lands are open to horses, unless posted otherwise. Marin Municipal Water District trails, a mixed lot regarding horse access, are usually well-signed. Horses are not permitted in Muir Woods National Monument. Remember that SIGNS AT TRAILHEADS, AND THE CURRENT REGULATIONS OF THE JURISDICTION MANAGERS, TAKE PRECEDENCE.

The two principal stables on the Mountain are both in Fairfax; Marin Stables at 139 Wood Lane (415/459-9455) and Sky Ranch at 106 Crest Road (415/459-9925). Other nearby stables are in Muir Beach, Tennessee Valley, and at Five Brooks. The Tamalpais Trail Riders, founded in 1939, represents many Mountain riders on local issues. Their address is P.O. Box 63, San Anselmo, California, 94960.

CAMPING

Overnight camping on Tamalpais was once all but unrestricted. Hundreds of people spent weekends, and some lived full-time, in the more popular camp sites or in remote nooks. Sharp-eyed visitors can still find old stashes of cooking utensils and other remnants of the camps. After the depression years of the 1930's, when camping on Tamalpais peaked, and particularly after the 1960's, when a new generation rediscovered living on the Mountain, restrictions against camping tightened. Today, overnight camping is permitted on Tam at only a handful of designated sites.

These campgrounds, all in Mt. Tamalpais State Park, are:

Camp Alice Eastwood - Camp Eastwood Road. Open only to groups by reservation, (415) 388-2070. Has water, outhouses.

Pantoll - Junction of Panoramic Highway and Pantoll Road. Wooded campsites all within a short walk of the parking area. First come, first served; usually filled early. Present fee is $10 a night. Firewood is sold and there is a telephone and restrooms with flush toilets. The Pantoll phone number is (415) 388-2070.

Shansky Backpack Camp - Coastal Fire Road between Highway 1 and Dipsea Trail. Closed at press-time due to storm damage. Four wooded campsites well off any auto-access road. Has an outhouse but no water. Fires and pets are not permitted. Reservations required through Pantoll, (415) 388-2070.

Steep Ravine Environmental Campground - Base of Steep Ravine Road below Highway 1. Six campsites on bluff above the ocean. There is water, outhouses, and a telephone. No pets allowed. Reservations required via MISTIX at (800) 444-PARK.

Horse Camp - Frank Valley Road near base of Heather Cutoff Trail. The newest campground, opened in 1989. Its few sites are geared to horse riders. Reservations are through Pantoll, (415) 388-2070.

Camping is also allowed, by advance permit only, on lands of the Marin County Open Space District.

NATURE STUDY

Many organizations offer natural history outings on Mt. Tamalpais. In addition to those listed in the hiking section above are:

California Native Plant Society - Concentrates on plant study and preservation of the native flora. Information on the Marin chapter can be obtained from Wilma Follette, 1 Harrison Avenue, Sausalito 94965.

College of Marin - Marin's community college regularly offers courses on area geology, wildlife (including marine life), plants, weather, etc. Most classes are open to adults of any age who register and pay the very nominal fees. Catalogs can be obtained from COM, College Ave., Kentfield 94904. The number for phone registration is (415) 382-0411.

Marin Discoveries - Originally part of the College of Marin, but now independent, Marin Discoveries offers a wide choice of outings. Groups are usually small and are led by professional naturalists. Marin Discoveries' office is at 11 1st St., Corte Madera 94925 (415/927-0410).

Audubon Society of Marin - Conducts scores of birdwatching walks annually. The local Redwood chapter's phone number is (415) 383-1770.

Terwilliger Nature Education Society - Outings usually are geared to younger people, but adults enjoy "tripping with Terwilliger" as well. The address is 50 El Camino Drive, Corte Madera 94925; phone number, (415) 927-1670.

FISHING

Lake Lagunitas was stocked with fish soon after it was filled in 1873, and angling has been a popular pastime on Tam ever since. The old fish hatchery beneath Lagunitas Dam is still visible. Fishing is permitted, and popular, at all MMWD lakes (Alpine, Bon Tempe, Kent, Lagunitas, and Phoenix) in the Tamalpais watershed. Bass and trout are periodically stocked. Beginning in the late 1980's, Lake Lagunitas has been managed as a self-sustaining trout fishery. The lake was drained, all the bass were removed, an aerator to provide oxygen during the hot summer months was installed, and 8,000 Shasta strain rainbow trout were planted. New regulations; fishing only with artificial lures and a single barbless hook, a catch limit of two, and no keeping of fish between 10 and 16 inches, were initiated at Lagunitas. At Phoenix, some 1,700 tires were placed on the lake bed after it was last drained in the mid-1980's to serve as breeding places for large-mouth bass.

Fishing is subject to the California Fish and Game Code. Be sure to CHECK AND OBSERVE POSTED REGULATIONS.

DOGS

Each of the Mountain's jurisdictions has regulations regarding dogs. Basically, dogs are not permitted at all in Muir Woods National Monument, other Golden Gate National Recreation Area lands on the Mountain, and in Mount Tamalpais State Park. They are allowed on leash on maintained Marin Municipal Water District trails unless otherwise posted. Dogs are permitted off-leash, but under voice control, on Marin County Open Space District trails, except those through designated wilderness areas. As always, TRAIL SIGNS AND PUBLISHED REGULATIONS PREVAIL.

SOME CAUTIONS

Almost all who spend time on Mt. Tamalpais come to view it as a friend, even as a protector. Still, there are a few matters that sometimes demand extra caution.

Ticks

Ticks are small blood-sucking arachnids that have long been a minor nuisance on the Mountain. There is a danger of infection if they become embedded in the skin. The problem has gotten more serious in recent years because of the spread, though it is still rare, of Lyme disease. The disease is caused by a bacterial spirochete *(Borrelia burgdorferi)*, only discovered in 1983, carried by the ticks. If left untreated, Lyme disease (named for Old Lyme, Connecticut, where the disease was first described in 1975) can be debilitating, causing arthritis and heart and nerve problems. Ticks, attracted to the warmth of warm-blooded mammals, brush off from foliage. They then quickly, and rather firmly, attach themselves to the skin. Our problem tick, the 1/8 inch long western black-legged *(Ixodes pacificus)*, is active just about all year.

Check yourself, or have a friend check, for ticks after trips, particularly if you went cross-country in grassland. If you find a tick, one age-old treatment is to dab petroleum jelly (Vaseline) on the tick to smother it, wait 15-30 minutes, gently pull the tick straight out with sterile tweezers, then thoroughly clean the area. Another technique is to hold a lighted match near the tick, which leads it to withdraw its hold. Some authorities, however, say these techniques are not effective. If any part of the tick remains embedded, if the tick has been lodged for a while, if the area shows any sign of infection, or if a circular, reddish rash has formed around the bite (the diagnostic symptom of Lyme disease), see a physician. Early treatment of Lyme disease with antibiotics is almost invariably successful.

Poison Oak

Contact with the oily sap of poison oak causes a dermatitis in most people, though the resulting degree of inflammation and itching varies widely. To compound the problem, poison oak may be the most abundant shrub on Mt. Tamalpais, common in many habitats. It also takes on a variety of appearances. It may be short and single stalked, tall and branching, a vine, or even a short tree. The three-lobed leaves, which turn reddish in late summer, are diagnostic (the old axiom is "leaves of three, let it be") and all Mountain visitors soon learn to recognize it at a distance. Even without its leaves in winter, poison oak can still be toxic. If you know, or think, you've touched poison oak, take a thorough shower soon after using a strong soap such as Fels naphtha.

Giardiasis

Through 1989, there were no documented cases of giardiasis, an intestinal ailment caused by the protozoan *Giardia lamblia,* resulting from drinking Mt. Tamalpais water. Still, to be safe, the Marin Municipal Water District has, on their lands, posted formerly commonly used water sources that are not treated as "non-potable." Readers must choose for themselves whether to drink untreated water. It is always wise, however, to TAKE AN ADEQUATE SUPPLY OF DRINKING WATER ON ANY TRIP ON THE MOUNTAIN.

Yellowjackets

These pesky wasps are yellow with black bands. They have, unfortunately for us, an amazing ability to sense lunch, our lunch! Keeping food well sealed is the best defense. They also congregate around water fountains, like those at the East Peak parking area. Stings are usually just mildly painful but can cause severe reactions in some people. Artifical respiration and other prompt medical attention may sometimes be required. Swelling commonly lasts about two days.

Rattlesnakes

Rattlesnakes live and breed on Mt. Tamalpais, but bites are extremely rare and fatal encounters nil. The Mountain's variety of the Western rattlesnake *(Crotalus viridus)* is usually 2-4 feet long. It has the characteristic broad, triangular head and the rattles, a segment of which is added each time the snake sheds its skin. Give a rattlesnake, even a dead one, a wide berth to avoid any problems. Gopher snakes, also found on the Mountain, bear some resemblance to rattlers, including a vibrating tail when aroused. They, and all other Mountain snake species, are harmless.

Homo sapiens

David Carpenter, the convicted "Trailside Killer," changed the complexion of Mt. Tamalpais, permanently for some, when he murdered several hikers in 1980. The fact is that the Mountain had long been a safe place, and is so again. Crimes of any sort on Tam are rare. There are occasional car break-ins; don't leave valuables in cars. Still, if you lose an item on a trail it will more likely than not be returned to you. Those wary to venture alone on the Mountain can always find companions from the groups listed above. Report any suspicious activities to a ranger.

Fire

Fires have always been a part of Mt. Tamalpais. In 1859, a fire burned for three months. In 1881, one scorched 65,000 acres. In 1929, a fire destroyed over 100 homes on the Mill Valley slope and lit up the night sky of San Francisco. The last major conflagration was in 1945, on the north side. Since lightning is rare on Tam, fires are usually man-made. At all times, but particularly during the tinder-dry, rainless months of summer and fall, Mountain visitors must exercise exceptional caution regarding potential fire causing activities.

CHRONOLOGICAL HISTORY

Unknown - Plate movements uplift the 65-150 million year old rocks of the Franciscan Complex to form the Tamalpais massif.

150,000 years before present - Erosion of less resistant rock leaves Mt. Tamalpais with a profile somewhat resembling today's shape.

18,000 years before present - The global ice age peaks; so much of the earth's water is tied up as ice that sea level is 30 miles west of Mt. Tamalpais. A warming trend begins, and the ocean advances to the present shoreline.

7,000 years before present - Coast Miwok Indians, migrants from Siberia, begin living along the ocean and bay margins of Mt. Tamalpais.

3,000 years before present - The Potrero Landslide, almost two miles long and nearly 3,500 feet wide, drops a huge chunk off the north side of Tamalpais.

1,200 years before present - The oldest redwood tree alive today in Muir Woods sprouts.

1542 - The Spanish explorer Juan Cabrillo sails past Tamalpais and may have been the first European to see it.

1792 - British navigator George Vancouver produces the first map of the San Francisco Bay Area that has Mt. Tamalpais distinctly identified, though not named.

1793 - Spaniards in Lt. Felipe de Goycoechea's overland expedition are believed to be the first Europeans to walk on the Mountain. Some historians say his party climbed to the summit; others believe the first ascent may have been decades later.

1817 - Mission San Rafael Arcangel is established, beginning European settlement in Marin County. Cattle grazing is introduced to Mt. Tamalpais shortly after, substantially altering the vegetation. The native Indian population is decimated, mostly by European diseases, falling 90% within a few decades.

1822 - Control of California passes from Spain to the new nation of Mexico.

1826 - British Captain Frederick Beechey prepares a detailed nautical map of the Bay Area and gives the name "Table Mountain," which persists for decades, to Mt. Tamalpais.

1834 - The first of several huge grants dividing Marin County is made by the Mexican government to John Reed, who, two years later, builds an adobe house and a sawmill in what is now Mill Valley.

1846 - Possession of Mt. Tamalpais, and all of Alta California, passes from Mexico to the United States.

1849 - The Gold Rush triggers a population and building boom in San Francisco that forever alters the area. Commercial logging, which clears the Mountain of virtually all its original growth redwoods, begins in earnest.

1873 - Lagunitas Creek is dammed to form Lake Lagunitas as a reliable source of drinking water. Dams forming Phoenix (1905), Alpine (1919), Bon Tempe (1949), and Kent (1954) lakes follow.

1880 - The last reliable report of a bear, taken in a trap, is made on the Mountain.

1884 - Eldridge Grade, the first stage route up the Mountain, opens.

1896 - The Mt. Tamalpais Railway lays 8.5 miles of track from Mill Valley to near East Peak and begins bringing passengers up on its steam powered trains. A spur to Muir Woods opens in 1907. The railway ceases operations, and the track is torn up, in 1930.

1898 - The first trail map of the Mountain is published by Sanborn and Knapp.

1901 - A marine observatory is built atop East Peak. It was rebuilt in 1937 and now serves as a fire lookout.

1904 - West Point Inn is built.

1905 - The first Dipsea Race is run.

1906 - The great San Francisco earthquake and fire begins another rush of development to Marin and the Mountain's slopes.

1908 - William Kent donates Muir Woods to the United States Government as the first public holding on Mt. Tamalpais.

1912 - The Marin Municipal Water District, which now manages most of Mt. Tamalpais, is created by a public referendum. It replaced earlier private water companies holding Mountain lands.

1912 - The Tamalpais Conservation Club is formed and organizes the first of its trail maintenance days, which continue to this day. The Tamalpais branch of the Tourist Club is founded the same year, and the California Alpine Club in 1914. Both still have clubhouses on the Mountain.

1912 - The original Mountain Home Inn opens.

1913 - The first Mountain Play, "Abraham and Isaac," is performed. The present amphitheater was constructed in the 1930's.

1917 - The Mt. Tamalpais Game Refuge is established.

1926 - Ridgecrest Boulevard, from Fairfax-Bolinas Road to near East Peak, is completed as a toll road.

1928 - Mt. Tamalpais State Park, one of the first in the California system, is created. Subsequent additions enlarge it from 500 to over 6,000 acres.

1929 - Panoramic Highway across the Mountain opens. The connection to Ridgecrest Boulevard (between Pantoll and Rock Spring) was finished the following year.

1929 - A devastating fire sweeps the Mountain's south side, destroying 117 Mill Valley homes.

1933 - The depression-inspired Civilian Conservation Corps sets up two camps on the Mountain and begins a variety of major building projects, including fire roads and the Mountain Theater.

1937 - Opening of the Golden Gate Bridge creates still another wave of construction around the Mountain.

1941 - The Army closes off parts of the Mountain, particularly around West Peak (the summit of which is still fenced), for military purposes.

1944 - Eight servicemen die when a Navy seaplane crashes into the southeast face of the Mountain.

1945 - One of the largest fires in the county's history burns out of control for a week on Tamalpais' north side.

1951 - The Mill Valley Air Force Station is built atop West Peak on land leased from the Marin Municipal Water District. The summit, then the Mountain's highest, is bulldozed from 2,604 feet down to 2,567 feet, making it lower than East Peak. The property was declared surplus in 1983, and the lease transferred to the Golden Gate National Recreation Area. In 1986, the first buildings were torn down by volunteers.

1962 - The Marin and Golden Gate Audubon Society chapters unite to purchase and protect Audubon Canyon Ranch. The Ranch later expands its Tamalpais acreage.

1971 - The Golden Gate National Recreation Area, now with extensive holdings on the south and west of the Mountain, is created.

1972 - The Marin County Open Space District, which subsequently acquires sizable parcels on the east side of the Mountain, is formed by a general election. One percent of Marin's property taxes are set aside to finance open space purchases.

1980 - David Carpenter creates an unprecedented atmosphere of fear on the Mountain by murdering several hikers. He was captured in 1981 and, later, found guilty and sentenced to death.

1989 - In recognition of its importance as a world resource, Mt. Tamalpais is named by the United Nations as an International Biosphere Reserve, one of just 250 on the planet.

FURTHER STUDY

HISTORY COLLECTIONS

Lucretia Little History Room - This treasure contains perhaps the most extensive collection of Mt. Tamalpais literature, maps, photographs, and artifacts to be found anywhere. It is presently open, staffed by volunteers, six hours a day. The History Room is in the basement of the Mill Valley Public Library at 375 Throckmorton Avenue; the phone number is (415) 388-4245.

Anne Kent California History Room - Kent is the family name most closely associated with Tamalpais. This Room is part of the Marin County Free Library, in the Civic Center in San Rafael, and is open during regular library hours. The phone number is (415) 499-7419.

Marin County Historical Society - The Society's headquarters, in the Louise Boyd Museum at 1125 B Street, San Rafael, have been closed for structural repairs but are due to reopen in 1990. The phone number is (415) 454-8538.

There are also fine collections in the Jack Mason Museum in Inverness, in the Bancroft Library at the University of California in Berkeley, and at public libraries in the communities that surround Mt. Tamalpais.

RECOMMENDED MAPS

"Trails of Mt. Tamalpais," published by the Olmsted Bros. Map Co., Berkeley. It features colored relief, forty-foot contour intervals, historical references, and covers from Pine Mountain to the Golden Gate.

"Trail Map of the Mt. Tamalpais Region," published by Erickson Maps, Oakland. As the successor to the famous, older Freese maps, Erickson shows many smaller details, such as footbridges.

BOOKS IN PRINT

Scores of books have been devoted entirely, or largely, to Mt. Tamalpais. The following are some of those in print in 1990:

"Mount Tamalpais, A History," by Lincoln Fairley (Scottwall Associates, San Francisco, 1987). A handsome book, with superb photos, lovingly researched by the late Fairley.

"The Crookedest Railroad in the World," by Ted Wurm and Al Graves (Trans-Anglo Books, Glendale, 1983). The definitive work on the Mt. Tamalpais Railway.

"Marin Flora," by John Thomas Howell (University Of California, Berkeley, second edition 1970). The authoritative compilation, for over 40 years, of the Mountain's trees, shrubs, wildflowers, and ferns.

"Mt Tam," by Don and Kay Martin (Martin Press, San Anselmo, Ca., 1986). Describes 32 suggested hikes.

"Dreams of Tamalpais," by Sharon Skolnick (Last Gasp, San Francisco, 1989). Explores the Mountain's spiritual significance.

"Steaming Up Tamalpais," is a charming, award-winning video, containing interviews and rare old footage, about the Mt. Tamalpais Railway. It was produced by Cris Chater and is sold at local outlets.

ORGANIZATIONS

Among many public membership groups concerned with Tamalpais, the following focus almost exclusively on the Mountain:

Golden Gate National Park Association (GGNPA) - This very active non-profit group supports the staff of the Golden Gate National Recreation Area, which includes Muir Woods and much of Tamalpais' western slope. The GGNPA publishes the quarterly "ParkEvents" and recently issued a handsome "Park Guide," the first official guidebook to the GGNRA. The GGNPA played a major role in the construction of the new Muir Woods Visitor Center. Membership information can be obtained through GGNPA, Fort Mason, Building 201, San Francisco 94123. Their phone number is (415) 556-2236.

Mt. Tamalpais History Project (MTHP) - This 100+ member group promotes historical research, restoration and preservation, and the dissemination of information. The Project can be reached through Fred Sandrock, 21 South Green, Larkspur CA 94939.

Mt. Tamalpais Interpretive Association (MTIA) - Founded in the early 1980's, the MTIA supports Mt. Tamalpais State Park staff by leading hikes, operating the Mt. Tam Visitor Center near East Peak, and fund raising. The MTIA can be reached via the Pantoll Ranger Station, 801 Panoramic Highway, Mill Valley; (415) 388-2070.

Tamalpais Conservation Club (TCC) - The 1,700 member TCC, whose motto is "Guardian of the Mountain," was founded in 1912. They played a major role in establishing Mt. Tamalpais State Park. The TCC is active in trail maintenance, conservation issues, and helping to finance public land acquisitions. Their address is 870 Market Street, Room 562, San Francisco 94102 and the phone number is (415) 391-8021.

APPENDIX

Trail	Miles*	Trailhead	Page
Alpine	.35	Pantoll	130
Alpine-Bon Tempe Pump F.R.	.50	Sky Oaks	180
Arturo	.49	East Ridgecrest	22
Azalea Hill	.8	Sky Oaks	181
Azalea Meadow	.9	Sky Oaks	182
Bald Hill	.71	Deer Park	12
Baltimore Canyon F.R.	.49	Old Highway 101	112
Barbara Spring	.34	Old Highway 101	113
Ben Johnson	1.27	Muir Woods	94
Benstein**	1.16	Rock Spring	164
Bill Williams	.64	Phoenix Lake	146
Blithedale Ridge F.R.	2.33	Mill Valley	40
Bon Tempe	3.96	Sky Oaks	183
Bootjack**	2.7	Muir Woods	95
Bridle Path F.R.	.3	Sky Oaks	185
Buckcyc	.24	Deer Park	13
Bullfrog F.R.	.83	Sky Oaks	186
Camp Eastwood Road	2.25	Mountain Home	74
Camino Alto-Marlin F.R.	1.19	Old Highway 101	114
Canyon	.69	Deer Park	13
Casey Cutoff	.51	Sky Oaks	187
Cataract	2.89	Rock Spring	165
Coastal	8.9	West Slope	226
Colier	1.5	Sky Oaks	188
Concrete Pipeline F.R.	2.78	Sky Oaks	189
Corte Madera Ridge F.R.	1.69	Old Highway 101	115
Corte Madera	.37	Mill Valley	42
Cross Country Boys	1.1	Sky Oaks	191
Dawn Falls	1.35	Old Highway 101	116
Deer Park F.R.	1.13	Deer Park	14
Deer Park F.R.	2.4	Muir Woods	98
Deer Park	.84	Deer Park	15
Dipsea	6.8	Mill Valley	44

Trail	Miles*	Trailhead	Page
East Peak Fire	1.2	Sky Oaks	192
Eastwood	.5	East Ridgecrest	23
Easy Grade	.60	Pantoll	131
Eldridge Grade	5.46	Phoenix Lake	147
Elliott	.63	Deer Park	16
Escalon-Lower Summit F.R.	1.26	Old Highway 101	118
Fern Canyon	1.03	Muir Woods	100
Fern Creek	.74	East Ridgecrest	24
Filter Plant Road	1.00	Sky Oaks	193
Fish Grade	.76	Phoenix Lake	149
Fish Gulch	.57	Phoenix Lake	150
Glen F.R.	.9	Mill Valley	49
Gravity Car Grade	.97	Mountain Home	76
H-Line F.R.	.89	Mill Valley	50
Harry Allen	1.3	Phoenix Lake	151
Harvey Warne	.18	Old Highway 101	119
Heather Cutoff	1.2	Muir Woods	102
Helen Markt	2.0	West Slope	230
Hidden Cove	.3	Sky Oaks	194
Hidden Meadow	.74	Phoenix Lake	152
High Marsh	2.1	West Slope	232
Hill 640 F.R.	.3	Pantoll	132
Hillside	.70	Muir Woods	103
Hogback F.R.	.61	Mountain Home	77
Hoo-Koo-E-Koo	4.04	Old Highway 101	120
Horseshoe F.R.	.28	Mill Valley	51
Huckleberry	.61	Old Highway 101	122
Indian F.R.	1.33	Old Highway 101	123
International	.52	East Ridgecrest	25
Junction	.25	Deer Park	16
Kent Canyon	.5	Muir Woods	104
Kent Fire	.7	Old Highway 101	124
Kent	3.85	Sky Oaks	195

Trail	Miles*	Trailhead	Page
Old Stage Road	1.83	Pantoll	133
Old Stove**	.3	West Slope	240
O'Rourke's Bench	.3	Rock Spring	172
Owl	.9	West Slope	240
Panoramic	.92	Mountain Home	83
Phoenix Lake	2.33	Phoenix Lake	153
Pilot Knob	.81	Sky Oaks	210
Pipeline	.3	Mountain Home	84
Plankwalk	.2	East Ridgecrest	33
Plevin Cut	.2	Mountain Home	85
Pumpkin Ridge	.72	Sky Oaks	211
Red Rock	.3	West Slope	242
Redwood	.74	Mountain Home	86
Redwood Spring	.43	East Ridgecrest	34
Ridge	1.09	Deer Park	18
Riding and Hiking	.4	Pantoll	135
Rock Spring-Lagunitas F.R.	3.39	Sky Oaks	212
Rock Spring	1.70	Rock Spring	173
Rocky Point	.3	West Slope	242
Rocky Ridge F.R.	1.78	Sky Oaks	215
Rocky Ridge Fire	.7	Sky Oaks	216
Ross	.6	Phoenix Lake	155
Scott Tank F.R.	.3	Sky Oaks	217
Shaver Grade	1.69	Phoenix Lake	156
Sierra	1.05	Mountain Home	87
Simmons	.95	Rock Spring	176
Six Points	.57	Deer Park	19
Sky Oaks-Lagunitas	1.07	Sky Oaks	218
Slide Gulch	.4	Mill Valley	60
Southern Marin Line F.R.	2.78	Old Highway 101	125
Stapelveldt	.9	Pantoll	136
Steep Ravine	2.05	Pantoll	137
Steep Ravine Road	1.1	West Slope	243
Stinson Gulch F.R.	.6	West Slope	244
Stocking	1.2	Sky Oaks	219
Sun	.69	Mountain Home	88
Sunset Point	.9	Pantoll	139

Trail	Miles*	Trailhead	Page
Tavern Pump	.3	East Ridgecrest	35
Taylor	.52	Sky Oaks	221
TCC	1.80	Pantoll	140
Telephone	.6	Mill Valley	62
Temelpa	1.48	Mill Valley	63
Tenderfoot	1.09	Mill Valley	65
Troop 80**	1.48	Mountain Home	89
Tucker	1.65	Phoenix Lake	157
Upper Berry	.45	Sky Oaks	222
Verna Dunshee	.68	East Ridgecrest	36
Warner Canyon F.R.	1.19	Mill Valley	67
Warner Falls	.5	Mill Valley	68
West Point	.8	Pantoll	142
Wheeler	.7	Mill Valley	69
Willow Camp	2.6	West Slope	245
Willow Meadow	.6	Sky Oaks	223
Worn Spring F.R.	2.51	Phoenix Lake	158
Yolanda	2.23	Phoenix Lake	160
Zig Zag	.50	Mill Valley	70

* When mileage is shown to two decimal places (hundredths of a mile), distance was measured with a surveyor's wheel.

** Trails containing spurs (spur's distance not included).

The author measuring Bill Williams
Trail with surveyor's wheel (K. Wilson)

BARRY SPITZ has been hiking and running almost daily on Mt. Tamalpais
for over 15 years. He's on the Board of Directors of the Mt. Tamalpais
History Project, Tamalpais Conservation Club, Marin Discoveries and,
formerly, of the Golden Gate Audubon Society. He serves on the Trails
Committee of the Marin County Open Space District. Barry leads hikes on
Tam for several groups. He is also a member of the Mt. Tamalpais
Interpretive Association, Tamalpa Runners, California Native Plant
Society, Sierra Club, Marin Conservation League, and Golden Gate
National Park Association. He ran the Quadruple Dipsea in 1987. Barry
was born in 1948. He is married, and lives in San Anselmo.

Additional copies of "Tamalpais Trails" may be ordered by sending a check
or money order for $16.95 each, plus $3 for tax and postage (paid by the
publisher on orders of 2 books or more), to:

Potrero Meadow Publishing Company
P.O. Box 3007
San Anselmo, CA 94960

Requests for personal inscriptions by the author will be honored. The
author also welcomes any comments, queries, additions, and corrections;
please direct them to the address above.